COOKBOOK COMMITTEE

COOKBOOK CHAIRMEN

Janis Loukas
1984–85

Patty Soule
1985–87

ASSISTANT COOKBOOK CHAIRMEN

Patty Soule
1984–85

Jan Mitchell
1986–87

CREATIVE DIRECTOR/PRINTING COORDINATOR
Linda Storm

MANAGING EDITOR
Patty Soule

WRITING/EDITING TEAM	RESEARCH	COMPUTER
Libby Malone	Jan Bailey	Becky Rivers
Jan Mitchell	Anne Edwards	Patty Soule
Patty Soule	Brooke Novelli	Diann Steed
Linda Storm	Patty Soule	
	Linda Storm	
	Stephanie Williams	

RECIPE TESTING CHAIRMAN
Janis Loukas

RECIPE TESTING COORDINATORS
Lynne Covert
Mary Margaret George
Martha Mitchell
Tina Westerkom
Cassie Weir

RECIPE TESTERS
Ann Boelens
Debbie Blackbird
Caren Elbrecht
Sally May
Jayne McGinnis
Beth Voorhees
Mary Wilson

SECRETARY
Diann Steed

TREASURER
Kristine Anderson

OFFICE COORDINATORS
Nan Alsup   Melinda Bowman   Linda Kreutz   Ruthie Oliver
Becky Rivers   Nancy Whitworth

MARKETING

Judy Carr
Wholesale

Kathy Davis

Mary Jane Moran
Retail

Assistant
Brenda Willson

Assistant
Anne Edwards

PUBLICITY
Elizabeth Coffin   Nancy Littlejohn   Dobi Zamarripa

EX-OFFICIO
Chris Attal   Regan Gammon   Mary Herman   Cindy Kozmetsky   Libby Malone

SUSTAINING ADVISORS
Eleanor Gammon   Kay McHorse   Elora Jane Smith

The Cookbook Committee wishes to acknowledge and thank the following people for their assistance and advice: Mildred Ardis, Clyde Bennett, Ann Clark, Edyth Giesecke, Bill Grosskopf, Jim Knight, Bob Lowe, Mark MacDonald, Henry Montgomery, Susan Mullins, Jenny van Rensburg, Charles Russell and John Soule.

COOKBOOK CHAIRMEN

Janis Loukas	1984–85
Patty Soule	1985–87
Jan Mitchell	1987–88
Patti Hirsh	1988–89
Nancy Marroquin	1989–90
Janice Hanks	1990–91
Suzanne Stewart	1991–92
Patsy Martin	1992–93
Jill Durkee	1993–94
Alison Campbell	1994–95
Hillary Anderson	1995–96
Cathy Wilson	1996–97
Sharman Reed	1997–98
Dinah Barksdale	1998–00
Donna Smith	2000–01
Mary Anne Potter	2001–02

Contributor's List

Necessities and Temptations is a collection of over 600 triple-tested recipes. The cookbook committee wishes to express sincere appreciation to the contributors and testers for their assistance and support.

Marilyn Moorman Adams
Denel Johnson Adkins
Dorothy Anne Alcorn
Jeanne Shaffer Alfandary
Nan Lillard Alsup
Kristine A. Anderson
Sarah Pearson Anderson
Peggy Reyburn Annis
Kathy Fulks Armstrong
Christina Kazen Attal
Cindy Henneberger Babel
Jan Buster Bailey
Linda Kattness Baker
Phyllis Francis Baker
Mary Delmore Balagia
Cindy Broussard Balderach
Jannis Stallworth Baldwin
Pam Primdahl Bannerot
Molly Smith Barbee
Claudia Jackson Barnard
Hallie Orr Barton
June Bivins Baumoel
Amanda Merritt Beck
Margene Thornton Beckham
Laura McLean Belisle
Mary Hooper Bell
Jan Noble Berend
Cynthia Thomas Berkman
Betsey Ann Bishop
Janelle Holter Bishop
Debbi McCurley Blackbird
Lynn Blakely
Karen Freese Boatright
Ann Waldie Boelens
Marnette Landrum Bonta
Bebe Moody Boone
Charla Ann Borchers
Peggi Purcell-Boston
Linda Kay Anderson Bowman

Mary Ann Lewis Bowman
Melinda McMahon Bowman
Eden Van Zandt Box
Lynn Langston Box
Zenobia Myers Bremond
Trisha Triesch Bridges
Maureen Copeland Britton
Noreen Quinn Brock
Kay Ann Buratti Broline
Judy Winkel Brooks
Celeste Brown
Janice Parks Brown
Patsy Read Browning
Peggy LePard Budd
Jan Weaver Busby
Allison Butler
Linda Richards Butler
Marty Mahaffey Butler
Mimi Holt Buzbee
Teresa de Silva Cain
Connie Clayton Camp
Nancy Bauerle Campbell
Judy Gant Carr
Ellen Steck Carter
Caroline Robinson Caven
George Ann Byfield Chalmers
Eleanor Tyler Chote
Joan Howard Church
Kate Eustis Clark
Ann Cox Coates
Lynn Danforth Coats
Elizabeth Jones Coffin
Lynn Miller Cohagan
Stella Conner
Peggy Conway
Madalyn McDonald Cooke
Peggy Wilson Cooley
Meredith Ross Cooper
Elizabeth Rogers Covert

Lee Ann Brown Covert
Lynne Shapiro Covert
Martha Woods Covert
Melinda Pratt Covert
Penny Montgomery Cowan
Margie Craig Cowden
Mac Duncan Cromwell
Julie Dryden Crow
Linda Gordon Cummins
Kathleen Cowen Cunningham
Suzanne Cunningham
Nancy Self Dacy
Jenefred Hederhorst Davies
Kathleen Penn Davis
Mollie Villeret Davis
Sherry Stafford Davis
Alice Ferrick deGraffenried
Holly Howell Decherd
Emily Kennard Derounian
Vicki Scott Donoghue
Louisa Mahone Donoghue
Cathryn Seymour Dorsey
Sharon Ladd Dowdle
Grace Odem Doyle
Susan Page Driver
Jon Anna Perry Dyer
Carol Foust Eckert
Susan Meason Edgar
Anne Davis Edwards
Amy Grimes Ehrlich
Caren Copus Elbrecht
Cynthis Strauss Eledge
Susan Carpenter Erickson
Judy Gund Fairey
Martha Poarch Farmer
Maydelle Foster Fason
Alice Heiligenthal Ferrick
Dorothy Sartin Fields
Elizabeth Rice Finks

Julia Corley Fish
Mary Lou Laughlin Fitzpatrick
Patty Forney Flack
Laura Lee Hill Ford
Cornelia Adams Foster
Janelle Jones Foster
Marcia Ungren Foster
Pam Jarvis Foster
Debra Fleming Gainer
Susie Sanford Gamble
Eleanor Stayton Gammon
Debbie Greenberg Garmon
Bonita Miller Garvey
George Ann Langford Geeslin
Karen Kee Gentry
Mary Margaret Marshall George
Jean Summers Gilbert
Karen Dombrowsky Glover
Sarah Goodearle
Jody Holland Goodson
Missy McCrary Gray
Carol Winters Green
Nancy Loughridge Green
Phyllis Toler Green
Cinda Arnold Greenlee
Jane Sentilles Greig
Martha West Griffith
Kay Smith Guleke
Diana Roth Guest
Cissy Brown Gully
Jeannette Smith Gutherie
Mary Anne Taylor Hackney
Nancy Chote Hagman
Elizabeth Hahn
Karen Scruggs Hall
Laurie Granger Hall
Rebecca Archer Hardeman
Carla Geise Harman
Debbie Hyde Harmon
Sally Seigfreid Harmon
Nancy Brown Harrison
Louise Burd Hart
Jere West Hayden
Kay Hayden-Polsky
Monica Hallahan Hearn

Catherine Stewart Heidrick
Bitsy Bailey Henderson
Mary Gideon Herman
Dealy Decherd Herndon
Karen Flesher Hertel
Virginia Nelson Hickey
Evelyn Oglesby Hill
Jane Ferguson Hill
Susan Robinson Hinton
Patti Hage Hirsh
Patty Patterson Hoffpauir
Beverly Enderle Holcomb
Bonnie Harper Holder
Judy Ryan Holmes
Sarah Holmes
Elizabeth McKee Holt
Joan King Holtzman
Mickey Murtha Holtzman
Janet Dahl Hooten
Hallie Powell Horton
Helen Newell Houston
Clare Ritchie Hudspeth
Jan Stone Hughes
Phoebe Foster Hughes
Sarah McMordie Hull
Marianne Wilkerson Jackson
Melissa Owens Jackson
Linda Sinclair Jacoby
Millicent Chapman Johns
Karen Ruble Johnson
Lucille Labue Johnson
Caroline Jones
Roberta Pankey Jones
Jean Zenner Kaelber
Ginger Villemez Kendall
Ann Turnbull Kidd
Martha Davis Kipcak
Pam Miller Knierim
Betty Bergfeld Knight
Nancy Knapp Kocurek
Cindy Hendrick Kozmetsky
Bev Allmen Krasovec
Natalie Attwill Kreisle
Kay Clark Lane
Sydney Thompson Langley

Laura Rainey Leshikar
Kim Fairey Lewis
Gail Hope Lindley
Annabel Bradshaw Linscomb
Nancy Ford Littlejohn
Kathy Jarmon Lockart
Ann Long
Lou Ann Curtis Looney
Jane Dryden Louis
Janis Wood Loukas
Lucie Wolf Lowrance
Susan Ablon Lubin
Mary Nobles Lyles
Diana Brinkley Maclin
Libby Snyder Malone
Catharine Glober Maloney
Sandra Moffett Martine
Sally Whittington May
Susan Fisher McCaleb
Missy Childs McCarroll
Marilyn Murray McDonald
Jayne Henderson McGinnis
Kay McKay McHorse
Nancy Wroe McMahon
Virginia Calhoun McMordie
Phoebe Hughes McMurrey
Kay Lynn Kriegel McNabb
Nancy Dinwiddie Mercer
Eugenia Betts Miller
Kitty Gordon Miller
Jacqueline Wheeler Milstead
Annabel Givens Minter
Jan Giesecke Mitchell
Martha Perry Mitchell
Lillian Chappell Montgomery
Mary Faust Moore
Mary Jane McBride Moran
Verna Mae Hardy Morrison
Elizabeth Ann Gates Morrow
Laurie Humphreys Morse
Missy Donnell Moscoe
Mary Mountcastle
Meredith Morton Moyer
Susan Major Mullins
Janet Hetherington Murdock

Margo Myers
Carol Gasaway Nalle
Lida Lea Nalle
Nancy Gates Nation
Melinda Wilson Neblett
Keni Cunningham Neff
Polly Lyons Nelon
Nancy Reese Newman
Lucille Dee Nuessle Norman
Nancy Smith Norvell
Brook Offutt Novelli
Lucy Wicker O'Brien
Ree Limmer O'Connell
Ruthie Herman Oliver
Karen Ross Oswalt
Lolla McNutt Page
Shelly Gerst Page
Dee Bulkley Painter
Lila Ann Parker
Susan Deegan Parker
Julibeth Swenson Parrish
Kathy Sellers Patman
Patricia Page Payne
Jane Large Peeler
Sue Wright Peschel
Karen Bailey Pettigrew
Sheryl Koschak Pfluger
Cynthia Tassos Phillips
Meg Phillips Phillips
Peggy Pickle
Louise Gose Pincoffs
Joan Sundbeck Polson
Kathy Moats Porter
Lea Gilbert Porter
Joyce Michels Prestridge
Betsy Berryman Puckhafer
Caroline Cardwell Puett
Sue Stapp Ramsey
Julie Lunsford Redding
Jayne Strain Richardson
Katy Durfee Ritts
Becky Barlow Rivers
Farrell Frederick Robertson
Mercedes Jensen Robinson
Pat Folmar Robinson

Becky Campbell Roche
Marthanne Burrow Root
Catherine Brown Rose
Mandy Rose
Patsy Patteson Rose
Gene Anne Cox Sandbach
Beverly Casal Sawyer
Alice Rotsch Scarbrough
Nancy Neal Scherer
Dianne Dies Schoch
Donna Tidwell Schneider
Linda Hughes Schrieber
Ann Schroeder
Linda McDaniel Schulze
Susie Boyce Schumacher
Debi Sistrunk Schutze
Ann Schwartz
Aileen Nation Secunda
Carolyn Bell Sharkey
Cynthia Lynch Sharp
Sara Dycus Sharp
Aimee Kane Sheehan
Lois Crow Sheffield
Linda Branch Shelton
Patty Hayes Shepherd
Marian Newsome Sherwood
Sharon Wade Shoop
Eleanor Long Simmons
Cathy Nelson Sisk
Judy Hext Skaggs
Karen Schmidt Slaughter
Elora Watt Smith
Glenda Holder Smith
Susan Smith
Joan Pratt Snodgrass
Susan Deal Somerville
Patty Arkwright Soule
Wesie Brenner Spires
Diann Crouch Steed
Laurie Miller Stephens
Molly Bowman Stephens
Nelle Buchanan Still
Jane Massey Stockton
Linda Campbell Storm
Colleen Dillworth Stroup

Claire Field Stuart
Marilyn Tankersley Taylor
Louann Atkins Temple
Donna Durham Thomas
Patricia Thomas Thomas
Jean Powell Thompson
Wissie Reynaud Thompson
Anne Morrow Tillett
Barbara Elliot Tindel
Dorie Dawson Throckmorton
Jackie Teague Thurman
Betty O'Brien Trimble
Jan Cooper Trimble
Eleanor Niggli Tyler
Jeanne Smith Umstattd
Debbie McCormick Vacek
Jeanne Bordini Vier
Penny Ramey Ruch Vineyard
Kay Tynan Vinson
Beth Daniel Voorhees
Nancy Butcher Wade
Bernie Kirby Wagner
Auddie Craig Walker
Randy Klopton Wallenstein
Jane Barbour Walters
Barbara Huber Ward
Adrienne Monnig Watt
Kathy Adams Weaver
Cassie Boyd Weir
Morey McGonigle Weldon
Marie Snodgrass Wentsch
Tina Hathaway Westerkom
Valerie Schott Weynand
Debbie Grounds Wheeler
Kay Jarvis White
Linda Gale Thompson White
Mary Koch White
Ruth Cash Whitehurst
Mercedes Baker Whittington
Nancy Denton Whitworth
Becky Meason Wiley
Betty Travis Wilkes
Pam Pitzer Willeford
Elizabeth Pendleton Williams
Gail Wommack Williams

Stephanie Williams
Judy Turner Williamson
Mona McKay Williamson
Brenda Bland Willson

Mary Pincoffs Wilson
Ann Johnson Winger
Joan E. Winter
Marilla Black Wood

Sherry Lutz Wooley
Ellen Robinson Yaun
Sandy Geyer Youman
Bobi Blankenship Zamarripa

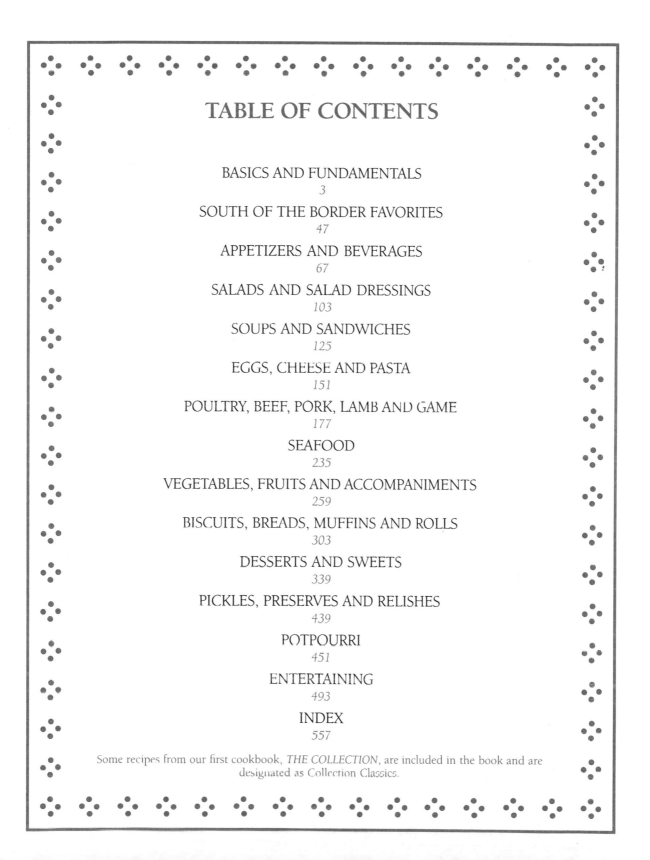

TABLE OF CONTENTS

Some recipes from our first cookbook, *THE COLLECTION*, are included in the book and are designated as Collection Classics.

INTRODUCTION

The Junior League of Austin proudly presents **Necessities and Temptations**, compiled, written and published exclusively by League volunteers committed to excellence and to the belief that this cookbook is unique in the marketplace. **Necessities and Temptations** contains carefully culled and tested recipes—both the easy and the elegant—that are the hallmark of any Junior League cookbook. But as you look closely, you will also discover special features that will make this book one of the most treasured resources in your kitchen.

Cooking and entertaining fundamentals are the framework for **Necessities and Temptations.** From the first chapter with its comprehensive and meticulously organized charts on everything from spices to substitutions to the last chapter that highlights all facets of entertaining from caterers to canapés, you will find information that is easy to read, accurate and useful. Here are the basic necessities for cooks of every level of experience.

Tempting ideas and recipes add flourish and flavor to our cookbook. New and original recipes are seasoned with classics from our first cookbook, the critically acclaimed *Collection*. The step-by-step clarity of the recipe format is ideal for today's efficiency-conscious cook. In the menu section, you will find the style and ambiance of Austin. The magic in the Potpourri section will transform your kitchen into a workshop of creativity and fun.

As you can see, **Necessities and Temptations** is really two books in one—a handy basic kitchen reference and a delightful community cookbook that captures the vitality of our city and the culinary artistry of our membership. Your enjoyment of this unique publication will give meaning to the countless, caring hours of volunteer work that made this cookbook possible. Your support of this effort will give substance to our many community service projects.

The Junior League of Austin

The Junior League of Austin
Volunteers Meeting Community Needs

In 1994, the Junior League of Austin will celebrate its Sixtieth Anniversary of providing funds and personnel to charitable causes in Central Texas. **Necessities and Temptations** is one of three methods employed by the organization to raise nearly $350,000 annually to contribute to the Austin community through the Community Assistance Fund, Teacher Grants, Sponsorships and Projects at local non-profit agencies. The 548 active members of the organization will freely give over 18,000 hours to the following projects supported by the Junior League of Austin in 1992-93.

- Create and manage a community food drive to fill the shelves at the **AIDS Services of Austin Food Bank**. League volunteers will inventory the food, stock the shelves and fill grocery orders for clients.

- Conduct, through the **City of Austin EMS/Star Flight**, A DWI awareness program for junior and senior high school students.

- Provide a well-structured and enriching program for abused and neglected children during their stay at the **Austin-Travis County Shelter**.

- Research, plan and initiate a **Cancer Program/Child Life Program** at Brackenridge Children's Hospital.

- Provide mediation services to assist people in solving their problems in an inexpensive alternative to the court system at the **Dispute Resolution Center**.

- Provide meals to the residents, relief to the house manager and help to the newsletter editor at the **Ronald McDonald House**.

- Plan and initiate a **Hispanic Mother/Daughter Program** in conjunction with the University of Texas whereby sixth grade Hispanic girls and their mothers are mentored by college students and encouraged to fulfill their potential through education.

- Renovate the interior of **The Spectrum**, a shelter for runaway teens sponsored by **Middle Earth Unlimited**.

(continued on next page)

Butter

If a recipe calls for: **You may use:**

1 c. butter

   a. ⅘ c. bacon fat (clarified)
      increase liquid in recipe by ¼ c.
   b. ⅔ c. chicken fat (clarified)
      increase liquid in recipe by ¼ c.
   c. ⅞ c. corn or nut oil plus a pinch of salt
   d. ⅞ c. lard/shortening plus ½ t. salt
   e. 1 c. margarine
   f. 1¼ c. 36–40% butter fat
      cream (whipping cream)
   g. 2½ c. 18–20% butter fat
      cream (half and half)

Seasoning and Spices

If a recipe calls for: **You may use:**

If a recipe calls for:	You may use:
1 t. dried herbs	1 T. fresh herbs
1 t. allspice	1 t. equal parts cinnamon, clove and nutmeg
1 t. basil	1 t. oregano
1 t. caraway	1 t. anise
1 t. cayenne	1 t. chile peppers
1 t. chervil	1 t. parsley or tarragon
1 t. fennel	1 t. anise or tarragon
⅛ t. garlic powder	1 small garlic clove
1 T. prepared mustard	1 t. dry mustard
1 t. nutmeg	1 t. mace
1 T. dehydrated, minced onion	1 small fresh onion
1 T. onion powder	1 medium fresh onion
1 t. oregano	1 t. marjoram
1 t. sage	1 t. thyme

Sugar and Sweeteners

If a recipe calls for: **You may use:**

Sugar

In the following three substitutions, reduce liquid in recipe by ¼ cup

1 c. sugar

                         a. 1 c. molasses plus ½ t. baking soda
                         b. ½ c. honey plus ½ t. baking soda
                         c. 1 c. maple syrup plus ¼ c. corn syrup
                         d. 1 c. maple syrup and ¼ t. baking soda

1 c. brown sugar   a. 1 c. white sugar plus ¼ c. molasses

Sweeteners

1 c. corn syrup   a. 1 c. sugar plus additional ¼ c. of any liquid in recipe
1 c. honey   a. 1¼ c. sugar plus additional ¼ c. any liquid in recipe
                         b. 1 c. molasses

CANNED FOODS

1. Purchase cans that are in good condition. Do not buy or use cans that are dented, rusted or bulging; they may not be safe.

2. Canned foods are graded and labeled based on quality. A United States Department of Agriculture (U.S.D.A.) grade shield will appear on the label. Price is based on the grade of the product.

3. The manufacturer of canned foods is required to list all ingredients used in preparation of the contents.

4. Canned foods should be stored at room temperature not to exceed 70° F.

5. The average shelf life of canned foods is one year.

CAN SIZES

Can Size	Average Weight	Approximate Measure	No. 4 Oz. Servings	Common Uses
6 oz.	6 oz.	¾ c.	6	juices (frozen concentrates)
8 oz.	8 oz.	1 c.	2	fruits, vegetables
No. 1 (10½-12 oz. picnic)	10½ to 12 oz.	1¼ c.	2–3	condensed soups, fruits, vegetables
12 oz.	12 oz.	1½ c.	3–4	fish products
No. 300	14 to 16 oz.	1¾ c.	3–4	pork n' beans, spaghetti, fruits, cranberry sauce
No. 1½ or 303	15 to 17 oz.	2 c.	4	fruit cocktail
No. 1 tall	16 oz.	2 c.	4	vegetables
No. 2	1 lb. 4 oz., 1 pt. 2 fl. oz. or 20 oz.	2½ c.	4–5	fruits, juices, vegetables
No. 2½	1 lb. 13 oz., 1 pt. 10 fl. oz.	3½ c.	7	fruits, vegetables, fruit cocktail, pumpkin
No. 3	2 lb. or 32 oz.	4 c.	8	fruits, vegetables
46 fl. oz.	46 oz.	5¾ c. or 1 qt. 14 fl. oz.	9–11	fruits, vegetables, juices
No. 5	52 oz.	6½ c. or 3 lb. 4 oz.	12–13	institutional size
No. 10	6 lb. 9 oz. to 6 lb. 14 oz.	12 c., 3–4 qts. or 1 gal.	25	institutional size

HERBS AND SPICES

True Spices—Allspice, cayenne, cinnamon, cloves, ginger, mace, nutmeg, paprika, pepper, saffron and tumeric

Blends of Spices—Chili powder, curry powder, fine herbs, pickling spices, poultry and seafood seasonings, pumpkin and apple pie spices

Modern Additions to Spice List—Dried celery flakes, garlic and onion in powdered or dehydrated forms

Aromatic Seeds—Anise, caraway, cardamom, celery, coriander, cumin, dill, fennel, mustard, poppy and sesame seeds; these seeds are not especially aromatic until cooked or crushed.

True Herbs—Basil, bay leaves, chervil, chives, dill, marjoram, mint, oregano, parsley, rosemary, sage, saffron, savory, tarragon and thyme; these are the leaves, seeds or flowers of aromatic plants.

Terminology of Fresh Herbs

Many recipes may call for a blend of herbs.

Sweet herbs—Thyme, sage, chives and mint

Pot herbs—Cabbage, spinach, dandelion greens and beet tops

Salad herbs—Any herbs used to flavor salads

Fines herbes—A blend of parsley, chives, tarragon and chervil are the classic fine herbs of French cooking and are most often used in egg and cheese dishes.

Herb bouquet or bouquet garni—These terms refer to a blend of herbs wrapped in cheesecloth and tied at the top. This spice bag is used during cooking, much like a tea bag is used in making tea. It is also used in soups, stews, sauces and vegetables.

   Classic bouquet—Consists of 2 sprigs of parsley, ½ bay leaf, 1 sprig of fresh thyme or ⅛ teaspoon of dried thyme

   Bouquet for lamb—Consists of rosemary, parsley and celery

   Bouquet for veal—Consists of parsley, thyme and lemon rind

   Bouquet for beef—Consists of basil, parsley, bay leaf and clove

Cooking with Fresh Herbs

1. A light touch is preferable when cooking with herbs, as the aromatic oils are very strong and a tiny pinch can be very intense.

2. Always finely chop or mince the herbs, so that the maximum flavor can be absorbed during the blending, marinating or cooking process.

3. Never blend the strong herbs such as rosemary, sage or basil because their flavors would compete with one another and overpower the dish, rather than enhance it.

4. Add herbs during the last 15 minutes of cooking, because cooking too long will cause the dish to be bitter or the herbs to lose their flavor entirely.

   Exception 1—Bay leaves may be used throughout the cooking process and removed at the end.

   Exception 2—Cold preparations, salad dressings or marinades require more time to absorb the flavors (at least 15 minutes).

   Exception 3—Some recipes specifically direct you to add herbs and spices early in the process.

5. One tablespoon of minced, fresh herbs is equivalent to ⅓ teaspoon ground or ½ tablespoon crushed, dried herbs.

Dried Herbs and Spices

1. Purchase dried herbs and spices in small quantities, if possible, or divide with a friend, as they only have a shelf life of 4 to 6 months.

2. Always store dried herbs and spices in airtight containers away from light, heat and moisture. Light robs the herbs and spices of their color, and heat affects their flavor and potency. Moisture causes dried herbs and spices to cake and harden.

3. Open herbs and spices once a month to check for freshness. If they are stale, throw them away and replace. Old herbs and spices can ruin a dish.

4. Use dried herbs and spices with caution. It is easy to add more, but complicated to correct over seasoning.

5. Avoid using too much of any herb or spice unless a recipe specifically calls for it, such as ginger in gingerbread, in which one spice dominates the flavor of the recipe.

6. Remember that herbs and spices are meant to enhance, not disguise, the flavor of food.

7. When a recipe is doubled or tripled, do not double or triple the herbs and spices. When doubling a recipe, use 1½ times the amount of herbs or spices called for. When tripling a recipe, use twice the amount of herbs or spices called for.

Cooking with Dried Herbs and Spices

1. Dried herbs and spices will release more flavor if they are crushed or crumbled before they are added to other ingredients.

2. Whenever possible, use freshly ground spices rather than ready ground or powdered spices. Whole spices have a longer shelf life than ready ground or powdered and a more intense flavor when freshly ground.

3. To reconstitute dried herbs, soak them for 10 minutes to 1 hour in any liquid called for in the recipe. If the recipe calls for butter, simmer the herbs in the butter before adding.

4. Add dried herbs and spices early in the cooking process of casseroles, soups and stews

5. In salad dressing recipes, add dried herbs and spices to the oil 15 to 30 minutes before serving.

Steps to Correct Over Seasoning

1. Add a raw, peeled and quartered potato and simmer for 15 minutes. Remove and discard potato before serving.

2. If the seasoning is still too intense after trying the raw potato method, prepare a second, unseasoned recipe and combine the two.

3. If the seasoning is too salty, add a quartered raw potato and then a little brown sugar. Begin with ¼ teaspoon of brown sugar, using up to 2 teaspoons if necessary.

4. If the seasoning is too sweet, add ½ to 1 teaspoon of lemon juice, cider or wine vinegar to adjust the flavor.

5. Use a large metal strainer to separate bits of herbs and spices.

HERB AND SPICE CHART

H—indicates herb

Herb or Spice	Description	Uses and Tips
Allspice	Flavor of clove, cinnamon and nutmeg	Baked goods, pot roasts, pickles, soups, lamb, fruit pies, pumpkin pie
Anise	Sweet, licorice-like, greenish-brown seeds	Baked goods, shellfish, poultry and veal, fruit and vegetable salads, cheese; Spanish, Italian and Mediterranean entrées
Basil[H]	Subtle, spicy, distinctive flavor	Mainstay of many Italian dishes, especially tomato dishes and sauces; salads, eggs, cheese, lamb, pork, veal and chicken

Herb or Spice	Description	Uses and Tips
Bay leaf[H]	Aromatic laurel tree leaf, used whole	Meat and fish dishes, soups and pasta sauces (remove before serving)
Caraway seeds	Dark brown seeds that add a warm, tangy taste	Rye bread, sauerkraut, cheeses, potato/cabbage dishes, beef and pork dishes
Cardamom	Blackish-brown seeds with green pods	Baked goods, pastries, fruits, soups and curries; wine and hot coffee
Cayenne pepper	Very hot, ground red pepper (also called chiles)	Mexican and Italian dishes, seafood, eggs, chili, soups, pork ribs, sausages and chicken
Celery seeds	Derived from a special variety of celery	Pickling, salads, cream cheese spreads, eggs and vegetables, stews and seafood
Chervil[H]	Lacy leaf; considered a fine herb	Soups, salads, egg and seafood dishes
Chili powder	Very hot blend of spices which includes cayenne pepper	Spanish and Mexican dishes, rice, beans, meat and chili
Chive[H]	Delicate onion flavor	Salads, soups, sauces, egg and fish dishes
Cinnamon	Spicy bark of a tree, either ground or in long sticks	Baked goods, drinks, desserts, pickles, stewed fruits and sugar syrups
Cloves	Dried flower buds which are spicy, strong and pungent	Used whole to stud ham, onions and oranges; used to flavor hot drinks; used like cinnamon when ground
Coriander	Seed with a perfumed, aromatic flavor	Curries, stews, pickling and baked goods
Curry powder	Golden yellow in color; a blend of many spices	Indian and Middle Eastern dishes, eggs, chicken, lamb, fish and cheese

Herb or Spice	Description	Uses and Tips
Cumin (comino) (whole or ground)	A seed with a bitter and aromatic character	Essential in Mexican dishes and Indian chutneys
Dill	Pickle taste	Poultry and seafood dishes, eggs, salad dressing, pickles, soups and cheeses
Fennel	Licorice character and aroma	Italian and Swedish dishes, seafood, salads and egg dishes
Garlic	Strong, onion-like odor and taste; gives a mild flavor when used unpeeled; for stronger flavor, mince the cloves; for an even stronger flavor crush or mash the cloves	Mediterranean dishes, including Italian and French cuisine; used with meats, fish, poultry, salads, salad dressings, sauces, soups and breads
Ginger	Irregularly shaped root with a sharp pungent fragrance	Used in Oriental dishes, baked goods, meats, preserves; may be purchased crystallized for sweetness, ground for cooking and whole to add texture to a dish
Marjoram[H]	Spicy odor but delicate flavor, member of the mint family	Egg and fish dishes, poultry, salads, sauces, soups, stews and vegetables (particularly spinach)
Mint[H]	Fresh, clean, cool taste with spearmint or peppermint character	Drinks, desserts, jellies, sauces, salads, lamb dishes, fruit and vegetables
Mustard	Sharp and spicy flavor	Pickles and relishes, salad dressings, dips, meat glazes, chicken and fish
Nutmeg	Mellow, spicy taste	Bread and cakes, vegetable and egg dishes, sauces, soups and drinks
Oregano[H]	Aromatic taste	Greek and Italian dishes; especially pasta, sauces, salad dressings, eggs and cheeses

Herb or Spice	Description	Uses and Tips
Paprika	A spicy red pepper with a mild, sweet, peppery flavor derived from the same plant as cayenne (but not nearly as hot)	To garnish, color and give a zesty taste to all kinds of foods; frequently used in Hungarian and Spanish dishes
Parsley[H]	Mildly bitter taste, considered a fine herb	In meat, fish, poultry, soups, salads, stews and as a decorative garnish
Pepper, black	Zesty and pungent taste	Generally used like salt
Pepper, white	Similar to black pepper with a more subtle flavor; stronger than black pepper (use only half as much when substituting)	Is used when a more subtle flavor is desired and when pepper should not show
Poppy seeds	Tiny blueish-black seeds with a grainy texture and nutty taste	Sprinkle on bread and rolls, noodles, dips, dressings and in some pork dishes
Rosemary[H]	Aromatic taste	Lamb, beef, chicken, Italian dishes, egg dishes; used frequently in French cuisine
Saffron	Pleasantly bitter taste; has a reddish-yellow color; costly	Seafood, rice and egg dishes; used frequently in Spanish and French cuisine
Sage[H]	Spicy, musty grayish-green leaf	Pork, sausage, fish, game, veal, poultry dishes; stuffings, soups and sauces
Savory[H]	Piquant dark green leaf; two varieties: summer and winter	Poultry dishes, eggs, salads and stuffings
Sesame seeds	Nutty taste	Sprinkled on bread and rolls, salads, soups and casseroles
Tarragon[H]	Slightly anise-like, sweet, green leaf	In poultry, meat, fish dishes, salads, sauces, dressings, soups and marinades (use sparingly on meat as it may become too sweet)

Herb or Spice	Description	Uses and Tips
Thyme[H]	Pungent flavor	In stuffings, soups, seafood, meat and poultry, stews, clam chowder and salad dressings
Tumeric	Rich, sweet and slightly spicy; reddish-orange color	Used in curry blends and pickling; may be substituted for saffron; adds color like saffron, but has different flavor

OVEN TEMPERATURE CHART

Term	Degrees Fahrenheit	Degrees Celsius
VERY SLOW	250°–275°	121°–135°
SLOW	275°–325°	135°–163°
MODERATE	325°–375°	163°–191°
HOT	375°–425°	191°–219°
VERY HOT	425°–475°	219°–246°
EXTREMELY HOT	475°–525°	246°–274°

Familiarize yourself with your oven and its temperature accuracy. Inexpensive oven thermometers are available at hardware and cooking stores or through mail order catalogues. These can be placed inside the oven to monitor the exact temperature of the oven. Make adjustments accordingly. It may be necessary to have your oven adjusted professionally.

When using glass ovenware, the oven temperature should be reduced by 25°.

TO DETERMINE OVEN TEMPERATURES WITHOUT A THERMOMETER

Sprinkle a small amount of flour in a pan and place in a heated oven. A piece of white tissue may be used instead of flour.

250°–325° F. Flour or tissue turns delicate brown in five minutes.

325°–400° F. Flour or tissue turns golden brown in five minutes.

400°–450° F. Flour or tissue turns deep brown in five minutes.

450°–500° F. Flour or tissue turns dark brown in three minutes.

CONVERSION FORMULA

To convert Centigrade to Fahrenheit: multiply by 9, divide by 5, add 32.

To convert Fahrenheit to Centigrade: subtract 32, multiply by 5, divide by 9.

TEMPERATURES AND TIMES USED IN BAKING

Type of Product	Oven Temperature (degrees F.)	Baking Time (minutes)
Breads		
Biscuits	425° to 450°	10 to 15
Cornbread	400° to 425°	30 to 40
Cream puffs	375°	60
Muffins	400° to 425°	20 to 25
Popovers	375°	60
Quick loaf breads	350° to 375°	60 to 75
Yeast bread	400°	30 to 40
Yeast roll (plain)	400° to 425°	15 to 25
Sweet	375°	20 to 30
Cakes (with fat)		
Cupcakes	350° to 375°	15 to 25
Layer	375°	20 to 30
Loaf	350°	45 to 60
Cakes (without fat)		
Angel food and sponge	350° to 375°	30 to 45
Cookies		
Drop	350° to 400°	8 to 15
Rolled	375°	8 to 10
Egg, meat, milk and cheese recipes		
Cheese souffle (baked in a pan of hot water)	350°	30 to 60
Custard (plain or corn) (baked in a pan of hot water)	350°	30 to 60

Type of Product	Oven Temperature (degrees F.)	Baking Time (minutes)
Macaroni and cheese	350°	25 to 30
Meat loaf	300°	60 to 90
Meat pie	400°	25 to 30
Rice pudding (raw rice)	300°	120 to 180
Scalloped potatoes	350°	60
Pies		
One-crust pie (unbaked shell) (custard type)	400° to 425°	30 to 40
Meringue or cooked filling in prebaked shell	350° to 425°	12 to 15
Pie shell only	450°	10 to 12
Two-crust pies with un-cooked filling	400° to 425°	45 to 55
Two-crust pies with cooked filling	425° to 450°	30 to 45

STORING AND FREEZING FOOD

Location is the main consideration in shelf storage of dry foods. It is wise not to store packaged foods too close to the stove top and oven or the dishwasher, as the heat distributed from these appliances can shorten shelf life. Herbs and spices should not be stored close to the stove top; heat can destroy their essence. They also have a relatively short shelf life, so it is better to buy small quantities or divide purchases with a friend. Note the purchase date on the container with a marker. Generally, foods stored at room temperatures will keep well if resealed properly. If this is not possible, use airtight storage containers or cannisters.

Shelf Storage of Common Staples

Food	Average shelf life	Storage suggestions
Baking powder and baking soda	18 months	Date container
Bouillon (cubes or instant)	1 year	Away from moisture or heat

Food	Average shelf life	Storage suggestions
Bread	5 to 7 days	Reclose wrapper with twist tie (will not keep as long during summer months but may be refrigerated)
Cake mixes	1 year	Away from moisture or heat
Canned foods	1 year	Date container
Chili sauce	1 month	Can be refrigerated
Coffee (instant)	6 months	Can be refrigerated or frozen
Coffee (vacuum packed)	1 year	Can be refrigerated or frozen
Dry cereals	4 to 6 months	Airtight container
Crumbs (packaged)	6 months	Airtight container or freeze
Flour (all-purpose)	1 year	Airtight container or freeze
Gelatin (plain or flavored)	18 months	Date container
Herbs and spices	6 months	Date containers
Honey	1 year	If honey crystallizes heat jar in hot water or remove lid and microwave briefly
Prepared horseradish	1 month	Refrigerate
Jams and jellies	1 year	Can be refrigerated
Ketchup	2 to 3 months	Refrigerate
Lard	8 months	Can be refrigerated
Mustard	2 to 3 months	Refrigerate

Food	Average shelf life	Storage suggestions
Noodles (egg)	6 months	Away from moisture and heat
Oil	3 months	Can be refrigerated
Pancake mixes	6 months	Airtight container
Pasta	1 year	Can be refrigerated
Peanut butter (unopened)	6 months to 1 year	Some varieties require refrigeration
Rice brown, wild or white	6 months to 1 year	Airtight container
Sugar brown, powdered or granulated	4 months to 2 years	Airtight container
Tea	6 months	Airtight container

Refrigerator Storage of Common Staples
(40° F. or slightly lower)

Food	Average refrigerator life	Storage suggestions
Butter	2 weeks	Tightly covered
Buttermilk	2 weeks	Reclose tightly
Cheese cottage	3 to 5 days	
		All cheeses should be tightly covered or wrapped
cream	2 weeks	
hard	2 months	
Parmesan	3 months	
sliced	2 weeks	
spreads	1 to 2 weeks	
Cream	3 to 5 days	Reclose tightly
Eggs	1 to 3 weeks (depending on freshness when purchased)	

Food	Average shelf life	Storage suggestions
Half and half	1 to 2 weeks	Reclose tightly
Mayonnaise	3 months	Reclose tightly
Meats		
bacon	1 to 2 weeks	Wrap tightly
cold cuts	2 weeks	
fresh from butcher	1 to 3 days	
hot dogs	1 to 2 weeks	
poultry	1 to 2 days	
Nuts	up to 3 months	Airtight container
Seafood	1 day	Double wrapped to prevent odor

Freezer Storage
(0° F. or lower)

Food should be wrapped in airtight, moisture proof/vapor proof material to prevent odors from penetrating the freezer and foods. It is wise to date frozen foods to determine when they should be used. When defrosting frozen foods, allow enough time to do so in the refrigerator. Do not refreeze food after it has thawed.

Foods Not Suitable for Freezing

bananas	onions	tomatoes
cabbage	pears	whites of
celery	processed meats	hard-cooked eggs
cucumbers	radishes	
mayonnaise	salad greens	

Freezer Storage of Common Foods

Foods	Average freezer life	Storage suggestions
Breads	2 to 3 months	Wrap in moisture proof materials
Butter or margarine	4 to 6 months	Freeze in unopened package
Cakes		
baked and unfrosted	2 to 6 months	Wrap tightly

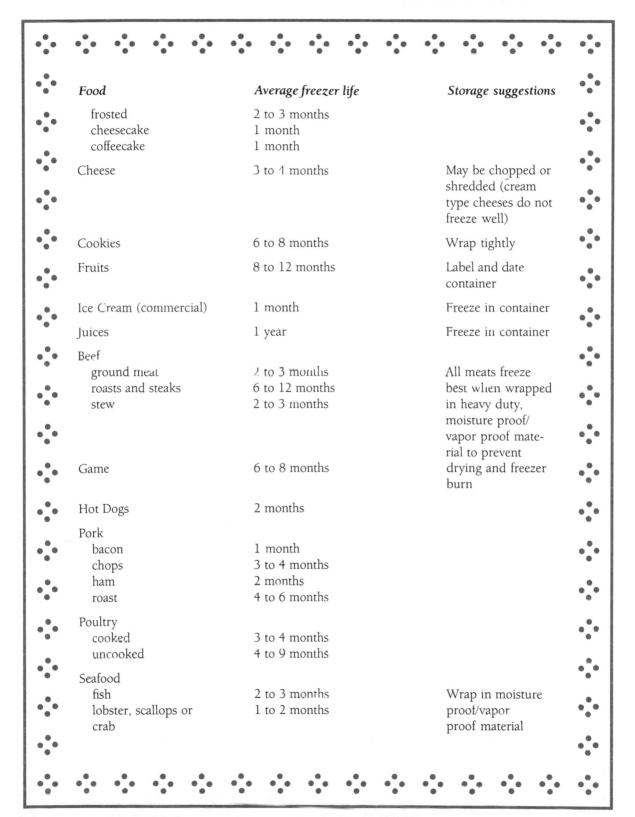

Food	Average freezer life	Storage suggestions
frosted	2 to 3 months	
cheesecake	1 month	
coffeecake	1 month	
Cheese	3 to 4 months	May be chopped or shredded (cream type cheeses do not freeze well)
Cookies	6 to 8 months	Wrap tightly
Fruits	8 to 12 months	Label and date container
Ice Cream (commercial)	1 month	Freeze in container
Juices	1 year	Freeze in container
Beef		
ground meat	2 to 3 months	All meats freeze best when wrapped in heavy duty, moisture proof/ vapor proof mate- rial to prevent drying and freezer burn
roasts and steaks	6 to 12 months	
stew	2 to 3 months	
Game	6 to 8 months	
Hot Dogs	2 months	
Pork		
bacon	1 month	
chops	3 to 4 months	
ham	2 months	
roast	4 to 6 months	
Poultry		
cooked	3 to 4 months	
uncooked	4 to 9 months	
Seafood		
fish	2 to 3 months	Wrap in moisture proof/vapor proof material
lobster, scallops or crab	1 to 2 months	

Food	Average freezer life	Storage suggestions
oysters (shucked)	1 month	
shellfish	3 to 4 months	
Milk	3 to 4 months	Freeze in unopened carton
Nuts (shelled)	6 to 12 months	Wrap tightly
Pies (fruit)	6 to 8 months	Wrap tightly
Pizza	3 to 5 months	Wrap tightly
Sandwiches	1 month	Wrap tightly and freeze individually
Soups	8 to 12 months	Airtight container

※ *Partially thawed fruit may be refrozen if it shows no sign of spoilage. If you are unsure, just use it as soon as possible.*

Fresh Vegetables

To freeze fresh vegetables, wash thoroughly, then blanch by briefly submerging in boiling water. Unblanched vegetables should never be frozen.

Time in Boiling Water	Vegetables
1 minute	Peas
2 minutes	Asparagus, green beans, limas, cauliflower and spinach
3 minutes	Broccoli
8 minutes	Corn on the cob

Lift vegetables from boiling water and submerge immediately in cold water for 4 to 5 minutes. Drain and place in containers. Store in containers, label and freeze.

※ Partially thawed vegetables may be refrozen only if ice crystals are still visible.

※ Many vegetables may be chopped and frozen in 1 cup portions for easy use in cooking. Green peppers, chives and celery are good examples.

Freezing Casseroles
(0° F. or below)

Dishes, such as casseroles, should be slightly undercooked if they are to be frozen. The cooking process will be completed when the dish is reheated. The following tip will keep dishes from being lost in the freezer. Line casserole dish with heavy foil, then pour partially cooked casserole into the foil-lined dish. Cool before freezing. After the casserole is frozen solid, remove from dish. Wrap tightly with foil; label and date contents. Return foil wrapped casserole to the freezer. When you are ready to prepare the casserole, remove the foil and reheat in the original casserole dish.

Freezing Fruits and Vegetables
(O° F. or below)

Fruit

Fruit can be frozen in a variety of ways. When preparing fruit, ascorbic acid may be added to prevent darkening. Package fruit, leaving headspace to allow for expansion during freezing. Liquid packed fruit, stored in wide-mouth containers, should have a headspace of ½ to 1 inch. Dry packed fruit, stored in wide-mouth containers should have a headspace of ½ inch. Liquid packed fruit, stored in narrow-mouth containers should have a headspace of ¾ to 1 ½ inches. Dry packed fruit, stored in narrow-mouth containers should have a headspace of ½ inch. Do not freeze fruit in a container larger than ½-gallon capacity. Food packed in larger containers freezes too slowly. The quality of the fruit will be inferior.

Syrup Pack Method: Combine sugar and warm water and mix until sugar is dissolved. The amount of sugar needed varies with the type of fruit to be frozen. (Tart fruit may require more sugar than naturally sweet fruit.) Use 2 to 4 cups of sugar to 4 cups of water, depending upon the desired sweetness. After dissolving the sugar in the water, chill the mixture. If necessary, add and dissolve ascorbic acid in the syrup just before pouring it over the fruit. Use enough syrup to cover the fruit. Store in containers, label and freeze.

Sugar Pack Method: Spread fruit evenly in the bottom of a shallow glass dish. If desired, sprinkle fruit with ascorbic acid that has been dissolved in water. Add desired amount of sugar. Stir gently to coat the fruit evenly and let stand 15 minutes. This allows the fruit juices to be drawn out and the sugar to dissolve. Stir again and package with the juices. Store in containers, label and freeze.

Liquid Pack Method: Fruit may be frozen, unsweetened, in chilled water or fruit juice to which ascorbic acid has been added. Store in containers, label and freeze.

Dry Pack Method: Place fruit, in a single layer, on a cookie sheet or jelly roll pan. Sprinkle fruit with ascorbic acid, if desired. Freeze until firm. Package individual pieces in desired serving sizes. Label and freeze.

Bruise—To pound or crush into fragments

Brûlé, brûlée—The French word for "burned"; used in cooking to describe foods glazed with caramelized sugar

Brunoise—A French term used to describe a method of dicing or shredding vegetables (used to flavor soups and sauces)

Brush on—To apply a liquid to the surface of food with a small brush

Butterfly—To split food down the center, without cutting all the way through, so that the two halves can be opened flat like butterfly wings

Canapé—A thin piece of bread, toast, cracker, etc., topped with a spread or tidbit

Caramelize—To melt sugar or food containing a high percentage of sugar over low heat, without scorching or burning, until a brown color and a characteristic flavor develops

Caviar—The salted roe of sturgeon or other large fish, usually served as an appetizer

Chapon—A chunk or slice of French bread rubbed with garlic and seasoned with oil and vinegar; (tossed with salad greens to give a subtle garlic flavor and to be discarded before serving)

Chiffonade—A soup garnish consisting of vegetables cut into fine strips (commonly a mixture of sorrel and lettuce cooked in butter)

Chill—To make cold, not frozen, in a refrigerator, in ice or ice water

Chinois—A fine-meshed, conical, strainer; also, little Chinese oranges that are preserved in brandy or crystallized

Chop—To cut food into small pieces with a knife or other sharp tool

Chutney—A pungent sauce or relish containing fruits, spices and herbs

Clarify—To clear a liquid, such as consommé, by adding slightly beaten egg white and egg shells; then straining

Clove—One small, section of a segmented bulb, such as garlic

Coat—To cover the surface of food with either a liquid or dry substance

Coat a spoon—Stage reached when a mixture forms a thin, even film on the back of a metal spoon

Coddle—In a liquid, to cook slowly just below the boiling point

Combine—To mix together two or more ingredients until blended

Compote—Fresh or dried fruits cooked and served in a sweetened, flavored syrup; usually served as a dessert

Condiment—Any seasoning added to food to enhance its flavor; this term often refers to a sauce, spice or relish eaten with food

Consommé—A clear, strong soup made by boiling meat and bones slowly for a long time

Cool—To remove from heat and allow to stand until heat has reduced

Core—To remove the inedible center portion of a fruit or vegetable

Correct seasoning—To taste food at various stages of the cooking process and to add more seasoning if necessary

Coq au vin—Chicken in red wine sauce with onions, mushrooms and bacon

Coquille—A shell or small dish made in the shape of a shell used for baking and serving various fish or meat dishes prepared with sauce

Court-bouillon—A well-seasoned broth flavored with vegetables, fish and meat; used for poaching and as a sauce

Cream—To beat butter or other fat alone with sugar or other ingredients until soft, smooth and fluffy

Crème fraîche—A thickened cream made from heavy cream and buttermilk and used as a topping for fresh fruits and pastries

Creole—A dish made with tomatoes and peppers; usually served over rice

Crêpes—Thin, light, delicate pancakes of egg and flour batter

Crimp—To seal the sides of a pie or pastry by pinching together to form a decorative edge

Crisp—To make leafy vegetables, such as lettuce, firm by rinsing in water and chilling; dry foods such as bread or crackers, by heating

Croissant—Flaky, crescent-shaped roll

Croquette—A thick, creamy mixture containing foods such as meat, vegetables and rice that is shaped, coated with egg and crumbs, then fried

Croûte—The French term for "crust" or "pastry"; en croûte means wrapped in or topped with a crust

Croûtons—Hard, toasted or fried pieces of bread, used to garnish certain preparations

Crumb—To break into small pieces

Crush—To pulverize by rolling with rolling pin or by mashing until dry food is the consistency of coarse powder; fruits, particularly berries, are usually crushed by mashing until they lose their shape

Cube—To cut into small squares, generally ¼ to ½ inch

Cure—To preserve meat, fish or cheese by salting, aging or smoking

Custard—A mixture of beaten eggs and milk, variously sweetened, flavored and cooked either over hot water or baked in an oven

Cut in—A method of mixing solid fat into dry ingredients until particles are desired size

Dash—Less than ⅛ teaspoon

Deep fry—To cook food immersed in deep, hot fat (about 360°F)

Deglaze—To loosen drippings from bottom of pan by adding stock, wine or other liquid and heating gently

Degrease—To remove the fat from the surface of a liquid

Demi-glace—A rich, brown sauce or gravy made by boiling down meat stock (usually flavored with Madeira or sherry)

Devein—To remove the black and white veins along a shrimp's back

Devil—To mix with hot or spicy seasonings, usually mustard and cayenne

Dice—To cut into very small pieces of uniform size and shape

Dilute—To add liquid to another liquid or semi-solid in order to thin or weaken it

Demitasse—A very small cup or a cup of very strong, black coffee

Disjoint—To cut or break fowl or meat into smaller pieces at the bone joints

Dissolve—To disperse a dry substance in a liquid to form a solution or to heat a solid until it melts

Dot—To place small pieces of butter or other substances over the surface of food

Dough—A thick, pliable mixture of flour and other ingredients, of varying density, with or without a leavening agent, which is baked as bread, pastry, etc.

Dragées (nonpareilles)—Miniature candies used for decorating cookies, cakes and candies

Drain—To remove liquid, usually by allowing food to stand in a colander until liquid has dropped off or by pouring off liquid

Draw—To remove the internal organs of poultry, game or fish

Dredge—To coat food with a dry mixture such as flour, bread or cracker crumb.

Drippings—The juices and melted fats of meat that come out during cooking

Drizzle—To pour liquid over the surface of food in a fine stream

Dust—To sprinkle the surface of food lightly with a dry substance such as flour, crumbs or sugar

Duxelles—A thick, pastelike mixture of minced, sautéed mushrooms, sometimes seasoned with shallots, salt and pepper, that is mixed into sauces and other recipes

Egg and crumb—To dip food into a slightly beaten egg and dredge with crumbs; (prevents food from soaking up fat)

En papillote—To cook and serve in a wrapping of foil or oiled paper

Enrich—To add cream, eggs or butter to food

Entrée—The main course of a meal

Escalope—A thin slice of meat or fish that has been slightly flattened and fried in fat

Essence, extract—Concentrated flavoring

Filet, fillet—A boneless strip of lean meat or fish

Fines herbes—A mixture of minced herbs: parsley, chives, tarragon and chervil

Flake—To break into small pieces with a fork

Flambé (blaze)—To set a match to food flavored with brandy or liqueur

Flan—An open tart filled with fruit, cream, stuffing or some other filling

Flavor—To enhance the taste of food by adding aromatics, condiments and spices

Flour—The finely ground meal of grain; to coat evenly with a thin layer of flour

Fold—To add ingredients of a delicate mixture into a thicker, heavier one, using a gentle over-and-over motion

Force meat—A paste-like mixture of finely ground meat, poultry or fish

Fricassée—To cook pieces of meat or chicken by braising in fat and then in a seasoned liquid until tender

Fritter—Meat, vegetable or fruit dipped in a batter and then fried in deep fat

Frizzle—To fry thinly sliced meat until crisp and curly

Frost—To spread with frosting or coat with sugar

Fry—To cook in hot fat

Fumet—A very strong stock used as a base for sauces

Ganache—An extremely rich butter cream (usually chocolate or mocha) used for filling pastries, tarts, etc.

Garnish—To decorate food by adding small pieces of colorful foods such as pimientos, mushrooms, olives and lemons before serving

Gazpacho—A cold soup made of raw, chopped vegetables

Gel—To form a jellylike substance with gelatin

Giblets—The edible heart, liver, gizzard and neck of a fowl

Glacé—A French word for a sweet, frozen liquid, usually ice cream

Glace—A French word used to describe any food that has been coated with a thin, sweetened syrup and cooked at high heat until the syrup forms a hard coating that cracks

Glace de viande—A concentrated brown meat glaze obtained by boiling meat stock down until dark and thick (adds flavor and color to sauces and gravies)

Glaze—A mixture applied to food which hardens, adds flavor and gives a glossy appearance

Grate—To cut food into small particles by rubbing them on the sharp teeth of a grating tool

Gratin—The thin crust that forms on the surface of certain dishes when they are browned under a broiler or grill

Grease—To rub fat on to the surface of food or utensils

Grill—To cook on a gridiron over embers or to put under a hot broiler

Grind—To cut food into small pieces or reduce to powder

Hollandaise—A delicate sauce of egg yolks, butter and lemon juice

Hors d'oeuvres—Small amounts of food served before a meal or as a first course

Ice—A frozen liquid dessert; also, to spread with icing

Icing—A sweetened, thick coating for cakes, cupcakes and cookies

Infuse—To steep herbs or other flavoring in a boiling liquid until the liquid absorbs the flavor

Jelly-roll style—To roll a flat piece of cake, meat, fish, etc. around a filling

Julienne—To cut fruits, vegetables and meats into match-like strips

Knead—To work dough with the heel of the hand; pressing, folding and turning until it has been worked into a smooth and satiny texture

Lard—To insert strips or pieces of fat into uncooked lean meat to keep it moist and succulent throughout cooking; can be placed on top of uncooked lean meat for the same purpose; also refers to the rendered fat of hogs

Leaven—To lighten the consistency and increase the volume of breads, cakes and cookies; (is done with leavening agents such as baking soda, yeast or baking powder that react with heat and elements in the dough)

Légumes—Vegetables, like peas and beans, which bear their fruit or seeds in a pod

Lyonnaise—A dish, usually potatoes, cooked with onions

Macédoine—A mixture of fruits or vegetables; it can be served either hot or cold

Macerate—To soften by steeping in a liquid, often with heat; also, to soak fruits in alcoholic liquors

Madrilene—A clear soup flavored with tomato juice; generally served chilled

Marinate—To allow food to stand in a liquid (marinade) to enhance its flavor and make it more tender

Marrow—The soft, fatty substance that fills the cavities of bones

Marzipan—A confection made from ground almonds, egg whites and sugar; (is frequently colored, flavored and molded into special shapes and decorated)

Mash—To soften and reduce to pulp; (usually done with a potato masher, the back of a spoon or by forcing food through a ricer or press)

Mask—To cover food completely with sauce or aspic before it is served

Medallion—Small, circular pieces of meat

Melt—To change fat and solid dissolvable foods into liquid by heating

Meringue—A snowy white combination of beaten egg whites and sugar; (can be formed into small cakes and baked or used as a topping on desserts and baked until browned)

Mince—To chop or cut into very small pieces

Minestrone—A thick vegetable soup

Mirepoix—A mixture of finely diced carrots, onions, celery and sometimes meat; it is cooked slowly in butter and used as flavoring for sauces, stuffings, stews and other dishes

Mix—To combine two or more ingredients until evenly distributed

Mocha—A combination of chocolate and coffee flavors

Mold—To chill, cook, or freeze in a container so that the food takes on the shape of the container

Roast—To cook, uncovered, in the oven by dry heat

Roe—Fish eggs

Roulade—A thin slice of meat rolled up, with or without a stuffing, and cooked in a seasoned liquid or sautéed

Roux—A mixture of flour and fat, sometimes browned and sometimes not, that is used as a common thickening agent in many sauces

Salt—To add salt to food; to rub with salt

Sauerbraten—Pot roast of beef marinated in spiced vinegar mixture, then braised

Sauté—To brown or cook food in a small amount of fat, turning frequently

Scald—To heat a liquid to a temperature just below the boiling point where tiny bubbles form at the edge of the pan

Scallop—To bake food which is usually cut into pieces, covered with a liquid or sauce and topped with crumbs

Score—To cut ridges or slits partway through the outer surface of food, usually in a diamond pattern (serves as a decoration and permits seasonings to permeate the food)

Sear—To brown the surface of food quickly, using intense heat

Season—To add salt, pepper, herbs, spices and other ingredients to increase the flavor of food

Seed—To remove seeds

Semolina—Coarse granules of cereal from which various pastas, puddings and soups are made

Separate—To divide egg yolks from egg whites

Set, set up—A condition in which liquids coagulate by heat or cold and retain their shape

Shirr—To cook whole eggs in ramekins with cream; occasionally a topping of bread crumbs may be used

Shred—To form small, thin strips by rubbing on a grater

Shuck—To remove the outer covering of food, such as the shell of clams, oysters or scallops; also, to remove husks from corn

Sieve—To strain liquid through a sieve

Sift—To pass sugar or other dry ingredients through a fine sieve

Simmer—To cook a liquid gently over a very low heat (180° F.)

Singe—To burn off small feathers of poultry or winged game by passing the plucked bird through a flame

Skewer—A wooden or metal pin on which various substances can be threaded before being grilled or fried

Skim—To remove, with a spoon or skimmer, a substance which rises to the surface of a liquid

Sliver—To cut into long, thin pieces

Snip—To cut into very small pieces with scissors

Soft peaks—To beat egg whites or whipping cream until peaks, with tips that curl over, are formed when beaters are lifted

Soufflé—A puffy egg dish with a flavored sauce or base into which stiffly beaten egg whites are folded

Spit—A utensil on which meat, etc., is threaded and then roasted or grilled by direct heat

Steam—To cook, covered, by means of vapor from boiling liquid rising through the food

Steep—To place a substance in a liquid, just below the boiling point, for a period of time to extract flavor, color and other qualities

Stiff peaks—To beat egg whites or whipping cream until peaks, with tips that stand up straight, are formed when the beaters are lifted; (peaks should be moist and glossy)

Stir—To mix with a round-and-round motion until ingredients are blended or reach a uniform consistency

Stir fry—Oriental method of quickly stirring foods as they fry

Stock—A liquid in which meat, poultry, fish, bones, vegetables and seasonings have been cooked; (used as a base for soups, sauces, stews and gravies)

Strain—To pass through a sieve for the purpose of separating liquids from solids

Stroganoff—Meat sliced thin and cooked with a sauce of broth, sour cream, seasonings and mushrooms

Stud—To insert whole cloves, pieces of garlic or other seasoning into food

Sukiyaki—A Japanese dish made with thin slices of beef and usually containing soy sauce, bean curds and greens

Sweetbread—The thymus gland of an animal, such as a calf or lamb

Tart—A small, individual pie filled with fruit, jam, custard or some other filling

Terrine—An earthenware dish in which minced or ground meat, game or fish are cooked; also used to refer to pâté when baked in this dish

Thicken—To make a liquid mixture more dense by adding an agent like flour, cornstarch, egg yolks, rice or potatoes

Timbale—A custard-like mixture of finely chopped meats, fish or vegetables along with eggs, milk and seasonings; (usually baked in ramekins and served unmolded)

Toasting—The application of direct heat until the surface of the food is browned

Toss—To mix ingredients lightly

Tripe—The stomach tissue of ruminents used as foodstuff

Truss—To secure poultry or other food with binding or skewers to hold its shape during cooking

Tryout—See render

Unmold—To remove from the mold

Velouté—A basic white sauce, made from chicken or veal, which is used as a base for a number of other sauces

Vinaigrette—A sauce made with vinegar to which other seasonings and herbs are sometimes added

Welsh rarebit—Melted cheese, usually mixed with milk, ale or beer, and served over toast or crackers

Whip—To beat rapidly until stiff; to increase volume by the incorporation of air

Wiener schnitzel—A cutlet of veal, coated with egg and bread crumbs, which is cooked in fat

Zest—The colored part of citrus rind used for flavoring; also, the oil pressed from the rind

COOKWARE AND CUTLERY

A wide variety of cookware is available to the modern cook. Selection may be based on a cook's personal preferences and needs, ease of care or storage advantages. Different kinds of cookware require special care to maintain desirable qualities. Most cooks own several different kinds of cookware, favoring one type over another.

POTS AND PANS

Aluminum: Cookware made of aluminum offers many advantages. It is second only to copper as the most efficient conductor of heat. The heat is distributed rapidly and evenly. Aluminum is light weight and easy to handle.

Most modern aluminum cookware is anodized or made of alloys to give it greater strength. Anodizing is a process by which the surface pores of the aluminum are sealed by an electrolytic process. The result is an aluminum pan with a smooth dark surface that does not react with foods, crack or chip. Anodized pans do require special care. Follow the manufacturer's instructions.

Aluminum cookware that is not anodized has disadvantages. Certain chemicals, in asparagus and artichokes, can react and darken aluminum. The vegetables also react to aluminum by darkening. Aluminum cookware can be treated to remove any discoloration. Fill another pan with a concentrated solution of vinegar and water, or two teaspoons of cream of tartar in water. Heat solution and pour into the discolored pan. Soak pan fifteen to twenty minutes.

Aluminum can buckle and warp if heated while empty. Extreme temperature changes can also cause cookware to buckle. Allow hot cookware to cool before washing in cold water. Constant high heat can warp aluminum, especially the bottoms of pans. When cleaning, never soak pans more than a couple of hours. These precautions will help preserve cookware and extend its use.

Steel: Cookware made of steel provides strength. Steel is a warp resistant material ideal for rapid and high heat cookery, which is why woks and crepe pans are often made of steel. Steel cookware requires extra care, and cooks often reserve it for special uses because it is so vulnerable to rust.

New steel cookware is often lacquered or oiled to prevent rust from forming. Steel cookware, treated by either method, must have these protective coverings removed before using.

Cookware treated with lacquer should be immersed completely in boiling water and simmered ten minutes. Remove the pan and allow it to cool. Then scour with steel wool, rinse and dry. This should remove all traces of lacquer. The cookware is ready for seasoning.

To remove covering on cookware treated with machine oil, scour it and rinse thoroughly. This process may need to be repeated in order to remove all traces of oil. The cookware is ready for seasoning.

Steel pans must be well seasoned, before use, to prevent rust. To season a steel pan, lightly coat the entire surface with unsalted oil (avoid corn or safflower oil). Heat the pan until it begins to smoke. Remove from heat and allow it to sit several hours. Wipe with a dry towel to remove excess oil. Store in a dry, moisture free place. If steel does rust, re-season it. Over a period of time a well seasoned pan will blacken with use, making its care less troublesome.

Always remember to dry steel cookware completely to prevent rust. Never use harsh abrasives or clean in the dishwasher.

Stainless Steel: Cookware made of stainless steel is very strong, maintains a high polish and is corrosion resistant. It does not react with acidic or alkaline foods or discolor. To qualify as stainless steel, the metal must contain 11% chromium. Other stainless steel classifications are based on combinations of metal content. Those made of 18 parts chromium and 8 parts nickel are labeled $^{18}\!/_8$. Higher grades of stainless are made of 18 parts chromium and 10 parts nickel and labeled $^{18}\!/_{10}$. This content stamp is evident on the pan. Stainless steel alone is a poor conductor of heat. Because of this, it is sheathed or sandwiched with copper or aluminum. Stainless steel is oven-proof and dishwasher safe unless it has wooden handles. It is easy to clean, and when combined with aluminum or copper, provides an ideal all-purpose cookware.

Cast Iron: Cast iron cookware has been used for many years and is still preferred for frying because of its slow and even heat distribution. Some modern versions are lined with enamel, which according to some experts, defeats the purpose of using cast iron. The traditional version must always be seasoned with oil. It acquires a patina with continued use. To season, brush cast iron with oil or rub with unsalted shortening, then heat uncovered, in a 350° oven for two hours. It may also be seasoned by brushing with oil, and thoroughly coating the pan. Lay the pan upside-down over a drip pan in a 350° oven for one hour. Frying pans may be seasoned on top of the stove. Coat the interior with oil and heat until the pan begins to smoke. Cool, wipe out excess oil and repeat the process. To prevent rust, allow cast iron to dry thoroughly or dry in a warm oven before storing.

Enameled Cast Iron: This variety claims to provide all the advantages of its cast iron predecessor without some of the problems. It does not require seasoning.

Copper: Copper is the Rolls Royce of cookware. It is preferred by chefs and gourmet cooks because it is the best conductor of heat. It heats instantly and distributes heat evenly. It cools as soon as it is removed from heat. Copper conducts heat so well that it is sometimes necessary to use lower temperatures. The interior is usually lined with a non-reactive metal such as tin, nickel or stainless steel because copper may react with certain foods. Never place an empty copper pan over heat as the lining will blister. Polishing copper can be difficult. Use a non-abrasive, non-chemical paste polish with a jeweler's rouge base. Use a soft cloth to clean off paste and to polish.

Unlined Copper: Unlined copper cookware is used for candy making or recipes using large amounts of sugar, such as jams and jellies. The high sugar content retards any reaction with the copper. Copper cookware is often sold with a protective lacquer coating which must be removed before using. To remove the lacquer, fill a large kettle with water.

Add one quart of baking soda per gallon of water. Bring to a boil. Submerge the lacquered piece into the boiling water bath and boil for at least fifteen minutes. Remove and allow to cool. The lacquer should peel easily from the surface. Rinse in cool water and dry thoroughly. The pan is now ready for use. Acetone may be used to remove lacquer from pieces too large to submerge.

Enameled Metals: Enameled metal includes cookware such as porcelain enamel, enamel ware, agate ware or granite ware. A metal pan is coated with layers and layers of porcelain. This cookware is nonporous and does not react with acid or alkaline foods. It is prone to chipping and cracking and requires careful handling.

Glass: Tempered glass cookware does not react with acid or alkaline foods and can tolerate higher temperatures than regular glass. It is not a good conductor of heat, but once heated, retains the heat very well. Even tempered glass cookware is not suitable for broiling. Glass cookware is prone to cracking and chipping, especially when subjected to temperature changes. Always read and follow the manufacturer's directions carefully.

Earthenware: Glazed clay cookware is hand painted and very colorful. The quality may vary enormously. European varieties are usually the best. Some Mexican varieties are poorly made and are glazed and fixed with toxic materials. They should only be used decoratively.

Terra Cotta: Terra cotta is characterized by its ability to cook slowly and evenly. Cookware of this type requires soaking to create a steaming process that prevents food from sticking. A popular version is the Romertopf or Russian Pot. These pots impart a brick-oven flavor. Clay or terra cotta will absorb and retain flavors, therefore, it should not be used to cook strong flavored foods.

Black Steel: This cookware is characterized by its black surface which is produced by chemical treatments or enameling. It does not require seasoning, but does react with acidic or salty foods. Bakers like black steel because it promotes even browning. The black surface does absorb heat rapidly and oven temperatures should be reduced fifteen to twenty degrees.

CUTLERY

Tang—This part of the blade extends from the middle of the handle to the end. The metal of a good knife will run the full length, extending from the tip of the knife point to the edge of the handle. This gives the knife greater strength and good balance.

Rivets—These are the round metal pieces that attach the tang to the handle. Some knives have handles of molded plastic that completely envelop the tang and do not require rivets.

BLACK BEAN SOUP

2	cups dried black beans	2	cloves garlic, pressed
5	cups water	¼	cup chopped fresh cilantro
1	onion, chopped	⅛	teaspoon dry mustard
1	rib celery, thinly sliced		Salt and pepper to taste
¼	pound smoked ham, diced	½	cup dry sherry

1. Cover beans with water and soak overnight. Drain.
2. Add five cups of water, onion, celery, ham, garlic, cilantro, mustard, salt and pepper.
3. Bring to a boil. Simmer, covered, 3½ to 4 hours, or until beans are tender.
4. Add sherry the last 15 minutes of cooking.
5. Pour soup into warmed tureen or cups.

Garnish with a dollop of sour cream, crumbled bacon, finely minced green onion or crispy croutons.

Serves 8

TORTILLA SOUP

Hot, spicy and delicious on a cold winter day! Serve with Tex-Mex Canapés and a crisp, green salad.

1	small onion, chopped	1	10¾-ounce can chicken broth
1	small fresh jalapeño pepper, seeded and chopped	1	10¾-ounce can tomato soup
		1½	cups water
2	cloves garlic, minced	1	teaspoon ground cumin
2	pounds stew meat	1	teaspoon chili powder
2	tablespoons vegetable oil	1	teaspoon salt
1	16-ounce can stewed tomatoes	1	tablespoon fresh cilantro
1	10-ounce can tomatoes and green chiles	6	corn tortillas, cut into ½-inch strips
1	10¾-ounce can beef bouillon	½	cup grated Cheddar cheese

1. Sauté onion, jalapeño, garlic and stew meat in oil.
2. Add tomatoes, soups, water and seasonings. Bring to a boil. Lower heat. Simmer, covered, 1 hour.
3. Add tortillas and cheese to soup. Continue cooking 15 minutes.

Serves 6

MIGAS
A Collection Classic

2 tablespoons butter
Dash Tabasco sauce

4 eggs, lightly beaten

2 tablespoons finely chopped onion

2 tablespoons finely chopped green bell pepper

¼ cup grated Cheddar cheese
Tostados, crumbled

1. Melt butter in a large skillet and allow to cool slightly.
2. Stir Tabasco into eggs and pour into skillet. Return to heat.
3. As soon as eggs begin to cook, add onion and bell pepper. Stir. When eggs are almost cooked, add cheese and turn heat to lowest setting.
4. Stir in crumbled tostados. Serve hot.

Serves 2

MEXICAN QUICHE

1 10-inch pie shell, or 2 8-inch pie shells, lightly browned

4 cups sliced mushrooms

1 small green bell pepper, chopped

½ red bell pepper, chopped

¼ cup chopped black olives

5 eggs

½ cup mayonnaise

1 tablespoon all-purpose flour

¼ cup milk

½ cup picante sauce

½ cup grated mozzarella cheese

½ cup grated Swiss cheese

½ cup grated Cheddar cheese

1. Preheat oven to 350°.
2. Combine mushrooms, bell peppers and olives.
3. In a separate bowl, beat eggs. Add mayonnaise, flour, milk and picante sauce. Stir vegetables into egg mixture.
4. In a separate bowl, combine cheeses.
5. Layer ½ the vegetable and egg mixture in crust. Sprinkle with cheese. Top with remaining vegetable and egg mixture. Quiche may be garnished with additional cheese, if desired.
6. Bake 40 to 50 minutes or until firm and lightly browned.

Serves 6 to 8

CHILAQUILES
A Collection Classic

2	large onions, coarsely chopped	1	tablespoon coriander
3	cloves garlic, chopped		Salt to taste
½	cup olive oil	24	corn tortillas
2	10-ounce cans tomatoes and green chiles, undrained	2	pounds Monterey Jack cheese, grated
1	16-ounce can tomatoes, undrained	2	cups sour cream

1. Sauté onion and garlic in olive oil until tender. Add tomatoes, coriander and salt. Simmer, uncovered, approximately 10 minutes.
2. In a separate skillet, heat shortening. Dip tortillas, 1 at a time, into hot shortening just until softened. Stack tortillas on paper towels and cut into fourths.
3. In a 9 by 13-inch baking dish, layer tortillas, sauce and cheese. This may be refrigerated or frozen.
4. When ready to serve, bake at 350° for 20 to 30 minutes or until hot.
5. Serve with sour cream on top.

Serves 8 to 10

MEXICAN RICE

½	cup chopped green bell pepper	2	tablespoons red wine vinegar
1	cup chopped onion		Salt and pepper to taste
1	clove garlic, minced	1	cup frozen green peas, thawed, optional
1	cup uncooked white rice		
2	tablespoons olive oil		Provolone or Monterey Jack cheese, grated, optional
1	14½-ounce can tomatoes		
¼	cup water		

1. Sauté bell pepper, onion, garlic and rice in olive oil until rice is lightly browned.
2. Finely chop tomatoes. Add tomatoes and juice, water, vinegar, salt and pepper to rice. Cover and cook until rice is done.
3. Add peas, stirring well. Pour mixture into a 1½-quart baking dish. Top with cheese and bake at 400° until cheese melts.

Serves 4 to 6

CHEESE ENCHILADAS

This is an unusual enchilada without a tomato base. Cocoa gives an intriguing depth of flavor to the sauce.

1 clove garlic, minced	¼ cup vegetable oil
4 tablespoons vegetable oil	12 corn tortillas
3 tablespoons all-purpose flour	8 ounces Monterey Jack cheese, grated
3 to 4 tablespoons chili powder	8 ounces Cheddar cheese, grated
2 cups water	½ cup chopped onion
1 tablespoon cocoa	
1 chicken bouillon cube	
Salt to taste	

1. Sauté garlic in oil until soft. Add flour and chili powder. Cook and stir to make a roux. Add water, cocoa, bouillon cube and salt. Bring to a boil. Reduce heat and simmer 5 minutes or until bouillon cube is dissolved.
2. Mix together Monterey Jack cheese, Cheddar cheese and onion.
3. Heat oil in skillet over medium heat. Quickly dip each tortilla in hot oil to soften.
4. Place 1 tablespoon cheese mixture in center of tortilla and roll. Place, seam side down, in baking dish.
5. Spoon sauce over enchiladas. Sprinkle with onions and remaining cheese. Bake at 350° for 20 to 30 minutes or until cheese melts.

Yields 12

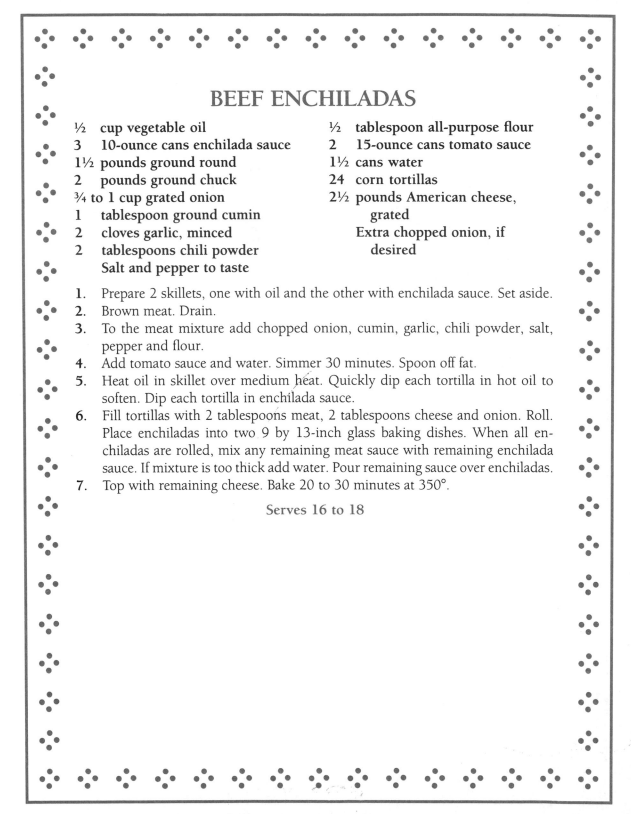

BEEF ENCHILADAS

½ cup vegetable oil	½ tablespoon all-purpose flour
3 10-ounce cans enchilada sauce	2 15-ounce cans tomato sauce
1½ pounds ground round	1½ cans water
2 pounds ground chuck	24 corn tortillas
¾ to 1 cup grated onion	2½ pounds American cheese,
1 tablespoon ground cumin	grated
2 cloves garlic, minced	Extra chopped onion, if
2 tablespoons chili powder	desired
Salt and pepper to taste	

1. Prepare 2 skillets, one with oil and the other with enchilada sauce. Set aside.
2. Brown meat. Drain.
3. To the meat mixture add chopped onion, cumin, garlic, chili powder, salt, pepper and flour.
4. Add tomato sauce and water. Simmer 30 minutes. Spoon off fat.
5. Heat oil in skillet over medium heat. Quickly dip each tortilla in hot oil to soften. Dip each tortilla in enchilada sauce.
6. Fill tortillas with 2 tablespoons meat, 2 tablespoons cheese and onion. Roll. Place enchiladas into two 9 by 13-inch glass baking dishes. When all enchiladas are rolled, mix any remaining meat sauce with remaining enchilada sauce. If mixture is too thick add water. Pour remaining sauce over enchiladas.
7. Top with remaining cheese. Bake 20 to 30 minutes at 350°.

Serves 16 to 18

BEEF AND GREEN CHILE ENCHILADAS

A wonderful enchilada with a cheese sauce in place of the traditional red sauce.

1 pound ground beef	*Sauce:*
1 medium onion, chopped	¼ cup butter
Salt and pepper to taste	3 tablespoons all-purpose flour
⅓ pound Cheddar cheese, grated	2 cups milk
1 dozen corn tortillas	½ teaspoon salt
Vegetable oil	½ pound Velveeta cheese
	1 4-ounce can chopped green chiles, drained

1. Preheat oven to 350°.
2. Brown ground beef with onion. Drain. Add salt, pepper and Cheddar cheese.
3. Heat oil in skillet over medium heat. Quickly dip each tortilla in hot oil to soften.
4. Drain tortillas on paper towels.
5. Place 1 to 2 tablespoons meat mixture in each softened tortilla. Roll.
6. Place each enchilada, seam side down, in a 9 by 13-inch baking dish, not touching.
7. To make sauce, melt butter, add flour, stirring constantly, cooking until mixture bubbles. Stir in milk and salt. Cook until mixture thickens and begins to bubble. Add Velveeta and green chiles. Stir until cheese is melted.
8. Pour sauce over enchiladas. Bake 30 minutes or until hot and bubbly.

Serves 6

CHICKEN ENCHILADAS

2 cups cooked, cubed chicken
2 4-ounce cans chopped green chiles
¼ to ½ cup salsa verde
½ teaspoon salt

Garlic salt to taste
12 corn tortillas
2 cups whipping cream, warmed
8 ounces Monterey Jack cheese, grated

1. Preheat oven to 300°.
2. Combine chicken, chiles, salsa, salt and garlic salt. Stir.
3. Dip each tortilla in warm cream.
4. Fill center of each tortilla with chicken mixture. Roll and place in a 2-quart glass baking dish.
5. Pour remaining cream over tortillas.
6. Top with grated cheese. Bake 10 to 15 minutes or until warm and bubbly.

Serves 6

SOUR CREAM CHICKEN ENCHILADAS

8 ounces sour cream
1 10¾-ounce can cream of chicken soup
1½ cups chicken broth
1 4-ounce can green chiles, chopped
12 flour tortillas

2½ to 3 pounds chicken, cooked, boned and shredded (reserve broth)
8 ounces Monterey Jack cheese, grated
4 ounces Cheddar cheese, grated

1. Combine sour cream, soup, broth and green chiles. Heat and stir until smooth and well blended.
2. To soften tortillas, heat a small amount of reserved chicken broth in a skillet. Place tortillas, 1 at a time, in broth for a few seconds. Remove and drain.
3. After draining, place tortillas, 1 at a time, directly into soup mixture.
4. Lift tortillas out of the soup mixture. Place 3 tablespoons chicken and 2 to 3 tablespoons of each cheese in the center of each tortilla.
5. Roll up and place, seam side down, in a 2-quart baking dish.
6. Pour remaining sauce over tortillas. Sprinkle remaining cheese on top.
7. Bake at 350° for 20 to 30 minutes or until bubbly.

Serves 4 to 6

AUSTIN FAJITAS

Provide guests with flour tortillas and bowls of salsa, refried beans, guacamole, grilled onions, grated cheese and chili con queso to make their favorite fajitas.

1½ to 2 pounds lean flank or skirt steak or 6 chicken breasts, boned and skinned

Marinade:
¼ cup vegetable oil
2 tablespoons lemon juice
2 tablespoons soy sauce
2 tablespoons chopped green onions

1 clove garlic, minced
1 teaspoon coarsely ground black pepper
1 teaspoon celery salt
1 teaspoon jalapeño juice, optional

1. Combine all marinade ingredients and mix well.
2. Remove any fat from steak and wipe well with paper towels.
3. Place steak and marinade in a shallow dish. Marinate at room temperature for at least 6 hours, turning frequently.
4. Drain liquid. Broil over hot coals. Cut steak diagonally.

Serves 4

PORK AND PINTO CHALUPAS

3 pounds boneless pork roast
1 pound package pinto beans
7 cups water
2 onions, chopped
2 cloves garlic, minced

2 to 3 tablespoons chili powder
1 tablespoon ground cumin
1 teaspoon oregano
1 4-ounce can chopped green chiles

1. Put all ingredients into a large Dutch oven and cook over low heat for 5 hours. Add more water as necessary.
2. When done, shred meat with a fork.

To make chalupas, serve meat and bean mixture on crisply fried corn or flour tortillas. Let guests choose from many ingredients to create their own specialties. Listed are some favorite toppings: shredded lettuce, chopped tomatoes, guacamole, sour cream, grated Cheddar cheese, finely chopped red onion and picante sauce.

Serves 10

SOUTH OF THE BORDER LASAGNA

This is a great dish for casual entertaining and can easily be doubled to serve a large crowd.

2	pounds ground chuck
1	onion, chopped
1	clove garlic, minced
2	tablespoons chili powder
3	cups tomato sauce
1	teaspoon sugar
1	tablespoon salt
½	cup sliced black olives
1	4-ounce can chopped green chiles
12	corn tortillas
	Vegetable oil
2	cups small curd cottage cheese
1	egg, beaten
8	ounces Monterey Jack cheese, grated
1	cup grated Cheddar cheese

Toppings:

Variation I:

½	cup chopped green onions
½	cup sour cream
½	cup sliced black olives

Variation II.

½	cup chopped pecans
½	cup raisins
½	cup sour cream

1. Brown meat. Drain. Add onions and garlic and cook until soft. Sprinkle chili powder over meat and mix well.
2. Add tomato sauce, sugar, salt, olives and green chiles. Simmer 15 minutes.
3. While mixture simmers, soften tortillas in hot oil. Drain on paper towels.
4. Beat together cottage cheese and egg. Set aside.
5. In a 9 by 13-inch casserole, place ⅓ meat mixture, followed by ½ the Monterey Jack cheese, ½ the cottage cheese and ½ the tortillas. Repeat process, ending with meat sauce on top. Cover with grated Cheddar cheese.
6. Bake 30 minutes at 350°.

Place toppings in individual bowls and let guests serve themselves.

Serves 8 to 10

CHILE RELLENO ESPECIAL

4 to 5 4-ounce cans whole green
    chiles, divided
1   pound lean ground beef
1   large onion, chopped
1 to 2 cloves garlic, minced
1   tablespoon ground cumin,
    divided
3   tablespoons chili mix, divided
    Salt to taste
8   ounces Monterey Jack cheese,
    grated
8   ounces sharp Cheddar cheese,
    grated

4   eggs, beaten
1   13-ounce can evaporated milk
1   tablespoon all-purpose flour
1   13-ounce can tomato sauce

Toppings:
1   cup sour cream
1   cup raisins
    Chopped pecans

1. Rinse chiles, open flat and remove seeds. Drain on paper towels.
2. Brown meat with onion and garlic. Drain.
3. Add 1 teaspoon cumin, 1½ tablespoons chili mix and salt. Stir.
4. In a greased 9 by 13-inch pan, layer chiles, beef and additional chiles.
5. Combine cheeses and sprinkle over chiles.
6. Beat together eggs, milk and flour. Pour over cheese mixture.
7. To the tomato sauce, add 2 teaspoons cumin and 1½ tablespoons chili mix.
   Pour over all.
8. Bake 30 to 45 minutes at 350°.

*If preparing ahead, do not cover with tomato sauce until time to bake. To serve, place
toppings in bowls and let guests help themselves.*

Serves 10 to 12

MEXICAN BAKED REDFISH

Sauce:

5   fresh tomatoes, peeled and diced
3   cloves garlic, minced
2   medium onions, chopped
1   jalapeño, seeded and chopped
2   green bell peppers, sliced
2   ribs celery, sliced
1   4-ounce can chopped green chiles
1   cup water
1   teaspoon pepper
1   teaspoon salt
3   6-ounce cans V-8 juice
2   dashes Worcestershire sauce

2½ pounds redfish fillets
    Creole seasoning
¼   cup water
1   cup grated Cheddar cheese
¼   cup grated Parmesan or Romano cheese
1½ cups sour cream
1½ green bell peppers, sliced
1   onion, sliced
⅓   cup chopped black olives

1. To make sauce, combine first 12 ingredients in a saucepan. Bring to a boil. Reduce heat and simmer 1 hour.
2. Season fish generously with Creole seasoning. Place in a buttered baking dish. Add ¼ cup water and sauce. Cover tightly with foil. Bake 45 minutes at 325°.
3. Remove from oven, uncover and sprinkle with cheeses. Place under broiler until cheeses melt.
4. Remove from oven and cover with sour cream, bell pepper, onion and black olives.
5. Return to oven and broil 3 to 5 minutes or until sour cream is heated.

Serves 6 to 8

GULF COAST CEVICHE

This may be served as an appetizer with chips or as an entrée.

2 medium onions	2 tablespoons seasoned salt
3 fresh jalapeños	3 pounds flounder or redfish
1 bunch cilantro	fillets, cut in bite-size pieces
2 cups fresh lime juice	or bay scallops
1 cup olive oil	5 to 6 ripe tomatoes, cut in bite-
1 cup dry white wine	size pieces

1. Chop onions, jalapeños, and cilantro together in food processor or by hand. Add lime juice, olive oil, wine and salt. Mix thoroughly.
2. Stir fish and tomatoes into lime juice mixture.
3. Marinate in a glass container in the refrigerator 24 hours, stirring occasionally.

Serve in avocado halves, warmed pita bread or on top of finely shredded lettuce.

Yields 4 quarts

TEXAS PRALINES

2 cups sugar	2½ cups pecan halves
1 cup milk	½ teaspoon vanilla extract
1 scant teaspoon soda	1 tablespoon butter

1. Cut a sheet of foil 2 feet long. Do not use wax paper.
2. In a 6-quart saucepan combine sugar, milk and soda. Cook over medium heat. Mixture should boil and turn brown. Stir, very slightly, around the edges.
3. When a soft ball forms (234°-240° F.) in water, remove from heat. Add vanilla, butter and pecans.
4. Beat with a wooden spoon until gloss is gone. This is a tricky step as candy can quickly turn to sugar if beaten too long. If mixture becomes too thick to "spoon out," add a few drops of hot water.
5. Quickly drop by spoonfuls on foil. When candy cools, store in a tightly covered container.

Yields 20 to 25 pieces

CREAMY PRALINES

¼ cup butter
1 cup brown sugar
1 cup white sugar
2½ tablespoons corn syrup

½ cup half and half
1½ tablespoons vanilla extract
¾ to 1 pound whole pecans

1. Combine butter, sugars, corn syrup and half and half in 6-quart saucepan.
2. Cook slowly to softball stage (234°-240° F.)
3. Remove from heat. Add vanilla and pecans.
4. Stir constantly until mixture loses its gloss.
5. Drop by spoonfuls onto a brown grocery bag. Allow pralines to cool. If mixture becomes too thick to "spoon out," add a few drops of hot water. Store in tightly covered container.

Yields 2 dozen pieces

BRANDIED PUMPKIN FLAN
A Collection Classic

¾ cup sugar
1 cup cooked pumpkin
1 cup milk
1 cup light cream
6 eggs, beaten

½ cup sugar
½ teaspoon salt
2 teaspoons vanilla extract
⅓ cup plus 2 tablespoons cognac

1. Heat sugar in heavy skillet until it is the consistency of light brown syrup.
2. Pour syrup into an 8-inch round baking dish. Rotate dish to cover bottom and sides. Set aside.
3. To make custard, blend pumpkin, milk and cream in saucepan. Heat over low heat, stirring constantly, until bubbles form around side of pan.
4. Add sugar, salt and vanilla to beaten eggs. Gradually stir in hot milk mixture. Add ⅓ cup cognac and stir. Pour into prepared baking dish.
5. Set dish in hot water bath. Bake at 350° for 1 hour. Cool.
6. Refrigerate overnight.
7. To serve, run spatula around edge of dish. Invert onto platter. Shake gently. Warm 2 tablespoons brandy. At the table, ignite cognac and quickly pour over flan.

Serves 12

APPETIZERS AND BEVERAGES

Quick Appetizers

✳ Wrap paper thin slices of prosciutto (Italian ham), Honey-baked or Smithfield ham around bite-size pieces of melon, fig, kiwi or pineapple. Secure with toothpicks. Thin slices of ham may also be rolled around fresh, blanched asparagus stalks.

✳ Wash, dry and slice tops off cherry tomatoes. Scoop out pulp and seeds with a melon ball scoop. Fill with chicken salad, crab salad, shrimp salad or deviled egg yolks and garnish with parsley, dill sprigs or dots of caviar.

✳ Blanch fresh snow peas or sugar snaps. Wrap each pod around peeled, cleaned and cooked shrimp. Secure with toothpicks.

✳ Blanch fresh green beans. Chill. Serve with Dill Dip with a Twist.

✳ Wash and dry Belgian endive. Trim leaves to same length. Fill end of each leaf with softened Boursin cheese. Garnish with alfalfa sprouts, freshly chopped parsley or dill.

✳ Marinate spears of jicama, 3 to 4 hours, in juice drained from pickled jalapeño peppers.

✳ Serve crackers with a softened block of cream cheese covered with one of the following:
1. Jalapeño, green chile or Tabasco jelly
2. Raspberry, blackberry or strawberry preserves
3. Steak sauce, Jezebel sauce or picante sauce
4. Fruit chutneys

JALAPEÑO CHEESE SPREAD

The number of jalapeños can be adjusted depending on the stamina of your guests.

1 small onion, quartered	¼ pound American cheese, grated
2 fresh jalapeños, seeded	¼ pound pimiento cheese spread
6 ounces cream cheese	¼ cup pecans
Juice of 1 lemon	Paprika
1 tablespoon Worcestershire sauce	Parsley
¼ pound New York sharp cheese, grated	

1. Finely chop onion and jalapeños in a food processor.
2. Add cream cheese, lemon juice and Worcestershire. Process until well blended.
3. In a medium bowl, combine remaining ingredients. Stir until thoroughly blended. Add jalapeño mixture. Mix well.
4. Shape on a serving plate. Garnish with parsley.

Serve with crackers or chips.

Yields Approximately 3 cups

BLUE CHEESE LOG

8 ounces blue cheese, softened	1 tablespoon chopped chives
8 ounces cream cheese, softened	½ to ¾ cup chopped pecans
¼ cup butter, softened	
1 4½-ounce can chopped black olives, well drained	

1. Mix all ingredients except nuts.
2. Shape into 1 large or 2 small logs. Roll log in pecans. Chill thoroughly before serving.

Yields 2 cups

BOURSIN CHEESE

A subtle blend of herbs in cream cheese. Makes a delicious food gift that is simple to prepare.

Base:
16 ounces cream cheese, softened
8 ounce carton unsalted, whipped butter, softened
2 cloves garlic, minced

Variation I:
1 teaspoon tarragon
1 teaspoon fresh parsley, chopped
1 teaspoon chervil
1 teaspoon chopped chives

Variation II:
½ teaspoon oregano
¼ teaspoon dill
¼ teaspoon marjoram
¼ teaspoon basil
¼ teaspoon thyme
¼ teaspoon pepper

1. Cream butter and cheese.
2. Mix in herbs as desired.
3. Cover and refrigerate at least 3 days for the best flavor.
4. Remove from refrigerator shortly before serving. Serve with dark breads and crackers.

Serves 16

BEER CHEESE

12 ounces cold pack Cheddar cheese, at room temperature
½ to ¾ teaspoon cayenne pepper
¼ to ½ teaspoon garlic powder
¼ to ½ teaspoon onion powder
Stale beer to taste

1. Combine all ingredients except beer. Mix well.
2. Add beer until mixture reaches desired spreading consistency. Chill.

Serves 15 to 20

BAKED PARTY BRIE

1 8-inch round Brie cheese	Fresh fruit
1 tablespoon butter, melted	Crackers and dark bread
¼ to ½ cup almonds, slivered	Nuts

1. Preheat oven to 350°.
2. Place cheese in oven-proof serving dish. Brush top and sides with melted butter. Sprinkle almonds on top.
3. Bake 10 to 15 minutes or until cheese just begins to melt.

Serve cheese with fruit wedges, crackers, breads and nuts.

Variation I:

Prick Brie with a fork. Lightly sprinkle with brandy and powdered sugar. Broil 1 to 2 minutes or until sugar caramelizes and the top is golden brown.

Serve with fruit wedges, crackers, breads and nuts.

Variation II:

1   16-ounce package puff pastry
1   8-inch round Brie cheese
1   egg yolk
1   tablespoon water

1. Thaw dough slightly at room temperature.
2. Place 1 sheet pastry on lightly floured surface.
3. With a floured rolling pin, roll out pastry. Cut 2 rounds, slightly larger than Brie round. Cut strips long enough to wrap around Brie.
4. Beat together egg and water.
5. Place 1 circle pastry on an ungreased cookie sheet. Center Brie on pastry. Brush sides of Brie with egg yolk mixture. Wrap pastry strips around Brie, using egg yolk mixture to hold pastry together. Place other round of pastry on top of Brie. Press edges of strips to seal dough. Decoratively score top of pastry. Brush all over with remaining egg yolk.
6. Heat oven to 400°. Bake Brie 10 minutes. Reduce temperature to 325° and bake an additional 15 to 20 minutes or until pastry is golden.
7. Let Brie reach room temperature before serving. If served hot, cheese will be soft and runny.

Serve cheese with fruit wedges, crackers, breads and nuts.

6 to 8 servings

CHICKEN CHEESE BALL

8 ounces cream cheese	1 tablespoon curry powder
1 cup finely chopped chicken or turkey	¼ teaspoon salt
⅓ cup mayonnaise	1½ cups chopped pecans, divided
	Parsley, optional

1. Combine first 5 ingredients. Add half the pecans. Mix thoroughly.
2. Shape mixture into a ball and roll in chopped pecans or parsley.

Serve with hearty crackers or toasted bread rounds.

Yields 2½ cups

QUICK CURRIED BLUE CHEESE DIP

Make this versatile dip several hours before serving to enhance flavor.

8 ounces cream cheese, softened	½ teaspoon dried, minced onion
1 0.7-ounce package blue cheese salad dressing mix	¼ teaspoon curry powder
⅓ cup mayonnaise	Dash Worcestershire sauce
	1 teaspoon lemon juice

1. Combine all ingredients and blend until smooth.
2. Chill thoroughly.

Serve with fresh vegetables or wheat crackers, or as a sandwich spread.

Yields 2 cups

SOUR CREAM HORSERADISH DIP

Use this in place of mayonnaise when making shrimp salad.

8 ounces cream cheese, softened	1 teaspoon salt
¼ cup prepared horseradish	½ cup sour cream
2 tablespoons minced parsley	Juice of ½ lemon
½ small onion, grated	

1. Mix all ingredients together.
2. Chill and serve with vegetables.

Yields 2 cups

CUCUMBER AVOCADO DIP

1 tomato	1 package dried Italian salad
2 cucumbers	dressing mix
2 cups sour cream	1 avocado, peeled and diced

1. Peel, seed and dice tomato.
2. Peel, split lengthwise, seed and dice cucumbers.
3. Thoroughly drain all liquid from tomato and cucumbers.
4. Mix all the ingredients and chill before serving.

Serve with chips or vegetables.

Serves 15 to 20

CURRY DIP

Serve this lively dip with fresh vegetables.

½ cup mayonnaise	1 teaspoon wine vinegar
½ cup sour cream	½ teaspoon Worcestershire sauce
1 to 2 teaspoons curry powder	1 tablespoon chopped chives
1 teaspoon garlic salt	1 teaspoon grated onion
1 teaspoon prepared horseradish	

1. Combine all ingredients.
2. Chill.

Serve with any combination of asparagus, broccoli, carrots, cauliflower, celery, cucumber, bell pepper, jicama, mushrooms, pea pods or zucchini.

Yields 1 cup

DILL DIP WITH A TWIST

Delicious when served with a variety of fresh vegetables.

8 ounces cream cheese	1 teaspoon seasoned salt
2 cups sour cream	2 to 3 teaspoons dried dill weed
1 1-ounce package Italian dressing mix	2 tablespoons lemon juice

1. Combine all ingredients.
2. Chill until ready to serve.

Yields 2½ cups

SUNNY'S SHRIMP DIP

1 4-ounce can shrimp	½ cup mayonnaise
1 rib celery, chopped	2 green onions, chopped
Dry sherry	1 clove garlic, minced
8 ounces cream cheese, softened	

1. Drain shrimp. Rinse. Soak in ice water 20 minutes. Drain.
2. Soak celery in sherry, to cover, 10 minutes. Do not drain.
3. Blend cream cheese and mayonnaise.
4. Stir in green onions, garlic, shrimp and celery. Chill thoroughly.

Serve with crackers or bread rounds.

Serves 12 to 15

SHRIMP AND CHEESE DIP

A hollowed-out purple cabbage makes an attractive container for this tasty dip.

1 cup mayonnaise	1 clove garlic, minced
1 cup grated sharp Cheddar cheese	1 teaspoon onion, grated
1 cup cooked shrimp	Salt and pepper to taste

1. Combine all ingredients and chill overnight.
2. Serve with crackers or Melba rounds.

Yields 3 cups

SPICY HOT CRAB DIP

An elegant entrée when served over rice or in pastry shells.

8 ounces cream cheese, softened	Juice of ½ lemon
1 tablespoon milk	2 tablespoons grated onion
8 ounces fresh lump crab meat	2 teaspoons prepared horseradish
2 tablespoons sherry	¼ teaspoon salt
1 teaspoon Worcestershire sauce	Dash cayenne pepper
¼ teaspoon garlic powder	
1 teaspoon Tabasco sauce	

1. Preheat oven to 375°.
2. Combine cream cheese and milk. Blend thoroughly.
3. Add remaining ingredients. Blend well.
4. Spread mixture in a baking dish.
5. Bake 15 to 20 minutes.

Serve with assorted crackers.

Serves 12 to 15

HOT CHEESE LOAF

A hollowed out bread loaf makes an unusual container for this snappy dip.

1	2 pound round sourdough loaf	1	tablespoon Worcestershire sauce
2	cups grated sharp Cheddar cheese	1	small jar dried beef, chopped
1½	cups sour cream	1	4-ounce can diced green chiles
8	ounces cream cheese	1	2-ounce jar pimientos, drained
1	bunch green onions, chopped		

1. Carefully slice top off bread loaf.
2. Remove bread from center of loaf in square chunks. Toast bread squares on a cookie sheet 15 minutes at 350°.
3. Combine all remaining ingredients.
4. Fill hollowed loaf with cheese mixture.
5. Place top slice on loaf and wrap in foil.
6. Bake 1½ hours at 325°.
7. Serve warm with toasted bread or chips for dipping.

Serves 12 to 16

BAKED CHEESE PUFFS

6	ounces cream cheese	4	egg whites, beaten
8	ounces sharp Cheddar cheese, grated		Cayenne pepper or paprika
1	cup butter	1	loaf French bread, cut into 1-inch cubes
	Dash cayenne pepper		

1. Combine cheeses, butter and cayenne in a double boiler to melt.
2. Fold a small amount of hot mixture into egg whites. Slowly add remaining mixture.
3. Dip bread cubes into cheese mixture with a fork. A knife may be needed to frost sides of cubes.
4. Sprinkle with cayenne or paprika.
5. Freeze or refrigerate overnight.
6. Bake 10 to 12 minutes at 400°. If frozen, bake 12 to 15 minutes at 400°. Serve hot.

Yields 8 dozen

MARINATED SHRIMP

This versatile dish makes a lovely salad when served in lettuce cups.

¼ cup vegetable oil
1 tablespoon prepared mustard
2 tablespoons lemon juice
2 whole green onions, minced
1 tablespoon minced onion

2 tablespoons minced celery
Salt and pepper to taste
1 pound medium shrimp,
   peeled, deveined and cooked

1. Mix first 7 ingredients.
2. Add shrimp and stir until thoroughly mixed.
3. Marinate in refrigerator overnight, stirring occasionally.
4. Remove shrimp from dressing and serve as hors d'oeuvres with toothpicks.

Variation:
Substitute Dijon mustard for prepared mustard.

Serves 4 to 6

SOPHISTICATED SHRIMP

2 pounds raw shrimp, peeled
   and deveined
¼ cup minced, fresh parsley
¼ cup minced fresh tarragon,
   optional

4 cloves garlic,
   minced
1½ cups olive oil
Salt

1. Place shrimp in a bowl with a marinade of parsley, tarragon, garlic and oil. Marinate overnight in refrigerator.
2. Remove shrimp from marinade and place in shallow pan. Sprinkle a little salt over shrimp. Broil 2 minutes on each side. Shrimp will be tough if overcooked.

Serves 6

CURRY CHEESE SPREAD

8 ounces cream cheese, softened
8 ounces sharp Cheddar cheese, grated
2 tablespoons sherry

1 teaspoon curry powder
Mild chutney
Green onions, chopped

1. Combine cheeses and mix well.
2. Add sherry and curry powder. Mix and mold.
3. When ready to serve cover with chutney and chopped green onions. Serve with wheat wafers or other favorite crackers.

Serves 6 to 8

HOT CLAM ROUNDS

If clams are a favorite, try this recipe.

1 loaf Pepperidge Farm white bread
½ cup butter
1 6½-ounce can minced clams, drained
8 ounces cream cheese, softened

2 teaspoons minced onion
¼ teaspoon Worcestershire sauce
Dash Tabasco sauce
Salt and pepper to taste
Mayonnaise
Cayenne pepper or paprika

1. Preheat oven to 350°.
2. Cut bread slices into 1½-inch rounds.
3. Lightly sauté in butter until golden brown on 1 side only. Rounds can be stored and frozen at this point.
4. Mix together next 6 ingredients.
5. Spread uncooked side of bread with mayonnaise and mound with clam mixture.
6. Sprinkle with paprika or cayenne.
7. Bake until puffy, approximately 10 minutes. Serve hot.

This mixture can be made a day or two ahead. When ready to serve, spread on bread and bake.

Yields 30 to 36 pieces

SMOKED OYSTERS IN CREAM CHEESE PASTRY

½ cup butter, softened
6 ounces cream cheese, softened
¾ cup sifted all-purpose flour
Dash salt

1 tablespoon cold water
3 3¾-ounce cans small smoked oysters, drained

1. Cut butter and cream cheese into flour and salt. Add water and mix lightly. Chill.
2. Working with a small amount of dough at a time, roll out on a floured board. Use plenty of flour to prevent sticking. Roll dough ⅛-inch thick. Cut with biscuit cutter.
3. Place oyster on half the round and fold over. Prick edges and top with a fork. Freeze.
4. When ready to serve, place frozen pastries on a cookie sheet. Bake 20 to 30 minutes at 450° or until golden brown.

Yields 36 pieces

EASY SALMON MOUSSE

May be served as a luncheon dish or as a first course in individual molds.

1 envelope gelatin
2 tablespoons lemon juice
½ bunch green onions, chopped (reserve tops)
½ cup boiling water
½ cup mayonnaise
½ teaspoon salt

⅛ teaspoon Tabasco sauce
½ teaspoon paprika
1 teaspoon dill weed
1 pound canned pink salmon, drained and deboned
1 cup whipping cream

1. Combine gelatin, lemon juice, onions and water in bowl. Mix until gelatin dissolves.
2. Add remaining ingredients except cream. Mix again.
3. Add cream gradually, blending until smooth. Pour into well buttered 2½-cup fish-shaped mold. Chill overnight.
4. Unmold on a chilled serving platter and garnish, using green onion tops for gills and an olive for the eye. Surround with parsley. Serve with crackers.

Yields 2½ cups

MIEKO'S EGG ROLLS

2 tablespoons sesame oil
1 to 2 cloves garlic, minced
3 ¼-inch slices ginger root, finely grated

Meat Filling:
1 pound lean ground beef, or 2 small cans crab, or 1 pound fresh cooked and peeled shrimp, or any combination

Vegetable Filling:
2 carrots, shredded
2 cups shredded green cabbage
1 bunch green onions, finely chopped
1 pound bean sprouts

Vegetable oil

Sauce:
2 teaspoons cornstarch
⅓ cup water
1 tablespoon soy sauce

Paste:
1 package eggroll skins
2 teaspoons cornstarch
½ cup water

1. Heat sesame oil in skillet.
2. Add garlic and ginger root to oil and sauté over medium heat.
3. Add meat filling to skillet. Cook until meat is almost done. Add vegetable filling and cook approximately 2 minutes.
4. To make sauce, dissolve cornstarch in water and soy sauce. Add to filling mixture.
5. Place 2 to 3 tablespoons of mixture in each egg roll skin. Roll up on the diagonal, folding in ends as you wrap. Seal eggroll with paste. Deep fry in oil 3 to 5 minutes on medium high heat.
6. Serve eggrolls with sweet and sour sauce, hot mustard or jalapeño jelly.

Serves 20 to 25

CASHEW NUT CHICKEN WITH SWEET AND SOUR SAUCE

Sauce:

1	6-ounce jar red currant jelly
1	6-ounce jar prepared mustard

¼ cup cornstarch
½ teaspoon sugar
2 egg whites, slightly beaten
1 teaspoon cognac
4 boned and skinned chicken breasts, cut into 1½-inch strips
1½ cups finely chopped cashew nuts
Peanut oil

1. To make sauce, simmer jelly and mustard. Stir until melted and well blended. Set aside.
2. Combine cornstarch and sugar. Stir in egg whites and cognac.
3. Dip chicken in egg white mixture. Roll in cashews.
4. Heat oil to 375°. Fry chicken until brown.

Serve chicken strips with sauce.

Yields 30 pieces

MUSHROOM CREAM CHEESE PASTRIES

Crust:

8	ounces cream cheese
1½	cups butter
3	cups flour

Filling:

¾	pound fresh mushrooms, chopped
½	cup butter
3	tablespoons all-purpose flour
¾	cup whipping cream
3	tablespoons chopped onion
1	teaspoon lemon juice

1. Preheat oven to 375°.
2. Combine cream cheese, butter and flour to make dough.
3. Form into 1-inch balls and press into small muffin tins.
4. Sauté mushrooms in butter.
5. Add flour and cook 1 minute.
6. Add remaining ingredients and cook until thick.
7. Place 1 teaspoon filling into each tin of dough.
8. Bake until brown. Serve hot.

Yields 3 dozen

SAUSAGE HORS d'OEUVRES

2	pounds ground sausage	1	15.2-ounce bottle Major Grey's
1	cup sour cream		chutney
½	cup dry sherry		

1. Shape sausage into small balls and brown in skillet. Drain.
2. Chop any large pieces of fruit in the chutney. Heat together sour cream, sherry and chutney.
3. Pour sauce over sausage.

Serve in a chafing dish with toothpicks.

Serves 20

CHICKEN LIVER MUSHROOM PÂTÉ WITH COGNAC

The addition of cognac makes this an elegant spread.

1	pound chicken livers	¼	teaspoon dill weed
½	pound fresh mushrooms, sliced	3	drops Tabasco sauce
		1	teaspoon salt
⅓	cup minced green onions	½	cup butter, softened
1	clove garlic, minced	¼	cup cognac
1	teaspoon paprika	⅓	cup clarified butter
¼	cup butter	2	hard-cooked egg whites, sieved
⅓	cup dry white wine	⅓	cup parsley, optional

1. Sauté chicken livers, mushrooms, green onions, garlic and paprika in ¼ cup butter.
2. Add white wine, dill weed, and Tabasco. Cover and cook over low heat 10 minutes.
3. Cool. Purée mixture until blended and light in texture. Stir in ½ cup butter, cognac and salt.
4. Spoon into desired serving container. Cover pâté with a thin layer of clarified butter. Garnish with sieved egg whites or parsley.

Yields 2 cups

MARINATED MUSHROOMS AND ARTICHOKE HEARTS

Serve as an appetizer or as a salad on lettuce leaves.

1½ cups water	½ teaspoon chervil
1 cup cider vinegar	1 bay leaf
½ cup vegetable oil	1 tablespoon chopped parsley
1 clove garlic, minced	1 onion, thinly sliced
1½ tablespoons salt	1 green bell pepper, thinly sliced
½ teaspoon whole black peppercorns	2 pounds fresh mushrooms
½ teaspoon dried thyme	2 9-ounce packages frozen artichoke hearts, thawed or 2 11-ounce cans, drained
½ teaspoon oregano	

1. Combine water, vinegar, oil, garlic, salt, peppercorns, thyme, oregano, chervil, bay leaf and parsley to make marinade.
2. Add remaining ingredients and toss. Refrigerate overnight.

Serves 10

CRISPY DEEP FRIED MUSHROOMS

Serve with Sour Cream Horseradish Dip.

½ cup all-purpose flour	⅓ cup milk
1 teaspoon salt	1 teaspoon sugar
½ teaspoon baking powder	1 pound small fresh mushrooms
⅛ teaspoon pepper	5 cups crushed Corn Chex cereal
1 egg, separated	Vegetable oil

1. Mix together flour, salt, baking powder and pepper.
2. Beat egg yolk and milk together.
3. Beat egg white until foamy. Add sugar. Beat until stiff and fold into egg yolk mixture.
4. Add dry ingredients to make a batter.
5. Dip mushrooms in batter and roll in crushed cereal.
6. Heat oil to 375°. Deep fry mushrooms until golden.

Mushrooms may be frozen and reheated in a 350° oven for 10 minutes.

Serves 8

STUFFED MUSHROOMS

Quick and easy!

2 pounds mushrooms	8 ounces cream cheese
1 package cheese and garlic salad dressing mix	Paprika or cayenne pepper

1. Preheat oven to 350°.
2. Wash mushrooms and remove stems.
3. Mix salad dressing and cream cheese. Stuff mushrooms.
4. Sprinkle with paprika or cayenne.
5. Bake approximately 10 minutes.

Yields approximately 40 pieces

HAPPY'S COCKTAIL VEGETABLES

This may be used as an appetizer or as a salad served on a bed of lettuce. Use any size jars of vegetables. These must be prepared ahead of time.

1 large head cauliflower	1 jar sour pickles, drained and sliced
1 pound carrots	2 1-ounce packages Italian dressing mix
1 jar cocktail onions, drained	
1 jar pitted black olives, drained	
1 jar stuffed green olives, drained	

1. Prepare dressing according to package directions.
2. Cut cauliflower into florets. Peel and slice carrots into ¼-inch rounds.
3. Combine with onions, olives and pickles. Toss with prepared dressing.
4. Prepare 2 to 3 days before serving. Store in a gallon jar in refrigerator. Shake jar occasionally.

Serve with cheese, crackers and fruit for a light lunch. Vegetables will keep up to 2 weeks in the refrigerator.

Yields approximately 1 gallon

SWISS CHEESE CREAM PUFFS

1 cup water
½ cup butter
1 teaspoon salt
1 cup all-purpose flour, sifted

1 teaspoon dry mustard
4 eggs
4 ounces Swiss cheese, finely grated

1. Preheat oven to 450°.
2. Combine water, butter and salt in a saucepan. Bring to a boil.
3. When water boils, quickly add flour and mustard. Remove from heat and beat with a wooden spoon until well blended.
4. Return mixture to medium heat, stirring well for 15 to 30 seconds to remove moisture.
5. Remove from heat and add eggs, 1 at a time. Beat approximately 30 seconds after each egg.
6. Fold in grated cheese.
7. Drop by spoonfuls onto a greased cookie sheet. Bake 20 minutes.

Serves 8 to 10

SPICY CRACKER SNACKS

Try this spicy alternative to purchased, seasoned cocktail crackers.

¾ cup vegetable oil
1 small package ranch dressing mix
1 teaspoon garlic powder
1 teaspoon dill weed

Dash cayenne pepper, optional
Dash lemon pepper
1 12-ounce package oyster crackers

1. Mix all ingredients except oyster crackers in a gallon jar or self-closing plastic bag.
2. Add crackers and shake well.
3. Let stand 2 hours, shaking frequently.

These keep well in the freezer and may be served without thawing.

Yields 4 cups

ROSEMARY WALNUTS

These are wonderful with cocktails.

6   tablespoons butter
1   tablespoon ground rosemary
1 to 2 teaspoons salt
½   teaspoon cayenne pepper
4   cups walnut halves

1. Preheat oven to 300°.
2. Melt butter in a large skillet.
3. Add remaining ingredients and sauté walnuts 5 minutes over medium heat. Stir constantly as walnuts will burn.
4. Pour walnuts into an oven roasting pan. Bake 20 minutes, stirring every 5 minutes.

Yields 4 cups

※ Before cracking nut meats, soak whole nuts in salted water overnight. The meats will come out whole.

MEDITERRANEAN CHEESE BITES

1   4¼-ounce can chopped black olives
2   tablespoons finely chopped onion, or more to taste
½ to ¾ cup vegetable oil
1   teaspoon curry powder
2   cups grated Cheddar cheese
6   English muffins

1. Preheat oven to 375°.
2. Mix first 5 ingredients.
3. Spread on split English muffins. Cut into quarters and place on cookie sheet.
4. Bake or broil until bubbly.

Leave muffins whole and serve as an accompaniment to soup.

Serves 6 to 8

TOASTED SAUSAGE BITES

Serve with soup for a quick winter lunch.

1	pound lean ground beef		Oregano to taste
1	pound ground sausage		Salt and pepper to taste
1	pound Velveeta cheese	2	loaves party rye or
	Garlic powder to taste		pumpernickel bread rounds
	Tabasco sauce to taste		

1. Brown meats separately. Drain and absorb all grease with paper towels.
2. Combine meats in 1 pan. Cube cheese and melt with meat. Add spices.
3. Spread 2 loaves of bread with meat mixture and place on a cookie sheet. (At this point, they can be placed in a single layer, on a cookie sheet, and frozen for later use. Store frozen in a plastic bag.)
4. Bake 15 minutes at 350° until bubbly and brown. If frozen, bake 45 minutes.

Variation:
Serve as a breakfast treat by spreading on white bread and omitting spices.

Yields approximately 50 pieces

CHEESE NUT WAFERS

1	pound Old English cheese, grated	2	scant teaspoons salt
			Dash cayenne pepper
1	pound butter, softened	1	cup finely chopped pecans
5	cups all-purpose flour		

1. Beat together butter and cheese until light and fluffy.
2. Stir in flour, salt and cayenne to taste. Stir in pecans.
3. Shape into long rolls approximately 1½-inch diameter. Wrap in wax paper. Chill or freeze.
4. Slice ¼-inch thick. Bake on a lightly greased cookie sheet at 350° approximately 15 to 20 minutes.
5. Remove from cookie sheet while hot and cool on a rack.

Yields approximately 10 dozen

BEVERAGES

Cocoa for Crowds

NO. OF SERVINGS	COCOA	SUGAR	SALT	COLD WATER	HOT MILK	VANILLA
25	1¼ c.	1¾ c.	1½ t.	1 pt.	1½ gals.	1 t.
50	2½ c.	3¼ c.	1 T.	1 qt.	2½ gals.	1½ t.
75	3¾ c.	5 c.	1½ T.	1½ qts.	3¾ gals.	2 t.
100	5 c.	6½ c.	2 T.	2 qts.	5 gals.	1 T.

Combine cocoa, sugar and salt until well mixed. Add water and stir well. Heat to boiling point. Add hot milk and return to boiling point. Stir and blend thoroughly; add vanilla and serve.

❋ As soon as it is made, beat cocoa until frothy. This will prevent a film from forming on the surface.

COFFEE

Americans drink more coffee than any other people in the world. We also prepare more variations and blends. From region to region, the flavor of brewed coffee may differ greatly because of the different blends and preparation techniques. New Orleans' chicory coffee and Hawaii's Kona coffee are examples of different and distinctive flavors of coffee. In early Texas, Cowboy Coffee was the standard fare around the campfire, hence the name. Milk, sugar and liquor were added to strong coffee. Elsewhere, coffee prepared similarly may be known by another name.

Allow ¾ cup water per serving to 2 tablespoons coffee for most types of coffee makers. For stronger coffee use 3 tablespoons coffee for ¾ cup water. Strength may be varied by increasing or decreasing one or the other ingredient.

❋ Freshly ground coffee is best. Never combine old coffee with newly purchased coffee.

❋ Always clean coffee residue from utensils to prevent bitter tasting coffee.

❋ Begin with cold water when preparing coffee.

❋ Never allow coffee to boil.

❋ Remove coffee grounds as soon as coffee is brewed.

※ Serve coffee immediately. The flavor deteriorates when coffee is kept warm for longer than one hour.

※ Do not reheat coffee.

Coffee for Crowds

NO. OF SERVINGS	COFFEE	WATER
25	½ lb.	1¼ to 1½ gals.
50	1 lb.	2½ to 3 gals.
75	1½ lbs.	3¾ to 4½ gals.
100	2 lbs.	5 to 6 gals.

Serving Variations

Cafe au lait—Brew strong black coffee. Simultaneously pour coffee and an equal amount of scalded milk into cup. Add sugar if desired.

Cafe Brulot—In a chafing dish, combine 6 teaspoons sugar, 6 to 8 whole cloves, 2 cinnamon sticks, 4 lemon twists and 4 orange twists. Pour 8 ounces of either cognac or Cointreau over mixture. Flame. Add 4 cups very strong hot coffee. Heat approximately 1 minute, stirring occasionally. Ladle into cups and serve.

Café Viennese—To a cup of strong hot coffee, add 1 ounce cognac. Top with sweetened whipped cream. Sprinkle with ground nutmeg.

Cappuccino—Italian steamed coffee. Add ½ cup scalded milk to 1 cup hot espresso. In a warm bowl, beat milk and espresso until foamy. Sugar may be added if desired. Pour into cup and sprinkle with cinnamon.

Café con Canela—To a cup of strong hot coffee, add 1 ounce coffee-flavored liqueur and 1 teaspoon vanilla extract. Top with sweetened whipped cream. Sprinkle with grated semi-sweet chocolate or cinnamon. Garnish with a cinnamon stick.

Demitasse—Brew double strength coffee. Serve in small cups. Sprinkle bits of chocolate in cup for a mocha flavor.

Irish coffee—To a cup of strong hot coffee, add 1 ounce Irish whiskey and 1 to 2 teaspoons sugar. Top with sweetened whipped cream.

Tropical coffee—To a cup of strong hot coffee, add 1 tablespoon coconut cream and 1 ounce dark rum. Top with sweetened whipped cream. Garnish with grated toasted coconut.

TEA

There are three varieties of tea: black tea, green tea and oolong. These teas differ according to preparation and fermentation of the leaves. Americans are most familiar with black tea, of which the favorite, orange pekoe, is a variety. Black tea leaves are fermented. Green tea is Oriental and varies in color from light yellow to olive brown. Green tea leaves are not fermented. Many old southern punch recipes call for green tea, which was popular in the mid to late 19th century. Oolong teas combine black tea leaves with green tea leaves to create a blend of both flavors. Oolong tea is considered partially fermented.

Herbal tea and spice tea combine the flavors of other leaves, flowers, herbs and spices. These are brewed by themselves or combined with standard teas for flavor variations.

Tea Preparation

Allow ¾ cup boiling water to 1 heaping teaspoon loose tea or 1 tea bag. Strength may be varied by increasing or decreasing one or the other ingredient.

Hot Tea For Crowds

NO. OF SERVINGS	TEA	BOILING WATER
25	6 to 7 T.	1¼ gals.
50	¾ to 1 c.	2½ gals.
75	1 c. + 2 T. to 1½ c.	3¾ gals.
100	2 c.	5 gals.

Put tea leaves in a cheesecloth bag or a large tea strainer, tightly sealed, so that the tea leaves do not filter into the tea. Pour hot water over the tea and allow to steep for at least 10 minutes. These measurements are for a 6 oz. tea cup. The tea may be diluted by adding more boiling water.

　※ Begin with cold water when brewing tea.

　※ When preparing larger quantities, allow tea to steep 5 minutes longer.

　※ When serving hot tea in a china cup, place a spoon in the cup. Pouring tea over the spoon helps avoid cracking the cup. The spoon absorbs the heat.

Iced Tea For Crowds

NO. OF SERVINGS	TEA	BOILING WATER	TAP WATER
25	¼ c.	2 gals.	1 gal.
50	½ c.	3 gals.	1½ gal.
75	1½ c.	4 gals.	2 gals.
100	2 c.	5 gals.	2½ gals.

Put tea leaves in cheesecloth bag. Pour boiling water over tea and allow to steep for at least 10 minutes. After 10 minutes, add tap water equaling half the measurement used for boiling water.

❋ Never boil tea.

❋ To prevent bitter tasting tea, remove tea bags after tea has steeped.

❋ When preparing iced tea for a crowd, vary the flavor by adding 6 ounces of frozen lemonade to 1 gallon of tea.

❋ Freeze fruit juice for ice cubes, add to tea and garnish with sprigs of fresh mint.

❋ Use simple syrup to sweeten large quantities of tea.

❋ If iced tea is sweetened while it is hot, it requires less sugar.

❋ Make ice cubes with left-over tea or coffee. These cubes added to a drink will not dilute the beverage.

SIMPLE SYRUP

1   cup granulated sugar   1   cup water

1. In a saucepan, add sugar to water. Bring mixture to a boil and stir continuously.
2. Reduce heat slightly and simmer until liquid clears. Cool completely before using.

Yields 1¼ cups

PUNCH

Punch for Crowds

Number of Servings		Punch	
32	4-ounce servings	1	gal.
96	4-ounce servings	3	gals.

Sparkling Ice Ring

When making an ice ring, use distilled or boiled water for crystal clear ice. Choose a ring or decorative mold. Fill with ½ to 1-inch water. Place berries, leaves or fruits in mold and freeze. Add water to the top of ring and freeze. To loosen ice, dip ring or mold in hot water. Invert and float ring in punch.

   ❊ Garnish punch with sliced lemons, limes, oranges, whole or sliced berries, green seedless grapes, cherries, sprigs of mint or twists of citrus rind.

   ❊ Rinse maraschino cherries in cold water to prevent bleeding.

   ❊ Color ice cubes and flavor them with liqueurs.

   ❊ To make decorative ice cubes, place cherries, mint leaves or other garnishes in each compartment when freezing.

   ❊ Frozen bunches of grapes may be used to chill punch.

APRICOT LEMON COOLER

4	teaspoons instant tea	1	6-ounce can lemonade
4	tablespoons sugar		concentrate, thawed
1½	cups apricot nectar	3	cups ginger ale
½	cup cold water		Orange slices and cherries

1. Mix together tea, sugar, apricot nectar and water. Stir until sugar is dissolved.
2. Just before serving, add lemonade and ice cubes. Slowly add ginger ale, stirring gently.
3. Garnish with orange slices or cherries.

Serves 6

LEMON ALMOND ICED TEA

2   cups water
3   tablespoons lemon-flavored
       instant tea mix
2   cups cold water
1   12-ounce can frozen lemonade
       concentrate, thawed

1   tablespoon vanilla extract
1   tablespoon almond extract
2   quarts cold water

1. Bring 2 cups water and lemon tea mix to a boil. Steep 5 minutes.
2. Add 2 cups cold water, lemonade, vanilla and almond extract.
3. When ready to serve, add 2 quarts water. Serve over ice.

Yields 3½ quarts

TEA AND LEMONADE COOLER

8   tea bags
3   quarts boiling water
¾   cup sugar
1   32-ounce bottle ginger ale,
       chilled

1   12-ounce can lemonade
       concentrate
Lemon slices
Mint

1. Place tea bags in boiling water and steep 10 minutes.
2. Remove tea bags. Add sugar and stir until dissolved.
3. Add lemonade. Chill.
4. Just before serving, add ginger ale. Pour over ice or serve as punch.

Garnish with lemon slice and sprigs of mint.

Yields 16 cups

SPECIAL FRUIT TEA

Chill well before serving.

2   cups sugar
4   cups water
1   tablespoon whole cloves
3   cinnamon sticks
1   46-ounce can unsweetened
      pineapple juice

1   46-ounce can orange juice
12 cups tea, unsweetened and
      diluted to desired strength
3 to 4 thinly sliced lemons
      Mint sprigs

1. Bring sugar and water to a boil.
2. Add cloves and cinnamon sticks. Boil 5 minutes.
3. Remove cloves and cinnamon. Cool.
4. Add pineapple juice, orange juice and tea.
5. Garnish with lemon slices and mint sprigs.

Yields 1½ gallons

CRANBERRY TEA

This is a delightful drink anytime, but a special treat for the holiday season.

3   cups water
3   small tea bags
⅓   cup sugar

1   tablespoon lemon juice
1   cup cranberry juice

1. Bring water to a boil. Add tea bags and steep 5 minutes.
2. Add sugar, lemon juice and cranberry juice.

This is wonderful served hot, but is equally good served cold.

Yields 3½ cups

Cloudy tea may be freshened by pouring hot water into tea already steeped.

KID'S FRUIT PUNCH

Children like this and moms are pleased that it's good for them!

2   12-ounce cans frozen, orange juice concentrate

1½ cups unsweetened pineapple juice

4   cups apple juice

1. Prepare orange juice according to directions. Mix with pineapple juice and apple juice.
2. Serve chilled.

Serves 24

CRANBERRY PUNCH

4   cups cranberry juice

1½ cups sugar

4   cups pineapple juice

1   tablespoon almond extract

2   liters ginger ale

Fresh fruit slices

Rum, optional

1. Combine first 4 ingredients. Stir until sugar is dissolved.
2. Chill.
3. Add ginger ale just before serving.
4. Garnish with fruit slices if desired.

Variation:
Rum, in any amount, can be added to this punch.

Serves 30

CRANBERRY LEMON PUNCH

2 quarts cranberry juice
1 6-ounce can frozen lemonade concentrate, thawed

½ cup maraschino cherry juice
2 liters lemon-lime soda, well-chilled

1. Combine all ingredients.
2. Serve over an ice ring in a punch bowl. Float additional lemon slices, orange wedges and maraschino cherries for garnish.

For a festive, attractive ice ring, freeze lemon slices, orange wedges and maraschino cherries in colored water or cranberry juice.

Serves 40

FROZEN BANANA PUNCH

A refreshing, versatile drink that can be prepared and frozen weeks before serving. Delicious for a brunch, tea or wedding reception.

2 12-ounce cans frozen orange juice concentrate, thawed
1 12-ounce can frozen lemonade concentrate, thawed
1 46-ounce can pineapple juice

6 ripe bananas
6 cups water
2 to 4 cups sugar
10 liters ginger ale or lemon-lime soda, chilled

1. In a large container, combine juices.
2. Using a blender, purée bananas two at a time with water and sugar. Add mixture to juices after thoroughly blending.
3. Freeze in quart containers.
4. When ready to serve, thaw until punch base is slushy. Add two liters ginger ale or lemon-lime soda to each quart of punch base.

Yields 5 quarts base
or
3¾ gallons punch

CHAMPAGNE PUNCH

4	sugar cubes	1	fifth champagne, chilled
2	dashes angostura bitters	1	fifth dry white wine, chilled
	Peel of ½ orange		Orange slices
½	cup apricot brandy		

1. In a glass bowl or pitcher, saturate sugar cubes with bitters. Add orange peel and brandy to sugar mixture. Stir until sugar is dissolved.
2. Chill mixture until ready to serve.
3. Add champagne and white wine. Garnish with orange slices.

Serves 10 to 12

CITRUS WINE WELCOMER

2	cups orange juice	1	25.4-ounce bottle dry white wine, chilled
1	6-ounce can frozen lemonade concentrate, thawed	1	liter club soda, chilled
1	cup Cointreau or other orange-flavored liqueur		Crushed ice
			Orange slices

1. Combine first 4 ingredients in a punch bowl. Stir.
2. Add club soda and crushed ice, stirring gently.
3. Garnish with orange slices.

Serves 10 to 12

HOT SPICED WINE

2 quarts hearty Burgundy	10 whole cloves
¾ fifth of brandy	8 to 10 cinnamon sticks
5 oranges, sliced	½ pound slivered almonds
5 lemons, sliced	8 ounces raisins
1 12-ounce can orange juice concentrate, thawed	½ cup sugar or to taste, optional

1. Bring first 7 ingredients to a boil.
2. Reduce heat to simmer. Add almonds, raisins and sugar.
3. Simmer 4 to 6 hours.
4. Strain before serving.

Leftover wine can be stored 2 to 3 days in refrigerator.

Serves 10 to 12

HOT SPICY ORANGE CUP

½ cup sugar	4 2-inch cinnamon sticks
2 cups water	2 quarts orange juice
12 whole cloves	1 quart sweet cider

1. Combine sugar, water and spices in a saucepan.
2. Simmer 10 minutes. Strain.
3. Add orange juice and cider, stirring well.
4. Serve piping hot in mugs with a cinnamon stick.

Serves 30 to 40

HOT GOLDEN FALL PUNCH

This tart wassail is good served with cookies or cake.

4	cups unsweetened pineapple juice	1	cup orange juice
1	12-ounce can apricot nectar	2	cinnamon sticks
4	cups apple cider	¼	teaspoon salt
		1	teaspoon whole cloves

1. Pour juices into electric percolator. Place remaining ingredients in basket and perk. Serve steaming hot.

Without a percolator, pour juices in a large pot. Simmer 10 minutes. Remove spices.

Serves 18 to 20

CREAMY ORANGE DELIGHT

6	eggs	1	6-ounce can limeade concentrate
1	cup sugar		
1	tablespoon vanilla extract	1	quart gin
1	12-ounce can orange juice concentrate		Lemon-lime soda

1. Place eggs in a blender and blend until frothy.
2. Pour eggs in a large pitcher. Add all ingredients except lemon-lime soda. Let punch base stand at least 1 hour.
3. Mix equal parts punch base and lemon-lime soda. Serve over crushed ice.

Serves 12

WINTER WASSAIL

4 cups apple cider
2 cups cranberry juice
½ cup orange juice
2 cups vodka
1 cup brandy

1 teaspoon whole allspice
1½ teaspoons whole cloves
2 cinnamon sticks
Cranberries, optional

1. Combine all ingredients and heat until warm. Strain.

If served in a punch bowl, garnish with fresh cranberries.

Serves 15 to 18

CAPPUCCINO

1 pound ground coffee
2 cinnamon sticks
1 teaspoon ground cinnamon
½ cup sugar

4 cups whipping cream, whipped
Shaved chocolate
Crushed peppermint candy

1. In a 30-cup percolator, filled with water, brew cinnamon sticks and ground cinnamon with coffee.
2. Add sugar to coffee after brewing.
3. On a tray, place bowls of whipped cream, shaved chocolate and crushed peppermint. Guests may prepare coffee as desired.

Serves 30

HEART WARMING HOT CHOCOLATE

½ ounce peppermint schnapps
½ ounce crème de menthe

½ ounce crème de cocoa
1 cup hot chocolate

1. Mix peppermint schnapps, crème de menthe and crème de cocoa together.
2. Prepare 1 cup of hot chocolate. When ready add liqueur mixture.

This can easily be adapted for a larger quantity.

Serves 1

BOURBON MILK PUNCH

1 gallon vanilla ice cream, softened	½ cup rum
1 cup bourbon	¼ cup brandy
	Freshly grated nutmeg

1. Place softened ice cream in a punch bowl. Add bourbon, rum and brandy. Stir until well blended.
2. Sprinkle with nutmeg and serve.

Serves 8 to 10

TRADITIONAL EGGNOG

1 dozen large egg yolks	4 cups bourbon
2 cups sugar	8 cups whipping cream

1. Blend bourbon and sugar. Let stand overnight, stirring occasionally.
2. Beat egg yolks until light and fluffy. Combine egg yolks and bourbon mixture, stirring constantly. Allow eggs and bourbon to stand 2½ hours.
3. Whip cream until stiff and gently fold into bourbon mixture.
4. Chill in refrigerator and serve in chilled cups.

Serves 30

QUICK CHOCOLATE EGGNOG

3 cups prepared eggnog, chilled	1 cup whipping cream
1 cup chocolate milk	2 tablespoons powdered sugar
½ cup crème de cacao	Shaved chocolate

1. In a pitcher, combine eggnog, chocolate milk and crème de cacao. Cover and chill.
2. Just before serving, whip cream to soft peaks and fold in powdered sugar.
3. Garnish each serving with a dollop of whipped cream and shaved chocolate.

This is especially festive served in a punch bowl with the whipped cream folded into the eggnog.

Yields 10½ cups

GIFT EGGNOG

A great gift idea for Christmas! Adults love it with a little bourbon, but it makes a delicious drink without the alcohol.

¾ cup sugar	1 tablespoon vanilla extract
3 eggs	Freshly ground nutmeg
1 quart whole milk	
2 tablespoons all-purpose flour	

1. Beat eggs in a mixer 3 to 4 minutes on high.
2. Place flour and sugar in the top of a double boiler. Add eggs and half the milk. Cook over hot water until thick.
3. Remove pan from heat. Slowly stir in remaining milk and vanilla.
4. Cool. Pour into a 1-quart glass jar or bottle. Store in refrigerator until ready to use.
5. When serving, place 1 or more tablespoons bourbon in a 6 to 8-ounce glass. Add eggnog, top with a dollop of whipped cream and sprinkle with nutmeg.

Yields approximately 1 quart

CHRISTMAS CAPPUCCINO

3 3-inch cinnamon sticks	6 cups boiling water
12 whole cloves	3 cups half and half, warmed
Cheesecloth	2 cups whipping cream, whipped
½ cup instant espresso or coffee	Freshly grated nutmeg
½ cup sugar	Extra cinnamon sticks

1. Tie cinnamon sticks and cloves in cheesecloth. Place in a 4-quart saucepan. Add coffee and sugar. Pour in boiling water to dissolve.
2. Cover and steep 5 minutes.
3. Remove spice bag. Add half and half.
4. Serve in warm mugs topped with whipped cream and nutmeg. Add a cinnamon stick to stir.

Serves 16

SALADS AND SALAD DRESSINGS

Types of Lettuce

1. **Iceberg** lettuce has a round, smooth, compact head with pale, crisp leaves. It retains its crispness and is especially useful for lunchbox sandwiches and salads.

2. **Romaine** or cos lettuce has an elongated head with narrow, dark green leaves. It is preferred for Caesar salad and is crisp and flavorful.

3. **Leaf** lettuce includes all ruffly types that do not form heads. Common types are red leaf, green leaf and Australian lettuce.

4. **Butter or Boston** lettuce has a rich, delicate flavor and a buttery texture. Its small, rounded head contains soft, medium-green leaves.

5. **Watercress** has a pungent, peppery flavor and small, round leaves. The leaves are delicious when young, but old leaves are bitter and tough.

6. **Endive** is the term given to a family of strongly flavored salad greens. Belgian endive is the most expensive because it is usually imported. The head is pointed and small. Escarole is used in Italian cooking and has wide, dark green leaves. Chicory (curly endive) has a bitter taste and large, curly leaves.

7. **Sprouts** are usually available in any produce market and are interesting additions to a salad. Alfalfa sprouts are wispy, green shoots while bean sprouts are pale and tender. Radish sprouts have a strong, distinctive flavor.

8. **Arugula** or rocket has a bittersweet flavor and small, narrow, dark green leaves. It is generally used as an accent.

9. **Cabbage** is always available in produce markets. There are several varieties including green, red, savory, curly and Chinese. They are delicious in salads and coleslaw.

10. **Spinach** is wonderful in salads by itself or in combination with other greens. It must be washed very well to remove sand and grit.

11. **Radicchio** is imported and looks like a small red cabbage. Its bitter flavor can be overwhelming when it is served alone, but it is good when tossed with other greens. Use sparingly.

Tossed Green Salads

※ Always tear lettuce for tossed salads, as cutting or slicing makes the lettuce bitter and browns the edges.

※ Use hands or tongs to gently toss green salads so that lettuce does not bruise.

※ Tomatoes will thin salad dressings, so add them at the last minute. Slice in wedges to keep them from losing their juices.

※ Avocado slices will not turn brown when added to a salad if they have been coated with lemon juice first.

Lettuce and Salad Greens

※ It is possible to revive wilted salad greens by dousing them quickly in warm water, then in ice water containing a small amount of vinegar.

※ Salad greens will retain their freshness and longevity if they are first rinsed, wrapped in paper towels, and then refrigerated in a sealable bag.

※ To core a head of lettuce, bang the core end on the kitchen counter, then twist and lift out the core. Do not cut out the core with a knife. This causes discoloration.

※ Lettuce will keep approximately two weeks if purchased fresh and stored at 32° F.

※ Parsley and watercress should be washed, drained and stored in air-tight containers in the refrigerator.

Types of Oils

1. **Olive oil** comes from the olive and has the same color, fragrance and taste. It is used when the oil contributes to the flavor of the dish. Quality is very important, but it is difficult to find a good olive oil on the market. Try several varieties. Once opened, a can of olive oil does not last indefinitely. It may become rancid; so it is best stored in bottles and covered with cheesecloth fastened to the neck with a rubber band. Store in a cool, dark place.

2. **Sesame oil** is made from roasted sesame seeds and is thick, light brown in color and very aromatic. It is used more for seasoning than for cooking because it burns easily. If the oil is well covered, the aroma remains indefinitely.

3. **Chile pepper oil** is used in Chinese cooking. It is also used in salads and dip sauces or is added during cooking. Chile pepper oil may be made by heating 1 cup of vegetable oil in a small saucepan until very hot. Turn heat to low and add ¼ cup crushed chile pepper flakes or 3 tablespoons powdered chile. Stir 1 minute and turn off heat. Allow to cool completely, then stir well. Strain the oil into a small bottle, using cheesecloth as a strainer. It may be kept for one month.

4. **Peanut oil** is thick and golden in color. It is a cooking oil commonly used in Chinese dishes. Its richness gives stir fry dishes an excellent flavor.

5. **Vegetable oil** is thick and light to medium yellow and is commonly used in American households. It is produced from a variety of vegetables.

6. **Corn oil** is thicker than vegetable oil. It is a rich, heavy oil and is best for frying foods.

7. **Safflower oil,** from safflower seeds, is light and yellow-clear in color. It may be used as an all-purpose oil.

8. **Sunflower oil,** made from sunflower seeds, is like safflower oil in color and texture and has fewer calories than vegetable and corn oil. It is used for frying.

Vinegars

1. **Cider vinegar,** amber in color, occurs naturally from the fermentation of apple juice. It is used in salad dressings as well as in cooking.

2. **Flavored vinegar** is made by adding fresh herbs, fruit, mint or garlic to wine vinegar.

3. **Distilled vinegar** has a strong flavor and is colorless.

4. **Wine vinegar** is red or white in color and is strong and aromatic. There are several varieties: white, red, sherry and rose wine. Its use is determined by its color.

5. **Rice vinegar** is sweet and light in flavor and is used often in Chinese cooking.

6. **Malt vinegar** is strong in flavor and has a light brown color. It is made from cereals or barley and is used in pickling.

7. **Spirit vinegar** also has a strong flavor and is colorless. It is used in sauces and for pickling.

Salad Dressings

※ To make a perfect oil and vinegar dressing, combine 1 part vinegar with 2 parts olive oil.

※ Salad dressings should be used sparingly; a thin coating is all that is necessary.

※ Try using rice vinegar in a vinaigrette instead of traditional vinegars. It gives a subtle, soft flavor.

※ Add zip to purchased French dressing by placing a clove of garlic in the bottle. Also, French dressing may be thickened just before serving by dropping an ice cube in it and stirring thoroughly.

Garnishes

The following is a list of ingredients you might add to your salads:

croutons	cheese
coconut	onion rings, marinated in beet juice
sunflower seeds	red bell peppers
sesame seeds	bacon
nuts	sausage
raisins	fresh flowers

Molded Salads

※ Never boil gelatin.

※ One tablespoon of gelatin (one envelope) sets two cups of liquid.

※ Before adding ingredients to gelatin, allow it to stand until it is the consistency of unbeaten egg whites.

✳ Add carbonated beverages by pouring slowly down the side of the bowl and stirring with an up and down motion.

✳ Be sure that frozen or canned fruits are drained thoroughly before adding to gelatin mixture.

✳ To chill gelatin quickly, place it in the freezer for ten minutes or place the bowl in ice water and stir.

✳ When unmolding gelatin, moisten the serving plate with cold water. This makes it easier to position the gelatin.

✳ To unmold, run a spatula around the edge to loosen, invert on a moistened serving platter and place a warm, damp dish towel over the mold. Shake gently.

OIL AND VINEGAR DRESSING WITH VARIATIONS

½	cup wine, cider or malt vinegar	¼	teaspoon white pepper
¾	teaspoon salt	1½	cups olive or vegetable oil

1. Combine vinegar and spices.
2. Beat well with a fork or in a blender.
3. Add oil slowly and continue beating until thickened.

Serve immediately or chill and use as needed.

Variations:

To 1 cup of the basic oil and vinegar dressing, add 1 of the following:

Bellevue (for fruit salads)—6 tablespoons sour cream and 1 tablespoon minced chives

Cottage cheese (for tomato salads)—3 tablespoons cottage cheese and 1 table spoon each of parsley or chopped sweet pickles

Curry (for green leafy salads)—1 teaspoon curry powder and 1 tablespoon minced shallots

Hot French dressing (for tossed vegetable salads)—2 teaspoons each parsley, green bell pepper, shallots and chervil all minced

Vinaigrette (for tossed green salads)—1 teaspoon each minced chopped green olives, parsley, chives, capers, gherkins and yolk of 1 hard-cooked egg, finely chopped

Bacon dressing (for spinach, cabbage or lettuce salads)—make basic oil and vinegar dressing but substitute hot bacon drippings for the 1½ cups oil.

CAESAR SALAD

A wonderful version of a traditional favorite.

½ clove garlic	Salt and freshly ground pepper
1 tablespoon red wine vinegar	to taste
1 tablespoon lemon juice	1 head romaine lettuce, torn into
Dash Worcestershire sauce	bite-size pieces
⅛ to ¼ teaspoon dry mustard	2 hard-cooked eggs, chopped
3 tablespoons olive oil	1 cup croutons
1 egg yolk	
3 heaping tablespoons grated	
Parmesan cheese	

1. Using a spoon, press garlic over the entire surface of a large wooden bowl. Discard garlic.
2. Add vinegar, lemon juice, Worcestershire and mustard. Stir dressing over entire surface of bowl.
3. Add oil, egg yolk and cheese. Whisk together. Cover the surface of dressing with salt and pepper. Whisk again.
4. Toss lettuce with dressing. Garnish with hard-cooked eggs and croutons.

Serves 4

CONFETTI CORN SALAD

1 12-ounce can shoe peg corn,	Salt and pepper to taste
drained	1 to 2 green onions, chopped
2 tablespoons mayonnaise	4 to 6 cherry tomatoes, sliced

1. Combine all ingredients and refrigerate.

Serves 4

CAULIFLOWER SALAD

Make ahead for a picnic.

½	head iceberg lettuce, torn into bite-size pieces	1	medium green bell pepper, chopped
1	head cauliflower, cut into very small florets	1	cup thinly sliced celery
		1	cup grated Parmesan cheese
½	purple onion, thinly sliced	⅛ to ¼ cup sugar	
1	pound bacon, crisply cooked and crumbled	½	cup mayonnaise
		½	cup sour cream

1. In serving bowl, layer lettuce, cauliflower, onion, bacon, bell pepper, celery and cheese. Repeat layers.
2. Sprinkle sugar over all. Mix mayonnaise and sour cream together and spread on top. Seal and chill in refrigerator overnight.
3. Toss well before serving.

Serves 12

CRUNCHY SALAD

¼	cup sesame seeds	½	head iceberg lettuce
½	cup sunflower seeds	½	head leaf lettuce
½	cup slivered almonds		

1. Preheat oven to 350°.
2. Roast sesame seeds, sunflower seeds and almonds approximately 15 minutes or until lightly browned.
3. Tear lettuce into bite-size pieces and add seed mixture. Toss with a favorite Italian dressing.

Serves 6

GARDEN SALAD WITH ALMONDS AND ORANGES

		Dressing:	
1	head iceberg lettuce	1	cup vegetable oil
1	head romaine lettuce	¼	cup vinegar
1	cup sliced or slivered almonds	¼	cup sugar
¼	cup sugar	1	teaspoon salt
6	green onion tops, thinly sliced		Dash black pepper
2	11-ounce cans mandarin oranges, chilled and drained		Dash red pepper
		1	tablespoon parsley flakes

1. Wash and prepare lettuce. Tear into bite-size pieces. Chill.
2. Combine almonds and sugar in a saucepan. Stir over medium heat until sugar melts and is browned. Cool caramelized almonds on a cookie sheet.
3. Combine all ingredients for dressing and chill.
4. When ready to serve, combine lettuce, green onions, almonds and oranges. Toss with desired amount of dressing.

Serves 6 to 8

MARINATED VEGETABLE SALAD

1	9-ounce package frozen Brussels sprouts, cooked and drained	1	10-ounce can small pitted black olives, drained
2	14-ounce cans artichoke hearts, cut in quarters	1	pint cherry tomatoes, halved
4	large ripe avocados, cut into bite-size pieces	1	cup Italian salad dressing

1. Mix vegetables in a clear glass salad bowl. Pour dressing over mixture. Toss gently.
2. Cover and chill 1 to 2 hours. This salad is not good when marinated too long. Toss gently before serving.

Serve on lettuce leaf or in half an avocado shell on a bed of shredded lettuce.

Serves 10 to 12

MARINATED SQUASH SALAD WITH FETA CHEESE

4 tablespoons white wine vinegar
2 cloves garlic, minced
1 teaspoon marjoram
½ cup olive oil
½ cup crumbled feta cheese

2 medium zucchini, sliced
2 medium to large yellow squash, sliced
1 medium purple onion, sliced
½ cup chopped black olives

1. In a large bowl, combine vinegar, garlic and marjoram. Gradually add oil, whisking continuously, until dressing is blended.
2. Add sliced vegetables and toss to coat. Refrigerate, stirring occasionally, 3 to 4 hours.
3. Drain vegetables. Add feta cheese before serving.

Serves 6

CREAMY POTATO SALAD

5 to 6 potatoes, boiled, peeled and cubed
1 hard-cooked egg
¾ cup chopped celery
1 tablespoon chopped pimiento
½ cup sliced green olives
⅓ cup sliced chives

1½ teaspoons prepared mustard
¾ to 1 cup mayonnaise
¼ cup finely diced green bell pepper, optional
¼ teaspoon dried dill
2 tablespoons finely chopped parsley

1. Place potatoes, chopped egg white, celery, pimiento, olives and chives in a large bowl.
2. Combine mustard, mayonnaise, and egg yolk in blender. Beat until smooth. Add salt, pepper, dill and parsley. Stir.
3. Pour over potatoes and toss. Chill 1 hour before serving.

Serves 6 to 8

RED, WHITE AND GREEN SALAD

Make ahead for a summer supper.

1	8-ounce can small green peas, drained
1	12-ounce can white corn, drained
1	16-ounce can French style green beans, drained
½	cup chopped purple onion
½	cup chopped white onion
½	small green bell pepper, chopped
½	small red bell pepper, chopped
1	cup chopped celery
1	2-ounce jar diced pimientos

Marinade:

½	cup vinegar
½	cup sugar
½	cup vegetable oil
½	teaspoon salt

1. Combine and mix all vegetables.
2. Combine marinade ingredients and pour over vegetables.
3. Toss and marinate in refrigerator at least 6 to 8 hours before serving.

Serves 10 to 12

ORIENTAL SALAD

1	head Chinese cabbage, coarsely chopped
½	cup green onions with tops, thinly sliced
1	3-ounce can Chinese noodles
1	cup thinly sliced mushrooms
½	cup slivered almonds

Dressing:

1	cup mayonnaise
¼	cup milk
¼	cup soy sauce

1. Combine mayonnaise, milk, and soy sauce to make dressing.
2. Combine salad ingredients and toss with dressing mixture. Serve immediately.

Serves 4 to 6

VEGETABLE ASPIC

½ envelope unflavored gelatin
1 13-ounce can clear consommé, divided
⅓ cup chopped celery
⅓ cup chopped carrots
⅓ cup fresh green beans, blanched
⅓ cup cauliflower, parboiled
Dash Tabasco sauce

1. Dissolve gelatin in a few teaspoons of consommé.
2. Bring remaining consommé to a boil and add to gelatin.
3. Add vegetables and seasonings.
4. Pour into a 3 to 4 cup mold.
5. Chill thoroughly before serving.

If desired, make a dressing of cream cheese, thinned with mayonnaise and seasoned with Dijon mustard.

Serves 3 to 4

SPINACH SALAD

This delicious dressing should be made at least six hours before serving. It is wonderful on spinach but is not a good choice for other greens.

Dressing:
1 cup vegetable oil
2 whole cloves garlic, minced
2 tablespoons minced parsley
5 tablespoons red wine vinegar
4 tablespoons sour cream
1½ teaspoons salt
½ teaspoon dry mustard
1 to 2 tablespoons sugar
Black pepper to taste
1 10-ounce package fresh spinach
4 hard-cooked eggs, sliced
8 slices bacon, crisply cooked and crumbled
8 ounces mushrooms, sliced
¼ pound red onion, thinly sliced

1. Combine first 9 ingredients to make dressing. Refrigerate at least 6 hours before serving.
2. Wash, drain and tear spinach into bite-size pieces.
3. When ready to serve, toss spinach with eggs, bacon, mushrooms, onions and dressing.

Serves 6

SPINACH MOLD WITH CUCUMBER SAUCE

This can also be used as a spread with crackers.

16 ounces cream cheese
7 10-ounce packages frozen
   chopped spinach, cooked
   and drained. Reserve ½ cup
   liquid.
1 tablespoon grated onion
2 tablespoons chopped
   cucumber
   Juice of ½ lemon
   Salt, pepper and paprika to
   taste

3 envelopes unflavored gelatin
1 10½-ounce can chicken broth
¾ cup toasted almonds

Sauce:
1 cup mayonnaise
1 tablespoon grated onion
3 tablespoons grated cucumber

1. Cube cream cheese and stir into hot spinach. Add onion, cucumber, lemon juice, salt, pepper and paprika.
2. Dissolve gelatin in cold spinach liquid. Add to chicken broth and heat until gelatin is completely dissolved. Add to spinach mixture.
3. Pour into a well greased 10-inch mold. Refrigerate.
4. To make sauce, mix all ingredients together. Chill in refrigerator until ready to serve. Unmold.

Serve with sauce and garnish with almonds.

Serves 24

SPECIAL SPINACH SALAD

Best when made a day before serving.

Dressing:
⅓	cup grated onion
1	cup vegetable oil
¾	cup sugar
¼	cup vinegar
⅓	cup ketchup
2	tablespoons Worcestershire sauce
½	teaspoon salt

Salad:
1	11-ounce can artichoke hearts, drained and quartered
1	11-ounce can mandarin oranges, drained
1 to 2	avocados, cut into bite-size pieces
1	10-ounce package fresh spinach
½	purple onion, thinly sliced and separated into rings

1. To make dressing, combine all ingredients in blender or food processor. Blend 2 minutes.
2. Six to eight hours before serving, combine artichoke hearts, oranges and avocados. Cover with dressing. Toss and refrigerate.
3. When ready to serve, combine spinach, onion and marinated ingredients. Toss and serve.

Dressing Yields 2 cups

Serves 8

CHICKEN APRICOT SALAD

The unusual combination of chicken and apricots is a treat!

¼	cup milk
2	tablespoons lemon juice
½	cup mayonnaise
1	cup sour cream
3	teaspoons prepared mustard

1	teaspoon salt
1	cup dried apricots, diced
3	cups cooked, diced chicken
1	cup chopped celery
⅓	cup chopped green onions

1. Mix ingredients in order.
2. Refrigerate several hours before serving. The mixture may appear soupy at first, but the apricots absorb most of the liquid while chilling.

This salad is attractive when served in avocado halves.

Serves 6 to 8

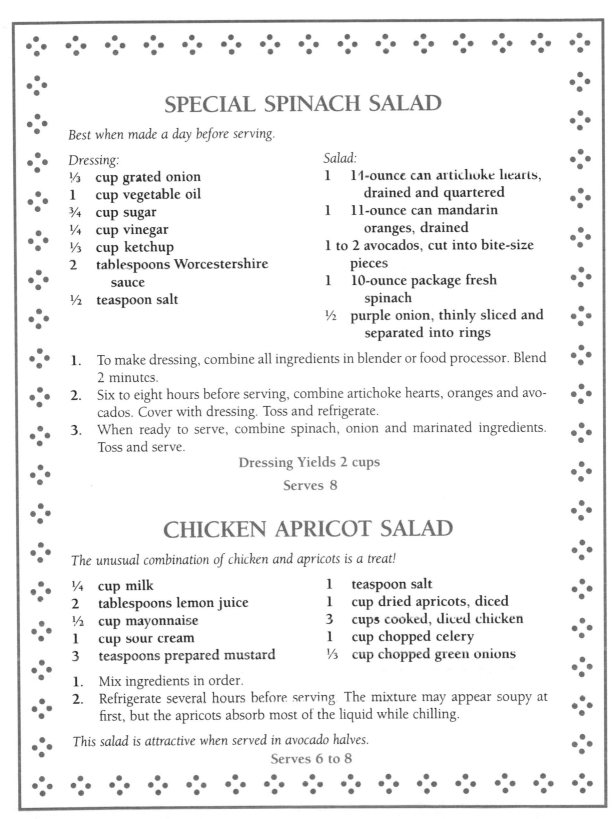

WILD RICE SALAD

Diced chicken, turkey or ham added to this salad makes a delightful main dish.

1	7 to 8-ounce package wild rice	3	cloves garlic, minced
6	ribs celery, chopped	1	cup chopped fresh parsley
2	large green bell peppers, chopped	2 to 4	tablespoons fresh lemon juice
2	large red bell peppers, chopped		Garlic salt to taste
1	onion, finely chopped		Black pepper to taste
			Creamy Italian dressing

1. Cook wild rice according to directions. Drain and cool.
2. Chop ingredients to desired size. Mix with rice, lemon juice, seasonings and enough dressing to bind ingredients.
3. Refrigerate overnight. Adjust seasonings to taste.

Serves 10

VEGETABLE RICE SALAD

1½	cups raw rice	¾	cup mayonnaise
1	green bell pepper, diced	2	tablespoons Dijon mustard
1	tomato, diced	2	tablespoons creamy Italian dressing
3	ribs celery, diced		
3	green onions, chopped		

1. Cook rice according to package directions. Cool. Combine rice and vegetables. Toss.
2. Make dressing by combining mayonnaise, mustard and Italian dressing. Pour over rice mixture, tossing gently. Chill overnight.
3. Serve in a bowl lined with lettuce leaves.

Variation:
If desired, serve with extra dressing on the side. Dressing made of ½ cup creamy Italian dressing and ¼ cup mayonnaise makes an excellent accompaniment.

Serves 8 to 10

CHICKEN SALAD WITH BACON AND ALMONDS

Bacon gives this salad a unique flavor.

4	cups cooked, cubed chicken	1	cup mayonnaise
2	cups chopped celery	1	cup sour cream
	Sliced mushrooms, optional	1	teaspoon salt
½	cup slivered almonds, toasted	2	tablespoons lemon juice
4 to 5 slices bacon crisply cooked			
	and crumbled		

1. Combine chicken, celery, mushrooms, almonds and bacon.
2. In another container, combine mayonnaise, sour cream, salt, and lemon juice.
3. Toss chicken mixture with dressing and chill thoroughly before serving.

Serves 8

COLD CURRIED CHICKEN SALAD

4	cups cooked, diced chicken	1	cup mayonnaise or to taste
1	cup cooked rice	2	teaspoons curry powder
3	hard-cooked eggs, chopped	½	teaspoon salt
½	cup peanuts, crushed	1	teaspoon ground ginger
1	bunch green onions, chopped	1	teaspoon white pepper
6	slices bacon, crisply cooked	1	tablespoon lemon juice
	and crumbled		

1. Combine first 6 ingredients.
2. Mix remaining ingredients and fold into chicken mixture.
3. Chill and serve on lettuce leaves. Garnish with avocado slices or mandarin orange sections.

Serves 10 to 12

CURRIED CHICKEN AND ARTICHOKE SALAD

A festive dish to serve at a luncheon or casual dinner party.

1	8-ounce box chicken flavored rice	2	6-ounce jars marinated artichokes (reserve ½ marinade from one jar)
2	cups cooked, cubed chicken	1½	cups mayonnaise
3	green onions, thinly sliced	½	teaspoon curry powder
½	medium green bell pepper, chopped		
15	green olives with pimentos, sliced		

1. Prepare rice according to package directions, omitting butter. Cool.
2. Mix mayonnaise with reserved marinade.
3. Combine all remaining ingredients. Toss until well mixed. Chill thoroughly.

Variation:
Substitute shrimp for chicken, using 1 pound shrimp, peeled, deveined and boiled. Cut into bite-size pieces.

This is best when made the day before serving.

Serves 6 to 10

CRANBERRY APPLE SALAD

An unusual, tart salad for Thanksgiving or Christmas.

1	pound fresh cranberries	¾ to 1	cup sugar
2	red apples	1	cup chopped pecans
2	cups miniature marshmallows	1	cup whipping cream

1. Grind or coarsely chop cranberries and apples together. Mix thoroughly.
2. Combine marshmallows, sugar and fruit. Refrigerate overnight. Drain.
3. Prior to serving, whip cream.
4. Fold cream and pecans into mixture.

Serves 8 to 10

SHRIMP AND AVOCADO SALAD

Dressing:

2	cups salad dressing	6	avocados
½	cup chili sauce	4	pounds shrimp, peeled, deveined and cooked
3	cups minced celery		
2	tablespoons lemon juice		
2	tablespoons vinegar		
8	teaspoons minced green onion		

1. Combine first 6 ingredients to make dressing.
2. Cut avocados into bite-size pieces. Set aside.
3. Combine shrimp and dressing.
4. Toss avocado pieces with shrimp mixture.
5. Serve on a bed of lettuce or in a large bowl.

Serves 12

ORIENTAL TUNA SALAD

1	10-ounce package frozen Italian green beans	½	cup mayonnaise
1	6½-ounce can white tuna, drained	1	tablespoon fresh lemon juice
1	cup chopped celery	1½	teaspoons soy sauce
			Dash garlic powder
		1	3-ounce can Chinese noodles

1. Cook green beans according to package directions. Drain and cool.
2. Combine with tuna, celery, mayonnaise, lemon juice, soy sauce, and garlic powder. Chill.
3. Before serving, add Chinese noodles to mixture. Toss.

Serves 5 to 6

APRICOT DELIGHT SALAD

A salad that can be prepared ahead for a buffet or weekend company.

1	16-ounce can crushed apricots
1	20-ounce can crushed pineapple
1	6-ounce package orange gelatin
3	cups boiling water
1	cup miniature marshmallows, optional

Topping:

1	cup pineapple juice
½	cup sugar
3	tablespoons butter
3	tablespoons all-purpose flour
	Dash salt
2	eggs, beaten
1	cup whipping cream
1	cup grated Cheddar cheese

1. Drain apricots and pineapple. Reserve 1 cup apricot juice. Crush apricots with a fork. Chill fruit.
2. Put gelatin in a 9 by 13 by 2-inch dish. Add boiling water and stir until gelatin is dissolved. Cool.
3. Add 1 cup apricot juice, chilled fruit and marshmallows to gelatin. Refrigerate until congealed.
4. Combine all ingredients of topping except whipping cream and cheese. Simmer, while stirring, over low heat until mixture thickens. Chill.
5. Beat whipping cream. Add topping mixture and continue to beat at low speed until mixture reaches a smooth consistency. Spread over gelatin. Top with grated cheese.

Variation:
Peaches may be substituted for apricots.

Serves 20

MANGO SALAD
A Collection Classic

3   3-ounce packages lemon
    flavored gelatin
3   cups boiling water
8   ounces cream cheese, softened
1   16-ounce can mangoes,
    drained, juice reserved

1   cup mango juice (if needed,
    add water to make 1 cup)
1   cup sour cream
1 to 2 tablespoons honey

1. Dissolve gelatin in boiling water.
2. In a blender, combine cream cheese, mangoes and mango juice.
3. Combine gelatin and cream cheese mixture. Stir well.
4. Pour into a 2½-quart mold and chill.
5. Serve with a dressing made of sour cream, sweetened with honey.

Serves 12 to 15

CREAMY GARLIC DRESSING

Serve over crisp salad greens, carrots, green beans and celery.

8   ounces sour cream
⅔   cup vegetable oil
5   tablespoons mayonnaise
2   teaspoons salt

5   tablespoons vinegar
2   large garlic cloves, minced
½   cup chopped fresh parsley,
    without stems

1. Combine and blend all ingredients in a blender.
2. Refrigerate. Shake well before serving.

Yields 2 cups

※ To crush garlic with little mess, put cloves in a small plastic bag and crush
   with a hammer.

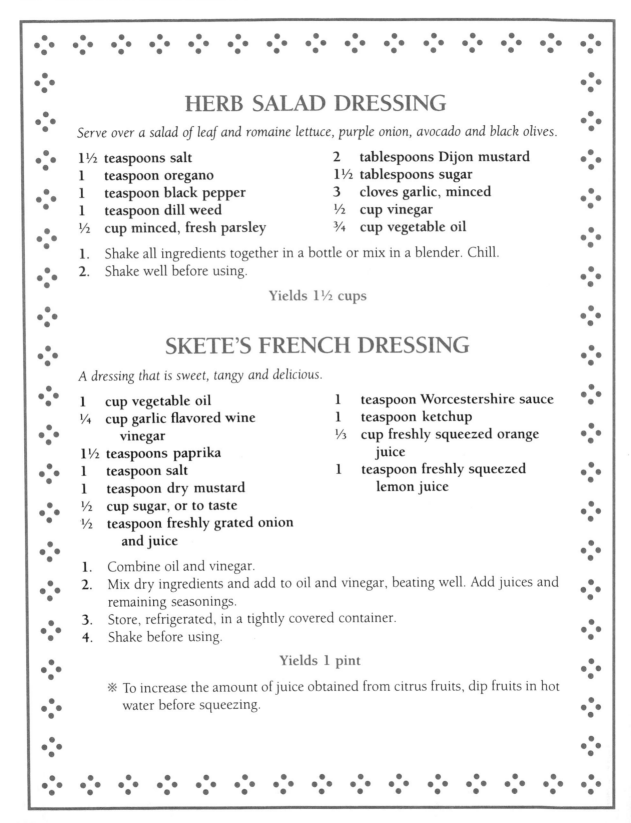

HERB SALAD DRESSING

Serve over a salad of leaf and romaine lettuce, purple onion, avocado and black olives.

1½	teaspoons salt	2	tablespoons Dijon mustard
1	teaspoon oregano	1½	tablespoons sugar
1	teaspoon black pepper	3	cloves garlic, minced
1	teaspoon dill weed	½	cup vinegar
½	cup minced, fresh parsley	¾	cup vegetable oil

1. Shake all ingredients together in a bottle or mix in a blender. Chill.
2. Shake well before using.

Yields 1½ cups

SKETE'S FRENCH DRESSING

A dressing that is sweet, tangy and delicious.

1	cup vegetable oil	1	teaspoon Worcestershire sauce
¼	cup garlic flavored wine vinegar	1	teaspoon ketchup
1½	teaspoons paprika	⅓	cup freshly squeezed orange juice
1	teaspoon salt	1	teaspoon freshly squeezed lemon juice
1	teaspoon dry mustard		
½	cup sugar, or to taste		
½	teaspoon freshly grated onion and juice		

1. Combine oil and vinegar.
2. Mix dry ingredients and add to oil and vinegar, beating well. Add juices and remaining seasonings.
3. Store, refrigerated, in a tightly covered container.
4. Shake before using.

Yields 1 pint

❋ To increase the amount of juice obtained from citrus fruits, dip fruits in hot water before squeezing.

THOUSAND ISLAND DRESSING

Try this dressing as a dip with crudites.

1	egg	1	cup chili sauce
2	tablespoons sugar	1	green bell pepper, minced
1	teaspoon salt	1	hard-cooked egg, chopped
	Dash cayenne pepper	1	small onion, grated
¼	cup cider vinegar		
1	cup vegetable oil		

1. In a blender, combine first 5 ingredients.
2. While blending, slowly add oil until mixture reaches the consistency of mayonnaise. Add chili sauce, bell pepper, egg and onion.
3. Blend only until all ingredients are mixed, not puréed.
4. Refrigerate.

Yields 2½ cups

FRESH FRUIT DRESSING

For a light summer dessert, serve over fresh melons or available fruits.

8	ounces sour cream	⅓	cup flaked coconut
⅓	cup chopped pecans	2½	tablespoons apricot preserves

1. Combine all ingredients. Mix well.
2. Chill slightly before serving.

Yields 1½ cups

HONEY DRESSING

A quick and easy dressing for all fruits and a perfect combination of sweet and tart.

½	scant cup sugar	5	tablespoons vinegar
1	teaspoon paprika	⅓	cup honey
1	teaspoon dry mustard	1	cup vegetable oil
1	teaspoon salt		

1. In a blender or mixer, combine sugar, paprika, mustard and salt. Blend in vinegar and honey.
2. Slowly add oil and beat well.
3. Chill.

Yields 1½ to 2 cups dressing

※ To liquify honey that has turned sugary, put the jar in a small amount of hot water.

SOUPS AND SANDWICHES

As a first course, soups should complement the entrée. Light or bland soups should be served with highly seasoned entrées. Cream soups should never be served with other creamed dishes. Soups with varied ingredients, flavors and textures add interest to a meal.

When serving soup as the first course, allow 1 quart for six servings. When serving soup as the main course, allow 1 quart for three to four servings.

Warm bowls when serving hot soup. Chill bowls when serving cold soup.

Types of Soup

Cream Soups—Consist of a vegetable base to which cream or milk and butter are added; may be thickened by the addition of barley, rice, oatmeal or eggs. Cream soups must never be boiled. Heat only to the boiling point or heat in the top of a double boiler.

Chowders—Consist of a thick fish, meat or vegetable base to which cream and other vegetables are added

Clear Soup—Broth, bouillon or stock made from meat or vegetables

Cooking Tips

※ To correct salty soup, place a raw, peeled potato into the pot of soup. Allow soup to boil for a short time. Remove potato before serving.

※ Salty soup may also be corrected by allowing soup to cool thoroughly, then adding 1 teaspoon of sugar to the mixture and reheating.

※ To remove grease from soup, place a lettuce leaf into the pot of hot soup. Remove the lettuce before serving.

※ Fat is easily removed from soup if pot is cooled in the refrigerator. Skim congealed fat off the top.

※ To eliminate excess liquid from soup, place a large colander into the pot and hold over solid ingredients. Spoon off excess liquid.

※ Spices that are to be removed at the end of the cooking process should be placed in a tea strainer. Hook the strainer on the side of the pot. Spices are more easily removed when it is time to serve the soup.

❋ To clarify stock: for each quart of stock allow 1 egg white and 1 crushed egg shell. Cool stock. Beat egg whites until soft peaks form. Stir egg whites and crushed egg shell into stock. Heat until foam forms. Remove from heat and allow to stand at room temperature for one hour. Strain through several layers of cheesecloth or a fine strainer.

❋ Add leftover stuffing to soups to enhance flavor and to thicken.

❋ When using alcohol in soups, add 1 tablespoon for each cup of soup. Too much liquor will make the soup bitter. Add just before serving. Do not let soup boil.

❋ For extra flavor, add bouillon cubes to canned or homemade soup.

❋ Cool soups uncovered.

Soup Garnishes

avocado slices	whipped cream dollops
bacon bits	popcorn
basil	poppy seeds
caraway	mint sprigs
carrots, grated	mushrooms, sliced
celery, diced	nuts, all varieties
cheese, grated	olive, ripe or green
chervil	Parmesan cheese
chili powder	pepitos
chives, snipped	peppers, diced
croutons	pimiento
cucumber, sliced	radishes
curry powder	sesame seeds
dill	scallions
eggs, hard-cooked	sour cream
fennel	sunflower seeds
herb butters	tarragon
lemon rind or slices	tomatoes
onion slices	tofu
orange rind or slices	watercress
parsley, minced	

COLD PIMIENTO SOUP

5 tablespoons butter	3 cups cream
4 tablespoons flour	16 ounces pimientos
5 cups chicken broth	

1. Strain and chop pimientos.
2. Place pimientos in pan with 2 cups broth and heat.
3. Pureé broth and pimiento mixture.
4. Melt butter, add flour and let mixture begin to boil. Add cream and simmer, stirring constantly until mixture thickens.
5. Stir in pimiento mixture and remaining broth. Simmer 3 minutes.
6. Chill

Garnish with parsley and pimientos before serving.

Serves 4

COLD CURRIED TOMATO SOUP

Prepare ahead and serve on a hot summer day.

1 46-ounce can tomato juice	Freshly ground black pepper to taste
1 tablespoon tomato paste	
8 green onions	Juice of 1 lemon
2 teaspoons salt	1 teaspoon sugar
⅛ teaspoon thyme	2 cups sour cream
1 teaspoon curry powder	Lemon slices

1. Mince green onions, separating white from green. Reserve green for garnish.
2. Combine all ingredients except sour cream in a blender. Blend until smooth.
3. Before serving, add sour cream. Blend again.

Serve cold. Garnish with tops of green onions or lemon slices.

Serves 6 to 8

CAULIFLOWER SOUP

1 medium head cauliflower, divided into florets
2 cups chicken stock
2 cups milk
6 tablespoons butter
4 tablespoons all-purpose flour
Salt to taste
White pepper to taste

⅛ teaspoon freshly grated nutmeg
1 cup grated Cheddar cheese
Paprika

1. Combine cauliflower and chicken stock in a soup kettle. Bring to a boil. Lower heat and simmer 7 minutes.
2. Strain, reserving stock. Set cauliflower aside.
3. Return stock to kettle. Add milk and bring to boiling point.
4. Make a cream sauce using butter, flour, and milk.
5. Add salt, pepper and nutmeg. Blend well.
6. Just before serving, add cauliflower and heat thoroughly.
7. Garnish each serving with cheese and paprika.

Serves 4 to 6

CORN CHOWDER

Enhance the flavor by preparing a day ahead.

¼ cup finely chopped onion
3 tablespoons butter
2 16-ounce cans creamed corn
2 10¾-ounce cans cream of potato soup

3 cups milk
1 tablespoon dried parsley
1 teaspoon salt
¼ teaspoon pepper
¼ teaspoon celery seed

1. Sauté onion in butter until transparent.
2. Add remaining ingredients, stirring well. Simmer 20 minutes.

Serves 8

MUSHROOM SOUP WITH PARMESAN

1 tablespoon butter
1 tablespoon olive oil
1 medium onion, finely chopped
1 clove garlic, split
1 pound fresh mushrooms,
   thinly sliced
3 tablespoons tomato paste
3 cups chicken stock
2 tablespoons vermouth
½ teaspoon salt
   Dash pepper
   French bread
   Butter

Optional Ingredients:
4 egg yolks
2 tablespoons chopped parsley
2½ tablespoons Parmesan cheese

1. In a heavy pan, melt butter. Add olive oil. Sauté onion.
2. Add garlic to butter and onion. Brown garlic slightly. Discard.
3. Stir mushrooms into onion mixture. Sauté 5 minutes.
4. Add tomato paste and mix well. Add chicken stock. Blend well. Add vermouth, salt and pepper. Simmer 10 minutes.
5. Cut bread into 1-inch slices and butter on 1 side. Grill buttered side only. Pour soup over bread in individual bowls.
6. For a thick, rich soup, beat together egg yolks, parsley and cheese. Beat into hot soup and serve over toasted bread.

Serves 4 to 6

SPICED PUMPKIN SOUP

1   cup chicken broth
1   cup canned pumpkin
2   tablespoons minced onion
½ to 1 teaspoon curry powder
¼   teaspoon ground cumin

¼   teaspoon ground coriander
     Salt to taste
½   cup half and half
     Lemon slices

1. Combine chicken broth, pumpkin, onion and spices in saucepan.
2. Whisk together while bringing mixture to a boil. Whisk in cream just before serving.
3. Garnish with lemon slices.

Serves 4

RED BELL PEPPER SOUP

This soup goes well with any dish because of its subtle flavor.

4   medium red bell peppers,
       chopped
2   leeks, white part only,
       chopped
1   medium carrot, sliced

1   medium onion, chopped
3   tablespoons butter
2   cups chicken stock
2   cups whipping cream
     Salt and white pepper to taste

1. Sauté vegetables in butter until softened.
2. Add stock and cream. Lower heat and simmer 30 minutes.
3. Purée in blender.
4. Simmer soup 15 minutes or more.
5. Season with salt and white pepper.

Soup may be served as an appetizer in demitasse cups.

Serves 4 to 6

ENGLISH POTATO AND LEEK SOUP

A wonderfully rich flavor and creamy texture.

1½ cups minced leeks
½ cup minced onion
1 clove garlic, minced
¼ cup butter
4 cups chicken broth
1½ cups peeled, diced, raw
    potatoes
1 cup whipping cream
1 teaspoon salt
⅛ to ¼ teaspoon pepper
    Chopped green onions or
    chives

1. Sauté leeks, onion and garlic in butter until transparent.
2. Add broth and potatoes. Cook until tender.
3. Purée in a blender or food processor.
4. Add cream and seasonings. Chill at least 24 hours. Serve cold or hot.
5. Garnish with chopped green onion or chives before serving.

Serves 6 to 8

OLD FASHIONED SPLIT PEA SOUP

1 pound dried, split green peas
8 cups water
2 ham hocks or 2 pieces smoked
    ham
1 pound can tomatoes, diced
1 cup chopped onion
1 cup chopped celery
½ cup shredded carrots
2 teaspoons dried parsley
2 tablespoons vinegar
½ teaspoon garlic powder
2½ teaspoons seasoned salt
½ teaspoon crushed, dried
    oregano
    Chicken broth

1. In a heavy pan, bring peas, water and ham to a boil. Boil slowly for 2 minutes. Turn off heat. Cover and let stand for 1 hour.
2. Add remaining ingredients. Cover pot and simmer 2½ hours.
3. If soup is too thick, thin with chicken broth.

Serves 10

TOMATO BISQUE

¼   cup butter
½   cup minced onion
½   cup all-purpose flour
1½ cups milk
1   cup chicken stock
2   14½-ounce cans Italian plum
      tomatoes, reserve juice

1   tablespoon honey
2   tablespoons minced parsley
1   teaspoon dill weed
¼   teaspoon basil
¼   teaspoon marjoram
1   whole bay leaf
      Salt and pepper to taste

1. Melt butter in pan. Add onions and sauté until transparent.
2. Lower heat. Add flour and cook, stirring constantly. Add milk and chicken stock. Whisk until smooth and thick.
3. Purée tomatoes in blender.
4. Add purée, including juice, to flour mixture. Add remaining ingredients. Simmer 45 minutes, stirring frequently.
5. Remove bay leaf and serve.

Serves 6

CRAB SOUP

1   package dried leek soup mix
2   cups water
1   6-ounce can claw crab meat,
      including liquid

1   cup whipping cream
      Salt and pepper to taste
½   cup white wine

1. Dissolve soup mix in water. Add crab liquid and whipping cream. Season with salt and pepper. Simmer 20 minutes.
2. Stir in wine. Heat. Serve warm.

Serves 6

FRENCH COUNTRY VEGETABLE SOUP

11 cups water	1 green bell pepper, finely chopped
1 10¾-ounce can beef broth	1 8-ounce can tomato sauce
2 cups finely chopped carrots	2 tablespoons tomato paste
2 cups finely chopped potatoes	3 cloves garlic, pressed
1 onion, finely chopped	¼ cup fresh basil or 1 tablespoon dried basil
2 tomatoes, diced	
1 tablespoon salt	½ cup grated Parmesan cheese
1 9-ounce package frozen cut green beans or 2 cups fresh	2 tablespoons all-purpose flour
2 yellow squash, finely chopped	¼ cup olive oil

1. In a 6-quart pot, combine water, broth, carrots, potatoes, onions, tomatoes and salt. Simmer 15 minutes.
2. Add green beans, squash, bell pepper and tomato sauce. Cook over medium heat 15 to 20 minutes.
3. In a small bowl, combine tomato paste, garlic, basil, cheese and flour. Beat in olive oil.
4. Before serving, slowly add 2 cups of broth to the tomato paste mixture. Add to soup pot. Heat.

For a spicy, hot soup, add crushed red pepper to each bowl.

Serves 12

ZUCCHINI SOUP

Delicious served hot or cold.

7 chicken bouillon cubes	1 onion, diced
4 cups water	8 ounces cream cheese, cubed
6 medium zucchini, thinly sliced	Salt and pepper to taste
2 carrots, grated	1 tablespoon fresh chives, optional

1. Dissolve bouillon cubes in boiling water. Add squash, carrots and onion. Cook 15 minutes or until ingredients are tender.
2. Put mixture in blender and purée.
3. Add cream cheese a little at a time. Add salt and pepper. Garnish with chives.

Yields 8 cups

VICHYSSOISE

½ cup butter
1 large onion, sliced
4 bunches green onions
4 cups chicken stock
3 medium potatoes, peeled and
   thinly sliced
Freshly ground pepper to taste
¼ teaspoon finely grated nutmeg
1 teaspoon salt
1 cup whipping cream
2 cups milk

Toppings for Variation:
Sour cream
1 14-ounce can julienne beets,
   seasoned with salt and
   pepper
Green onion tops

1. Melt butter in a large saucepan.
2. Slice green onion, separating white from green. Reserve green for garnish.
3. Add sliced onions to butter and cook until transparent.
4. Add chicken stock, potatoes, pepper, nutmeg and salt. Bring to a boil. Lower heat and simmer until potatoes are cooked.
5. Working with a small amount of liquid at a time, purée mixture in a blender. Return mixture to pan.
6. Add cream slowly, stirring constantly. Add milk. Store in refrigerator 24 hours. This step is very important. Additional milk may be added if thinner consistency is desired. Serve hot or cold.

This may be frozen up to 1 month.

Variation:
To serve a la russe: Serve cold, garnished with a large spoonful of sour cream, topped with drained julienne beets and sprinkled with green onion tops.

Serves 6 to 8

HEARTY CHEDDAR CHOWDER

4 medium potatoes, peeled and diced
1 medium onion, finely chopped
1 cup thinly sliced carrot
½ cup diced green bell pepper
3 cups chicken broth
⅓ cup butter
⅓ cup all-purpose flour

3½ cups milk
4 cups grated sharp Cheddar cheese
1 2-ounce jar diced pimiento, drained
¼ teaspoon Tabasco sauce, optional

1. In a large soup kettle, combine potatoes, onion, carrots, bell pepper and chicken broth. Cover and simmer 15 minutes or until vegetables are tender.
2. Make a white sauce using butter, flour and milk. Add cheese, stirring until melted.
3. Stir cheese sauce, pimiento and Tabasco into vegetable mixture. Do not boil.

Serve hot.

Serves 8 to 10

CREAMY SPINACH AND CRAB SOUP

2 pounds fresh spinach or 2 10-ounce packages frozen, chopped spinach, well drained
4 to 6 small green onions, chopped
6 cups chicken stock, divided
⅓ cup butter

6 tablespoons all-purpose flour
Salt and pepper to taste
2 cups half and half
1 cup fresh crab meat
½ teaspoon freshly grated nutmeg

1. Cook spinach and onions in a small amount of water. Drain.
2. Combine spinach and onions with 2 cups chicken stock. Purée in a blender or food processor.
3. Melt butter. Add flour, salt and pepper. Stir in remaining 4 cups of chicken stock and puréed spinach mixture. Simmer 10 minutes, stirring occasionally.
4. Stir in half and half and crab meat. Heat, but do not boil. Sprinkle with nutmeg and serve.

Serves 8 to 10

OYSTER STEW

A Christmas Eve tradition in many homes.

6 tablespoons butter, melted
3 tablespoons minced green onion
3 tablespoons minced celery
2 tablespoons minced green bell pepper
3 tablespoons all-purpose flour
2 cups scalded milk
1 teaspoon salt
½ teaspoon black pepper
1 cup half and half

1 pint raw oysters, cleaned and drained, reserving ½ cup oyster liquid
Cayenne pepper or Tabasco sauce
¼ cup minced parsley
⅛ teaspoon freshly grated nutmeg
Additional butter for each soup bowl

1. In the top of a double boiler, combine butter, onion, celery and bell pepper. Over direct heat, cook and stir until onions are transparent.
2. Add flour and mix well.
3. Add hot milk and whisk until smooth.
4. Season with salt and pepper.
5. Place top of double boiler over hot water. Add cream and oyster liquid. Heat thoroughly.
6. Add oysters and heat over hot water 7 to 10 minutes, until oysters are cooked and edges fluted. If overcooked, oysters will be tough.
7. Add parsley, grated nutmeg, a few drops of Tabasco or a dash of cayenne.
8. Serve piping hot in heated bowls that have ½ teaspoon butter in the bottom.

Serves 5 to 6

WILD RICE AND CHICKEN SOUP

½ medium onion, chopped
½ cup butter
½ cup all-purpose flour
3 cups chicken broth
2 cups half and half
2 cups cooked wild rice
½ teaspoon salt

2 cups cubed, cooked chicken
1½ cups thinly sliced carrots, cooked
½ cup chopped celery
½ cup sliced mushrooms
½ cup parsley

1. Sauté onion in butter. Add flour to make a thick roux.
2. Slowly add broth and half and half using a whisk. Cook over medium heat stirring constantly until slightly thickened.
3. Add rice, salt, chicken, vegetables and parsley. Simmer 5 to 10 minutes. If soup is too thick, thin with extra broth.

Serves 8

BEEF AND EGGPLANT STEW

2 medium onions, sliced
2 green bell peppers, coarsely chopped
1 pound ground beef
2 tablespoons olive oil
1 small eggplant, peeled and cubed

2 16-ounce cans tomatoes
1 1½-ounce package spaghetti sauce mix
¼ pound mozzarella cheese, grated
Salt and pepper to taste

1. Cook onions, peppers and beef in oil until meat is brown and vegetables are slightly soft. Drain.
2. Add eggplant, tomatoes and spaghetti sauce mix to meat mixture. Bring to a boil. Cover and simmer 15 minutes or until eggplant is tender. Add salt and pepper to taste.
3. Spoon into individual serving bowls while very hot. Cover with cheese.

Serves 4 to 6

RICH CHICKEN SOUP

Serve this hearty soup with a crisp green salad and crusty rolls for a complete meal.

2½ to 3 pounds chicken	¼ teaspoon thyme
1 medium onion, chopped	1 bay leaf
6 sprigs parsley	6 cups water
4 carrots, chopped	1½ cups dry white wine
1 rib celery with leaves, chopped	¼ cup butter
1 clove garlic, minced	¼ cup all-purpose flour
¼ teaspoon peppercorns	6 cups chicken stock
1½ teaspoons salt	2 egg yolks, beaten
	1 cup whipping cream, warmed

1. In a large soup kettle, bring to a boil chicken, onion, parsley, carrots, celery, garlic, peppercorns, salt, thyme, bay leaf, water and wine. Simmer 1 hour.
2. Remove chicken. Bone and chop into bite-size pieces. Remove vegetables with a slotted spoon. Discard peppercorns and bay leaf. Save vegetables. Strain stock through a fine sieve. Set stock aside.
3. Make a thin white sauce using butter, flour and chicken stock.
4. Add a small amount of sauce to egg yolks. Whisk while returning yolk mixture to sauce. Add cooked vegetables and chicken.
5. Whisk soup briskly while adding cream.

Serves 6 to 9

ROUND STEAK STEW

½   cup butter
½   cup all-purpose flour
8   cups water
2   pounds round steak, cut in 1-inch cubes
3   tablespoons butter
1   cup chopped onions
1   cup chopped carrots
1   cup diced celery

1   10-ounce package frozen mixed vegetables
1   tablespoon Accent
3 to 4 beef bouillon cubes
1   teaspoon garlic powder
    Salt and pepper to taste
2   medium potatoes, peeled and cubed

1. Melt butter in a large Dutch oven. Stir in flour to make a smooth paste. Stir constantly over medium-high heat until flour is browned.
2. Add water and heat until paste is fully dissolved.
3. In a separate pan, sauté round steak in butter until browned.
4. Remove steak and add to flour mixture in Dutch oven. Add all remaining ingredients, except potatoes. Simmer 3 hours, stirring frequently.
5. Add potatoes. Simmer 30 minutes.

This may also be baked for 3 hours in a 350° oven.

Serves 6 to 8

NUTMEG NOODLES

These are good in turkey or chicken soup.

2   eggs
28 saltine crackers, crushed
1   teaspoon freshly grated nutmeg

4   tablespoons all-purpose flour
2   tablespoons butter
½   teaspoon salt
2 to 5 tablespoons soup stock

1. Beat eggs and mix with cracker crumbs, nutmeg, flour, butter and salt.
2. Moisten lightly with soup stock.
3. Roll into small balls and drop into boiling soup. Cook 4 to 6 minutes.

Serves 8

CELESTIAL POTATO SOUP
A Collection Classic

2 medium potatoes, peeled and diced
2 carrots, grated
1 rib celery, finely chopped
1 turnip, peeled and diced
3 tablespoons minced onions
1 tablespoon dried vegetable flakes
1 teaspoon monosodium glutamate

Salt and pepper to taste
3 tablespoons butter
2 tablespoons all-purpose flour
1½ cups milk
1½ cups sour cream
3 slices bacon, crisply cooked and crumbled

1. Combine potatoes, carrots, celery, turnip, onion, vegetable flakes, monosodium glutamate, salt and pepper. Cover with water and simmer 30 minutes.
2. In another saucepan, melt butter and stir in flour. Add a small amount of liquid from potato mixture to form a paste. Cool and stir in milk and sour cream.
3. When vegetables are cooked, mash or purée them. Add flour and milk mixture. Do not boil. Garnish with bacon and serve.

For a change, this may also be served cold.

Serves 6

Freezes

PIMIENTO CHEESE SPREAD

1   pound mild Cheddar cheese,
    grated
1   4-ounce jar diced pimientos,
    drained

Seasoned salt to taste
Cayenne pepper to taste
½   cup mayonnaise or to taste

1. Combine all above ingredients.
2. Add ingredients from variations below if desired.
3. Refrigerate and chill thoroughly until ready to serve.

Variations: Choose one of the following:

Add 1 chopped, roasted and peeled red pepper.

Add ⅓ cup finely chopped walnuts.

Add 1 small clove minced garlic.

Add finely chopped jalapeños to taste.

Add ¼ cup chopped black olives and ¼ cup dried green chives.

Add 2 hard-cooked, finely chopped eggs, ½ cup thinly sliced celery and 3 tablespoons sweet pickle relish.

Yields 4 cups

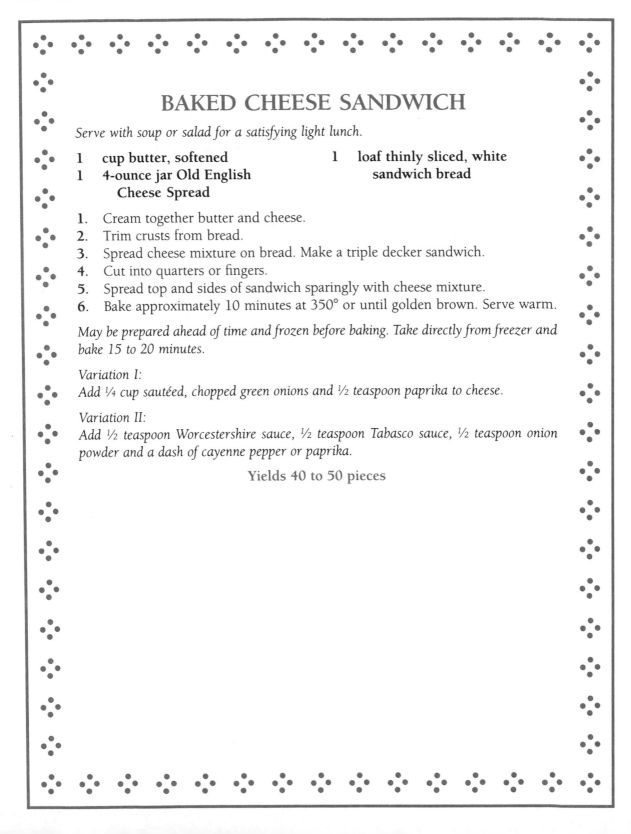

BAKED CHEESE SANDWICH

Serve with soup or salad for a satisfying light lunch.

1 cup butter, softened	1 loaf thinly sliced, white
1 4-ounce jar Old English	sandwich bread
Cheese Spread	

1. Cream together butter and cheese.
2. Trim crusts from bread.
3. Spread cheese mixture on bread. Make a triple decker sandwich.
4. Cut into quarters or fingers.
5. Spread top and sides of sandwich sparingly with cheese mixture.
6. Bake approximately 10 minutes at 350° or until golden brown. Serve warm.

May be prepared ahead of time and frozen before baking. Take directly from freezer and bake 15 to 20 minutes.

Variation I:
Add ¼ cup sautéed, chopped green onions and ½ teaspoon paprika to cheese.

Variation II:
Add ½ teaspoon Worcestershire sauce, ½ teaspoon Tabasco sauce, ½ teaspoon onion powder and a dash of cayenne pepper or paprika.

Yields 40 to 50 pieces

SWISS BACON SANDWICH WITH AVOCADO DRESSING

Avocado adds a new twist to the traditional bacon sandwich.

Avocado dressing:

1	medium to large ripe avocado	8	slices bacon
4	teaspoons lemon juice	4	slices mixed-grain bread
¼	cup mayonnaise		Mayonnaise
¼	cup thinly sliced green onions	4	slices Swiss cheese
	Salt and pepper		Alfalfa sprouts
			Tomatoes, sliced

1. To make dressing, halve, seed, peel and purée avocado. Mix with lemon juice and mayonnaise until blended. Stir in green onions, salt and pepper.
2. Cook bacon until crisp. Drain and keep warm.
3. Toast bread lightly. Spread 1 side of each slice with mayonnaise.
4. Place cheese on bread.
5. Broil until cheese is softened.
6. Cover generously with sprouts. Spoon ¼ cup avocado dressing over sprouts. Top with bacon.
7. Serve with tomatoes and extra sprouts.

Dressing yields 1½ cups

Serves 4

HOT ITALIAN SANDWICH

3 loaves frozen bread dough	1 8-ounce can mushroom pieces, drained
1 pound ground chuck	1 8-ounce can chopped black olives, drained
1 pound ground sausage	
1 onion, chopped	1 4-ounce jar diced pimientos, drained
1 green bell pepper, chopped	
¼ teaspoon garlic salt	¾ cup grated mozzarella or Cheddar cheese
½ teaspoon salt	
¼ teaspoon pepper	
1 jalapeño pepper, finely chopped	3 tablespoons butter, melted

1. Thaw bread dough. Let it rise according to package directions.
2. Preheat oven to 350°.
3. Brown chuck, sausage, onions and bell pepper. Drain. Pat with paper towels to remove additional grease.
4. Mix in remaining ingredients, except cheese and butter.
5. Roll each loaf flat like pizza dough. Brush with melted butter. Cover with meat mixture.
6. Top with cheese. Roll jelly-roll fashion. Tuck ends in and seal well. Place in a bread pan. Brush with butter. Bake 30 minutes or until golden brown.
7. Cut in slices and serve warm.

Can be frozen after baking. To serve, thaw, cover with foil and reheat 30 minutes at 350°.

Yields 24 slices

HOT ASPARAGUS AND PARMESAN FINGER SANDWICHES

1 6 to 8-ounce can asparagus spears, drained	2 hard-cooked eggs, sieved
4 ounces cream cheese	12 thin slices white bread
1 teaspoon seasoned salt	½ cup butter, melted
	½ cup grated Parmesan cheese

1. Blend asparagus, cream cheese and salt in food processor. Blend in eggs.
2. Trim crusts from bread. Spread mixture on 1 slice of bread and top with second slice.
3. Cut in thirds for finger sandwiches.
4. Dip or roll sandwiches in melted butter. Coat with Parmesan cheese.
5. At this point, sandwiches may be frozen until ready to broil. Broil on both sides until lightly browned and serve warm.

Yields 6 sandwiches
or 18 finger sandwiches

PARSLEY BACON SANDWICH FILLING

An unusual filling for party sandwiches.

2 bunches fresh parsley or watercress finely chopped	Dash Worcestershire sauce
1 pound bacon, crisply cooked and crumbled	1 teaspoon garlic powder
	1 cup butter, softened
⅓ to ½ cup mayonnaise	1 loaf sandwich bread

1. Combine parsley, bacon, mayonnaise, and Worcestershire to spreading consistency.
2. Mix garlic powder and butter.
3. Trim crusts from bread and flatten pieces lightly with a rolling pin.
4. Spread bread with butter mixture.
5. Spread bread with parsley and bacon mixture.
6. Spread top slice of bread with garlic butter and place on bottom half.
7. Cut into triangles or finger sandwiches.

Yields 9 dozen finger sandwiches

DELI ROLL UPS

2	loaves frozen bread dough	½ pound lunch meat, thinly sliced
¾	pound ham, thinly sliced	
½	pound salami, thinly sliced	½ pound sliced American cheese
¾	pound pepper ham, thinly sliced	½ pound sliced Swiss cheese
		½ pound provolone cheese

1. Thaw bread dough and let it rise according to package directions.
2. Preheat oven to 350°.
3. Cut each loaf in half.
4. Roll each section into a flat 10 by 12-inch rectangle.
5. Layer meats and cheeses.
6. Roll jelly-roll fashion. Tuck ends in and seal well.
7. Place loaves on cookie sheet. Bake 45 minutes.
8 Let them stand 10 minutes. Slice and serve warm.

Roll ups can be frozen after baking. To serve, thaw and cover with foil. Reheat at 350° for 30 minutes.

Variation:
Sprinkle meats and cheeses with 1 cup sliced black olives.

Yields 4 loaves
or 32 slices

CRUNCHY GERMAN SANDWICHES

3	cups finely shredded cabbage		Butter
⅔	cup mayonnaise	1	pound Virginia baked ham, thinly sliced
3	tablespoons chili sauce		
1	tablespoon minced onion	1	pound Swiss cheese, thinly sliced
¼	teaspoon salt		
12	slices rye bread		

1. Lightly mix first 5 ingredients. Refrigerate 1 hour or until well chilled.
2. For each sandwich, lightly spread each slice of bread with butter.
3. On 1 slice of bread, generously layer ham and cheese slices. Spread with cabbage mixture. Top with second piece of bread.
4. Cut sandwich into thirds, crosswise, and fasten with picks.

Serve with Old-Time Ice Box Pickles on page 448.

Serves 12 to 15

HAM AND CHEESE BUNWICHES

Make these by the dozen and freeze.

Spread:
½ cup butter
¼ cup Dijon mustard
¼ cup minced onion
2 teaspoons poppy seeds

Sandwich:
8 torpedo rolls
8 slices ham
8 slices Swiss cheese
8 slices Muenster cheese

1. Combine all spread ingredients.
2. Spread both sides of split torpedo rolls with butter spread.
3. Layer ham and cheeses on roll.
4. Wrap each bunwich in foil.
5. At this point, bunwiches may be frozen.
6. Thaw and bake 30 minutes at 350°.

Baskets of foil wrapped bunwiches can be served with assorted chips, dips and iced drinks for a delicious picnic. Give a basket of these to friends.

Serves 8

FREEZER MUFFIN PIZZAS

These are fun for children to prepare at a party; and are good to have in the freezer for Saturday lunch.

24 English muffins, split and buttered	1 teaspoon garlic salt
2 pounds ground beef	2 16-ounce jars processed cheese spread
1 large onion, diced	1 14-ounce jar pizza sauce
1 teaspoon salt	½ cup minced fresh parsley
1 teaspoon pepper	½ cup Parmesan cheese

1. Brown beef and onion in a large skillet. Drain.
2. Season with salt, pepper and garlic salt.
3. Spread 2 teaspoons of cheese spread and 2 teaspoons pizza sauce on each muffin. Spoon meat mixture onto pizza sauce. Sprinkle with parsley and Parmesan cheese.
4. Place on a cookie sheet and freeze. Wrap in plastic wrap or foil. Store in freezer until ready to use.
5. Bake frozen, approximately 20 to 30 minutes, at 350° or until bubbly.

Yields 48 mini pizzas

PEPPERONI PIZZA

Children and teenagers will find this to be a fun do-it-yourself meal.

1 16-ounce package hot roll mix	Red pepper to taste
1 8-ounce can tomato sauce	1 3-ounce package pepperoni
1 pound ground meat, browned	sausage
and drained	¼ cup chopped green bell pepper
1 teaspoon thyme	½ pound Cheddar cheese, grated
1 teaspoon oregano	
1 6-ounce package sliced	
mozzarella cheese	

1. Prepare hot roll mix according to package directions. Spread dough on a greased cookie sheet into a 14-inch diameter circle.
2. Mix together tomato sauce, meat and spices. Spread mixture over pizza. Top with mozzarella cheese, pepperoni sausage, bell pepper and Cheddar cheese. Sprinkle with red pepper if desired.
3. Bake 20 minutes at 150°.

Serves 4 to 6

CHEESE SPREAD FOR HOT POOR BOYS

1 cup finely shredded Cheddar	2 tablespoons chopped green
cheese	onions
3 ounces cream cheese, softened	2 teaspoons prepared mustard
3 tablespoons mayonnaise	½ teaspoon Worcestershire sauce
¼ to ½ cup chopped black olives	

1. Combine all ingredients and spread on poor boy sandwich buns.
2. Any combination of the following may be added: sliced ham, turkey, roast beef, salami, pastrami, sliced tomato, chopped onion, chopped bell pepper, pickles, bacon, chopped egg, lettuce, sprouts, cucumber slices and sliced mushrooms. Be creative. There are many more possibilities.
3. Wrap sandwich in foil. Heat at 350° approximately 10 to 15 minutes or until sauce is bubbly. Serve hot.

Serves 6 to 8

MOUFFELATA SPREAD

A spread that makes fabulous poor boy sandwiches. Serve with cold cuts and your guests and family will love it!

1	cup chopped onion	½	cup lemon juice
1	cup chopped celery	2	6-ounce jars marinated
1	cup chopped green bell pepper		artichokes, drained
1	cup chopped black olives	2	cans anchovies, drained
¾	cup olive oil	2	tablespoons Italian seasoning

1. Combine all ingredients in food processor or blender. Blend until well mixed.
2. Will keep 2 weeks stored in a glass jar in refrigerator.

Use as a spread for poor boy sandwiches, ham, turkey or salami, two cheeses, mustard and mayonnaise on a French roll.

Yields spread for 16 to 20 sandwiches

WINE MUSTARD FOR HAM SANDWICHES

Makes a nice gift from the kitchen.

1	cup dry mustard		Pinch salt
1	cup red or white wine vinegar	5	drops Tabasco sauce
2	eggs		Watercress, optional
1	cup sugar		

1. Mix dry mustard and vinegar. When mixture is smooth, cover and refrigerate 7 hours or overnight.
2. Beat eggs until fluffy.
3. Slowly add sugar, beating well until mixture is very thick.
4. Combine egg and sugar mixture with mustard and vinegar mixture. Add salt and Tabasco.
5. In double boiler, over boiling water, cook several minutes until thick, whisking constantly.
6. Divide into several small jars.
7. Cool and refrigerate.
8. Spread on deli rolls. Add slices of ham. Watercress may be used as a garnish.

Yields 2 cups

EGGS, CHEESE AND PASTA

EGGS

Eggs have been called the perfect food. They play a major role in all aspects of cooking whether they are used as the main ingredient, or as a binding agent. However, the quality of an egg cannot be determined by its exterior appearance.

The United States Department of Agriculture, (U.S.D.A.) has established guidelines for grading eggs. There are four grades, ranging from the top quality, Grade AA, to the lowest quality, Grade C. The size of an egg is determined by weight per dozen, not by the size of an individual egg.

Egg Size Chart

Jumbo: 30 ounces per dozen
Extra Large: 27 ounces per dozen
Large: 24 ounces per dozen
Medium: 21 ounces per dozen
Small: 18 ounces per dozen

Egg Whites

1. To store egg whites, place in a tightly sealed container and refrigerate. Egg whites may be kept for several weeks.
2. To freeze egg whites, place 1 egg white in each section of an ice cube tray. When frozen, place cubes in a storage bag.
3. Refrigerated eggs separate more easily than those at room temperature. However, egg whites will yield more volume if they are room temperature when beaten.
4. To easily separate the egg white from the yolk, simply crack the egg in your hand and let the white run through your fingers into a cup, then carefully place the yolk in another cup. This is less trouble than using the shell or an egg separator.
5. A copper bowl is best for beating egg whites. If this is not possible, add a pinch of cream of tartar when egg whites reach the foamy stage. The cream of tartar adds acidity which helps increase the volume and stability of the egg whites.

Egg Yolks

1. When using only the white, save the yolk by covering with cold water or oil and store in the refrigerator.
2. When separating eggs, if yolk gets in the white, remove with a piece of shell.
3. When slicing hard cooked yolks, wet the knife to prevent crumbling.

Curdling

When adding eggs to custards and sauces, take care not to overcook the egg or use too high a heat. This can cause curdling or instant scrambled eggs and completely ruin the result. To prevent this, use the following technique, called tempering, for adding eggs to hot mixtures.

1. Beat the eggs slightly.
2. Add approximately ¼ cup of the hot mixture to the beaten egg, warming the egg gradually. This tempers the egg mixture so it can be added to the remaining hot mixture.
3. Continue cooking, stirring constantly, until the mixture thickens and is smooth and creamy.

Fried Eggs

To prepare the perfect over easy egg, fry until the underside is done, add approximately ¼ cup of water to the pan and cover with a lid. Steam cooks the top half of the egg perfectly and preserves the yolk, eliminating the turning process.

Hard-cooked Eggs

Hard-cooked eggs or hard-boiled eggs are relatively easy to prepare if you follow a few simple rules:

1. Before you begin, prick the large end with a pin or tack. This makes peeling easier and prevents cracking during cooking.
2. Limit the quantity you cook at one time to twelve. Place the eggs in a single layer on the bottom of a saucepan. Cover the eggs with at least 1 inch of cold tap water.

3. Add 1 teaspoon salt or vinegar to the water to prevent egg white from escaping a cracked shell.
4. Quickly heat the eggs to almost boiling and remove from heat.
5. Let the eggs stand, covered, for 15 to 17 minutes (longer if the eggs are extra large and shorter if they are particularly small).
6. Immediately run cold water over the eggs, or place in a bowl and pour ice water over the eggs. This prevents the gray-green discoloration of the yolk.
7. Cool 20 minutes, then peel gently.
8. Hard-cooked eggs can be refrigerated, in the shell, for 2 to 3 days.

Poached Eggs

There are numerous ways to poach eggs. Eggs can be contained during poaching with metal egg rings or can be poached in special poaching pans.

To poach eggs without a ring or pan, follow these steps:

1. Bring 2 inches of water to a boil in a deep skillet.
2. Reduce the heat and let the water simmer.
3. Carefully break 1 egg at a time into the simmering water. Do not crowd.
4. Add a pinch of salt or a few drops of vinegar to the water. This will harden the whites and help them retain their shapes.
5. Poach 3 to 5 minutes, then quickly remove the eggs with a slotted spoon or spatula.
6. Use water or milk for the poaching liquid or flavor the water with bouillon. If milk or bouillon is used reserve the liquid and pour over the egg when served on toast.

Omelets

Omelets are one of the most versatile ways to prepare eggs and one of the most popular. The fillings for omelets are endless, providing great variety with very little effort. Basic omelet mixtures may vary slightly. To prepare a perfect omelet, select a good pan, designed for this purpose. In this section, we have compiled an omelet page with a basic recipe and different filling suggestions.

Basic Omelet Recipe

3   eggs   Salt and pepper to taste
2   tablespoons butter

1. With a whisk, beat eggs until well blended.
2. In an omelet pan, melt butter over medium heat.
3. Pour eggs into pan and cook until edges begin to thicken.
4. With a fork, lift edges allowing unset egg to run into pan. Shake pan frequently to prevent eggs from sticking.
5. Remove from heat when entire bottom is thickened, but top is still moist. Allow omelet to stand a few seconds.
6. Add filling and fold omelet.
7. Serve immediately as eggs become tough when they cool.

The varieties of ingredients for omelets are limited only by your imagination. Create your own fillings by choosing appealing combinations of ingredients. Add desired amounts of ingredients and seasonings. Sauté vegetables in a small amount of butter before cooking eggs.

Fried, drained and crumbled bulk pork sausage, sliced mushrooms and sour cream

Diced ham, chopped parsley and shredded American or Cheddar cheese

Cooked crumbled bacon, finely chopped onion, and shredded Swiss cheese

Chopped avocado blended with mayonnaise and lemon juice, finely chopped onion and alfalfa sprouts

Shredded Monterey Jack cheese, thinly sliced green onion, diced green chile, diced tomato and sour cream

Chopped artichoke hearts and grated Parmesan cheese or Romano cheese

Sliced sautéed mushrooms and sour cream

Caviar and sour cream

Chutney and grated mozzarella cheese

Grated and drained zucchini, thinly sliced green onion, diced tomato, basil and shredded Swiss cheese

Cooked scallops, lobster, crab meat, shrimp or a combination with shredded Swiss cheese

Picante sauce, thinly sliced green onions, finely chopped jalapeño pepper or finely chopped green bell pepper and shredded Monterey Jack cheese

Quiche

Quiche is a mixture of cream, eggs and a variety of flavorings baked in a pastry shell until the mixture is firm and the top is golden brown. The possibilites for creating mixture combinations is endless. Quiche is simple to prepare.

To prevent a quiche crust from becoming soggy, place a piece of buttered aluminum foil on top of the crust. Cover foil with a layer of dried beans. Place pastry shell in a 425° oven for 15 or 20 minutes until bottom is set and sides are lightly browned. With a pastry brush, coat entire shell with egg yolk. Return shell to the oven for 2 minutes.

Shake the pan gently to see if quiche has set or gently insert a knife into the center of the quiche. If it comes out clean, the quiche is done.

Soufflé

A soufflé is a thick sauce, enhanced with egg yolks and flavorings, that doubles in volume when egg whites are carefully added to the mixture. There are three simple parts to a soufflé: the base or sauce, the flavorings and the egg whites. The flavorings or ingredients that give a soufflé its taste should be finely chopped or puréed. These ingredients are usually cooked before they are added to the sauce base. The egg whites cause the mixture to expand and double in size when it is heated. Adding the egg whites to the mixture may be the single most important step of creating a perfect soufflé. The egg whites should be carefully folded into the mixture. This preserves the delicate texture of the egg whites.

Several varieties of soufflé dishes are available, but the straight-sided glass or china variety seems to be the most successful. The straight sides give the soufflé greater strength during baking. The soufflé may be reinforced by making a wax paper, parchment or foil supportive collar. This collar must first be folded and then tied around the dish, extending at least four to five inches above the rim of the dish to support the sides of the soufflé during baking.

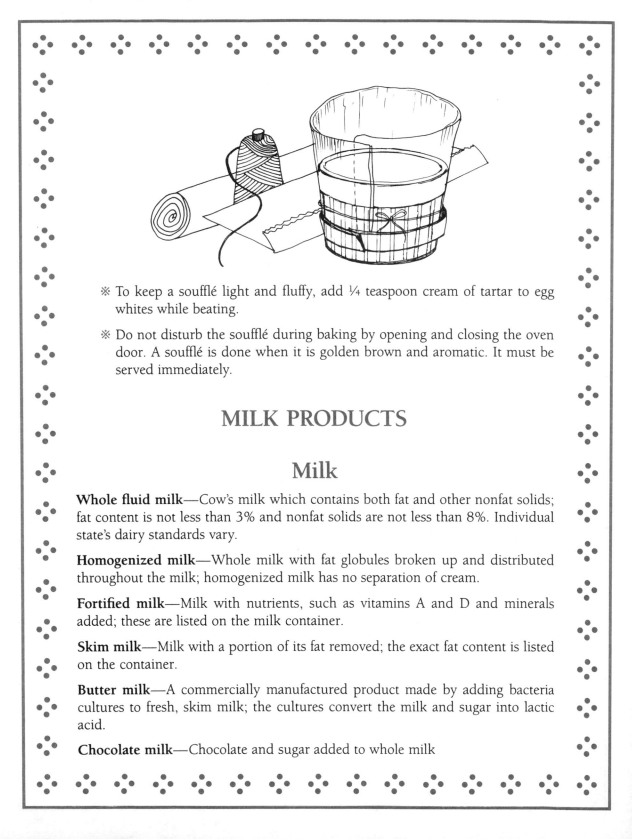

✳ To keep a soufflé light and fluffy, add ¼ teaspoon cream of tartar to egg whites while beating.

✳ Do not disturb the soufflé during baking by opening and closing the oven door. A soufflé is done when it is golden brown and aromatic. It must be served immediately.

MILK PRODUCTS

Milk

Whole fluid milk—Cow's milk which contains both fat and other nonfat solids; fat content is not less than 3% and nonfat solids are not less than 8%. Individual state's dairy standards vary.

Homogenized milk—Whole milk with fat globules broken up and distributed throughout the milk; homogenized milk has no separation of cream.

Fortified milk—Milk with nutrients, such as vitamins A and D and minerals added; these are listed on the milk container.

Skim milk—Milk with a portion of its fat removed; the exact fat content is listed on the container.

Butter milk—A commercially manufactured product made by adding bacteria cultures to fresh, skim milk; the cultures convert the milk and sugar into lactic acid.

Chocolate milk—Chocolate and sugar added to whole milk

Canned and Dry Milk Products

Evaporated milk—Sterilized, homogenized milk from which about 60% of the water has been removed

Sweetened condensed milk—Whole milk from which approximately 50% of the water has been removed; sugar has been added as a preservative.

Dry whole milk—Whole milk from which the water has been removed; add water to reconstitute.

Nonfat whole milk—Whole milk from which both water and fat have been removed; add water to reconstitute.

Cream

Cream—The substance that rises to the top of milk; contains more than 18% milk fat

Heavy or whipping cream—Cream with 30 to 36% milk fat

Light whipping cream—Between 30 to 36% milk fat

Heavy whipping cream—More than 36% milk fat

> ※ Whipping cream doubles in volume when air is forced into the cream.

> ※ Freeze dollops of whipped cream on wax paper. After cream is frozen, carefully remove and wrap individual dollops in plastic wrap. Store in a protective container in the freezer.

> ※ Cream whips quickly if the bowl and beaters are chilled.

Light cream—Also called coffee or table cream; contains between 18 to 36% milk fat

Half and half—A mixture of milk and cream; usually contains 10 to 12% milk fat

Sour cream—Sweet cream that has been soured by adding lactic acid culture; has a milk fat content of 18 to 20%

Other Milk Products

Ice cream—A frozen mixture of milk, cream, sugar and flavorings

Ice milk—Like ice cream, with less milk fat and more nonfat milk solid

Sherbet—Frozen mixture of lowfat milk solids, sugar, food acid, water and fruit juices

Yogurt—A cultured milk product made from partially skimmed or concentrated whole milk; often contains flavorings

BUTTER

Butter is fresh or soured cream that has been churned. Law requires it to contain at least 80% milk fat. The remaining 20% is largely water with some milk solids added. Butter can be salted or unsalted (often called sweet butter).

Butter is manufactured in three grades:

U.S. Grade AA—Has a pleasant aroma and a sweet flavor

U.S. Grade A—Most often found in stores

U.S. Grade B—Made from sour cream and does not have the sweet fresh flavor of the other superior grades

Cooking With Butter

Butter adds a rich creamy flavor to foods. It is a perfect flavoring for breads, cooked vegetables, meats and sweets. Check recipes for the type of butter recommended. The type of butter used will affect the taste of the recipe.

How to Clarify Butter:
1. Melt butter, in a heavy pan, over low heat.
2. Skim white froth, as it forms, on top of the melted butter.
3. Pour off clear liquid yellow butter. Make sure the sediment of the milk solids is not poured off.
4. Discard sediment.
5. Keep refrigerated or frozen.

※ Whipped butter has air or gas whipped into it, increasing its volume. It is generally unsatisfactory for cooking. Remember, when measuring butter, equal amounts of whipped butter cannot be substituted for non-whipped butter.

FLAVORED BUTTERS

Anchovy Butter

½   cup butter, softened
4   anchovy fillets, mashed

½   teaspoon lemon juice
Dash cayenne

1. Cream butter until light and fluffy.
2. Add remaining ingredients. Blend thoroughly.
3. Store in a tightly sealed container. Refrigerate.

Serve on meat or fish.

Bercy Butter

½   cup dry white wine
1   tablespoon finely chopped
       shallots
⅓   cup butter, softened

2   teaspoons finely chopped
       parsley
Salt and pepper to taste

1. Boil wine in saucepan until volume of liquid is reduced by half.
2. Cream butter until light and fluffy.
3. Add remaining ingredients. Blend mixture thoroughly into wine.

Serve on meat or fish.

Chives Butter

½   cup unsalted butter, softened
½   cup finely chopped chives

Salt to taste
Freshly ground pepper to taste

1. Cream butter until light and fluffy.
2. Add remaining ingredients. Blend thoroughly.
3. Store in an airtight container. Refrigerate.

Serve over meat, fish and vegetables.

Fines Herbes Butter

½ cup butter, softened
1 green onion, white only
2 tablespoons chopped parsley

½ teaspoon dried tarragon
½ teaspoon dried chervil
Dash freshly ground pepper

1. Cream butter until light and fluffy.
2. Add remaining ingredients. Blend thoroughly.
3. Store in a tightly sealed container. Refrigerate.

Serve on vegetables or fish.

Garlic Butter

2 to 3 cloves garlic
½ cup butter, softened

2 tablespoons finely chopped
   parsley, optional

1. Boil garlic in water 4 to 5 minutes. Drain.
2. Dry garlic and crush well.
3. Cream butter until light and fluffy.
4. Add garlic and parsley. Blend thoroughly.
5. Store in a tightly sealed container. Refrigerate.

Serve on vegetables, fish, meat or bread.

Lemon Butter

¼ cup butter
1 tablespoon lemon juice

Dash white pepper

1. Melt butter. Add lemon juice and pepper. Blend thoroughly.

Serve on fish and vegetables.

Mustard Butter

½ cup butter, softened	½ teaspoon Worcestershire sauce
2 teaspoons dry mustard	¼ teaspoon garlic salt
2 tablespoons chopped parsley	Dash freshly ground pepper

1. Cream butter until light and fluffy.
2. Add remaining ingredients. Blend thoroughly.
3. Store in a tightly sealed container. Refrigerate.

Serve as a sandwich spread or over meats and vegetables.

Paprika Butter

½ cup butter, softened   1 tablespoon paprika

1. Cream butter until light and fluffy.
2. Add paprika. Blend thoroughly.
3. Store in a tightly sealed container. Refrigerate.

Delicious served on fish and vegetables.

Parsley Butter

½ cup butter, softened   ¼ cup finely chopped parsley
Dash freshly ground pepper

1. Cream butter until light and fluffy.
2. Add remaining ingredients. Blend thoroughly.
3. Store in a tightly sealed container. Refrigerate.

Serve on meat and vegetables.

Tarragon Butter

½   cup butter, softened
1   tablespoon fresh tarragon

1   tablespoon tarragon vinegar

1. Cream butter until light and fluffy.
2. Add remaining ingredients. Blend thoroughly.
3. Store in a tightly sealed container. Refrigerate.

Serve with poultry, fish or meat.

Orange Butter

¼   cup frozen orange juice
      concentrate
⅔   cup unsalted butter

16   ounces powdered sugar
¼   teaspoon grated orange rind

1. Cream butter until light and fluffy.
2. Add remaining ingredients. Blend thoroughly.
3. Store in a tightly sealed container. Refrigerate.

Serve on hot rolls and breads.

Strawberry Butter

1   10-ounce package frozen
      strawberries, thawed

1   cup unsalted butter
½   cup powdered sugar

1. Cream butter until light and fluffy.
2. Add remaining ingredients. Blend thoroughly.
3. Store in a tightly sealed container. Refrigerate.

Serve on hot rolls and breads.

Spice Butter

½ **cup unsalted butter**   ¼ **teaspoon cinnamon or nutmeg**

1. Cream butter until light and fluffy.
2. Add cinnamon or nutmeg. Blend thoroughly.
3. Store in a tightly sealed container. Refrigerate.

Serve on muffins, pancakes or butter breads.

CHEESE

There are hundreds of varieties of cheese available today. Sample as many kinds as possible and experiment with different varieties of the same type of cheese. For example, in our recipe for Tex-Mex Canapés we offer a choice of either Cheddar cheese or Monterey Jack cheese, two varieties of hard cheese. The results are essentially the same, but with subtle taste differences. A different type of cheese can alter the character of a dish. You may be pleasantly surprised to find a new approach to one of your old favorites.

To insure freshness when selecting cheese, check the packaging and date. Avoid cheese with a wet or sticky wrapper. Do not purchase cheese that is shrinking from the rind. Do not purchase cheese containing blue or green veins that exhibits brownish discoloration near the veins. Also, check for drying and cracking in hard and semi-firm cheeses. If unsure, ask the counter attendant for assistance.

Cheeses can be categorized according to hardness and aging period. Hardness refers to the labeling: hard, firm, soft and unripened varieties of cheese. Cheese may be processed, unripened or mature according to the time involved in producing the particular variety.

Processed cheese—Velveeta, Cheese Whiz

Mature or natural cheese—Swiss, Cheddar, Brie, Camembert, Gruyère and Parmesan

Unripened or fresh cheese—Ricotta, curd or cream cheeses, Neufchâtel, cottage and mozzarella

Serving Tips

1. Soft cheese should be served chilled.
2. Hard and semi-firm cheese tastes best when served at room temperature.

   a. Remove from refrigerator 30 minutes before serving.
   b. Microwave for 15 seconds on high to speed the process; this also helps to soften cheese spreads, such as pimiento cheese, if they have hardened during refrigeration.

Grating and Slicing

1. Allow ¼ pound for 1 cup of shredded cheese.
2. Shredded hard cheese may be frozen.
3. Cheese grates more easily when chilled.
4. Use a knife, that has been warmed by running water, when slicing hard or semi-firm cheese.

Storage

1. Always tightly rewrap freshly cut cheese to prevent drying.
2. Store strong smelling cheese, such as Roquefort, in a plastic container with a tight fitting lid in the bottom of the refrigerator (usually the coldest part of the refrigerator).
3. Fresh, unripened cheese should be used as soon as possible after purchasing and should carefully be rewrapped.
4. Natural and processed cheese will stay fresh for several months, unopened and wrapped tightly, but only up to six weeks if it has been opened.
5. Hard and semi-hard cheese may be frozen up to two months. Freezing soft cheese is not recommended as this changes its flavor and texture.
6. If cheese develops a mold, do not discard; simply cut the mold off before using.

Cooking With Cheese

Cheese is already cooked and does not need additional cooking time, just enough to heat and melt evenly or blend well.

1. Low heat is best. High heat or overcooking may cause cheese to become tough and stringy and may cause fat to separate. Flavor may be lost.

2. When adding cheese to a sauce, it is best to grate or dice it first so that it will melt and blend quickly.
3. Processed cheese is too soft to grate, and works best if diced and then added to a recipe.
4. When topping a casserole with grated cheese, add during the last 5 minutes to prevent the cheese from becoming hard and brittle.
5. When making an omelet, add grated cheese after the omelet is cooked, just before folding.

PASTA

Pasta is an Italian word for dried, hardened dough paste made in a great variety of shapes and sizes. Fresh pasta may be cooked immediately after preparation or dried and stored. Commercially prepared pasta is available in many varieties. Fresh pasta is more readily available now and can be found in the refrigerated sections of grocery stores or specialty shops.

Cooking Pasta

1. To prevent pasta from sticking to the pan, add lime juice or oil to the water.
2. To prevent water from boiling over, add 2 tablespoons of oil.
3. If pasta is prepared for a hot dish, rinsing is not necessary. But, if you are preparing it for a cold pasta salad, rinse it in cold water and add the salad dressing or marinade while the pasta is still warm, then refrigerate.
4. Pasta is considered done when it is firm or "al dente", Italian for "to the bite".
5. Another test for pasta readiness after designated cooking time calls for pulling a piece or strand from the boiling water and flinging it at a vertical surface. If it sticks, it is supposedly done.
6. When preparing noodles for a casserole, reduce the cooking time by $1/3$. The cooking process will be completed during the baking of the casserole.
7. Generally, pasta may be substituted interchangeably measure for measure or by weight if measurement is not possible because of shape.
8. Servings and yields of pasta:

   ※ Six or seven ounces or two cups of macaroni yields four cups cooked pasta.

   ※ Seven or eight ounces of spaghetti yields four cups cooked or four to six servings.

   ※ Eight ounces or four to five cups of egg noodles yields four to five cups cooked or four to six servings.

BRUNCH EGG CASSEROLE

A wonderful casserole for weekend company or brunches.

6	slices white bread, crust removed	6	eggs
1	pound ground sausage	1	teaspoon salt
4	cups shredded Cheddar cheese	1	teaspoon dry mustard
		2	cups half and half

1. Lightly butter each slice of bread.
2. Place bread in a 9 by 13-inch buttered glass baking dish.
3. Brown sausage. Drain and pat with paper towels. Sprinkle sausage over bread.
4. Sprinkle cheese over sausage.
5. Beat eggs. Add salt, dry mustard and half and half. Beat again.
6. Pour egg mixture over bread, sausage and cheese.
7. Cover with foil and refrigerate overnight. At this point, it may be frozen until ready to use. Remove from freezer and thaw overnight in refrigerator.
8. Remove foil. Bake 45 minutes at 350° or until casserole is bubbly and lightly browned on top. This dish reheats easily.

Variation I: Texas Brunch Casserole

1. Brown sausage with 2 finely chopped onions.
2. Sprinkle 4-ounces drained, chopped green chiles and 1 fresh chopped jalapeño over sausage.
3. Sprinkle with 4 cups grated Monterey Jack cheese.
4. Add 1 teaspoon seasoned salt and 1 rounded teaspoon ground cumin to 6 beaten eggs. Add 1 teaspoon dry mustard and half and half. Mix well.
5. Pour over all. Bake as above.

Variation II: Twenty-Four Hour Sandwich

1. Prepare 12 slices of bread. Place 6 slices in a greased baking dish.
2. Cover bread with 3 cups shredded ham and 4 cups shredded Cheddar cheese. Top with remaining bread.
3. Combine eggs, mustard and salt with 3 cups half and half. Pour over layers. Bake as above.

This casserole is best when it stands 30 minutes after baking.

Serves 16

SAUSAGE RING WITH COTTAGE SCRAMBLED EGGS

Sausage Ring:
2   eggs, slightly beaten
½   cup milk
1½ cups cracker crumbs
¼   cup minced onion
1   cup peeled and diced apple
2   pounds ground pork sausage

Cottage Scrambled Eggs:
3   tablespoons butter
3   tablespoons all-purpose flour
1   cup milk
10 eggs
1   cup cottage cheese
½   teaspoon salt
    Pepper to taste

1. To make sausage ring, combine all ingredients and mix well.
2. Line a 6½-cup ring mold with plastic wrap. Press sausage mixture into mold.
3. Unmold sausage ring onto a jelly roll pan. Remove plastic wrap.
4. Bake one hour at 350°.
5. Slide ring onto a serving dish. Fill center with eggs and garnish with paprika and parsley.
6. To make cottage scrambled eggs, make a cream sauce of butter, flour and milk.
7. Combine eggs, cottage cheese, salt and pepper. Stir into sauce.
8. Cook, stirring occasionally until eggs are firm. (Too much stirring gives eggs a grainy texture.)
9. Spoon into and around sausage ring.

Sausage ring can be prepared ahead of time and baked when ready to serve.

Serves 8

CRAB MEAT QUICHE

3	eggs, slightly beaten	3	tablespoons butter
1	cup sour cream	½	pound Swiss cheese, coarsely grated
½	teaspoon Worcestershire sauce		
¾	teaspoon salt	½	pound fresh white lump crab
1	white onion, thinly sliced	1	baked pastry shell

1. Preheat oven to 325°.
2. Combine eggs, sour cream, Worcestershire and salt.
3. In a large skillet, sauté onion in butter. Stir in cheese, crab and egg mixture.
4. Pour into baked pastry shell.
5. Dot with butter. Bake 55 to 60 minutes or until custard is set and knife inserted in center comes out clean. Serve hot.

Serves 4 to 6

CRUSTLESS SAVORY QUICHE

This delicious quiche is a full meal when served with a spinach or fruit salad.

3	eggs		Pepper to taste
1	3-ounce package cream cheese	½	cup milk
1	12-ounce carton small curd cottage cheese	1	cup grated Cheddar cheese
		½	cup cooked chopped ham, bacon, shrimp or crab
¼	cup butter, softened		
¼	cup all-purpose flour	2	tablespoons minced green onion
½	teaspoon baking powder		
¼	teaspoon salt	½	cup sliced fresh mushrooms

1. Preheat oven to 350°.
2. Grease a 9-inch pie plate. Set aside.
3. In a large mixing bowl, beat eggs. Beat in cream cheese, cottage cheese and butter until almost smooth.
4. In a small bowl, combine flour, baking powder, salt and pepper. Stir in egg mixture until thoroughly blended. Beat in milk. Pour into prepared pie plate.
5. Sprinkle with cheese and meat or shellfish. Sprinkle with green onions and mushrooms.
6. Bake 30 to 40 minutes.

Serves 8

TURKEY AND DRESSING QUICHE

2½ cups cornbread dressing (or
    prepared chicken stuffing
    mix)
1 cup chopped, cooked turkey
1 cup shredded Swiss cheese

4 eggs, beaten
1 5⅓-ounce can evaporated milk
⅛ teaspoon white pepper
    Tomato wedges, optional
    Paprika, optional

1. Press dressing into a 9-inch pie plate forming a crust. Bake 10 minutes at 400°.
2. Combine meat and cheese.
3. In another container, combine eggs, milk and pepper.
4. Sprinkle meat and cheese mixture into hot crust. Pour milk mixture on top. Bake 30 to 35 minutes at 350° or until center is set.
5. Cool at least 10 minutes before serving.
6. Garnish with tomato wedges and paprika if desired.

Serves 6

CHEDDAR CHEESE SOUFFLÉ

¼ cup butter
¼ cup all-purpose flour
1 cup milk
½ teaspoon salt
    Dash cayenne pepper

½ pound sharp Cheddar cheese,
    grated
4 eggs, separated
    Paprika

1. Preheat oven to 375°.
2. Melt butter and blend in flour. Gradually add milk and cook over low heat until thick, stirring constantly. Add salt, cayenne and cheese. Stir until cheese melts. Remove from heat.
3. Beat yolks until thick and lemon colored. Slowly add cheese mixture to yolks, stirring constantly. Cool mixture.
4. Beat egg whites until stiff and fold into cheese mixture. Pour into a buttered 1½-quart soufflé dish. Sprinkle with paprika. Bake 25 minutes.

Serves 4

FAUX FETTUCCINI ALFREDO

Juice of 1 lime
1 pound egg fettuccini
2 eggs

¾ cup Parmesan cheese
¼ cup Romano or Gruyère cheese
1 tablespoon butter

1. In a large pot, boil water. Add lime juice and fettuccini. Cook fettuccini al dente.
2. Drain. Return fettuccini to pot.
3. Add eggs and butter. Toss until eggs begin to turn creamy.
4. Add cheeses and continue to toss gently until cheese melts and coats pasta.

Serves 6

LINGUINE WITH CRAB SAUCE

2 cloves garlic, minced
¼ cup olive oil
¼ cup butter
½ cup dry white wine
¼ cup water
2 tablespoons chopped parsley
½ cup sliced, fresh mushrooms

2 tablespoons butter
1 teaspoon basil
½ teaspoon salt
1 cup lump crab meat
½ pound spinach linguine, cooked according to package directions

1. Sauté garlic in oil and butter.
2. Add wine, water and parsley. Simmer, uncovered, 10 minutes.
3. Sauté mushrooms in 2 tablespoons butter.
4. Add mushrooms, basil, salt and crab to garlic mixture.
5. Toss with linguine. Serve immediately.

Variation:
Substitute shrimp for crab. Add ¼ teaspoon red pepper flakes.

Serves 6

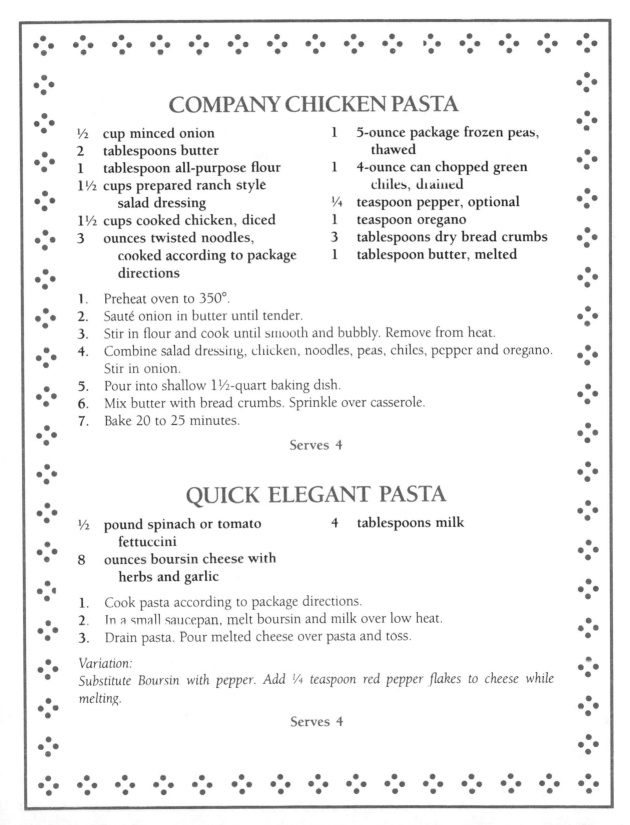

COMPANY CHICKEN PASTA

½ cup minced onion
2 tablespoons butter
1 tablespoon all-purpose flour
1½ cups prepared ranch style
    salad dressing
1½ cups cooked chicken, diced
3 ounces twisted noodles,
    cooked according to package
    directions

1 5-ounce package frozen peas,
    thawed
1 4-ounce can chopped green
    chiles, drained
¼ teaspoon pepper, optional
1 teaspoon oregano
3 tablespoons dry bread crumbs
1 tablespoon butter, melted

1. Preheat oven to 350°.
2. Sauté onion in butter until tender.
3. Stir in flour and cook until smooth and bubbly. Remove from heat.
4. Combine salad dressing, chicken, noodles, peas, chiles, pepper and oregano. Stir in onion.
5. Pour into shallow 1½-quart baking dish.
6. Mix butter with bread crumbs. Sprinkle over casserole.
7. Bake 20 to 25 minutes.

Serves 4

QUICK ELEGANT PASTA

½ pound spinach or tomato
    fettuccini
8 ounces boursin cheese with
    herbs and garlic

4 tablespoons milk

1. Cook pasta according to package directions.
2. In a small saucepan, melt boursin and milk over low heat.
3. Drain pasta. Pour melted cheese over pasta and toss.

Variation:
Substitute Boursin with pepper. Add ¼ teaspoon red pepper flakes to cheese while melting.

Serves 4

ANGEL HAIR PASTA WITH HAM AND PEAS

10 ounces angel hair pasta
1½ cups chopped ham
1   8-ounce package frozen green
     peas, thawed

1   cup whipping cream, warmed
1   cup grated Parmesan cheese

1. Cook pasta in rapidly boiling, salted water approximately 3 minutes. Drain thoroughly.
2. Add ham and peas.
3. Add cream and Parmesan cheese. Stir.
4. Toss pasta mixture with cream until well coated. Serve immediately.

Serves 4 to 6

CANNELLONI

8   ounces manicotti or cannelloni
     shells

Filling:
1   clove garlic, minced
1   onion, finely chopped
2   tablespoons olive oil
2   tablespoons butter
1½ pounds ground chuck
1   10-ounce package frozen
     chopped spinach, thawed
     and drained
8 to 10 ounces mozzarella cheese,
     shredded
2   eggs, lightly beaten
2   tablespoons whipping cream or
     half and half
½   teaspoon basil
½   teaspoon oregano
3   tablespoons parsley, chopped
3   tablespoons bread crumbs
     Salt and pepper to taste
2 to 3 tablespoons Marsala wine

Sauce:
1   clove garlic, minced
1   onion, chopped
2 to 3 tablespoons olive oil
1   14-ounce can Italian plum
     tomatoes
1   12-ounce can tomato purée
2   teaspoons sugar
1   tablespoon basil
½   teaspoon oregano
     Red pepper to taste
¼   cup grated Romano cheese
½   cup red wine or bouillon or ¼
     cup Marsala wine
½   pound mozzarella cheese,
     grated
     Romano cheese

1. Preheat oven to 350°.
2. Boil manicotti shells 3 minutes in rapidly boiling salted water. Drain and dry.
3. Brown garlic and onions in olive oil and butter.
4. Brown meat. Drain. Add remaining filling ingredients and set aside.
5. To make sauce, sauté garlic and onion in olive oil. Add tomatoes, purée, sugar, basil, oregano, red pepper, cheese and wine. Simmer 1½ hours until thickened.
6. Stuff shells with meat mixture.
7. Coat bottom of a 9 by 13-inch flat baking dish with a thin layer of sauce. Arrange shells in single layer in baking dish. Coat with sauce and cover with mozzarella cheese. Sprinkle with additional Romano cheese.
8. Bake 20 minutes.

Cannelloni can be prepared 1 to 2 days ahead and refrigerated or frozen. Bring to room temperature, bake and serve.

Serves 8

FETTUCCINI WITH ZUCCHINI AND MUSHROOMS

2 tablespoons salt
1 tablespoon olive oil
12 ounces fettuccini
1 cup whipping cream, divided
8 ounces fresh mushrooms, sliced
¼ cup butter
1¼ pounds small zucchini, cut into 2½-inch strips

¼ to ½ cup butter, cut up
¼ to ½ cup grated Parmesan cheese
¼ cup chopped parsley
Salt and freshly ground pepper to taste

1. Bring 4-quarts water to boil. Add salt and oil. Cook pasta in boiling water for 7 minutes. Drain. Toss with ¼ cup cream.
2. Sauté mushrooms in ¼ cup butter 2 minutes. Add zucchini, remaining cream and butter. Bring to a boil. Simmer, covered, 3 minutes.
3. Add pasta to mushroom mixture. Add Parmesan cheese and parsley, tossing thoroughly. Season with salt and pepper. Serve at once. Sprinkle with additional Parmesan, if desired.

Serves 8

MARINARA SAUCE

⅓ cup olive oil
1 large garlic clove, peeled
2 medium onions, quartered
4 sprigs parsley
1 large green bell pepper, cut into 12 pieces
3 14½-ounce cans whole tomatoes, drained

1 teaspoon sugar
½ teaspoon oregano
½ teaspoon freshly ground pepper
1 tablespoon fresh basil, chopped

1. In a 3-quart saucepan, heat oil over medium heat.
2. Position steel blade in food processor. With machine running, drop in garlic. Quickly add onions and parsley. Chop finely.
3. Add onion mixture to oil and sauté 10 minutes.
4. With steel blade, chop bell pepper. Add to onion mixture.
5. Drain tomatoes and almost purée in processor.
6. Add tomatoes to onion mixture.
7. Stir in sugar, oregano, pepper and basil. Cook over low heat for at least 1 hour.

Variation:
Marinara sauce poured over boned, skinned, chicken breasts, topped with mozzarella cheese and baked until tender, makes a wonderful main dish.

Serves 4 to 6

CHICKEN AND DILL PASTA SALAD

2 ounces green noodles
2 ounces spiral noodles
1¼ cups cooked chicken breast, cubed
1 cup julienne carrots
1 cup julienne zucchini
2 tablespoons minced fresh parsley, or 1 tablespoon dried parsley

20 snow peas
⅓ cup mayonnaise
⅓ cup sour cream
2 teaspoons minced dill or ½ teaspoon dried dill
Salt to taste

1. Cook noodles separately according to package directions. Rinse with cold water and drain.
2. Combine spiral noodles, chicken, carrots, zucchini, parsley, and snow peas.
3. Mix mayonnaise, sour cream and dill. Combine with chicken mixture. Chill thoroughly. Serve on a bed of green noodles and sprinkle with additional parsley.

Serves 6

PASTA SALAD WITH RASPBERRY VINAIGRETTE DRESSING

Can be served lukewarm or cold. Great picnic fare!

½   cup olive oil
¼   cup raspberry wine vinegar
2   cloves garlic, minced
¼   cup chopped green onions
¼   cup minced parsley
Scant ¼ cup minced fresh basil

¼   teaspoon salt
Freshly ground pepper to taste
1   28-ounce can plum tomatoes
¼   cup sliced black olives
1   12-ounce package spiral pasta
½ to ¾ cup Parmesan cheese

1. Combine olive oil and vinegar. Whisk until well blended. Add garlic, green onions, parsley, basil, salt and pepper. Stir.
2. Drain tomatoes. Slice in half. Squeeze slightly to extract as many seeds and as much juice as possible. Dice tomatoes.
3. Add tomatoes and olives to the oil and vinegar mixture.
4. Prepare pasta al dente. Rinse with cold water and drain. Transfer pasta to a deep serving platter.
5. Add tomato mixture and toss lightly. When ready to serve, add cheese and toss well. Refrigerate.

This is best when made a day ahead.

Serves 4 to 6

SPINACH PASTA SALAD

2 ounces spinach noodles
2 ounces plain noodles
6 spinach leaves, washed and blotted dry
8 pitted black olives
1 large tomato, cut in chunks
⅓ cup feta cheese, crumbled

Marinade:
3 tablespoons olive oil
3 tablespoons liquid from black olives
   Pinch garlic powder
¼ teaspoon garlic salt

1. Cook noodles according to package directions. Rinse with cold water and drain.
2. Combine spinach, olives, tomato and cheese. Toss with noodles.
3. Combine marinade ingredients. Pour over noodles and toss. Cover and chill overnight.

Serves 2

PASTA SALAD DIJON

8 ounces thin egg noodles
4 ounces canned shrimp, rinsed and drained
1 tablespoon vinegar
½ teaspoon salt
⅛ teaspoon pepper
½ teaspoon celery seeds

3 green onions, chopped
2 large ribs celery, chopped
1 tablespoon Dijon mustard
3 tablespoons sweet relish
¾ cup mayonnaise
1 to 2 tablespoons fresh lemon juice

1. Cook noodles according to package directions. Rinse with cold water and drain.
2. Add shrimp. Combine vinegar, salt, pepper, celery seed and green onions. Pour mixture over noodles to coat.
3. Add remaining ingredients. Chill well.

Variation:
Tuna may be substituted for shrimp.

Serves 4

POULTRY, BEEF, PORK, LAMB AND GAME

Poultry

Poultry is the all-purpose term applied to birds that are raised for the table. Chicken, turkey, squab or pigeon, guinea fowl, pheasant, duck and goose fall into this category. (The term game refers to wild birds or animals that are killed seasonally for sport.)

Chicken

Chicken has a high protein content and is relatively low in fat. Of all poultry, it is the most widely used and is a staple in American diets. The following terminology applies to the age and weight by which chicken may be purchased.

Poussin or Squab Chicken—Young chicken weighing up to 1 pound, no more than 4 to 6 weeks old

Broiler-Fryer—Older bird weighing from 2 to 4 pounds; raised specifically for the table

Roasting Chicken—A variety weighing from 4 to 8 pounds; it is up to 10 weeks old and is very plump and perfect for roasting.

Boiling and Stewing Hen or Fowl—Older bird that was possibly a layer or broiler breeder; it is tough and needs to be cooked by a long, slow and moist method to achieve tenderness. It weighs from 2½ to 7 pounds and is best when used for soup, stew or recipes calling for ground or chopped chicken.

Heavy Hen—A term the poultry industry applies to a plump, meaty laying hen, weighing from 4½ to 6 pounds

Capon—A castrated cock that is full breasted and very tender; these birds are specifically raised to produce a high proportion of meat to bone. It weighs from 6 to 10 pounds.

New York Dressed—A term referring to a bird that has been hung for a few days to develop flavor; the chicken is displayed intact, with its feathers removed. At the time of purchase, the butcher will clean it for you. When sold with innards removed, it is called eviscerated.

Giblets—A cleaned chicken will have a package of giblets in the body cavity. Giblets consist of the neck, liver, gizzard and heart and may be used for making gravy. Always remember to remove package before cooking or storing.

Turkey

Turkey is a favorite and traditional holiday fare and is becoming more widely used year round. It is available fresh or frozen and is sold in cut portions. A turkey can weigh from 6 to 26 pounds. Both male and female birds are raised for the table. Hens have a higher proportion of flesh to bone and are often preferred. Allow approximately 12 ounces of raw turkey per serving when estimating what size bird to purchase. Turkey, like chicken, comes with a giblet package stored in the cavity. Turkey is also classified according to age and weight.

Fryer-Roaster—A young, tender turkey of either sex, usually weighing 4 to 10 pounds

Young Hen and Young Tom—A female or male turkey between 5 to 7 months old; it is best when roasted. Weight may vary according to type of breed.

Yearling Hen and Yearling Tom—A female or male turkey just over 1 year of age; the meat is not as tender as younger varieties.

Mature Hen and Mature Tom—A female or male turkey more than 15 months old; because of age, these turkeys are tough and are not generally marketed in stores.

Turkeys are categorized according to size

small—4 to 10 lbs.
medium—10 to 19 lbs.
large—20 lbs. or more

Turkey Thawing Chart

In Refrigerator

Weight	Time
8 lbs.	1 day
8 to 12 lbs.	1½ to 2 days
12 to 16 lbs.	2 to 3 days
16 to 20 lbs.	3 to 4 days
20 to 24 lbs.	3 to 4 days

※ Never thaw a bird at room temperature unless using cool-water immersion method.

※ Never let a thawed bird stand at room temperature, refrigerate instead.

※ Never stuff a bird until ready to roast.

These precautions are necessary to avoid food poisoning.

Turkey Roasting Chart
(cooked whole and uncovered)

Weight (cleaned and trimmed)	Oven Temperature	Cooking Time	Meat Thermometer Temperature
4 to 8 lbs.	325° F	1¾ to 2¾ hours	180°–185° F
8 to 12 lbs.	325° F	3½ to 4 hours	180°–185° F
12 to 16 lbs.	325° F	4 to 4½ hours	180°–185° F
16 to 20 lbs.	325° F	4½ to 5 hours	180°–185° F
20 to 24 lbs.	325° F	5 to 6 hours	180°–185° F

※ Always remove giblet package from body cavity.

※ When turkey needs to be cooked more quickly than the classic roasting method, wrap the prepared turkey in heavy foil after brushing with butter or fat. This method is faster. However, the bird will be more steamed than roasted.

Wrapped Turkey Cooking Chart

Weight	Oven Temperature	Cooking Time
6 to 8 lbs.	450° F	1½ to 2 hours
8 to 12 lbs.	450° F	2 to 2½ hours
12 to 16 lbs.	450° F	2½ to 3 hours
16 to 20 lbs.	450° F	3 to 3½ hours
20 to 24 lbs.	450° F	3½ to 4 hours

※ To brown, uncover for the last 30 minutes of cooking and baste if needed.

Placement of Turkey

Breast-up Method (whole bird)—This method calls for placing the bird breast up in an uncovered pan. During cooking, the bird may be periodically basted for a golden brown result.

Breast-down Method (whole bird)—The uncovered bird is placed on a rack in a pan with the breast down. This produces a juicy bird. Cover rack with a non-stick vegetable cooking spray to prevent bird from sticking.

Duck and Goose

Raised ducklings range from 6 weeks to 3 months old and are available fresh in the spring and summer, but are most often found frozen. Duck has a very rich flavor and a high proportion of fat. A 3 to 4 pound duck will serve four. A duckling will serve two.

Geese, raised for the table are processed while they are still goslings. Geese are very fat birds and are best when roasted. Generally, they weigh 4 to 14 pounds when marketed.

How to Cook Duck or Goose
(Cooked Whole and Uncovered)

1. Prepare for cooking as recipe directs, then rub inside of body cavity with lemon juice.
2. Prick skin with sharp fork to allow fat to drain, and baste during cooking.
3. Rub with salt for a crisp skin.
4. Place bird breast up on a rack in a shallow pan. Drain drippings as needed.

   ※ Always remove giblet package from body cavity.

Duck and Goose Roasting Chart

Duck

Weight	Oven Temperature	Cooking Time
4 to 5½ lbs.	350° F	2¼ to 2¾ hours

Goose

Weight	Oven Temperature	Cooking Time
4 to 6 lbs.	325° F	2¾ to 3 hours
6 to 8 lbs.	325° F	3 to 3½ hours
8 to 12 lbs.	325° F	3½ to 4½ hours
12 to 14 lbs.	325° F	4½ to 5 hours

Poultry Tips

※ Always thaw frozen poultry in the refrigerator, if possible, and allow plenty of time. The larger the bird, the longer the process takes. Place covered bird in a shallow pan to catch drippings.

※ Skinning poultry, particularly chicken, is easier if it is slightly frozen.

※ Allow ¾ to 1 pound per person when purchasing in raw weight.

※ Meat thermometers are handy, but not completely reliable. Insert the probe into the large, meaty muscle on the inside of the thigh. Be sure that the thermometer does not touch the bone. A thermometer may also be inserted through the carcass to the center as long as it does not touch the bone.

※ To insure a golden brown glaze, brush bird with butter or a special glaze the last 20 to 30 minutes of cooking. Glazes can be made from juices, jams and sugar, and add a delicious flavor.

Meat

Meat must adhere to specific government standards and pass inspection to be sold in the United States. For each variety of meat there are classifications and weight standards that determine the price. The meat is inspected and stamped at the wholesale level, before it is divided into individual cuts that are purchased at the meat counter.

Beef

Beef is the meat of mature cattle that is specifically raised to be slaughtered. The classifications of beef are Prime, Choice, and Good.

Prime beef is richly marbled with fat and is the most tender and flavorful of the beef cuts. Naturally, because it is the highest quality, it is also the most expensive.

Choice beef is the most available variety found at meat counters. It has less fat than prime beef, but still has enough to produce a good flavor.

Good beef is usually sold as economy meat and of course has very little fat marbling. It may also be sold as "lean" and is generally not as tender as the other grades of beef. Nutritionally, it is just as good, however.

Aged beef is stored and hung in a meat locker from two to six weeks, allowing for the natural process of tenderizing. Usually, true aged beef is only available to restaurants. Because of the shipping process, all beef is aged to some extent.

In addition to the various grades of beef, the particular cut of meat determines the degree of tenderness. The source of the cut also dictates the cooking method used to prepare the meat. Less tender cuts require longer cooking at lower temperatures. Marinating helps tenderize tougher cuts of beef. Tender cuts only require brief cooking to seal the natural juices and enhance the flavor.

Cuts of Beef

Chuck—Chuck is cut from the shoulder and consists of the neck, blade, arm and shoulder. Chuck meat is a tough cut of beef.

Rib—Rib is cut from the forequarter section, directly behind the shoulder and along the backbone. Rib steaks, rib eyes, and rib roasts come from this section.

Loin—Loin is cut from the mid-section, in front of the hips, and is the most tender portion of beef cattle. Cuts include sirloin strips, filet mignon, tenderloin or tenderloin roast.

Round—Round is cut from the rump and hind leg section. Cuts from this section are tougher and include roasts and steaks.

Flank—Flank is cut from the underside belly section. It is a boneless section but is relatively tough. Flank steak or fajita meat comes from this section.

Brisket—Brisket is cut from the breast and foreleg section. It is a tough cut, but is ideal for long, slow cooking which makes it tender.

Much of the tougher sections of beef are ground or chopped to make hamburger meat. Hamburger is either lean or fat, based on the quantity of fat included in the grinding process. Ground chuck contains the most fat and ground round has the least fat. Sirloin is sometimes ground for high quality hamburger meat.

All cuts of beef may be prepared in many ways but the most popular methods for steaks and hamburgers are broiling and grilling. Both styles are quick cooking methods.

Broiling positions the meat in the oven directly under the heat source. The meat should be placed 5 to 6 inches from the heat source.

Grilling cooks the meat over a bed of coals or in a cast iron griddle over a burner. The thickness of the cut determines the length of time it must be cooked to achieve rare, medium rare, medium or well-done.

Oven Broiling Chart

Very Rare	3 minutes per side
Rare	4 minutes per side
Medium Rare	5 minutes per side
Medium	6 minutes per side
Well-done	7 minutes per side

Times are based on 1-inch thickness. Double time, per side, for each additional ½-inch of thickness of meat. These settings are based on 3 to 4-inch distance from heat source and are approximations. Different oven broilers vary slightly to exact temperature.

Grilling Chart
(moderately hot coals)

Very Rare	6 to 7 minutes per side
Rare	8 to 9 minutes per side
Medium Rare	10 to 12 minutes per side
Medium	14 to 16 minutes per side
Well-done	18 to 20 minutes per side

Grilling Chart (continued)

Times are based on 2-inch thickness cooked approximately 4 to 5-inches from the coals. Increase the time, per side, 3 to 5 minutes for each additional ½-inch of thickness.

Roasting is another popular cooking method. To determine if a roast is done, insert a meat thermometer for a brief period of time toward the end of the cooking process.

Roast Beef Chart
(Oven Temperature 325° F.)

Cut	Approximate Weight (lbs.)	Meat Thermometer Temperature	Minutes Per lb.	Total Time (hrs.)
Rib Roast	4 to 6	140° (rare)	26–32	1¾–3¼
		170° (well)	40–42	2¾–4¼
	6 to 8	140° (rare)	23–25	2¼–3¾
		160° (medium)	27–30	2¾–4
		170° (well)	32–35	3¼–4¾
Rolled Rib Roast	5 to 7	140° (rare)	32	2¾–3¾
		160° (medium)	38	3–4½
		170° (well)	48	4–5½
Rib Eye Roast	4 to 6	140° (rare)	18–20	1¼–2
		160° (medium)	20–22	1¼–2¼
		170° (well)	22–24	1½–2¼
Rolled Rump Roast	4 to 6	150°–170°	25–30	1¾–3
Sirloin Tip Roast	3½ to 4	150°–170°	35–40	2–2¾
Tenderloin Roast (whole) (oven temp. 425° F.)	4 to 6	140° (rare)	45–60	3–6
Tenderloin Roast (half) (oven temp. 425° F.)	2 to 3	140° (rare)	45–60	1½–3

VEAL

Veal comes from calves or young cattle. Veal is milk fed and approximately four months old. It is a grayish, pale pink color and is tender because it is young meat. It must be carefully prepared to prevent drying because it has so little fat. Some roast and joint cuts should be well oiled or greased during cooking. Thin slices of veal are often sautéed in a delicate butter sauce with herbs and spices.

The tender cuts of veal come from the rib section (roasts and chops), the loin section (roasts and chops), and the sirloin section (roasts and steaks). Other sections of veal are less tender and should be used in stew or cut meat dishes. Veal is also graded Prime, Choice and Good. Again, various cuts dictate method of preparation due to degree of tenderness. Cuts from the shoulder should be braised. The rib section produces the crown rib roast, the premier cut of veal, which should be roasted. Leg cuts are good for veal scallops that are sautéed. Rolled and breaded cutlets may be prepared from this cut of veal.

LAMB

Lamb is a meat that is sometimes approached with hesitancy. It is highly prized as a superior meat elsewhere in the world, and in some cultures is more valued than beef.

Lamb is the meat of a young sheep, up to one year of age. Milk-fed or baby lamb is between six and eight weeks old. Spring lamb is three to five months old. When lamb is butchered at one year, it is mutton. Lamb is graded Prime, Choice or Good like other meats. Young lamb is pink. The older the lamb, the redder the meat. True mutton is dark red and is easily distinguished from lamb. Cuts of lamb and mutton are the same, but vary in size with age. Any recipe that calls for lamb may be substituted with mutton, but the taste will differ.

PORK

Of all meat, pork is the most versatile and varied. Literally, all parts of the pig may be used except for the snout. Pork is graded 1,2,3,4, utility, and cull, but is usually graded by packers as premium or star grade. The tender cuts include the loin section which yields roasts, chops, Canadian bacon, back ribs, and fat back. The tenderloin, spare ribs, bacon and ham leg are also tender sections of pork. Less tender sections include the shoulder, jowl, picnic, hock and feet.

There are as many ways to prepare pork as there are different pork cuts. The primary rule of cooking pork is to cook it long enough to reach an internal temperature of 185° F. to insure safety. Pork of any kind should never be eaten rare or undercooked.

It is always important to read instructions on the packaging, as some hams are pre-cooked and require different preparation.

Basic Ham Preparation

1. Unwrap ham and remove any cording or cloth covering.
2. Rinse under lukewarm water to remove any preservatives.
3. If necessary, remove the rind on the outside.
4. Under the rind there will be a thick layer of fat which should be trimmed to a ¼ to ½-inch layer.
5. Place on a rack or cover the ham with a glaze of brown sugar, vinegar, honey or fruit preserves and bake.

Country cured ham must be soaked in cold water for 8 to 12 hours before roasting. These special hams come with very detailed instructions for preparation and cooking.

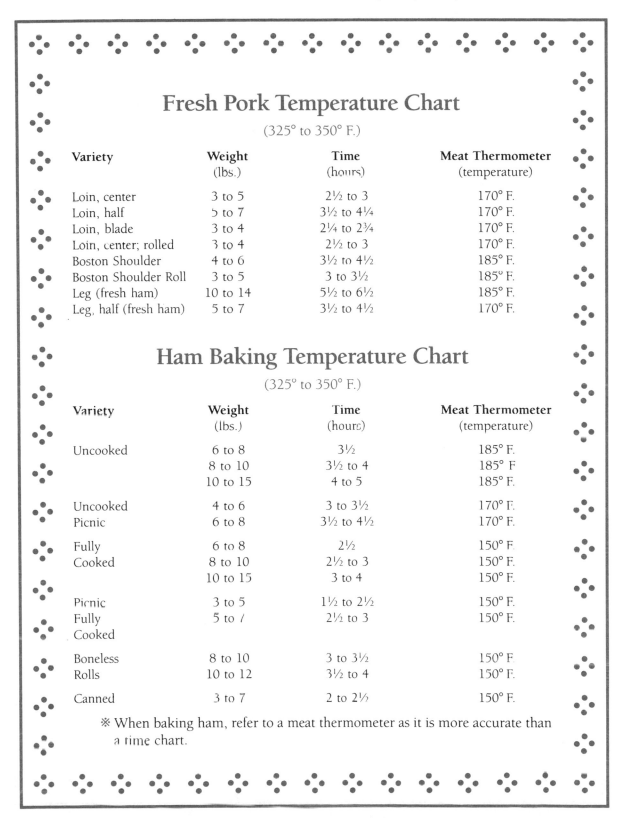

Fresh Pork Temperature Chart

(325° to 350° F.)

Variety	Weight (lbs.)	Time (hours)	Meat Thermometer (temperature)
Loin, center	3 to 5	2½ to 3	170° F.
Loin, half	5 to 7	3½ to 4¼	170° F.
Loin, blade	3 to 4	2¼ to 2¾	170° F.
Loin, center; rolled	3 to 4	2½ to 3	170° F.
Boston Shoulder	4 to 6	3½ to 4½	185° F.
Boston Shoulder Roll	3 to 5	3 to 3½	185° F.
Leg (fresh ham)	10 to 14	5½ to 6½	185° F.
Leg, half (fresh ham)	5 to 7	3½ to 4½	170° F.

Ham Baking Temperature Chart

(325° to 350° F.)

Variety	Weight (lbs.)	Time (hours)	Meat Thermometer (temperature)
Uncooked	6 to 8	3½	185° F.
	8 to 10	3½ to 4	185° F
	10 to 15	4 to 5	185° F.
Uncooked	4 to 6	3 to 3½	170° F.
Picnic	6 to 8	3½ to 4½	170° F.
Fully Cooked	6 to 8	2½	150° F.
	8 to 10	2½ to 3	150° F.
	10 to 15	3 to 4	150° F.
Picnic Fully Cooked	3 to 5	1½ to 2½	150° F.
	5 to 7	2½ to 3	150° F.
Boneless Rolls	8 to 10	3 to 3½	150° F.
	10 to 12	3½ to 4	150° F.
Canned	3 to 7	2 to 2½	150° F.

※ When baking ham, refer to a meat thermometer as it is more accurate than a time chart.

LEMON GRILLED CHICKEN BREASTS

Juice of 6 large lemons
1½ cups olive oil
4 cloves garlic, minced
2 tablespoons rosemary

1 teaspoon salt
1½ teaspoons coarsely ground
   black pepper
8 chicken breast halves

1. Combine first 6 ingredients to create a marinade.
2. Place chicken breasts in marinade. Cover and refrigerate at least 12 hours, stirring occasionally.
3. Grill over hot coals with mesquite chips for best flavor.

Grilling time will depend on size of chicken breasts.

Serves 8

FOIL BAKED CHICKEN AND VEGETABLES

An excellent dish that can be prepared ahead of time.

4 chicken breast halves, boned
   and skinned
2 carrots, cut into 1-inch slices
8 ounces fresh mushrooms,
   sliced ¼-inch thick
1 large zucchini, sliced

4 tablespoons butter
8 tablespoons cooking sherry or
   chicken broth
Pepper to taste
Seasoned salt to taste

1. Preheat oven to 350°.
2. Tear off 4 12-inch pieces of foil.
3. Place 1 chicken breast on each piece of foil.
4. Cover each piece of chicken with vegetables, butter, sherry and seasonings, dividing ingredients equally.
5. Fold foil around each breast to make a tight pouch.
6. Place foil packages on a cookie sheet and bake 30 to 40 minutes.

Variation:
Many combinations of vegetables can be used in this dish. Onions, yellow squash, potatoes and green beans are other favorites.

Serves 4

VERSATILE BAKED CHICKEN

Begin with 8 boned chicken breasts. Select one of the ingredient variations. Follow the preparation directions.

Butter Mixture	*Crumb Mixture*

Variation I:

¾	cup butter	1	cup crushed sesame crackers
1	tablespoon lemon juice	1	teaspoon garlic salt
		½	teaspoon pepper

Variation II:

½	cup butter	½	cup Italian bread crumbs
2	cloves garlic, minced	1½	cups grated Cheddar cheese
		¼	cup grated Parmesan cheese
		1	teaspoon salt
		½	teaspoon pepper

Variation III:

½	cup unsalted butter	2	cups bread crumbs
2	cloves garlic, minced	½	cup grated Parmesan cheese
1	teaspoon Worcestershire sauce	⅓	cup chopped parsley
1	teaspoon dry mustard	1	3-ounce can onion rings, crushed

1. Preheat oven to 350°.
2. Choose desired variation. Melt butter and add all ingredients under butter mixture column.
3. Combine all ingredients for desired crumb mixture.
4. Dip chicken breast in butter and then roll to thoroughly coat in crumb mixture. (At this point chicken may be frozen for later baking.)
5. Place chicken pieces in a 2-quart baking dish. Drizzle any remaining butter on top and sprinkle with any remaining crumbs.
6. Bake 45 to 60 minutes or until tender.

Serves 6 to 8

OVEN FRIED CHICKEN

2½ to 3 pound chicken, cut up or
   any choice of pieces
Salt and pepper to taste

All-purpose flour
½ cup butter, melted

1. Preheat oven to 350°.
2. Salt, pepper and flour chicken.
3. Melt in a 9 by 13-inch pan, lined with foil.
4. Dip prepared chicken pieces in butter. Place skin side up in pan.
5. Bake 45 minutes or until chicken is brown and tender.

Variation:
Any combination of herbs may be added to flour for a change in taste.

Serves 4

CHILI BEER CHICKEN

2½ to 3 pound chicken, cut up or
   any choice of pieces
½ cup all-purpose flour
½ teaspoon salt
½ teaspoon pepper

6 tablespoons butter
2 onions, thinly sliced and
   divided
1 12-ounce bottle of beer
1 cup chili sauce

1. Preheat oven to 325°.
2. Combine flour, salt and pepper. Dredge chicken in flour to coat.
3. Melt butter in a skillet. Add chicken and 1 sliced onion. Cook until chicken is brown on all sides.
4. Place chicken and cooked onion in a large baking dish.
5. Combine beer and chili sauce. Pour over chicken.
6. Place remaining sliced onion on top of chicken. Bake 45 minutes.

Serves 4

CHICKEN AND TORTILLA DUMPLINGS

A quick alternative to chicken and dumplings.

4 to 6 chicken breast halves   **Salt and pepper**
**1   12-ounce package flour
      tortillas**

1. Boil chicken in 3 quarts of water for 1 to 1½ hours to make a rich broth.
2. Remove chicken. Measure 2 quarts of broth. Bring to a hard, rolling boil. Add 1 teaspoon salt.
3. Cut tortillas into 1½-inch strips. Add strips to broth, 1 at a time, stirring with a large cooking fork to prevent sticking. Lower heat. Simmer 15 to 20 minutes.
4. Remove dumplings from heat. Partially cover and let stand 2 to 3 hours before serving. (If dumplings are completely covered, they will become soggy.) Dumplings will absorb broth as they stand. If they become too dry, add more broth.
5. Bone and dice chicken.
6. Just before serving, add chicken. Season heavily with salt and pepper. Heat and serve.

These can be refrigerated and successfully reheated.

Serves 12

RUSSIAN CHICKEN

**6 to 8 chicken breast halves, 4 legs
   or thighs**
**1   8-ounce bottle Russian salad
      dressing**

2   envelopes dry onion soup mix
**1   8-ounce jar apricot jam or
      preserves**

1. Preheat oven to 300°.
2. Place chicken pieces in a large baking dish.
3. Mix all other ingredients. Spread over chicken.
4. Bake 2 hours.

Serves 6 to 8

DEVILED CORNISH GAME HENS

8	Cornish game hens	3	tablespoons minced shallots
	Salt and pepper to taste	½	cup butter
8	tablespoons Dijon mustard		White wine
⅔	cup seasoned bread crumbs		

1. Preheat oven to 400°.
2. Rub each bird with salt, pepper and 1 tablespoon mustard. Sprinkle with bread crumbs.
3. Place in a large roasting pan.
4. Sprinkle hens with shallots and dot with butter. Pour 3 tablespoons of white wine over each.
5. Seal hens with foil and bake 50 minutes.
6. Remove foil and brown 10 minutes.
7. Pour pan drippings over birds.

Serve with wild rice and a favorite green salad.

Serves 8

CHICKEN BREASTS WITH ORANGE SAUCE

2½	cups chicken broth	2	teaspoons sugar
12	boned chicken breast halves	½	cup orange juice
2	tablespoons butter	1	tablespoon lemon juice
2	tablespoons all-purpose flour		Grated rind of 1 orange
½	cup reserved chicken broth		Pinch white pepper
½	teaspoon salt		Parsley

1. Simmer breasts in broth, approximately 30 to 40 minutes. Do not boil. Reserve ½ cup broth.
2. In a saucepan, make a sauce with butter, flour and broth.
3. Add remaining ingredients. Cook 3 to 4 additional minutes.
4. Pour sauce over chicken. Garnish with parsley.

Serves 12

CHICKEN IN MADEIRA WINE

2   pounds boned, skinned
chicken breasts or veal
¾   cup all-purpose flour
1   teaspoon salt
¾   teaspoon freshly ground
pepper
¼ to ½ cup butter
1   cup Madeira wine

½   cup water
2   tablespoons lemon juice
1   teaspoon minced garlic
¼   cup butter
1   pound fresh mushrooms,
sliced
Cherry tomatoes
Parsley sprigs

1. Pound breasts ¼ to ⅛-inch thick.
2. Mix flour, salt and pepper. Dredge chicken in flour mixture. Shake off any excess.
3. In a large skillet, heat ¼ cup butter over moderate heat. Add 3 or 4 breasts and cook 2 to 3 minutes on each side until lightly browned.
4. Remove from skillet. Arrange in a 9 by 13 by 2-inch baking dish. Repeat with remaining breasts adding more butter to skillet as necessary.
5. Drain and discard fat. Add wine and water to skillet. Cook over medium heat, stirring constantly. Add lemon juice and garlic. Cook 2 to 3 minutes until liquid boils and looks syrupy. Pour over chicken breasts.
6. Add ¼ cup butter to skillet and melt over moderately low heat. Add mushrooms and cook 5 to 7 minutes. Stir frequently, until softened and moisture has evaporated. Spoon over breasts.
7. Cover tightly with foil. At this point chicken may be refrigerated up to 24 hours before baking.
8. Bake 50 minutes at 350°.

Garnish with cherry tomatoes and parsley.

Serves 4

CHICKEN PAPRIKA

2½ to 3 pound chicken, cut into
    pieces or 4 chicken breast
    halves
½   cup butter
1   clove garlic, minced
2   chicken bouillon cubes

2   cups boiling water
3   tablespoons paprika
1   cup whipping cream, room
    temperature
Cooked rice

1. Melt butter in a skillet.
2. Add garlic and chicken to butter. Brown over low heat.
3. Dissolve bouillon cubes in boiling water. Set aside.
4. Sprinkle paprika over browned chicken. Add ½ cup bouillon.
5. Bring chicken to a boil. Lower heat. Cook, covered, 30 minutes.
6. Turn chicken and cook 30 additional minutes. Add bouillon as needed.
7. Remove chicken after 1 hour. Add whipping cream to drippings. Cook to thicken sauce.
8. Pour sauce over chicken and hot, fluffy rice. Serve immediately.

Serves 4 to 6

※ Leftover cooked rice can be frozen. Steam, covered, in a colander to reheat.

SAFFRON CHICKEN

Guests will enjoy this colorful and elegant dish.

6   chicken breast halves, boned
    and skinned
6 to 8 tablespoons butter
1½   pounds mushrooms, chopped
2   green bell peppers, thinly
    sliced
3   red bell peppers, thinly sliced,
    or 3 whole pimientos, sliced

Salt and pepper to taste
1   large pinch saffron
1½   teaspoons cornstarch,
    dissolved in 1 tablespoon
    whipping cream
½   cup whipping cream

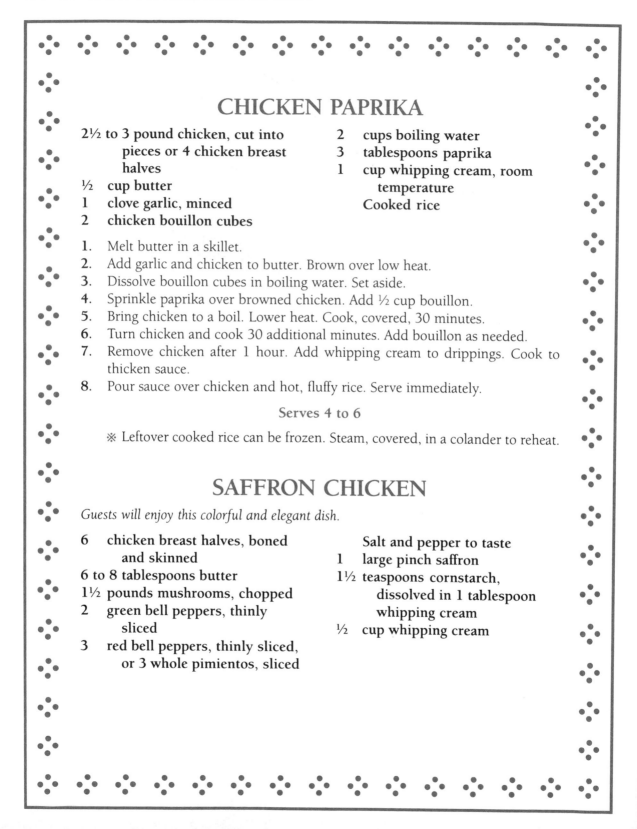

1. Sauté chicken breasts in butter 15 minutes, turning occasionally. Remove.
2. Increase heat, add mushrooms. Sauté until liquid evaporates.
3. Add peppers and lower heat. Cook until soft. Season with salt and pepper.
4. Using slotted spoon, remove vegetables to serving platter.
5. Combine saffron, cornstarch and whipping cream. Whisk into pan.
6. Continue stirring until mixture boils, is smooth and is slightly thickened.
7. Arrange chicken on top of vegetables and pour sauce over all.

Serves 6

CHICKEN CRÊPES

Batter:

1	cup all-purpose flour	6	chicken breasts
¼	cup butter	2	jalapeños
½	teaspoon salt	1	tablespoon diced pimientos
2	eggs, well beaten	1	tablespoon chopped onion
1	cup milk		Salt to taste
			White pepper to taste
		1½	pounds Swiss cheese, grated
		2	cups whipping cream

1. Mix flour, butter, salt, eggs and milk for crêpe batter.
2. One tablespoon batter will yield 1 4-inch crêpe. Cook as a pancake in a small skillet. Turn crêpes once and cook until done, not brown.
3. Boil chicken in water until tender.
4. Bone chicken, slice and cut into 1-inch pieces.
5. Add chopped jalapeños, pimientos, onions, salt and pepper. Mix well. Add 1 pound cheese and stir well.
6. Place approximately 2 tablespoons of the chicken mixture in center of each crepe. Roll. Place in a large baking dish.
7. Sprinkle remaining cheese over all. Pour cream around crêpes.
8. Place in oven at 350° until heated throughout and cheese is melted.
9. Remove and serve immediately.

Serves 20

CHICKEN MARSALA

Serve with buttered fettuccini and a green salad.

2	chicken breast halves, skinned and boned		Dash pepper
2	tablespoons butter	1	teaspoon lemon juice
6	large mushrooms, sliced	3	green onions, chopped
1	cup Marsala wine	2	teaspoons chopped fresh parsley
½	teaspoon salt		

1. Place each piece of chicken between 2 sheets of wax paper. Using a meat mallet or rolling pin, pound chicken to ¼-inch thickness.
2. Melt butter in a medium skillet. Add chicken. Over low heat, cook each side of chicken until tender and golden brown.
3. Remove chicken breasts and place on a serving platter.
4. Add next 6 ingredients to skillet. Cook until mushrooms are tender.
5. Pour wine mixture over chicken. Sprinkle with parsley.

Serves 2

COUNTRY STYLE CHICKEN KIEV

½	cup fine bread crumbs	⅔	cup butter, melted
2	tablespoons Parmesan cheese	4	chicken breast halves
1	teaspoon oregano	¼	cup white wine or apple cider
1	teaspoon basil	¼	cup chopped green onions
½	teaspoon garlic salt	¼	cup chopped parsley
¼	teaspoon salt		

1. Preheat oven to 375°.
2. Combine first 6 ingredients.
3. Dip chicken in butter, then bread crumb mixture.
4. Place prepared chicken in baking dish.
5. Bake 50 to 60 minutes.
6. To remaining butter, add wine, green onion and parsley. When chicken is golden brown, pour butter sauce over chicken. Continue baking 3 to 5 minutes.

Serves 4

CHICKEN AND MUSHROOM CRÊPES

2 cups sliced fresh mushrooms
1½ cups butter, divided
1 cup flour
8 cups cooked, cubed white
   chicken
4 cups chicken broth
2 cups whipping cream
2½ cups milk, divided

1 cup vermouth or dry white
   wine
1 teaspoon seasoned salt
   White pepper to taste
2 egg yolks
   Grated Parmesan cheese
   Paprika
2 dozen crêpes

1. Preheat oven to 375°.
2. Sauté mushrooms in ½ cup butter. Combine with chicken. Set aside.
3. Melt remaining 1 cup butter. Add flour and stir until smooth and bubbling.
4. Slowly add chicken broth, cream, 1½ cups milk and vermouth. Cook until smooth and thick. Add seasoned salt and white pepper. Stir.
5. Remove from heat and divide in half.
6. Add egg yolks to the first half. Combine with chicken and mushrooms.
7. Fill crêpes and place in 2 greased 3-quart baking dishes.
8. Add remaining 1 cup of milk to remainder of sauce and pour over crêpes.
9. Dot with butter and sprinkle liberally with Parmesan cheese and paprika.
10. Bake 30 minutes until bubbly and slightly brown.

These can be made a day ahead and refrigerated until baking time.

Variation I:
This sauce is delicious served over vermicelli or in pastry shells. Shrimp can be substituted for chicken.

Variation II:
Add 1½ pounds grated Swiss cheese to sauce before dividing. Omit Parmesan and sprinkle with Swiss cheese.

Variation III:
For a Central Texas flavor when using variation 2, add 2 chopped jalapeños, 1 teaspoon pimiento, and 1 teaspoon finely chopped onion.

Serves 12

CHICKEN ALFREDO

Cheese sauce:

1	cup whipping cream
¼	cup water
¼	cup butter
½	cup grated Romano cheese
¼	cup chopped parsley

6	chicken breast halves, boned and skinned
½	cup all-purpose flour
3	eggs, beaten
3	tablespoons water
½	cup grated Romano cheese
½	teaspoon salt
1	cup bread crumbs
3	tablespoons butter
2	tablespoons vegetable oil
4 to 6	ounces mozzarella cheese, grated
¼	cup chopped parsley

1. To make cheese sauce, heat cream, water and butter in a saucepan until butter melts. Add cheese. Cook and stir over medium heat 5 minutes. Stir in parsley.
2. Preheat oven to 425°.
3. Mix eggs, water, Romano cheese, parsley and salt.
4. Coat chicken pieces with flour. Dip chicken pieces in egg mixture, then in bread crumbs.
5. Heat butter and oil in large skillet.
6. Cook chicken breasts over medium heat until brown, approximately 15 minutes.
7. Place chicken in a 2-quart baking dish.
8. Pour cheese sauce over chicken. Top each piece with extra grated mozzarella cheese. Sprinkle with parsley.
9. Bake until cheese melts, approximately 8 minutes.

Serves 6

ITALIAN CHICKEN AND NOODLES

2½ to 3 pound chicken, cut into pieces
2 tablespoons oil
1 onion, chopped
3 cloves garlic, minced
3 tablespoons dry sherry
1 tablespoon Italian herbs

1 12-ounce package spinach noodles
1 cup sour cream
½ cup chopped green onions
1 4-ounce can mushrooms
Crushed red pepper
Parmesan cheese

1. Brown chicken in oil.
2. Add onion and garlic. Sauté a few minutes.
3. Add sherry and Italian herbs.
4. Cover and cook 1 hour or until tender.
5. Cook noodles according to package directions. Drain.
6. Remove chicken from skillet. Add cooked noodles to skillet drippings.
7. Stir in sour cream, chopped green onions, Parmesan cheese and mushrooms.
8. Cook briefly until ingredients are warm. Remove from heat.
9. Serve noodles around chicken pieces on large platter.
10. Pass extra Parmesan cheese and crushed red pepper.

Serves 4

CHICKEN CACCIATORE

An easy family meal. Serve with green salad and garlic bread.

2½ to 3 pound chicken, cut into
    pieces or 4 chicken breast
    halves
1   tablespoon olive oil
1   large onion, chopped
8   ounces fresh mushrooms,
    sliced
1   8-ounce can tomato sauce
1   6-ounce can tomato paste

¼ to ½ cup water
1   teaspoon dried basil
½   teaspoon dried oregano
2   cloves garlic, minced
    Salt and pepper to taste
1   10-ounce can sliced black
    olives, optional
3   cups cooked rice

1. In a large Dutch oven, brown chicken in oil.
2. Remove chicken. Add onion and mushrooms. Sauté until lightly browned.
3. Remove and discard oil.
4. Add tomato sauce, tomato paste and water to Dutch oven.
5. Stir in herbs, garlic, salt and pepper.
6. Add chicken, mushrooms and onions. Simmer, covered, 20 minutes. Add sliced olives and simmer 15 to 20 minutes. Serve over hot, fluffy rice.

Serves 4

Slice mushrooms with an egg slicer.

CHICKEN AND VEGETABLE STIR FRY

2 pounds boned chicken breast	¼ cup sliced almonds
¼ cup soy sauce	2 to 4 cloves of garlic, minced
2 tablespoons sherry	1 onion, coarsely chopped
2 tablespoons orange marmalade	1 green bell pepper, coarsely chopped
1 teaspoon cornstarch	
½ teaspoon ground ginger	1 8-ounce can sliced water chestnuts, drained
1½ teaspoons crushed red pepper flakes	1 6-ounce package frozen snow peas, thawed
4 tablespoons peanut oil, divided	

1. Cut chicken into ½-inch strips and place in a large glass bowl.
2. Combine next 6 ingredients. Pour over chicken and stir to coat.
3. Heat 2 tablespoons of oil in wok or heavy skillet.
4. Add almonds. Stir fry 1 minute. Remove and drain on paper towels.
5. Add remaining oil, garlic, onion and bell pepper.
6. Stir fry 2 to 3 minutes. Push to the side. Add chicken and marinade. Stir fry 2 to 3 minutes.
7. Add water chestnuts, snow peas and almonds.
8. Mix all ingredients and stir fry 2 to 3 minutes or until heated thoroughly.
9. Serve over hot cooked rice.

Variation:
Any choice of fresh vegetables such as broccoli or French style green beans may be used. Shrimp may be substituted for chicken.

Serves 4 to 6

ITALIAN CHICKEN

This easy chicken has a sauce that is delicious over wild rice.

8	chicken breast halves	1	package dry onion soup mix
4	tomatoes, quartered	½	teaspoon oregano
8	ounces fresh mushrooms	2	bay leaves
1	8-ounce bottle Italian dressing		

1. Preheat oven to 350°.
2. Place chicken breasts, tomatoes and mushrooms in a 9 by 13-inch baking dish.
3. Combine dressing, soup mix, oregano and bay leaves.
4. Pour sauce over chicken and vegetables.
5. Bake 1 to 1¼ hours.

Variation:
For the calorie conscious, skin chicken breasts and use diet Italian dressing.

Serves 8

ALMOND CHICKEN

½	cup butter	1	4-ounce can sliced mushrooms
6 to 8	chicken breast halves	1¾	cups chicken broth
¼	cup chopped onion	½	cup half and half
2	tablespoons all-purpose flour	¼	cup slivered almonds, toasted
¼	teaspoon salt	3	cups hot, fluffy rice
	Pepper to taste		

1. In a large skillet, melt butter. Add chicken.
2. Cover skillet. Brown chicken 10 minutes over medium heat.
3. Turn chicken and continue cooking 10 minutes.
4. Remove chicken. Add onions to butter in skillet. Sauté until lightly browned.
5. Add flour, salt and pepper. Stir. Gradually add broth and half and half. Stir until thickened.
6. Add chicken breasts and mushrooms.
7. Heat, without boiling, 15 to 20 minutes. Stir frequently.
8. Combine toasted almonds with rice. Serve chicken breasts over rice.

Serves 6 to 8

ORIENTAL CHICKEN WITH NUTS

1 pound skinned, boned, and
   cubed chicken

Marinade:

2 teaspoons crushed ginger
3 tablespoons soy sauce
1 teaspoon Accent
1 tablespoon wine

Batter:

1 egg white
1 tablespoon cornstarch
½ cup vegetable oil

Vegetable mixture:

1 cup bamboo shoots
1 cup green bell peppers, cut
   into 1-inch squares

½ cup mushrooms, quartered
1 clove garlic, minced
¼ teaspoon salt
1 tablespoon soy sauce
1 teaspoon Accent
1 tablespoon sugar
1½ cups roasted or sautéed nuts:
   walnuts, almonds, cashews,
   or a combination

Glaze:

2 teaspoons cornstarch
½ cup chicken broth

1. Combine marinade ingredients. Marinate chicken 1 hour.
2. Beat egg white and add 1 tablespoon cornstarch.
3. Dip chicken in batter. Fry in ½ cup oil until chicken is lightly browned.
4. Remove chicken from oil.
5. Pour off oil until ¼ cup remains.
6. Stir fry bamboo shoots, bell pepper, mushrooms and seasonings until vegetables are tender.
7. Add marinated chicken and liquid. Stir fry.
8. To the 2 teaspoons of cornstarch, add ½ cup chicken broth. Pour over mixture in pan.
9. Add nuts and stir until well coated.

Serves 4

BEEF WELLINGTON

4 to 5 pound beef filet
    Salt and pepper to taste
    Butter

    Puff Pastry
1   **egg yolk**
3   **tablespoons milk**

Duxelles:
½   **cup minced onion**
2   **tablespoons butter**
½   **cup minced parsley**
2   **cups minced mushrooms**
⅛   **teaspoon nutmeg**
    Salt and pepper to taste

1. Preheat oven to 450°.
2. Sprinkle filet with salt and pepper. Spread butter over surface of filet.
3. Roast filet: 10 minutes per pound for rare
              12 minutes per pound for medium rare
              15 minutes per pound for medium
4. Cool meat thoroughly.
5. Sauté onions in butter. Do not brown.
6. Wring parsley and mushrooms until thoroughly dry in a cloth towel. Add parsley and mushrooms to onions.
7. Add nutmeg, salt and pepper. Cook, while stirring, 5 to 10 minutes.
8. Remove from heat and allow to cool thoroughly.
9. To assemble Wellington, roll out puff pastry, to ⅛-inch thickness. Cut a piece large enough to wrap filet.
10. Spread ½ duxelle mixture into center of puff pastry. Place filet upside down on duxelles.
11. Arrange remaining duxelles on top and around sides of filet. Wrap pastry around filet. Seams may be sealed with water.
12. Turn Wellington seam side down and place on a baking sheet sprinkled with water.
13. Decorate Wellington with puff pastry cut outs. Refrigerate overnight.
14. Brush pastry with combined egg yolk and milk.
15. Bake in a preheated 425° oven until golden brown. The timing should be approximately the same as when roasting the filet above.
16. Remove and let meat stand 10 minutes before serving.

A serrated knife is preferred for slicing. Serve with Madeira or Béarnaise sauce.

Serves 8 to 10

BÉARNAISE SAUCE

1 shallot, finely chopped	12 tablespoons butter
1 tablespoon tarragon	1 pinch cayenne pepper
1 teaspoon chervil	3 tablespoons finely chopped
4 peppercorns	parsley
2 tablespoons white wine	¾ to 1 cup concentrated sauce
vinegar	Espagnole or sauce
4 tablespoons dry white wine	demi-glace
4 egg yolks	

1. Boil first 6 ingredients until 1½ teaspoons of liquid remains.
2. Strain liquid into top of a double boiler. Discard onions and other solids.
3. Add egg yolks to liquid. Cook over boiling water, beating until creamy.
4. Add butter, melted but not hot, little by little to egg yolks, still whipping to maintain frothiness.
5. Add cayenne and parsley. Add warmed, but not hot Espagnole sauce or demi-glace (undiluted, beef bouillon works well).

Yields 1½ cups

EASY BEEF BOURGUIGNONNE

3 pounds stew meat or beef chuck, cut into ¾-inch cubes	1 10¾-ounce can beef broth
Shortening to brown	1 cup Burgundy wine
3 tablespoons all-purpose flour	1 cup sliced fresh mushrooms, sautéed in 1 tablespoon butter
½ teaspoon salt	
½ teaspoon pepper	2 16-ounce jars small white onions, rinsed
½ teaspoon thyme	

1. Preheat oven to 325°.
2. Brown meat in shortening.
3. Add flour, salt, pepper and thyme.
4. Place in a 2-quart baking dish. Add beef broth and wine. Stir. Cover and bake 2 hours.
5. Add mushrooms and onions. Bake an additional 1½ hours.
6. Add equal portions of wine and water if meat appears too dry.

Serves 6

GRILLADES

2 pounds beef or veal round steak, ½-inch thick
2 tablespoons bacon fat
1 tablespoon all-purpose flour
2 medium onions, finely chopped
1 clove garlic, minced
1 green bell pepper, chopped
2 cups peeled and sliced or chopped tomatoes
1 tablespoon chopped parsley
2 sprigs of thyme or ¼ teaspoon powdered thyme
Salt and pepper to taste
2 tablespoons vermouth, optional

1. Cut meat into individual serving pieces. In a large skillet, brown meat on both sides in hot bacon fat. Remove and set aside.
2. In remaining fat, brown flour, onions and garlic.
3. When brown, add bell pepper, tomatoes, parsley and thyme. Stir until well blended.
4. Return meat to skillet and season with salt and pepper.
5. Cover and cook over low heat 1½ to 2 hours, or until meat is tender.
6. If gravy becomes too thick, stir in a small amount of hot water.
7. Five minutes before serving, whisk in vermouth.

Delicious served with grits, noodles or mashed potatoes.

Serves 6

BEEF TENDERLOIN
A Collection Classic

4 pound beef tenderloin, room temperature
Worcestershire sauce
3 cloves garlic, slivered
Bacon slices

1. Preheat oven to 400°.
2. Sprinkle tenderloin generously with Worcestershire.
3. Arrange garlic and bacon on meat.
4. Place, uncovered, on a rack in a roasting pan. Roast approximately 35 minutes for rare tenderloin.

Serves 8

VEAL PICCATA

1 pound veal scaloppine	1 whole shallot, minced
1 cup all-purpose flour, seasoned with salt and pepper	3 tablespoons fresh lemon juice
6 tablespoons butter	¾ cup dry white wine
3 tablespoons olive oil	3 tablespoons dried parsley
3 to 4 cloves garlic, minced	3 to 4 teaspoons capers
½ pound fresh mushrooms, sliced	3 teaspoons caper juice
	½ lemon, sliced

1. Dredge veal in seasoned flour.
2. Brown in olive oil and butter. Remove veal and set aside.
3. In the same pan, sauté mushrooms, garlic and shallots 1 minute. Add wine, lemon juice, parsley, capers and caper juice.
4. Return veal to skillet. Simmer 15 to 20 minutes, or until tender.
5. Serve garnished with lemon slices.

Serves 4

BAKED LEMON VEAL SCALOPPINE

1 pound veal scaloppine	4 tablespoons butter, divided
1½ cups milk	2 tablespoons olive oil
1 to 2 eggs	Juice of ½ lemon
¾ cup bread crumbs, plain or Italian	Garlic salt
	Parsley, chopped

1. Pound meat and soak in milk for 1 to 2 hours. Drain.
2. Dip veal in egg, then bread crumbs.
3. Melt 2 tablespoons butter and 2 tablespoons oil in skillet and brown veal.
4. Melt 2 tablespoons butter in 9 by 12-inch pan. Coat bottom of pan evenly with butter.
5. Place browned veal in pan. Sprinkle with lemon juice, garlic salt and parsley.
6. Cover with foil. Bake 20 to 30 minutes at 325°.

Serves 4

VEAL CORDON BLEU

12	veal scaloppine, divided	All-purpose flour
6	thin slices ham	Bread crumbs
6	thin slices Swiss cheese	Salt and pepper to taste
3	eggs, beaten	Butter

1. Pound veal. Place 1 slice ham and 1 slice cheese on 6 pieces of veal.
2. Salt, pepper and cover with remaining 6 slices of veal.
3. Pound edges to seal.
4. Dip each piece in flour, then egg, then crumbs.
5. Sauté in butter approximately 5 minutes on each side, until lightly browned.

Serves 6

FLEMISH BEEF RAGOÛT

3	tablespoons butter	1	bay leaf
3	medium onions, chopped	¼	teaspoon thyme
2	tablespoons butter	½	teaspoon paprika
2 to 2½	pounds lean boneless beef, cubed	8	ounces fresh mushrooms, optional
2	tablespoons all-purpose flour		Pepper to taste
⅔	cup beef bouillon, undiluted	1	12-ounce package medium egg noodles, cooked according to package directions
1	cup beer		
1	tablespoon fresh parsley		

1. Melt 3 tablespoons butter in Dutch oven. Sauté onions until transparent.
2. Remove onions. Set aside.
3. Melt remaining 2 tablespoons butter. Add meat and brown.
4. Sift flour over browned meat and stir until absorbed.
5. Stir in bouillon, beer and remaining ingredients. Add cooked onions. Cover tightly. Simmer over low heat 3 hours.
6. Add more bouillon, if more liquid is necessary.
7. Serve over hot, tender noodles.

Serves 4 to 6

SWISS STEAK

1 large Swiss steak, cut into 6
   serving pieces
All-purpose flour
Shortening
1 10¾-ounce can cream of
   mushroom soup

1 soup can of water
⅓ cup cocktail onions and juice
¼ to ½ cup sherry

1. Preheat oven to 300°.
2. Dredge meat in flour.
3. Brown meat in hot shortening. Remove.
4. Place in a 3-quart glass baking dish. Do not salt meat.
5. Add remaining ingredients to pan drippings. Cook over medium heat, stirring drippings into liquid. Pour over meat.
6. Bake, covered, 2½ hours.

Serve over noodles or hot fluffy rice.

Serves 6

PERFECT ROAST BEEF

Boneless roast, back of rump
   (or other tender cut)
2 to 3 garlic cloves, slivered
Lemon pepper marinade

Seasoned salt
Accent
Wondra Flour

1. MEAT MUST BE AT ABSOLUTE ROOM TEMPERATURE TO BEGIN. Preheat oven to 500°.
2. Rub meat with cut garlic cloves. Cut small pockets in meat and insert garlic slivers.
3. Rub with lemon pepper, seasoned salt and Accent.
4. Sprinkle roast with flour.
5. Rinse roasting pan with warm water.
6. Place roast in pan and bake at 5 minutes per pound. After this time turn off heat. Do NOT open door for 2 hours.
7. Medium rare roast is then ready to serve.

4 to 5 pound roast serves 6 to 8

BEEF à la DEUTSCH
A Collection Classic

1 pound ground beef	1 5-ounce package thin egg
1 8-ounce can tomato sauce	noodles, cooked and drained
1 clove garlic, minced	1 cup sour cream
2 teaspoons salt	3 ounces cream cheese
Pepper to taste	6 green onions, chopped
2 teaspoons sugar	1½ cups grated Cheddar cheese
1 16-ounce can tomatoes, undrained	

1. Brown meat. Drain. Add tomato sauce, garlic, salt, pepper, sugar and tomatoes. Simmer, covered, over low heat 45 minutes.
2. Preheat oven to 350°.
3. Combine hot noodles with cubed cream cheese. Stir to melt cheese. Add sour cream and green onions.
4. In a greased 3-quart baking dish, layer meat, noodles and cheese alternately.
5. Bake, uncovered, 35 minutes.

Serves 4 to 6

FAVORITE ROUND STEAK

2 pounds round steak, approximately ½-inch thick	2 10¾-ounce cans tomato soup
	1 can water
All-purpose flour	1 onion, thinly sliced
2 tablespoons vegetable oil	Salt and pepper to taste

1. Trim fat from meat and cut into serving size pieces.
2. Dust with flour, salt and pepper.
3. In a large skillet, brown meat in oil. Add onion and soup that has been mixed with water.
4. Lower heat. Simmer, covered, 1 to 1½ hours or until tender.

Serves 4

OVEN MEATBALL DINNER

1	pound ground round
½	small onion, chopped
½	small green bell pepper, chopped
⅛	teaspoon pepper
¼	cup cornmeal
1	teaspoon salt
1½	teaspoons dry mustard
2	teaspoons chili powder
¼	cup evaporated milk
¼	cup water

1	egg, slightly beaten
¼	cup all-purpose flour
2 to 4	tablespoons shortening
2	8-ounce cans tomato sauce
1	cup water
2	teaspoons Worcestershire sauce
3	large potatoes, quartered
1	pound carrots, sliced in strips
2	large onions, quartered

1. Combine first 11 ingredients. Mix and form into 12 to 14 meat balls.
2. Roll in flour. Brown in hot shortening. Remove and set aside.
3. Add tomato sauce, water and Worcestershire to pan drippings. Stir and bring to a boil. Remove from heat.
4. Layer meatballs and vegetables in a deep 4-quart casserole dish.
5. Pour sauce over all.
6. Bake, covered, 1 hour at 350°.

Carrots are very crisp after cooking. If well cooked vegetables are preferred, microwave carrots and potatoes several minutes before adding to casserole.

Serves 6

PEPPER STEAK

4　8-ounce sirloin or New York
　strip steaks
1　teaspoon salt
2　tablespoons black peppercorns
2　tablespoons white peppercorns
¼　cup butter, melted

1　tablespoon vegetable oil
1　teaspoon all-purpose flour
¼　cup beef broth
2　tablespoons whipping cream
1　teaspoon Dijon mustard
½　cup brandy

1. Sprinkle both sides of meat with salt.
2. Place peppercorns in a small plastic bag and crush them with a hammer or rolling pin.
3. Spread crushed peppercorns on a cutting board and press them into 1 side of each steak.
4. Brush the other side of steak with butter. Chill meat a moment to set butter.
5. Just before serving, sauté steaks in oil, butter side down, 5 to 6 minutes. Turn and sauté 5 additional minutes and remove to a platter. Keep warm.
6. To the pan, add 1 teaspoon butter, flour, beef broth, cream, mustard and brandy.
7. Simmer, whisking 3 to 4 minutes. Pour over steaks and serve.

Serves 4

FRUITED POT ROAST

3 to 4 tablespoons all-purpose
　flour
　Salt and pepper to taste
4　pounds chuck, arm or rump
　roast
　Butter
1½　onions, sliced
¼　teaspoon ground ginger

¼　teaspoon cinnamon
3　whole cloves
2　tablespoons sugar
1　cup apple cider or juice
12　dried apricots
2　apples, cored and quartered
½　cup raisins
12　dried prunes

1. Dredge meat in seasoned flour.
2. In a Dutch oven, brown meat in butter.
3. Add onions, spices and sugar.
4. Carefully pour apple juice around meat, but not on top.
5. Cover and simmer on stove 1 hour or bake 1 hour at 250°.
6. Add fruits and continue cooking, covered, 1 to 1½ hours or until done.
7. Thicken sauce with flour and water or cornstarch and water.

Serve roast and fruit over hot fluffy rice.

Serves 6 to 8

MEAT STUFFED PEPPERS

For a colorful entrée, use green, red and yellow peppers.

6 large bell peppers	*Tomato sauce:*
2 tablespoons vegetable oil	1 tablespoon olive oil
2 pounds ground meat	1 onion, chopped
1 onion	1 16-ounce can tomatoes, chopped and seeded, but not drained
Salt and pepper to taste	
1 tablespoon Worcestershire sauce	1 bay leaf
	Salt and pepper to taste

1. Cut tops from peppers. Set tops aside. Seed and core peppers. In a baking dish, stand peppers in 1-inch of water. Bake 10 to 15 minutes at 450°. Drain any remaining water.
2. Heat oil in a skillet. Add ground meat.
3. Process onion and tops of peppers in a food processor 1 minute. Add to meat. Lightly brown. Season with salt and pepper. Add Worcestershire.
4. Spoon mixture into peppers. Place any additional stuffing around peppers.
5. To make sauce, simmer oil, onion, tomatoes, salt, pepper and bay leaf 15 minutes.
6. Pour sauce around peppers in the pan.
7. Bake, covered, 25 minutes at 350°. Remove cover and continue baking another 10 to 20 minutes.

Serves 6

SPINACH MEAT LOAF

1½ pounds lean ground beef
5   ounces fresh spinach, finely
    chopped
1   tablespoon Worcestershire
    sauce
1   egg, beaten
¾   cup tomato juice, V–8, or
    tomato soup

¼   cup Parmesan cheese
¼   cup fine dry bread crumbs
    Garlic powder to taste
    Salt and pepper to taste
2   carrots, grated

1. Preheat oven to 325°.
2. Combine all ingredients and mix well. The mixture should be fairly moist. If
   not moist enough, add more tomato juice.
3. Form into a loaf. Place in a 1-quart loaf pan.
4. Bake 1 hour.

Serves 6 to 8

ZUCCHINI MOUSSAKA

Can be prepared ahead of time and refrigerated until time to cook.

3   medium zucchini, peeled and
    cut into ¼-inch slices
2   tablespoons vegetable oil
1   onion, sliced
1   pound ground round
1   8-ounce can tomato sauce

1   clove garlic, minced
½   teaspoon salt
¼   teaspoon cinnamon
1   cup small curd cottage cheese
1   egg, slightly beaten
¼   cup grated Parmesan cheese

1. Preheat oven to 350°.
2. In a skillet, lightly brown zucchini and onion in oil.
3. Place zucchini in bottom of a 9 by 13-inch baking dish.
4. In the same skillet, brown beef. Drain.
5. Stir in tomato sauce, garlic, salt and cinnamon.
6. Spoon this mixture over zucchini and onion.
7. Blend egg and cottage cheese. Spoon over meat.
8. Sprinkle Parmesan cheese over cottage cheese topping.
9. Bake 30 minutes.

Serves 6

BEEF GUMBO

2 tablespoons shortening	1 tablespoon Worcestershire sauce
1 onion, chopped	2 cups stew meat, venison, or leftover roast
½ green bell pepper, chopped	Salt to taste
½ cup sliced okra	Water, if necessary
1 16-ounce can tomatoes	
2 teaspoons chili powder, or to taste	
5 drops Tabasco sauce, or to taste	

1. Sauté chopped onion, bell pepper and fresh okra in shortening 5 minutes. Add tomatoes and juice.
2. Season generously with chili powder, Tabasco and Worcestershire.
3. Cook over low heat 1½ hours.
4. If using meat that has already been cooked, add after first hour. If using stew meat, add after first 30 minutes. Venison cooks the entire 1½ hours.

Serve over hot fluffy rice.

Serves 6 to 8

SANTA FE STEW

2 tablespoons vegetable oil	1 tablespoon rosemary
2 pounds chili meat, cubed	1 tablespoon thyme
2 onions, chopped	1 tablespoon marjoram
4 garlic cloves, minced	1 tablespoon parsley
4 cups water	8 carrots, chopped
4 beef bouillon cubes	3 ribs celery, chopped
1 tablespoon oregano	3 large potatoes, chopped
1 tablespoon ground cumin	2 4-ounce cans mild green chiles

1. In a Dutch oven, add oil, meat, onions and garlic. Brown. Drain.
2. Add water, bouillon cubes and spices. Simmer, covered, 2 hours.
3. Add vegetables. Simmer 30 additional minutes or until vegetables are tender.

Serves 8 to 10

SAVORY ISLAND MEAT PIE

A delightful dish that can be prepared ahead of time and refrigerated. It is a lot of work, but well worth it. It will not freeze.

Dough:

¼	cup sugar
¼	cup slightly softened butter
¼	teaspoon salt
1	egg, beaten
2	tablespoons cold milk
1⅓	cups all-purpose flour

1¼	teaspoons salt
1¼	teaspoons paprika
1	teaspoon basil
⅓	pound ground beef
1½	cups packed, unpeeled red potatoes, coarsely grated
1	cup beef stock

Filling:

½	cup butter
1	cup chopped onion
½	cup chopped celery
⅓	pound ground pork
2	teaspoons minced garlic
¾	teaspoon dried thyme
2	teaspoons cayenne pepper
1½	teaspoons black pepper

Topping:

8	ounces cream cheese, softened
¾	cup whipping cream
¾	teaspoon dried oregano
¾	teaspoon dried thyme

1. To make dough, place sugar, butter and salt in food processor. Process on high until creamy.
2. Add egg and milk. Process. Add flour and beat until blended.
3. Mold dough into a flat, round circle.
4. Dust with flour, cover and let it rest 1 hour.
5. To make filling, melt butter in a large skillet. Add onions and celery. Sauté until onions are transparent. Reduce heat. Add pork, garlic and seasonings. Cook, scraping pan bottom well.
6. Add beef and mix thoroughly. Lower heat. Simmer 5 minutes, stirring frequently, and scraping pan bottom.
7. Stir in potatoes and stock. Cook 10 minutes over medium heat, stirring constantly.
8. Using a strainer, drain mixture thoroughly and cool at least 15 minutes before filling pie dough.
9. To make topping, beat the ingredients until smooth and thoroughly blended.
10. On a lightly floured surface, roll dough ¼-inch thick to fit an 8-inch round cake pan (1½-inch deep).

11. Fit dough into the greased and floured pan. Press onto sides and bottom of pan.
12. Refrigerate for 15 minutes.
13. Bake unfilled for 30 minutes at 350° or until bottom looks dry. Cool 5 minutes.
14. Spoon meat filling into crust. Spread cheese topping over filling. Being careful not to get any filling into topping.
15. Return to oven and bake until crust is golden brown, approximately 45 minutes. Cool 10 minutes before serving.

Serves 6

CADILLAC CHILI

This is not for the faint-hearted. If milder chili is desired, use less cayenne pepper.

1 medium onion, chopped	2 tablespoons ground cumin
1 green bell pepper, chopped	½ to 1¼ teaspoons cayenne pepper
1 clove garlic, minced	1 teaspoon oregano
¾ pound ground chuck	¼ teaspoon liquid smoke
4 tablespoons tomato paste	1 tablespoon salt
1 15-ounce can dark kidney beans, drained	1¼ cups water

1. Brown onion, bell pepper, garlic and meat.
2. Add tomato paste, beans, cumin, cayenne, oregano, liquid smoke, salt and water.
3. Simmer 2½ hours. Add more water as needed.

For spicier chili, substitute chopped jalapeño pepper for bell pepper.

Serves 4

FAVORITE TEXAS BRISKETS

Variation I:

5 to 6 pound brisket   **Garlic salt**
  Worcestershire sauce   1   **10¾-ounce can beef broth**
  Salt and pepper

1. Liberally sprinkle Worcestershire on all sides of meat.
2. Season with salt, pepper and garlic salt. Pat in seasonings.
3. Place meat in a pan lined with heavy duty foil. Place meat under the broiler and brown on both sides.
4. Seal brisket in foil. Bake 4 to 6 hours at 325°.
5. Remove meat. Pour broth and pan drippings plus 1 cup water into a sauce-pan. Boil until liquid is reduced to 1 cup. Serve with brisket.

Variation II:

5 to 6 pound brisket   **Seasoned salt**
  Liquid smoke   **Cracked black pepper**
  Worcestershire sauce

1. Place brisket on a sheet of heavy duty foil.
2. Rub both sides with liquid smoke and Worcestershire.
3. Sprinkle fat side of meat with salt and pepper.
4. Wrap and seal tightly. Place in a pan.
5. Bake 1 hour at 450°. Reduce heat to 350° and bake 1 hour. Reduce heat to 250° and bake 1 hour and hold at this temperature until ready to serve.

Variation III:

5 to 6 pound brisket   2   **tablespoons sugar**
½ **cup vegetable oil**   1   **teaspoon salt**
1   **can beer**   3   **whole cloves**
1   **clove garlic, minced**   1   **envelope dry onion soup mix**
2   **tablespoons lemon juice**

1. Marinate brisket overnight in a mixture of all ingredients except onion soup mix.
2. Discard marinade. Sprinkle top of meat with soup mix.
3. Wrap meat tightly in foil.
4. Bake 4 to 5 hours at 275°.

Serves 10 to 12

LYLES RANCH BAR-B-QUE SAUCE

½ medium onion, chopped
2 cloves garlic, minced
½ cup butter
¼ cup fresh lime juice, do not substitute
½ cup Worcestershire sauce

1 cup strong black coffee
2 cups ketchup
2 fresh serrano or jalapeño peppers, seeded and chopped

1. Sauté onion and garlic in butter.
2. Add remaining ingredients and simmer at least 15 minutes.

Keeps two weeks in refrigerator.

Yields 5 cups

BAR-B-QUE SAUCE

Great for basting hamburgers, steaks or chicken.

2 cloves garlic, minced
½ cup butter
1 large onion, sliced
1 tablespoon black pepper

2 to 3 cups ketchup
1 16-ounce bottle Worcestershire sauce
2 small limes

1. Sauté garlic, butter and onion over medium heat until onion is transparent.
2. Add pepper and cook 5 minutes.
3. Add ketchup and Worcestershire. Squeeze juice of limes into saucepan and add whole rinds. Cook 5 minutes.
4. Remove rinds. Use immediately or store in refrigerator.

Yields 4 to 5 cups

HEARTY SPAGHETTI SAUCE

2	green bell peppers, chopped	2	12-ounce cans tomato paste
3	ribs celery, chopped	2	cups water
2	medium yellow onions, chopped	2	tablespoons salt
¼	cup vegetable oil	1½	teaspoons pepper
3	pounds ground beef	1	teaspoon sugar
3	cloves garlic, minced	1	tablespoon dried basil
2	3-ounce cans sliced mushrooms, undrained	2	tablespoons bouquet garni
2	16-ounce cans whole tomatoes	2	tablespoons dried oregano
3	15-ounce cans tomato sauce	1	cup chopped fresh parsley
		2	bay leaves

1. Sauté bell pepper, celery and onions in oil in a large pot until soft.
2. Add meat and garlic. Brown.
3. Add remaining ingredients. Simmer 2 hours.

Serve over cooked spaghetti.

Freezes

Serves 16 to 18

ORIENTAL MARINADE FOR FLANK STEAK

Also try this on chicken or pork.

¼	cup soy sauce	½	teaspoon garlic powder
3	tablespoons honey	½	teaspoon ginger
2	teaspoons vinegar	½	cup vegetable oil

1. Place all ingredients in a jar and shake to blend.
2. Pour over 1 to 2 pounds meat that has been pierced with a fork. Marinate overnight.
3. Broil meat over hot coals until done to taste.

Meat can be prepared early. Slice, cover with extra marinade and wrap in foil. Warm before serving.

Serves 4 to 6

SHERRY GARLIC MARINADE

A tasty marinade for steak.

½	cup fresh lemon juice		½	teaspoon cayenne pepper
1	cup vegetable oil		1	medium onion, sliced
1½	cups very dry sherry		1	tablespoon black pepper
1	teaspoon Tabasco sauce		1	tablespoon dry mustard
2	tablespoons Worcestershire sauce		1½	teaspoons salt
2	cups water		4	cloves garlic, minced

1. Combine all ingredients.
2. Marinate steak in a shallow dish for 24 hours, turning several times.
3. Cook steak over hot coals, basting with marinade.

Yields 5 cups

ELEGANT PORK TENDERLOIN

2	1½-pound pork tenderloins		¼	cup water
¼ to ½	teaspoon Creole seasoning		¼	cup Burgundy
½	cup butter		1	tablespoon chopped parsley
½	cup all-purpose flour		2	cups sliced, fresh mushrooms
¼	teaspoon pepper			Cooked rice
2	10¾-ounce cans beef bouillon			
	Juice of 1 lemon			

1. Preheat oven to 325°.
2. Sprinkle tenderloin lightly with Creole seasoning. Using a meat thermometer, roast tenderloin uncovered, approximately 30 to 45 minutes or until internal temperature is 185°.
3. While meat is roasting, melt butter in medium saucepan. Add flour and pepper. Cook over medium heat, stirring constantly until brown.
4. Add broth to pan, stirring constantly. Add lemon juice, wine, water and parsley. Simmer and stir until thickened. Add mushrooms and cook 10 additional minutes.
5. Pour ¼ of the sauce over tenderloins when done. Slice and serve with rice and remaining sauce.

Serves 6 to 8

DECORATED HOLIDAY HAM

This beautiful ham will be the center of attention and will become a delicious family favorite.

1	7-pound uncooked ham	1	cup port wine
	Whole cloves	1	cup brown sugar
1	8¼-ounce can chunk pineapple, reserve juice		Red cherries

1. If ham is cured, place in cold water and boil 20 minutes to remove salt. Do not remove any fat.
2. Before baking, remove casing and most of the fat. With a sharp knife, score ham ¼-inch deep in a decorative pattern. Stud with cloves and pineapple chunks, secured with toothpicks. Stick cherries on ends of toothpicks.
3. Simmer pineapple juice, wine and brown sugar in a saucepan. Use this sauce to baste ham.
4. Bake 1½ to 2 hours at 350° if boiled first. Cook 30 minutes longer if ham was not boiled. Baste ham frequently during baking.

Serves 12 to 15

SIMMERED HERBED PORK CHOPS

4 to 6 loin pork chops, 1-inch thick		1	tablespoon butter
	Salt and pepper	¾	cup tomato juice
1	teaspoon basil	¾	cup beef stock or bouillon
1	teaspoon thyme		

1. Rub seasonings generously into both sides of pork chops.
2. Sauté pork chops in butter 7 minutes on each side, or until browned.
3. Add tomato juice and bouillon to skillet.
4. Cover and simmer 30 minutes over low to medium heat.

To vary flavor, add ¼ cup chopped green chiles or ½ cup rice to skillet.

Serves 4 to 6

SWEET AND SOUR PORK

1	pound lean pork, cut in cubes		Pinch salt
1	cup all-purpose flour	1	teaspoon sugar
½	teaspoon monosodium glutamate, optional	1	teaspoon Worcestershire sauce
1	teaspoon salt	1	tablespoon dehydrated onion flakes
2	eggs, beaten	1	tablespoon cornstarch
1	14-ounce can pineapple chunks	2	tablespoons water
¼	cup ketchup	1¼	cup vegetable shortening
2	tablespoons vinegar	1	medium green bell pepper, cut in strips

1. Combine flour, monosodium glutamate and salt. Coat pork cubes with flour mixture. Dip in egg, dredge in flour again. Set aside.
2. Drain pineapple chunks, reserving ½ cup juice. Mix juice with ketchup, vinegar, salt, sugar, Worcestershire and onion flakes.
3. Mix cornstarch and water until smooth. Set aside.
4. Heat shortening until very hot. Fry pork cubes until crisp, turning to brown evenly. Remove and drain on paper towel. Pour off all but 1 tablespoon of fat.
5. Pour pineapple liquid and cornstarch mixture into pan drippings. Cook over low heat, stirring constantly, until thick.
6. Add pepper strips, pineapple chunks and pork cubes. Heat through, but do not boil.

Serve over hot, fluffy rice.

Serves 4 to 6

PORK CHOPS WITH RICE AND VEGETABLES

4	thick pork chops	4	rings of green bell pepper
	Salt and pepper	4	thick slices tomato
1	cup raw wild rice		Black olives, sliced
1	cup raw white rice		Mushroom slices
1	10¾-ounce can beef consommé	½ to 1 can water
4	rings of onion		

1. Preheat oven to 375°.
2. Season pork chops with salt and pepper. Brown.
3. Put rice in 2-quart casserole. Pour consommé over rice and stir.
4. Place pork chops on rice. Top with onion, bell pepper, tomato, olives and mushrooms. Add water.
5. Cover and bake 1 hour.

Serves 4

BUSY DAY PORK CHOPS

A favorite to put in the oven as school children come home. Dinner cooks while mother drives carpools.

1	cup ketchup	¼	cup lemon juice
½	cup water	4	thick center cut pork chops
¾	cup brown sugar, lightly packed		

1. Preheat oven to 250°.
2. Combine ketchup, water, brown sugar and lemon juice.
3. Place pork chops in 2-quart glass baking dish and pour sauce over pork chops.
4. Bake, uncovered, 2½ to 3 hours.

Garnish with thinly sliced lemon and parsley.

Serves 4

HAM AND POTATOES AU GRATIN

8 small new potatoes	2 cups cottage cheese
1 cup cooked diced ham	1 cup sour cream
½ cup finely chopped onion	Salt and pepper to taste
1 clove garlic, minced	1 cup Cheddar cheese, grated

1. Boil potatoes in water until tender. Drain.
2. Mix together all ingredients except cheese. Pour mixture into a 1½-quart glass baking dish. Cover with cheese.
3. Bake at 350° for 30 to 45 minutes.

Serves 6

SKILLET CHOPS AND HOT SLAW

6 pork chops	1 teaspoon salt
Salt and pepper	4 teaspoons Worcestershire
2 tablespoons bacon grease	sauce
2 tablespoons water	1 teaspoon celery seed
½ cup water	5 cups shredded cabbage
½ cup vinegar	1 cup shredded carrot
2 tablespoons all-purpose flour	½ cup chopped onion
2 tablespoons sugar	½ cup chopped green bell pepper
2 tablespoons prepared mustard	

1. Trim pork chops of excess fat. Season with salt and pepper.
2. Brown chops in hot bacon fat in a large Dutch oven. Add 2 tablespoons water. Cover and simmer 20 minutes.
3. As pork chops cook, blend ½ cup water, vinegar, flour, sugar, mustard, salt, Worcestershire and celery seed.
4. Remove pork chops. Set aside.
5. Add vinegar mixture to pan drippings. Stir until thickened.
6. Add vegetables. Cook and stir until covered with sauce. Place pork chops on vegetables. Simmer, covered 15 minutes.
7. Salt and pepper slaw to taste before serving.

Serves 6

HAM LOAF WITH MUSTARD SAUCE

A delicious alternative to beef meat loaf, and a good way to use the last of the ham.

1½ pounds ham (with some fat)	1 tablespoon prepared horseradish
½ pound ground pork	2 tablespoons finely minced green bell pepper
½ cup fresh bread crumbs	
½ cup milk	1 teaspoon dry mustard
1 tablespoon brown sugar	2 eggs, beaten
¼ teaspoon salt	
¼ teaspoon pepper	

1. Preheat oven to 350°.
2. Grind ham and pork together in a food processor.
3. Soak bread crumbs in milk. Mix all ingredients together. Shape into a loaf. Place in a 4 by 10-inch bread pan which has been lined with foil.
4. Bake 30 minutes. Turn oven to 300°. Bake another 45 minutes.
5. Serve with mustard sauce.

Serves 8 to 10

MUSTARD SAUCE

1 cup half and half or evaporated milk	¼ teaspoon salt
	1 egg yolk
¼ cup light brown sugar	½ cup vinegar
1 tablespoon dry mustard	2 tablespoons chopped chives, optional
1 tablespoon all-purpose flour	

1. Place all ingredients in blender or food processor. Process 15 to 30 seconds.
2. Transfer to a saucepan. Heat, stirring until thickened. Serve warm.

Yields 1½ cups

GLAZED HAM BALLS

Serve this delicious brunch or lunch dish with cheese grits and a green salad.

1½	pounds ground ham	½	cup vinegar
1½	pounds ground pork	1½	teaspoons dry mustard
¼	cup milk	½	cup water
2½	cups fresh bread crumbs	1	10-ounce jar orange
1½	cups brown sugar		marmalade

1. Preheat oven to 350°.
2. Mix first 4 ingredients. Let stand 1 hour.
3. Form balls into bite-size pieces and place in a 9 by 13-inch glass baking dish.
4. Combine brown sugar, vinegar, mustard and water in a saucepan. Simmer 15 minutes.
5. Pour sauce over ham balls. Bake 30 minutes. Pour orange marmalade over balls. Bake another 30 minutes.
6. Transfer to a chafing dish or serving bowl.

Yields 90 balls

ITALIAN SAUSAGE SKILLET DINNER

1	16-ounce can tomato sauce	2	links sweet Italian sausage
1	16-ounce can beef broth	2	links hot Italian sausage
2	teaspoons thyme	8	ounces rigatoni, cooked and
2	medium bay leaves		drained
2	teaspoons marjoram		Parmesan cheese
1	teaspoon oregano		

1. In a saucepan, combine tomato sauce, beef broth, thyme, bay leaves, marjoram and oregano. Bring to a boil. Lower heat. Simmer 30 minutes.
2. Remove casings from sausages. Fry and crumble until lightly browned. Drain. Return to skillet.
3. Remove bay leaves from sauce. Add sauce to sausage. Simmer 10 minutes.
4. Add pasta. Heat thoroughly.

Serve with Parmesan cheese.

Serves 6

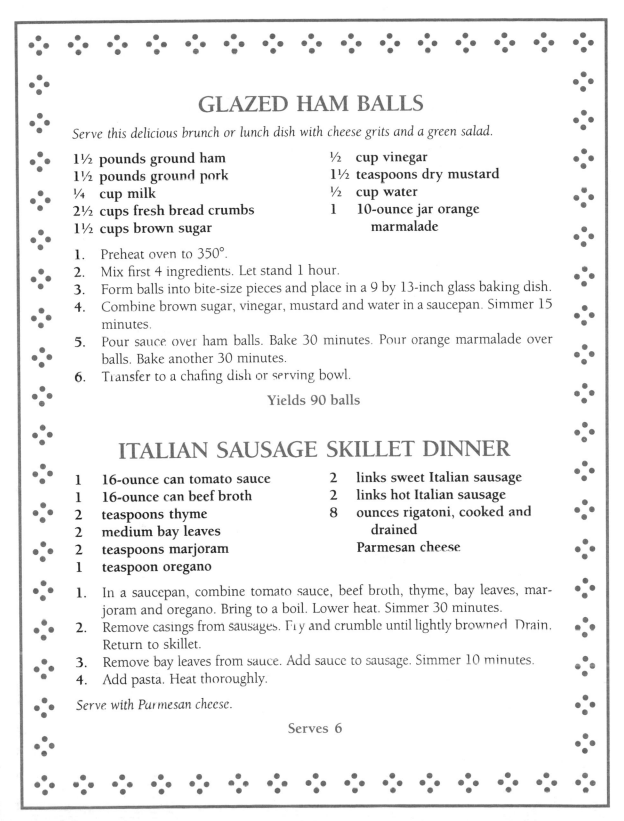

CHILI-RUBBED PORK ROAST

½ teaspoon salt
½ teaspoon garlic salt
2½ teaspoons chili powder, divided
4 pounds boneless pork roast, rolled and tied

1 cup apple jelly
1 cup ketchup
2 tablespoons vinegar

1. Preheat oven to 325°.
2. In a small bowl combine salt, garlic salt and ½ teaspoon chili powder. Rub roast with mixture.
3. Place roast, fat side up, on a rack in a shallow roasting pan. Roast, uncovered, approximately 2 hours.
4. While meat cooks, combine jelly, ketchup, vinegar and remaining chili powder in a medium saucepan. Bring to a boil. Reduce heat and simmer, uncovered, 2 minutes. Set aside.
5. About 15 minutes before roast is done, baste meat with jelly mixture.
6. When roast is done, remove from oven and let stand 10 minutes before carving.
7. Mix ½ cup of pan drippings with the remaining jelly mixture. Reheat sauce, if necessary, and serve with roast.

Serves 10

DADDY'S SAUSAGE STUFFING

This can be served as a side dish with Cornish hens, roast chicken or any poultry. It is enough dressing to stuff a 10 pound turkey.

2 pounds pork sausage
3 raw potatoes, grated
2 onions, finely chopped
3 eggs, beaten
5 slices white bread, moistened with water and the moisture squeezed out

1 tablespoon poultry seasoning
Salt and pepper

1. Preheat oven to 350°.
2. Brown sausage with potatoes and onions. Drain.
3. Add beaten eggs, bread and seasonings.
4. Place in a greased 3-quart baking dish.
5. Bake 30 minutes, or until dressing is set.

Try using leftovers in Turkey and Dressing Quiche.

Serves 8 to 10

SPICY ITALIAN MEAT SAUCE

2	tablespoons olive oil		1	15-ounce can tomato paste
1	onion, chopped		1	15-ounce can water
1	green bell pepper, finely chopped		3	tablespoons chopped fresh parsley
1	clove garlic, minced		1	bay leaf
6	large mushrooms, sliced		1	teaspoon sugar
1	carrot, peeled and diced		2	teaspoons oregano
1	pound ground beef		2	tablespoons basil
1	pound Italian sausage		¼	teaspoon red pepper flakes
1	28-ounce can tomatoes		¼	teaspoon cinnamon

1. Remove sausage from casings.
2. Sauté first 8 ingredients until meat is browned. Drain.
3. Add remaining ingredients and simmer 45 minutes to 1 hour.

Serve over fresh pasta or use as a sauce for lasagna.

Serves 8

ALICE'S LAMB

5 to 8 pound leg of lamb, boned
    Salt and pepper to taste
8 to 10 slices onion
1   8-ounce
    jar crabapple jelly
1   12-ounce bottle chili sauce
1   teaspoon whole cloves

1   teaspoon allspice
1   tablespoon brown sugar
    Salt
2   cups pan drippings
2   tablespoons red wine
1 to 3 cups water

1. Place boned leg in roaster, fat side up.
2. Salt and pepper lamb. Place onion slices over surface.
3. Pour water into pan to 1-inch. Cover.
4. Roast at 325°. (12 to 18 minutes per pound for rare, 130°–135° F.; 14 to 21 minutes per pound for medium rare, 140°–145° F.; 18–25 minutes for medium, 150°–160° F.) Let meat stand 15 to 20 minutes before carving.
5. Pour drippings into a 10-inch skillet. Add jelly, chili sauce, spices and sugar. Add salt to taste. Cook over low heat until blended. Add flour and enough water to thicken gravy. Strain. Add wine.

Variation:
Bourbon may be substituted for wine. Add ¼ cup bourbon to 2 cups of pan drippings.

Serves 6 to 10

※ Roast bones 2 hours before adding lamb to pan. This enriches the flavor of the drippings.

STUFFED GRAPE LEAVES

1   pound ground beef, if lean
    meat is used add ½ cup
    butter
½   cup raw rice, soaked briefly
    and drained
1   teaspoon salt

¾   tablespoon black pepper
⅛   teaspoon cinnamon
35 small grape leaves, about 3 to
    4-inches in diameter
3 to 4 pieces lamb shoulder bones
½   cup lemon juice

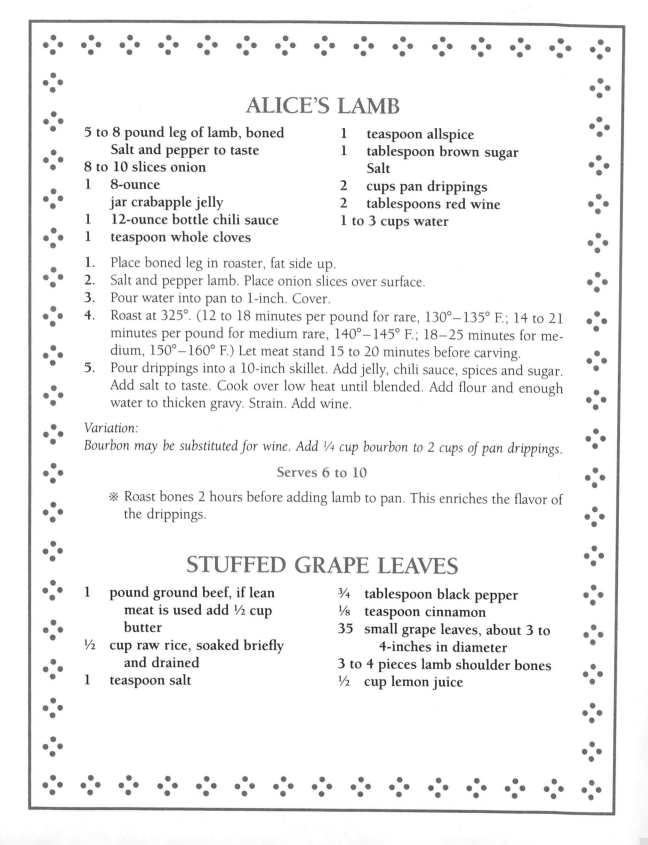

1. Blend meat, rice and seasonings thoroughly, moistening with water or beef stock to mix completely.
2. Place 1 tablespoon filling in center of underside of grape leaf. Turn in edges around filling and roll into a firm neat cylinder. Repeat with remaining grape leaves.
3. Place lamb bones in bottom of a 6-quart baking dish.
4. Layer stuffed grape leaves over lamb bones.
5. Fill pan with water up to, but not covering, top layer of rolled leaves.
6. Heat until water simmers. Lower heat. Cover and cook 5 minutes.
7. Add ½ cup lemon juice and continue cooking approximately 40 minutes or until tender.

※ If fresh grape leaves are used, wilt in hot water before using.

Yields 30 to 35 stuffed leaves

GRILLED LAMB CHOPS

Marinade:

1 to 2 cloves garlic
  Fresh ginger root to taste, grated
1 cup Burgundy wine
½ cup salad oil
2 tablespoons soy sauce
2 tablespoons vinegar
2 teaspoons sugar
1 teaspoon salt
1 teaspoon Accent
1 teaspoon marjoram
1 teaspoon rosemary

8 loin lamb chops

1. Combine all marinade ingredients.
2. Place lamb chops in a glass or enamel pan and pour marinade over them. Marinate 24 hours, turning meat periodically and spooning sauce over it.
3. Grill over charcoal until done to taste.

Serves 4

LAMB SHISH KEBAB

Marinade:

4   cloves garlic, minced
1½   teaspoons salt
½   teaspoon ground ginger
½   teaspoon ground allspice
½   teaspoon ground cloves
½   teaspoon pepper
½   teaspoon crumbled bay leaves
8   ounces sour cream

1   5-pound leg of lamb, boned
     and cut into 1-inch cubes
     Green bell peppers
     Cherry tomatoes
     Mushrooms
     Small onion, parboiled

1. Combine marinade ingredients in a large bowl. Place lamb pieces in mixture
    and stir until cubes are well coated.
2. Cover pan tightly and marinade at least overnight.
3. Thread meat on skewers alternately with vegetables.
4. Grill over charcoal approximately 5 minutes per side or until done to taste.

Serves 6 to 8

EGGPLANT SUPREME

1   large onion, chopped
¼   cup pine nuts, optional
1   tablespoon olive oil
1½   pounds lean ground lamb or
     beef
     Salt and pepper to taste

1   teaspoon cinnamon
1   15-ounce can tomato sauce
1   can water
4   medium eggplants, peeled and
     sliced lengthwise, ½-inch
     thick

1. Preheat oven to 375°.
2. In a Dutch oven, sauté onions and pine nuts in oil until onions are transparent.
3. Add meat and sauté until cooked. Drain.
4. Add spices, tomato sauce and water.
5. Simmer 15 minutes.
6. Layer bottom of 9 by 13 by 2-inch glass baking dish with eggplant.
7. Pour ⅓ meat sauce mixture over eggplant and continue to alternate sauce and
    eggplant ending with meat sauce.
8. Bake, uncovered, 30 minutes.

Serves 6

COMPANY DOVES

18 doves, whole or breasted
All-purpose flour
Salt
¾ cup butter
Bacon grease
½ cup chopped onion

1 8-ounce can chopped
mushrooms, reserve juice
2 teaspoons chopped parsley
1 cup dry white wine
1 cup whipping cream

1. Rub mixture of flour and salt into doves.
2. Sauté doves in butter and a small amount of bacon grease.
3. Remove doves and place in greased baking dish, breast side down.
4. Sauté onion, mushrooms and parsley in remaining butter. Add wine and mushroom juice. Pour mixture over birds.
5. Bake, covered, 2 hours at 300°. Baste frequently.
6. Add cream and bake 30 additional minutes.

Serves 6 to 8

KAT'S WILD DUCK

2 ducks
Vinegar
1 cup butter
1 8-ounce jar mushrooms
1 cup chopped parsley

2 medium onions, chopped
2 cloves garlic, minced
1 cup red wine
Wild rice

1. Marinate ducks in vinegar and water overnight.
2. Place ducks in heavy pot. Add butter, mushrooms, parsley, onion and garlic. Cover.
3. Cook on top of stove 1 hour. Add wine. Cook 1 additional hour.
4. Cook rice according to package directions. Serve duck over a bed of rice.

Serves 4

QUAIL OR DOVE SMOTHERED

12	birds		Lemon pepper
½	cup butter	½	cup all-purpose flour
½	cup chopped onion	½	cup butter
1	cup sliced mushrooms	½	cup water
	Salt and pepper	½	cup white wine

1. Sauté onion and mushrooms in butter until tender. Add wine and water.
2. Salt and pepper birds.
3. Stuff breast cavity with a small pat of butter.
4. Place birds, breast side down, in an 8 by 8-inch greased dish.
5. Sprinkle liberally with flour. Pour sauce over birds.
6. Cover and bake at 250° for 4 hours.

Serves 4

VENISON BEEF STEW

2	pounds stew meat	1	12-ounce can whole tomatoes
2	pounds venison ham, cubed	2	8-ounce cans tomato sauce
2	tablespoons vegetable shortening	2	bay leaves
	Salt and pepper to taste	1	pound carrots, peeled and diced
2	onions, chopped	2	ears of corn
4	ribs celery, diced	4 to 5	potatoes, peeled and diced
1	green bell pepper, diced		

1. Brown beef and venison in shortening. Add salt and pepper.
2. Add onions, celery, bell pepper, tomatoes, tomato sauce and bay leaves to meat. Add hot water to cover. Simmer 20 minutes.
3. Parboil carrots.
4. Remove corn from cob.
5. Add carrots, corn and potatoes to stew. Simmer an additional 30 minutes.

Serves 8 to 12

SEAFOOD

Thanks to fast transportation and improved methods of preservation, a large variety of fish and shellfish are now available. It is necessary to find a good fish market. A reliable market should receive daily deliveries and be willing to order almost any fish you desire, if available. It should also behead and clean the fish to your exact specifications. Fresh fish does not smell "fishy". It should be firm, plump and elastic and should not leave an impression when pressed. The eyes should be clear, not sunken or foggy. Frozen fish may actually provide a better alternative because many fishermen have facilities to freeze fish immediately. If frozen fish is purchased, it must be stored at once, and should not be allowed to thaw. When thawed, it must be cooked on the same day. Thawed or fresh fish does not keep more than one day in the refrigerator. This rule applies to all seafood. Most of it is best when prepared as soon as possible after purchasing. Thaw frozen seafood in the refrigerator. Recipes containing cooked seafood should be refrigerated and eaten within three days of preparation.

Fish may be classified as oily or lean, according to fat content.

OILY VARIETIES	LEAN VARIETIES	
Amberjack	Black Seabass	Shark
Bonito Blue	Gill	Sheepshead
Butterfish	Cod	Sole
Carp	Crappie	Speckled Sea Trout
Freshwater Catfish	Croaker	Triggerfish
Herring	Dolphin	Turbot
King Mackerel	Flounder	Walleye
Lake Trout	Grouper	Whiting
Mullet (Red or Gray)	Haddock	
Rainbow Trout	Halibut	
Sablefish	Ocean Catfish	
Salmon	Ocean Perch	
Sardines	Pike	
Shad	Pollack	
Spanish Mackerel	Pompano	
Swordfish	Red Snapper	
Tuna	Rock Fish	
Whitefish	Scrod	

SALT WATER FISH

Some fish are known by many different names. The following list provides alternate names.

Bluefish—Tailor, Skipjack
Butterfish—Harvest Fish
Croaker—Hardhead, Tom Cod
Black Drum—Oyster Cracker, Oyster and Sea Drum
Red Drum—Channel Bass, Redfish and Sea Drum
Grouper—Sea Bass
Red Hake—Mud Hake
White Hake—Common Hake
King Mackerel—Cero, Kingfish

SHELLFISH

Shellfish include clams, cockles, crabs, crayfish or crawfish, lobsters, mussels, octopus, oysters, scallops, shrimp, squid and whelks.

CLAMS

Clams may be purchased in the shell or shucked. Clam shells should be tightly closed. The shell will not close if the clam is dead. After cooking, discard any clams that have not opened. Allow six clams per serving.

CRAB

Two types of crab usually available are the hard-shell and the soft-shell. Most whole crabs on the market today are already cooked. The shells of cooked crab are usually tinged with red. When purchasing live crab, look for movement in their legs. Keep crabs alive until ready to cook. After cooking, crabs should be red and have no unpleasant odor. Whether fresh or thawed, crab should be used within a day after purchasing. Four pounds of crab in the shell yields about one pound of crab meat.

BASIC CRAB AND SHRIMP BOIL

½   cup salt
3   tablespoons cayenne pepper
¼   cup celery salt
¼   cup dry mustard
¼   cup ground cloves
2   tablespoons mace
2   tablespoons ground ginger

1. Mix all ingredients together.
2. Use ½ cup crab boil seasoning for each 6 to 8 crabs or 12 shrimp.

※ Add ½ cup vinegar (tarragon or wine) to the boiling pot for every 6 crabs. This eliminates the odor and retards frothing.

LOBSTER

Live lobster is available at many seafood markets. When purchasing live lobster, look for moving legs. When the lobster is picked up, its tail should curl under its body. Lobster may be refrigerated briefly, but should be cooked soon after buying.

Cooked lobster is also available. Many seafood markets will steam them while you wait. The shell of a cooked lobster should be bright red. There should be no unpleasant odor.

There is little meat in a lobster. One live 1¼-pound lobster yields ¾ to 1 pound of meat.

OYSTERS

When purchasing live oysters, the shells should be tightly closed or should spring closed when tapped. If the shell does not close, the oyster is dead and should not be used. The shell opens when the oyster is cooked.

Oysters can be kept alive in the refrigerator several days.

When buying shucked (shelled) oysters, look for those that are plump and cream-colored. The liquor surrounding the oysters should be clear rather than milky. Do not rinse the oysters before cooking as the liquor enhances the flavor.

Oysters are graded by size. The weight is indicated on the package. Allow six to twelve oysters per person, or approximately four ounces per person if served as an entrée; less, if used as an appetizer.

SCALLOPS

Scallops are available fresh or frozen. The large, common variety is the sea scallop which ranges in color from white to orange to pink. The small, delicately flavored bay scallops are creamy white, pink or light tan. These may be used interchangeably.

Fresh scallops may be kept in the refrigerator for several days. If scallops are frozen, they should be thawed in the refrigerator. If the scallops are sandy, rinse them in cool water and pat dry with paper towels. One pound of scallops serves three to four.

SHRIMP

Fresh shrimp are available raw or cooked (in the shell or peeled). Fresh shrimp should be firm and have no unpleasant odor. Frozen shrimp should be ivory in color. If they are white, they are freezer-burned. Store any shrimp, fresh, frozen or thawed in the refrigerator. Use within one day after purchase.

Shrimp are sold by size and range from very small to jumbo. Grading is based on the number of shrimp per pound.

When buying shrimp, allow at least ten small, seven medium or six large shrimp per serving.

BEER BOIL

5	pounds unpeeled shrimp	2	tablespoons black pepper
2	quarts water	2	tablespoons dry mustard
2	quarts beer (5 12-ounce cans)	2	tablespoons celery seed
5	tablespoons salt	2	cups tarragon vinegar

1. Combine all ingredients except shrimp. Bring mixture to a boil.
2. Add shrimp and boil 8 to 10 minutes.
3. Drain and leave shrimp in shells for 30 minutes.

SHRIMP TO THE POUND	HEADS ON COUNT	TAILS ON COUNT
Small	31 to 33	51 to 60
Medium	26 to 30	41 to 50
Large	19 to 21	31 to 35
Jumbo	13 to 15	21 to 25

※ To eliminate the odor of boiling shrimp, add a few fresh celery leaves to the pot.

※ Place shells, heads and tails in an airtight freezer bag and store in freezer until garbage collection day.

SHRIMP WITH FETA CHEESE

1	large onion, chopped	2	small dried red chiles or ½ teaspoon cayenne pepper
½	cup olive oil		
1	16-ounce can tomatoes, drained and chopped	2	cloves garlic, minced
		2	pounds shrimp, peeled and deveined
2	tablespoons chopped, fresh cilantro		
		½	pound feta cheese
1	teaspoon salt	¼	cup vodka, optional

1. Sauté onion in oil until transparent. Add tomatoes, cilantro, salt, chiles and garlic. Cover. Simmer 40 minutes.
2. Add shrimp to sauce. Pour into scallop shells or a 3-quart baking dish.
3. Crumble cheese over shrimp.
4. Bake 10 to 15 minutes at 350°.
5. Remove from oven. Pour heated vodka over shrimp and flame.

This is wonderful served with rice or new potatoes.

Serves 6 to 8

SHRIMP DILL

An elegant meal that can be prepared in minutes.

6 tablespoons butter
4 cups shrimp, peeled, deveined and cooked
3 4-ounce cans sliced mushrooms, drained
2 cups sour cream
2 teaspoons salt
2 teaspoons Worcestershire sauce
1½ teaspoons dried dill weed, or 2 tablespoons fresh dill, chopped
Dash paprika
2 to 3 teaspoons lemon juice
8 cups hot, fluffy rice

1. Melt butter in a large skillet. Add cooked shrimp and mushrooms. Warm over low heat.
2. Drain ½ the butter from shrimp and mushroom mixture.
3. Combine sour cream, salt, Worcestershire, dill weed and paprika. Add to shrimp. Heat in pan.
4. Cook, stirring occasionally, until thoroughly heated. Do not boil.
5. Sprinkle with lemon juice and serve over rice.

Serves 6

SPICY NEW ORLEANS SHRIMP

Serve in large soup bowls with lots of sauce and lots of napkins!

1 pound butter
1 16-ounce bottle Italian dressing
Juice of 4 lemons
2 ounces black pepper
4 pounds large shrimp, unpeeled

1. Melt butter and mix with dressing, lemon juice and pepper.
2. Pour sauce over shrimp and marinate several hours.
3. Bake 40 minutes at 325°.

Serves 8 to 10

CREOLE SHRIMP AND CHICKEN

1 pound medium shrimp peeled and deveined
1 teaspoon salt
4 chicken breast halves
3 tablespoons vegetable oil
½ cup green bell pepper, diced
1 small onion, diced
1 10-ounce can tomato sauce with chunks
½ cup dry sherry

1½ teaspoons salt
1 tablespoon Worcestershire sauce
¼ teaspoon pepper
¼ teaspoon thyme
1 to 2 tablespoons parsley
1 cup half and half
   Cooked long grain and wild rice

1. Preheat oven to 350°.
2. Boil shrimp in salted water for 2 to 3 minutes. Drain and chill.
3. Brown chicken breasts in oil. Set aside. Sauté pepper and onions in oil.
4. Combine sautéed vegetables, tomato sauce, sherry, salt, Worcestershire, pepper, thyme and parsley. Cut chicken breasts into pieces. Add to vegetable and tomato mixture.
5. Bake in a 4-quart casserole 45 minutes.
6. Add shrimp and cream to chicken mixture. Heat thoroughly. Serve over hot, fluffy rice.

Serves 6

SHRIMP, RICE AND ARTICHOKE CASSEROLE

Make ahead for a great dish.

1 medium onion, chopped	½ cup tomato sauce
2 ribs celery, chopped	1 cup whipping cream
3 cloves garlic	¾ teaspoon cayenne pepper
2 green bell peppers, chopped	Salt to taste
2 bay leaves	2 14-ounce cans artichoke
4 tablespoons butter	hearts, drained and halved
3 pounds shrimp, peeled,	1 to 2 cups grated Cheddar or
deveined and boiled	Swiss cheese
4 cups cooked rice	

1. Preheat oven to 350°.
2. Sauté onion, celery, garlic, bell pepper and bay leaves in butter. Add cooked shrimp. Remove garlic.
3. Add rice. Stir until hot.
4. Add tomato sauce, cream, cayenne, salt and artichokes. Stir well. Remove bay leaves.
5. Pour into a 9 by 13 by 2-inch glass baking dish. If casserole is not to be baked immediately, cover and refrigerate until ready to bake.
6. Before baking, cover with cheese.
7. Bake, covered, 30 minutes or until all ingredients are thoroughly heated.

Serves 6 to 8

PENANG SHRIMP CURRY

2 pounds shrimp, peeled and deveined
1 onion, sliced
2 shallots
1 rib celery, coarsely chopped
1 carrot, sliced lengthwise
1 apple, quartered
1 green bell pepper, quartered
1 chile pepper, seeds removed
1 tomato, quartered
1 clove garlic, minced
1 sprig parsley

½ teaspoon thyme
1 bay leaf
2 whole cloves
2 sprigs mint
½ teaspoon basil
Salt and pepper to taste
¼ teaspoon each marjoram, nutmeg, and cayenne pepper
1 tablespoon curry powder
Grated rind of 1 lime
2 tablespoons all-purpose flour
2 tablespoons butter

1. Cook shrimp in boiling, salted water for 7 minutes. Save 1 quart of liquid. Set aside.
2. In a large saucepan, combine remaining ingredients, except flour and butter. Add reserved liquid and bring to a boil.
3. Mix flour and butter to make a paste. Stir into mixture and simmer 1 hour.
4. Strain liquid and add shrimp. Simmer 2 minutes.

Serve over hot, fluffy rice.

Serves 5 to 6

RUM SHRIMP

A rum flavored dish that can be served in bowls with French bread to soak up liquid, or over rice.

3 dozen large, shrimp, peeled except for tail
½ cup butter

½ cup light rum
2 large cloves garlic, minced

1. Place shrimp flat in bottom of shallow baking pan.
2. Melt butter. Add garlic and rum. Pour mixture over shrimp, distributing garlic evenly.
3. Cover. Marinate 30 to 60 minutes at room temperature.
4. Remove cover. Place pan under broiler. Broil shrimp 3 minutes. Turn each shrimp over and broil an additional 3 minutes.

Serves 6

CURRIED SEAFOOD WITH AVOCADO

7 tablespoons butter, divided
4 tablespoons all-purpose flour
2 teaspoons curry powder
1 teaspoon salt
2 cups milk

1 pound large shrimp, peeled and deveined
3 tablespoons dry sherry
½ pound lump crab meat
½ cup soft, white bread crumbs
2 avocados, sliced

1. Melt 4 tablespoons butter in saucepan. Whisk in flour, curry powder and salt until bubbly. Add milk. Cook, stirring, until thick and bubbly.
2. In a skillet, melt 2 tablespoons butter and sauté shrimp 1 minute. Add sherry and cook 1 minute. Add crab and sauté 2 to 3 minutes.
3. Stir seafood into curry sauce and pour into a greased 1-quart casserole.
4. Melt remaining 1 tablespoon butter. Toss with bread crumbs. Sprinkle crumbs on top of casserole. Broil until bubbly and lightly toasted.
5. Serve on avocado slices.

Variation:
Shrimp can also be served over rice and topped with peanuts, raisins, chopped eggs and toasted coconut.

Serves 6

BAKED SHRIMP IN SCALLOP SHELLS

1½ pounds shrimp, boiled, peeled and deveined
¼ cup chopped green onion
1 clove garlic, minced
2 tablespoons melted butter
¼ cup all-purpose flour
½ teaspoon salt
1½ cups half and half

½ cup dry white wine
¼ cup soft bread crumbs
2 tablespoons grated Parmesan cheese
2 teaspoons chopped parsley
¼ teaspoon paprika
1½ tablespoons melted butter

1. Preheat oven to 350°.
2. Cut shrimp in half lengthwise.
3. Sauté onion and garlic in 2 tablespoons butter until transparent.
4. Stir in flour and salt. Remove from heat. Gradually add half and half, stirring constantly, until very thick. Stir in wine and shrimp.
5. Spoon shrimp mixture into a buttered 7 by 11-inch casserole or 6 large buttered scallop shells.
6. Combine bread crumbs, cheese, parsley, paprika and 1½ tablespoons butter. Mix until crumbly. Sprinkle crumb mixture over shrimp.
7. Bake 15 to 20 minutes or until lightly browned on top.

Serves 6 as a main course
or 8 to 10 as an appetizer

CLASSIC SHRIMP CURRY

1 cup finely chopped onion
1 cup finely chopped celery
1 cup finely chopped green bell
   pepper
½ cup finely chopped
   red bell pepper
1 cup butter
½ teaspoon salt
1 teaspoon black pepper
2 teaspoons curry powder

⅛ teaspoon cayenne pepper
1 tablespoon Worcestershire
   sauce
2 cups chicken broth
1 tablespoon cornstarch
1 cup half and half
1½ pounds shrimp, peeled,
   deveined, boiled and cut
   into bite-size pieces

1. Sauté onion, celery and bell peppers in butter until soft, but not brown. Add salt, pepper, curry powder, cayenne, Worcestershire and chicken broth. Bring to a boil. Reduce heat and simmer ½ hour.
2. Dissolve cornstarch in a small amount of half and half. Add remainder of half and half.
3. Stir cream and cornstarch into vegetable and curry mixture. Cook until thickened.
4. Add shrimp 5 minutes before serving. Heat thoroughly.

Serve over hot, fluffy rice.

Variation:
½ cup raisins may be simmered in the sauce.

Serves 6

CRAB AND SHRIMP BAKE

1	green bell pepper, chopped	1	teaspoon Worcestershire sauce
1	onion, chopped	1	cup mayonnaise
1	cup chopped celery	1	pound shrimp, peeled and
4	tablespoons butter		deveined
½	teaspoon salt	4	ounces fresh crab
⅛	teaspoon pepper	½	cup buttered bread crumbs

1. Preheat oven to 350°.
2. Sauté bell pepper, onion and celery in butter until softened.
3. Combine vegetables with remaining ingredients, except crumbs. Place in a buttered 3-quart baking dish.
4. Sprinkle with crumbs and bake 30 minutes.

Serves 6 to 8

CRAB WITH GRUYÈRE SAUCE

Delicious and easy to prepare.

White Sauce:

¼	cup butter	1	cup grated Gruyère cheese
¼	cup all-purpose flour	1	small green bell pepper,
½	teaspoon salt		chopped
¼	teaspoon pepper	2	5-ounce cans sliced water
2	cups milk		chestnuts, drained
		1	2-ounce jar diced pimientos,
			drained
		1	pound fresh crab

1. Melt butter over low heat. Add flour, salt and pepper. Heat, stirring constantly, until bubbly. Add 2 cups milk. Remove from heat.
2. Blend well. Return to heat. Bring to a boil, stirring constantly. Boil 1 minute. Add cheese. Stir until melted.
3. Add bell pepper, water chestnuts, pimientos and crab. Return to heat. Stir until thoroughly heated.

Serve over warmed English muffins, rice, pastry shells or boiled new potatoes and peas.

Serves 4 to 6

CRAB MEAT IMPERIAL

2 pounds lump crab meat
1 onion, finely grated
1 green bell pepper, finely chopped
¼ cup butter
½ cup chopped pimiento

Cream Sauce:
4 tablespoons butter
4 tablespoons all-purpose flour
2 cups hot milk
½ teaspoon salt
½ to ¾ teaspoon cayenne pepper
Noodles or rice

1. Sauté onion and bell pepper in butter. Add crab and pimiento.
2. In a small saucepan, melt butter, blend in flour and add milk. Whisk constantly until sauce thickens. Season with salt and cayenne. Add crab. Mix thoroughly.
3. Serve over hot rice or noodles.

Serves 12

CRAB MEAT AU GRATIN

4 tablespoons butter
½ garlic clove, minced
4 tablespoons all-purpose flour
1 cup milk
⅔ cup half and half
1 teaspoon salt
White pepper to taste
Tabasco sauce

¼ to ½ cup Madeira wine
1 cup grated Gruyère or Swiss cheese
¼ cup minced parsley
1 pound fresh crab meat
½ cup cracker crumbs
3 tablespoons butter

1. Preheat oven to 400°.
2. Melt 4 tablespoons butter. Add garlic and simmer 2 to 3 minutes. Add flour and blend until smooth. Add milk and cream. Stir until thickened. Add seasonings and wine. Heat thoroughly. Remove from heat. Cool.
3. Fold in cheese and parsley. Gently stir in crab.
4. Sauté crumbs in 3 tablespoons butter.
5. Place crab mixture in a greased baking dish and cover with bread crumbs.
6. Bake 10 minutes or until thoroughly heated and crumbs are brown.

Serves 6

HERBED CRAB CASSEROLE

4 ribs celery, chopped
1 large green bell pepper, chopped
1 bunch green onions, chopped
1 medium onion, chopped
¼ cup butter
1 pound claw crab meat
3 eggs

3 hard-cooked eggs, grated
4 cups seasoned stuffing mix
⅛ teaspoon cayenne pepper
Garlic salt to taste
Seafood seasoning to taste
2 cups half and half
Dried parsley flakes
Paprika

1. Preheat oven to 375°.
2. Sauté celery, bell pepper, scallions and onions in butter until soft.
3. Let mixture cool. Add crab, raw eggs, hard-cooked eggs and 3 cups stuffing mix. Season with cayenne, garlic salt and seafood seasoning. Mix well. Add half and half until desired consistency.
4. Pour into a greased 9 by 13-inch baking dish or into 8 individual, greased shells. Sprinkle remaining stuffing mix, parsley and cayenne on top.
5. Bake 20 minutes.

Serves 8

SCALLOPS WITH SNOW PEAS

1 tablespoon cornstarch
2 teaspoons soy sauce
½ cup water
1 tablespoon vegetable oil
1 pound sea scallops, cut in half or bay scallops

2 leeks, sliced
½ pound snow peas
1 cup Chinese mushrooms
1 teaspoon grated ginger root
Red pepper flakes to taste

1. In a small bowl, mix cornstarch, soy sauce and water until smooth.
2. Heat oil in a wok over high heat. Add scallops. Stir fry one minute. Add leeks, peas, mushrooms, ginger and pepper. Stir fry 1 minute.
3. Pour cornstarch mixture over scallops and vegetables. Stir until thickened.

Serve over hot, fluffy rice.

Serves 4

SCALLOPED OYSTERS

Seasonings:

1 pint oysters	Nutmeg
½ cup butter	Dried parsley
2 cups coarsely crumbled saltines	Pepper
¼ teaspoon salt	
½ cup half and half	
1 teaspoon Worcestershire	

1. Place ⅓ of cracker crumbs in bottom of a greased 1½ quart casserole.
2. Cover with ½ the oysters. Sprinkle with nutmeg, parsley and pepper.
3. Repeat layers, beginning with crackers and ending with seasonings.
4. Combine cream, Worcestershire and salt. Pour this mixture over layers.
5. Add remaining ⅓ of crackers.
6. Bake at 350° for 40 minutes or until lightly browned and bubbly.

Serves 6 to 8

SWAN'S PATH SCALLOPS

4 tablespoons butter	Salt and pepper to taste
½ clove garlic, minced	¼ cup finely chopped parsley
2 pounds scallops	½ cup buttered cracker crumbs
½ cup half and half	

1. Preheat oven to 400°.
2. Melt butter. Add garlic and sauté until garlic is soft.
3. Pour into an 8 by 8-inch buttered, baking dish.
4. Drain scallops well. If sea scallops are used, slice in half.
5. Dip scallops in garlic butter. Arrange in a single layer in baking dish.
6. Pour cream over scallops. Add salt and pepper. Spread chopped parsley over scallops. Sprinkle buttered cracker crumbs on top. Bake exactly 15 minutes.

Variation I:
¼ teaspoon dry mustard and ¼ teaspoon paprika may be combined with bread crumbs.

Variation II:
4 green onions may be chopped and added to garlic.

Serves 6

EASY SKEWERED SCALLOPS

1 pound scallops	Butter
Salt and pepper	Fresh white bread crumbs
All-purpose flour	Bay leaves

1. Salt and pepper scallops. Coat with flour. Dip in melted butter and roll in bread crumbs.
2. Placing a bay leaf between every 2 scallops, thread on a small, sharp skewer.
3. Broil 2 to 3 minutes on each side until scallops are browned and springy to the touch. Scallops will be tough if overcooked.

Serve over rice pilaf.

Serves 4

SCALLOPS IN WINE CHEESE SAUCE

1½ pounds scallops	3 tablespoons all-purpose flour
½ cup dry white wine	½ cup half and half or whipping
½ teaspoon salt	cream
Heavy dash cayenne pepper	1 cup grated Swiss or ½ Swiss
¼ cup finely minced onion	and ½ Parmesan cheese
3 tablespoons butter	

1. Preheat oven to 400°.
2. Place scallops in saucepan with wine, salt, cayenne and onion. If sea scallops are used, cut into bite-size pieces. Simmer, covered, 2 to 3 minutes. Drain. Reserve 1 cup liquid.
3. Melt butter in saucepan and blend in flour. Add reserved liquid and half and half. Whisk to make a smooth cream sauce. Add grated cheese and scallops.
4. For an appetizer, bake in individual scallop shells. For a main course, bake in a 1½-quart casserole 10 to 12 minutes. Serve over hot, fluffy rice.

Scallops can be prepared in the morning and refrigerated until ready to bake.

Serves 8 to 10 as a main course
12 to 14 as an appetizer

SOLE WITH LIME MAYONNAISE

2   pounds fillets of sole, flounder,
        or redfish ½ to ¾-inch thick
    Salt and white pepper to taste
¼ to ½ cup seasoned bread crumbs

6   tablespoons butter
2   tablespoons fresh lime juice
¾   cup dry white wine

1. Preheat oven to 375°.
2. Season fish fillets with salt and white pepper. Arrange fish in a large, shallow baking dish. Sprinkle with bread crumbs, covering well.
3. In a saucepan, combine butter,lime and wine. Simmer 5 minutes.
4. Pour sauce over fish. Bake 20 minutes.
5. Remove from oven and turn on broiler. Broil 5 minutes or until bread crumbs are crusty.
6. Serve with lime mayonnaise.

LIME MAYONNAISE

½   cup mayonnaise
2   teaspoons Dijon mustard

2   tablespoons fresh lime juice

1. Combine all ingredients. Beat until smooth.
2. Serve with sole, flounder or redfish.

Serves 6

SPINACH STUFFED TROUT

Spinach is a delicious addition to this traditional stuffing.

6   whole trout, cleaned, washed, and boned
Salt and pepper
¼   cup grated onion
1   tablespoon butter
¼   cup butter, softened
1   10-ounce package chopped spinach, cooked and drained

Salt and pepper to taste
1   egg
¼   cup milk
1   teaspoon salt
¾   cup toasted bread crumbs
½   cup shredded Swiss cheese
2   tablespoons butter

1. Preheat oven to 500°.
2. Wash trout and pat dry. Salt and pepper inside of fish.
3. Sauté onion in 1 tablespoon butter.
4. Combine ¼ cup butter, spinach, onion, salt and pepper. Spread mixture inside fish cavity.
5. Place egg, milk and 1 teaspoon salt in a bowl. Beat well.
6. In another bowl, combine bread crumbs and cheese.
7. Dip each fish into egg mixture and roll in crumbs.
8. Place fish in a single layer in a greased, shallow baking dish. Sprinkle with any remaining crumbs. Dot with 2 tablespoons butter.
9. Bake 15 to 20 minutes or until fish are tender and browned.

Serve with tartar sauce, hollandaise or salsa.

Serves 6

BROILED SALMON IN WINE BUTTER

1½ cups dry white wine
3 tablespoons minced shallots
3 tablespoons whipping cream
1½ cups unsalted butter, chilled
    and cut into small pieces

Juice of ½ lemon
Salt and white pepper to taste
8 salmon steaks

1. Boil wine and shallots in a small, heavy saucepan until liquid is reduced to 2 tablespoons.
2. Remove from heat. Whisk in cream and two pieces of butter.
3. Over low heat, whisk in remaining butter, one piece at a time.
4. Strain sauce. Season to taste with salt and white pepper. Add lemon juice.
5. Broil salmon steaks until lightly pink.
6. Spoon sauce over steaks.

Serves 8

FAVORITE BROILED FISH

2 pounds skinned fish fillets
2 tablespoons lemon juice
½ cup grated Parmesan cheese
¼ cup butter, softened
3 tablespoons mayonnaise

3 tablespoons chopped green onions
¼ teaspoon salt
Dash Tabasco sauce

1. Place fillets in a single layer on a well-greased broiler pan. Brush fish with lemon juice.
2. Combine Parmesan cheese, butter, mayonnaise, green onions, salt and Tabasco. Set aside.
3. Broil fish 4 to 6 minutes, or until it flakes easily with fork.
4. Remove fish from heat. Spread with cheese mixture.
5. Broil 2 to 3 minutes or until lightly browned.

Serves 6

BAKED FISH FILLETS

2   pounds fish fillets
    Salt
1   cup sour cream
1   cup mayonnaise

1   small package ranch style
    salad dressing mix
2   2.8-ounce cans French fried
    onion rings, crushed

1. Cut fish into serving size pieces. Sprinkle with salt.
2. Combine sour cream, mayonnaise and dressing mix.
3. Dip fish into 1 cup sour cream mixture. Roll in crushed onion rings.
4. Place in a greased 9 by 13-inch baking dish. Bake at 350° for 20 minutes.
5. Serve with remaining sour cream mixture.

Serves 4 to 6

FISH CROQUETTES

1   pound fresh or frozen fish
    fillets
1   package finely ground saltine
    crackers (45)
3   eggs, beaten
¼   cup finely chopped green
    onion

⅓   cup finely chopped green bell
    pepper
⅓   cup finely chopped celery
    Salt and pepper to taste

1. Add fish to simmering salted water. Cover. Remove from heat and let stand 5 minutes. Drain fish. Flake with a fork.
2. Combine fish, eggs, cracker crumbs, green onion, bell pepper and celery. Season to taste. Roll into 1-inch balls.
3. Brown in hot fat. Turn once while frying.

Serve with tartar or cocktail sauce.

These may be prepared ahead of time and fried when ready to use.

Yields 24 balls

SEAFOOD AND OKRA GUMBO

Gumbo is traditionally better when prepared one day and refrigerated, then heated and served the next.

½	cup vegetable oil
½	cup all-purpose flour
2	cups finely chopped fresh okra
1	cup finely chopped celery
1	cup finely chopped onion
½	cup finely chopped green onions
1	16-ounce can tomatoes
1	8-ounce can tomato sauce
2	10¾-ounce cans beef broth and 2 cans water or 2 quarts beef stock
2	pounds shrimp, peeled and deveined
1	cup lump crab meat
1	pint oysters, drained

Seasonings:

¼	teaspoon minced garlic
1	teaspoon black pepper
2	teaspoons salt
½	teaspoon seasoned salt
3	bay leaves
¼	teaspoon thyme
⅛	teaspoon oregano
2	tablespoons sugar
1	teaspoon Tabasco sauce
½	teaspoon cayenne pepper
1	tablespoon dry sherry

1. Make a roux by combining oil and flour in a large, heavy pot. Being careful not to burn, cook, stirring constantly over low to medium heat until mixture is a deep dark brown. This will take approximately 30 minutes.
2. Combine okra, celery, onion and green onions. Sauté in roux until tender.
3. Add tomatoes, tomato sauce, broth and seasonings.
4. Simmer 2 to 3 hours. Add seafood the last 10 minutes.

Serve over rice in large bowls.

Serves 8 to 10

CREOLE RÉMOULADE SAUCE

2 cloves garlic, minced
3 tablespoons grated onion
1 cup mayonnaise
½ cup oil
½ cup ketchup
1 teaspoon black pepper
1 tablespoon Worcestershire
 sauce

1 tablespoon water
1 tablespoon vinegar
1 teaspoon Creole mustard
1 teaspoon prepared horseradish
 Dash Tabasco sauce

1. Blend all ingredients in blender.
2. Chill in refrigerator until ready to use. Refrigerate any remaining sauce.

Yields 2¼ cups

RED SEAFOOD SAUCE

1 cup ketchup
1 cup chili sauce
2 tablespoons cider vinegar
1 tablespoon lemon juice

¼ cup prepared horseradish
1 teaspoon Tabasco sauce
2 teaspoons Worcestershire
 sauce

1. Combine all ingredients.
2. Store in refrigerator.

Yields 2½ cups

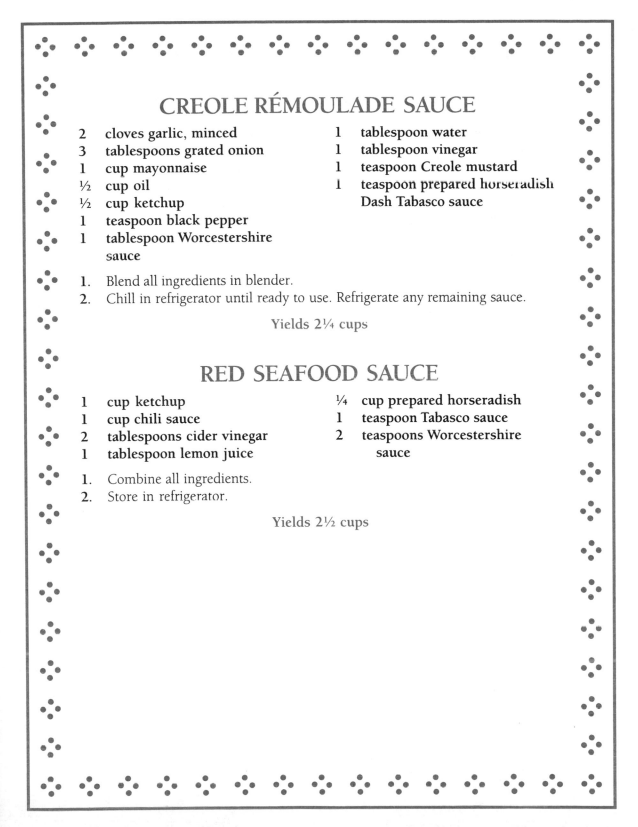

SPICY CHILI SAUCE FOR SEAFOOD

2   cups mayonnaise
½   cup ketchup
4   tablespoons water
1   clove garlic, minced
1   onion, grated
2   teaspoons prepared mustard
1½ tablespoons Worcestershire
      sauce

Dash Tabasco sauce
Dash paprika
1   teaspoon salt
2   tablespoons vinegar
½   cup chili sauce
1   cup vegetable oil
2   teaspoons pepper
1   teaspoon cayenne pepper

1. Mix all ingredients together.
2. Store in refrigerator.

Yields 1 quart

VEGETABLES, FRUITS AND ACCOMPANIMENTS

Leafy Vegetables or Greens

These are the most varied and available of all fresh vegetables. They are extremely perishable and should be used as soon as possible after purchasing. Thorough washing and trimming is the only preparation required, as they are often used raw in salads or on sandwiches. They may be cooked, but cooking time should be kept to a minimum to preserve color, flavor and texture.

Kinds and Varieties

Members of the Lettuce Family (detailed in the salad section)

Mustard, Collard, Beet and Turnip greens

Spinach

Sorrel

Vine leaves

✳ Spinach can be very difficult to clean and should never be drained in a colander, as grit will settle on the leaves. It is best to separate the leaves and soak in a full sink or very large bowl for 30 minutes. Drain the sink, rinse it and repeat the process.

✳ Some leafy vegetables should have the core removed before cooking to avoid any bitter taste.

The Cabbage Family

This family encompasses a large and varied group of vegetables and offers a great range in texture and flavor.

Kinds and Varieties

Head Cabbage—Includes red, green, Savoy and Brussels sprouts that are all tightly rolled leaves of vegetables compressed into a compact sphere shape

Cylindrical Cabbage—A cabbage with a loose-leaf, elongated shape

Kohlrabi—A cabbage/turnip-like vegetable with an edible stem

Broccoli—A variety with green buds on a fleshy, tough stalk

Cauliflower—Actually a compressed flower

❊ To prevent odor when cooking cabbage, place a half cup of vinegar next to the stove top. Also, a piece of bread placed near the stove top will absorb odors.

ROOTS AND TUBERS

Roots and tubers are vegetables grown underground, such as beets, carrots, rutabagas, parsnips, potatoes, sweet potatoes, turnips and Jerusalem artichokes. Potatoes, beets, turnips and carrots are best when harvested while relatively young. Other roots and tubers are left in the ground to mature. When purchasing these vegetables, look for ones that are firm and blemish free. Store, unwashed, in a moisture free area. Moisture encourages decay. If the vegetable has tops, cut off before storing. (The tops draw moisture from the root of vegetable.)

Potatoes

❊ Soak potatoes first in salty water to speed the baking process.

❊ Wrap buttered or greased potatoes in foil to insure tender skins.

❊ When crisp skins are desired, bake buttered or greased potatoes unwrapped.

❊ Soak raw, peeled and cut potatoes in cold water for 30 minutes before frying. This makes a crisper french fry.

❊ Add a pinch of baking soda along with milk and butter to insure light, fluffy potatoes.

PODS AND SEEDS

This family consists of lima and broad beans, corn and peas, green and wax beans, snow peas, bean sprouts and okra. They should be young and tender, small and brightly colored.

MUSHROOMS

Mushrooms are generally cultivated indoors. The caps should be closed, showing no gills on underside. Refrigerate unwashed. Mushrooms keep only 1 or 2 days. Do not wash in water. Simply wipe off with a damp paper towel.

VEGETABLE FRUITS

Avocados, eggplant, peppers and tomatoes are technically fruits.

Avocados

Avocados are available in several varieties and should feel slightly soft but not mushy. They freeze well when peeled and mashed. Thaw in refrigerator.

Eggplant

Eggplant is bitter and contains a large amount of water that should be removed before cooking. Peel and slice the eggplant, then salt the pieces and allow to stand for thirty minutes. This draws out the excess moisture and bitter juices.

Peppers

Peppers are best when firm and glossy. Color should be bright. They are available in many varieties ranging from hot to sweet. Some change color as they ripen, but may be used at any time during the ripening process.

Kinds and Varieties

Anaheim peppers—A favorite in Southwestern cooking; often called mild green chiles; mild flavor

Ancho peppers—Used in Mexican and Southwestern cooking; often called poblano peppers; dried peppers often used in enchiladas; often mashed and used in mole sauce; may be mild or hot

Banana peppers—Range from shiny yellow (sweet) to red (hot) during the ripening process; usually sold in yellow stage and often used for pickling

Bell peppers—Very common and used in many recipes; may be green, yellow, brown or red; a very sweet, mild flavor

Chiltecpin peppers—Very small, red or green round peppers; extremely hot in flavor; may be used interchangeably with tepin peppers

Jalapeño peppers—Very common hot peppers; range from mild to hot; used in Mexican and Southwestern cooking

Pimiento peppers—Processed peppers sold in jars; mild, almost bitter taste; used in many recipes

Serrano peppers—Resemble jalapeños but are much smaller; range from hot to extremely hot; used in Mexican cooking or served fresh

Peeling Peppers

Peppers are generally roasted before peeling. Slit each pepper to prevent bursting during roasting. The following methods of roasting are used most often.

1. Place peppers on a baking sheet and place on uppermost rack. Turn peppers often while roasting.

2. Place peppers directly on rack in oven (550°). Do not turn. Watch carefully.

3. Use a skewer or a long fork to roast pepper over the flame of a gas burner at a moderate or medium setting. Pepper is done when brown on all sides.

Be careful to avoid contact with skin while handling peppers and wash hands thoroughly when finished. Wear gloves if possible.

Tomatoes

Tomatoes should be stored at room temperature, not in the refrigerator. Cold inhibits the ripening process. To induce and speed ripening, place in a paper bag with slits cut in the side.

Seeding—Slice tomato in half, then squeeze to force the seed out. If the tomato is overly ripe, try scooping the seeds out with a spoon.

Peeling—When peeling a large quantity of tomatoes, drop in boiling water for fifteen to thirty seconds, then quickly submerge in cold water. The skins should slip off easily.

Stuffing—Scoop out seeds and pulp and turn upside down on a paper towel to drain.

THE SQUASH FAMILY

The squash family consists essentially of gourds which are fleshy vegetables with seeds on the inside and protective rinds on the outside. There are numerous varieties of squash.

Summer Varieties (April through August) include zucchini, yellow crookneck and scalloped squash; the smaller they are, the more tender they will be.

Winter Varieties (October through February) include acorn, butternut, buttercup, Hubbard, spaghetti squash, pumpkins, and chayote.

Many varieties can be kept up to 3 months in a cool, dry place.

STALK VEGETABLES

Stalk vegetables are those with plant stems that are fibrous and stringy, with tops or leaves. They are best when young and must be trimmed of tough fibers that do not soften when cooked.

Asparagus—February to June

Celery—year round

Fennel—fall and early winter

Swiss chard—June through October

Bok Choy—year round

Do not wash squash before storing. Moisture promotes decay.

THE ONION FAMILY

Strong flavored vegetables such as onions, garlic, shallots, leeks and scallions are used as seasonings.

Spanish yellow and white onions are very pungent. They are cured, dried and available year round. They should be firm and dry when purchased. If shoots are evident, they have been stored too long at a high temperature.

Leeks and Scallions are sold fresh year round and should be refrigerated.

Garlic bulbs should be tightly closed with unwrinkled skins.

ARTICHOKE

Artichoke is actually an edible thistle that is grown in California. It is best when purchased from March to June. The leaves should be closed tightly and should be bright green with no discoloration. From November to March the leaves may be somewhat discolored due to frost. However, the leaves may actually be thicker and have more meat.

RICE

Rice is a staple grain of which there are more than 7,000 varieties throughout the world. Varieties, preparation and cooking methods vary from country to country. The following types of rice are generally found everywhere.

Brown rice has a slightly chewy texture and a nutty flavor. It is whole grained (containing more nutrients) and unpolished, with both the hull and a small amount of bran removed.

Converted rice is also called parboiled or processed rice. Parboiled rice retains the nutrients that make rice an excellent staple. It cooks into plump, separate grains that are somewhat bland.

Precooked rice, or instant rice, is a long grained white variety that has been commercially cooked then rinsed and dried before packaging. Precooked rice is dry but tender with a bland flavor. When cooked, it does not separate well like parboiled rice. It is excellent for use in casseroles, desserts, soups and dishes that have a simultaneous cooking process.

Regular rice is milled to remove the hull, germ and most of the bran. It is like converted rice without the nutrients. Regular white rice may have long or short grains. It has a tender texture and bland flavor.

Wild rice is the seed of a grass which grows in shallow lakes and marshes and is not a true rice. It is a long grained, green, tan and brown variety, with a chewy texture and distinct nutty flavor.

※ Do not rinse rice after cooking because some of the nutrients may be lost.

※ Leftover cooked rice will freeze. To reheat, steam, covered in a colander, until thoroughly heated. Fluff with a fork.

Vegetable Flavoring Mixtures

Finely chopped combinations of vegetables, herbs and spices may be used to flavor other preparations. The most frequently used mixtures are French in origin, such as mirepoix, duxelles and a persillade, listed below. Also included is a sofrito, which is Spanish in origin.

Duxelles—Finely chopped mushrooms and onions or shallots cooked in butter to a purée consistency; often used in stuffings, vegetable casseroles or gratins

Mirepoix—Finely diced carrots combined occasionally with celery, seasoned with parsley, thyme and bay leaf; (Cook mixture in butter and sauté over low heat for 30 minutes until soft, but not brown.)

Persillade—Finely chopped combination of parsley and garlic which may or may not be sautéed in butter when served with grilled meats

Sofrito—Primarily consists of chopped tomatoes and onions, sometimes includes peppers and garlic along with meats, such as ham and sausage; may be used in stuffings and gratins

BASIC METHODS OF VEGETABLE COOKERY

Boiling And Steaming

There are several basic methods of boiling.

One calls for immersing green vegetables in a large pot of boiling water and cooking uncovered. This method, often referred to as the French Method or Chip Method, preserves the color, flavor and texture of the vegetable.

Another method of boiling requires that the vegetables be cooked in very little water. This preserves most of the nutrients of the vegetables.

Parboiling is a process in which the vegetables are partially cooked. The cooking process is usually continued in a later preparation.

For all methods, the cooking time should be as brief as possible. Most vegetables should be boiled in salted water.

Steaming

The steaming process involves suspending the vegetables over boiling water in a pierced insert or steaming basket, covering the pan and then cooking until tender.

Frying

There are two basic methods of frying: deep frying in a large amount of oil or frying in as little oil as possible. When frying, using either method, the vegetables should be cut into small pieces to ensure that they will be done throughout.

Selecting the Correct Oil or Fat

Heat tolerance and flavor should be considered when selecting an oil or fat in which to fry. Some varieties of oil will smoke when heated to high temperatures, others will give vegetables a distinct taste or flavor. Pure olive oil has the richest flavor, but it has a low heat tolerance. The oils with high heat tolerance include corn oil, soy bean oil, sunflower oil and peanut oil.

After frying, the oil or fat may be strained of particles and reused. Every time it is reused however, the heat tolerance is lowered.

Stewing and Braising

Both of these methods involve cooking vegetables very slowly in a small amount of liquid to combine the flavors.

Braising—The preparation of one vegetable in a small amount of liquid

Stewing—The process which calls for simmering or boiling slowly in very little liquid

The liquid used in cooking vegetables by either method can alter the end result. When using wine or other acidic liquids such as lemon juice for stewing or braising, the vegetables remain soft and intact throughout the cooking process. Both of these methods rely upon the use of delicate herbs and spices to enhance the final result.

Baking, Broiling and Grilling
Baking

Baking whole vegetables in their skins produces a mellow, yet concentrated flavor. This method is ideal for root vegetables such as potatoes, as well as winter squashes and eggplant. These vegetables have tough outer skins that protect the interior meat or flesh of the vegetable from drying out during the cooking process.

Besides baking vegetables whole, there are other baking methods that provide a great variety of texture and flavor.

Filling and stuffing are methods which utilize the vegetable as a cooking container, filling it with a mixture of other vegetables. This method blends flavors. Tomatoes, artichokes and onions are easily prepared by this method.

Gratin is a baking method that involves chopping the vegetables, then topping with crumbs or cheese to create a crisp brown top with delicately flavored vegetables underneath. Gratins can be cooked with cream to create a moist, rich flavor.

Vegetable Puddings and Soufflés

Vegetable puddings combine puréed vegetables with eggs, grated cheese and butter, and are baked in a mold.

Soufflé—The same ingredients used in vegetable puddings may be used to create a soufflé. Adding beaten egg whites to the mixture creates the lightness that characterizes a soufflé.

Broiling

Broiling utilizes the intense heat of the upper heating unit in an oven by cooking the vegetables approximately six inches from the heat source. This method requires close attention, as it is very quick and browning can take place very rapidly. Soft vegetables such as summer squash, eggplant and tomatoes should be lightly oiled to keep them moist. Always preheat the broiler for 15 to 20 minutes to ensure a hot, even temperature.

Grilling

Grilling outdoors over a charcoal fire is a difficult technique, because it is hard to control the heat of the coals. Vegetables may be cooked directly on the grill or sealed in foil, then placed on the grill. They should be grilled six inches from the coals. Cooking times vary. Test for tenderness by piercing with a long fork.

Preparation of a Whole Artichoke

When shopping for artichokes, purchase those with tightly closed leaves. Avoid those with spreading leaves, as they are tough. Discoloration indicates age and damage and is not desirable, except during the period between October and March when frost may cause browning. During these months, this variation in color is natural and does not affect the flavor of the artichoke.

1. Wash the artichoke in cool water.

2. Using a sharp, stainless steel knife, cut the stem flush with the base so the artichoke will stand upright. (Carbon steel turns artichokes black.)

3. Cut off the top ⅓ of the artichoke.

4. Cut off the thorny tips of leaves and remove any small, coarse or discolored leaves.

5. Rub the cut edges with lemon juice or immerse the whole artichoke in acidulated water to prevent discoloration.

※ The choke may be removed either before or after the cooking process.

Before Cooking—To remove the choke before cooking, first parboil the artichoke for 5 minutes. Plunge it into cold water and drain. Remove small interior leaves and the choke by scooping into the center of the artichoke with a stainless steel spoon. Lift under the hairy fibers of the choke, separating it from the heart. Lift the choke out and discard. At this point, the artichoke is ready to be cooked. It may be boiled or steamed with a variety of seasonings.

After Cooking—To remove the choke after the cooking process is completed, follow the preceding directions from the parboiling stage. After removing the choke, squeeze lemon juice into the empty cavity to prevent discoloration.

Preparation of Fresh Asparagus

1. Wash in cool water to freshen and remove any sand.
2. Hold each stalk near its base and bend it. The stalk will break or snap easily, just below the most tender part. Discard lower portion.
3. The stalks may be peeled with a vegetable scraper if desired.

Cooking Fresh Asparagus

The most frequently used method for cooking asparagus is one in which tied bundles of asparagus are immersed in a large quantity of boiling water.

1. Reserve one loose stalk to check for doneness.
2. Cook for 8 minutes when the water has returned to a boil, after initially placing the bundle in the pan.
3. When this amount of time has elapsed, remove the loose stalk, which should be tender yet firm to the bite, and remove the bundle of asparagus.

FRUIT

Fruit is best when fully ripe and eaten raw. However, some fruits are too bitter or tart to be eaten raw and are only palatable after being cooked. Malaga and Seville oranges are not tasty when fresh, but do provide great flavor when made into marmalade. Some fresh berries, such as gooseberries, are also too tart and are best when cooked and sweetened.

Whether fresh or prepared, fruit is a versatile accompaniment to meals and, depending upon the preparation, can be served for different courses.

Purchase the freshest fruit possible, checking for blemishes and bruises. Never buy overly ripe fruit for preserving. Slightly damaged fruits may be used for pies, puddings, chutneys and wine making. Choose only firm, perfect fruits for freezing. When washing fruit, handle gently and run under cool water or wipe with a dampened towel. When cooking, use as little liquid as possible and do not cook too long, (Nutrients are destroyed during a long cooking process.)

Today, packing and shipping methods are sophisticated and it is possible to find a wide variety of fruits. Also, exotic fruits are beginning to appear on market shelves, providing ingredients for foreign recipes.

Berries

Berries are great delicacies because they are available for a brief time during the short growing season. They are soft and fragile and very perishable, so even with advanced shipping techniques they are available in less quantity than other fruit because of supply limitations. Some berries may be grown in hot houses during off season months, but never seem to have the flavor of those produced during the prime growing season (late spring through summer). Handle berries with care and gently rinse with cool water to clean. Drain in a colander or spread on towels to dry. Berries are delicious fresh or when prepared in a variety of ways such as pies, cobblers, preserves, jams, jellies and other delicious concoctions.

Varieties of Berries—Bilberries, Blueberries, Blackberries, Cranberries, Currants, Gooseberries, Loganberries, Raspberries and Strawberries

Citrus Fruits

Citrus fruits are grown all over the world and are usually available year round. The most common varieties are lemons, limes, oranges and grapefruit. Special varieties of citrus fruit include tangerines, satsumas and clementines. Oranges are available in many varieties and flavors. Citrus fruits can be stored at room temperature or refrigerated. The acidic taste complements fatty meats such as duck and goose, but also tastes good with lamb, pork and poultry. Most of the flavor in citrus fruit can be derived from the rinds when cooking. The juice is used as a multipurpose additive for a wide variety of foods.

Orchard Fruits

Stone Fruits

These fruits are characterized by a center stone or seed that is surrounded by the fruit flesh and covered with a thin protective skin. They are often referred to as orchard fruits. Each has a defined season and is best during that time. These fruits are delicious fresh, but can be prepared in a multitude of ways.

Stone Fruit Varieties—Apricots, Cherries, Nectarines, Olives, Peaches and Plums

Gently wash the fruit and remove the stone before preparing. Some varieties have skins which may be removed by plunging into boiling water briefly, then removing and submerging in cold water. After this process, the skin should easily separate from the fruit.

Grapes

Grapes grow on vines and can be black, white or red, with or without seeds. Raisins, currants or sultanas are dried grapes. Fresh grapes complement many foods, but are particularly good served with cheese. Special varieties of grapes are used to make wine, and these, naturally, would not appear in the market. Grapes should be firm and attached securely to their stems. Store in a cool, dark place. Grapes refrigerate well. Below, are the table varieties, listed by color.

Red Grapes—Cardinal, Catawba, Delaware, Emperor and Red Malaga

Black Grapes—Concord and Ribier

Green/White Grapes—Almeria, Muscadine, Niagara, and Thompson Seedless

Grapes are found year round, but are best from September to November.

Apples and Pears

Apples

Apples are available year round, but are best in the fall. Select firm fruit with no blemishes, and store in a cool, dry place.

Cooking and Baking Varieties—Granny Smith, Pippin, Starr and Rome Beauty

Pies—Cortland, Rhode Island Greening, McIntosh and Yellow Transparent

Eating Varieties—McIntosh, Jonathan, Winesap and Golden or Red Delicious

Always taste the apple before cooking and compensate for its flavor. If it is tart, add a bit more sugar; if it is sour, add a pinch of salt. If it is very sweet, slightly reduce the amount of sugar called for in the recipe. If the apple is juicy, slightly reduce the amount of liquid in the recipe.

After slicing or peeling, sprinkle apples with lemon juice to keep them from turning brown.

Pears

Pears are not as readily available as apples, but appear sporadically throughout the year because different varieties are best at different times. Pears are best in late summer through fall.

Dual Purpose Varieties—(can be used for cooking and eating) Anjou, Bosc, Clapp, Seckel and Winter Nelis

Eating Varieties—Asian, Bartlett and Cornice, which is the most valued as a dessert pear

Tropical Fruits

Tropical fruits do not have a particular season; they come from a tropical climate with a constant temperature where they can grow year round.

Tropical Fruits—Dates, Figs, Guavas, Lychees, Kiwi Fruit, Mangoes, Passion Fruit, Paw-Paws, Pineapples and Pomegranates

These fruits are commonly eaten fresh, although some are used as key ingredients in recipes.

Fruits may be categorized according to physical similarities and methods of growing. Below, fruits are listed according to this criteria, and cooking and eating varieties are noted.

Bananas

Bananas are available year round and are always in season because they are a tropical fruit and flourish constantly. Bananas are most commonly eaten raw, but can be baked. They enhance and complement bacon and chicken. Overly ripe bananas can be used for bread and puddings, but slightly green bananas are best for baking. Because bananas do not freeze or refrigerate well, they should be stored at room temperature.

Melons

Melons are members of the gourd family and there are many varieties that offer a wide range of flavors. They are characterized by hard outer rinds with a crisp, sweet flesh inside. Melons are found throughout the year, but are best from June to September, during the peak growing season. They may be ripened at room temperature and then chilled in the refrigerator. Melons are served by themselves or in fruit salads. They can be used in chilled soups or ices.

Melon Varieties—Cantaloupe, Casaba, Charentais, Crenshaw, Honeydew, Honeyball, Persian, Spanish and Watermelon

LEMON DRESSING FOR VEGETABLES

¼ cup lemon juice
¼ teaspoon paprika
¼ cup vegetable oil
1 tablespoon sugar

1 clove garlic, minced
½ teaspoon salt
1 tablespoon chopped onion

1. Mix all ingredients. Refrigerate several hours before serving.
2. Shake well and pour over freshly cooked vegetables.
3. Refrigerate any left over dressing.

Yields ¾ cup

ASPARAGUS AND CELERY VINAIGRETTE

30 asparagus spears
30 ribs celery

Dressing:
⅓ cup white wine vinegar
1 teaspoon salt
1 tablespoon Dijon mustard
⅔ cup olive oil

Topping:
2 hard cooked eggs, chopped
¼ cup white wine vinegar
6 tablespoons oil
2 green onions finely chopped
Salt and freshly ground pepper
to taste
Paprika

1. Remove tough stalks from asparagus. Steam asparagus until tender.
2. Cut celery ribs the length of asparagus. Place in pan with salted water to cover. Steam until celery is tender and can be cut with a fork. Drain.
3. Combine dressing ingredients and pour over celery and asparagus. Marinate in refrigerator for several hours. Drain off marinade.
4. Insert asparagus spears into celery. Place in a 2-quart baking dish and pour topping over vegetables.
5. Garnish with paprika and serve chilled.

Serves 8 to 10

ASPARAGUS AND TOMATOES WITH BACON

3 strips bacon, crisply cooked
   and crumbled
¼ cup sliced green onions
3 tablespoons vinegar
1 tablespoon water

2 tablespoons sugar
¼ teaspoon salt
1½ pounds fresh asparagus cut in
   1½-inch pieces
3 tomatoes cut in wedges

1. Sauté onion in bacon grease until transparent.
2. Add vinegar, water, sugar and salt. Bring to a boil. Add asparagus. Cover and cook 5 minutes.
3. Add tomato wedges. Cover and cook 3 minutes.
4. Baste vegetables with liquid during cooking.
5. Sprinkle with bacon and serve.

Serves 6 to 8

STUFFED BROILED AVOCADOS

2 tablespoons chopped green
   onion
¼ cup olive oil
1 16-ounce can whole tomatoes,
   drained and chopped
4 tablespoons soft bread crumbs,
   divided

¼ cup fresh Parmesan cheese
3 avocados
2 tablespoons butter, melted
½ teaspoon salt
½ teaspoon white pepper

1. Sauté onion in oil. Stir in tomatoes and cook 5 minutes. Add 2 tablespoons bread crumbs. Keep warm over very low heat.
2. Mix 2 tablespoons bread crumbs and cheese. Cut avocados lengthwise. Remove pits. Brush with butter and sprinkle with salt and pepper. Fill with tomato mixture. Sprinkle with crumbs and cheese mixture. Broil 2 minutes.

Serves 6

※ Mashed avocados can be frozen. Add a generous ½ teaspoon of ascorbic-acid mixture to each cup of avocado. Put into freezer containers leaving ½-inch head space. Freeze. Thaw for use in sandwiches, dips, etc.

ASPARAGUS WITH LEMON CRUMBS

1½ pounds asparagus
3 tablespoons butter
Juice of 1 lemon

⅓ cup bread crumbs
Twisted lemon rind
Salt and pepper

1. Place asparagus and butter in a large skillet. Cover and cook over medium high heat 10 minutes, stirring frequently.
2. Transfer asparagus to a serving platter.
3. Add lemon juice to skillet, then bread crumbs.
4. Cook, stirring constantly approximately 3 minutes, until bread crumbs are crisp.
5. Sprinkle crumbs over asparagus. Garnish with twisted lemon rinds and serve.

Serves 4

PARMESAN BROCCOLI BAKE

1 egg white
¼ cup mayonnaise
3 tablespoons grated Parmesan cheese
2 tablespoons chopped parsley
Grated peel of ½ lemon

2 pounds fresh or 2 10-ounce packages frozen broccoli spears, cooked and drained
2 tablespoons butter, melted
Sesame seeds
Paprika

1. Beat egg white until soft peaks form.
2. Fold in mayonnaise. Stir in cheese, parsley and lemon peel.
3. Arrange cooked broccoli in an oven-proof serving dish. Pour melted butter over broccoli. Top with egg white mixture.
4. Sprinkle with sesame seeds and paprika.
5. Bake 5 minutes at 450° or until puffy and lightly browned.

Serves 4 to 6

RED CABBAGE

½ cup butter
2 tablespoons sugar
½ teaspoon salt
2 tablespoons cider vinegar

2 tablespoons water
1 head red cabbage, shredded
½ cup currant jelly
Pinch ground cloves, optional

1. In a 6-quart Dutch oven, melt butter over low heat. Add sugar, salt, vinegar and water. Add cabbage. Cover and simmer 1 hour.
2. Just before serving, add currant jelly and cloves if desired. Serve hot with pork chops.

Serves 4 to 6

COMPANY CABBAGE

A good dish to serve with chicken or pork.

4 ribs celery
1 small green bell pepper
3 medium carrots
¼ cup butter
1 teaspoon chopped onion

1 small head green cabbage, shredded
Salt and pepper to taste
Seasoned salt to taste

1. Cut celery, bell pepper and carrots into julienne strips.
2. Melt butter in a large Dutch oven. Add celery, bell pepper, carrots and onion.
3. Season cabbage. Place over other vegetables.
4. Cover pan tightly. Cook over high heat until vegetables begin to sizzle. Reduce heat. Cook 15 to 20 minutes. Do not stir.
5. When cabbage is cooked, turn upside down into a serving bowl.
6. Sprinkle with coarse black pepper.

Serves 6 to 8

※ When cooking cabbage, place a small container of vinegar on the stove near the cabbage. It will help absorb the odor from it.

DEVILED BRUSSELS SPROUTS

1   10 to 12-ounce package frozen
    Brussels sprouts
½   cup butter, melted
2   teaspoons prepared mustard

¾   teaspoon salt
1   teaspoon Worcestershire sauce
    Dash cayenne pepper

1. Cook Brussels sprouts according to package directions.
2. Combine butter, mustard, salt, Worcestershire and cayenne.
3. Pour over cooked sprouts.
4. Serve hot.

Serves 6

CAULIFLOWER à la CRÈME

1   small head cauliflower
    Salt to taste
⅓   cup hot water
2   tablespoons butter, melted

2   tablespoons whipping cream
    Paprika
    Snipped chives and parsley

1. Wash and remove lower stalks from cauliflower. Thinly slice entire head.
2. Place cauliflower in skillet. Sprinkle lightly with salt and add water.
3. Cook, covered, 5 to 7 minutes or until crisp tender. Do not drain.
4. Add butter and whipping cream. Heat 1 minute stirring with a fork.
5. Serve at once garnished with paprika, chives and parsley.

Serves 4

※ When cooking cauliflower, add a small amount of milk to the water. The cauliflower will remain white.

SESAME CAULIFLOWER SAUTÉ

1 head cauliflower	½ cup sliced green onions
¼ cup sesame seeds	¼ cup chopped parsley
4 tablespoons butter	Salt and pepper to taste
1 small onion, chopped	Lemon wedges
¼ cup water	

1. Break cauliflower into florets. Cut florets into ¼-inch slices and set aside.
2. In a large skillet, cook sesame seeds until golden brown, stirring frequently. Set seeds aside.
3. To the skillet, add butter and onion. Cook until onion is transparent. Add cauliflower and water. Cover and cook approximately 10 minutes or until cauliflower is tender. Stir in green onions, parsley, sesame seeds, salt and pepper.
4. Cook, stirring 1 to 2 minutes, to blend flavors.
5. Pass lemon wedges to squeeze over cauliflower.

Serves 6

SHOE PEG CORN

A good picnic dish.

½ cup butter, softened	2 12-ounce cans shoe peg corn, drain one can only
8 ounces cream cheese, softened	1 4-ounce can chopped green chiles, drained

1. Combine butter and cream cheese.
2. Add corn and green chiles. Mix well.
3. Place in a square 1½-quart glass baking dish.
4. Bake at 350° for 30 minutes.

Leftovers can be refrigerated, sliced in squares and served cold as a salad.

Serves 6

SOUTHERN FRIED CORN

10 ears of corn
3 tablespoons bacon grease
¼ cup milk, if corn is too dry
2 tablespoons butter

1 tablespoon salt
Pepper to taste
1 teaspoon sugar

1. Cut corn off cob.
2. Sauté corn in bacon grease 5 minutes, stirring often.
3. Add milk and butter. Cook over low heat approximately 20 minutes or until tender.
4. Add salt, pepper and sugar the last 10 minutes of cooking.

Serves 8 to 10

EGGPLANT MONREALE

1 14-ounce can tomatoes
1 8 ounce can tomato sauce
2 tablespoons onion flakes
1 teaspoon basil
1 teaspoon oregano
¼ teaspoon garlic powder
1 tablespoon wine

1 medium eggplant, peeled
2 eggs, beaten
½ teaspoon salt
Bread crumbs
Olive oil and vegetable oil
Grated Parmesan cheese
Mozzarella cheese, grated

1. Preheat oven to 325°.
2. Mix tomatoes, tomato sauce, onion flakes, seasonings and wine together. Simmer 20 minutes.
3. Slice eggplant approximately ¼-inch thick.
4. Add salt to beaten egg. Dip eggplant into egg and then into dry bread crumbs.
5. Sauté eggplant, until golden brown, in a mixture of half olive oil and half vegetable oil.
6. Place eggplant in single layers in a baking dish. Pour tomato mixture on each slice of eggplant.
7. Sprinkle Parmesan and mozzarella cheese on top.
8. Bake 15 to 20 minutes.

Serves 8 to 12

MEDITERRANEAN LAYERED VEGETABLES

A hearty dish that goes well with lamb or beef.

1   eggplant, unpeeled and cut into ¾-inch slices

2   large white onions, cut into ¼-inch slices

2   large, green bell peppers, cut into ½-inch slices

3   large tomatoes, cored and cut into ½-inch slices

Salt and pepper to taste

Parmesan cheese

1.   Preheat oven to 350°.
2.   Grease a 9 by 13 by 2-inch metal baking pan with olive oil.
3.   Layer vegetables in pan beginning with eggplant, then onion and bell pepper. Season lightly with salt and pepper. Bake 30 minutes.
4.   Top with tomatoes. Dot with butter. Sprinkle generously with Parmesan cheese.
5.   Bake 15 minutes and serve.

Serves 6 to 8

COUNTRY FRESH GREEN BEANS

4   slices bacon

3   medium onions, sliced

4   cups fresh green beans, thinly sliced

2   cups fresh tomatoes, peeled, seeded and diced

1   teaspoon salt

½   teaspoon freshly ground pepper

⅓   cup boiling water

1.   In a Dutch oven, sauté bacon until crisp. Remove and crumble.
2.   In remaining bacon fat, sauté sliced onions until tender and light brown. Add green beans and lightly sauté.
3.   Add tomatoes, salt, pepper and water. Simmer, covered, 30 minutes or until beans are tender.
4.   Stir in bacon and serve.

Serves 6 to 8

GREEN BEANS FAR EAST

2 pounds fresh green beans cut, or 2 9-ounce packages frozen French style green beans
1 5-ounce can sliced water chestnuts, drained
½ cup finely chopped onion

2 tablespoons butter
1 teaspoon sugar
1 teaspoon seasoned salt
1 teaspoon vinegar
Dash pepper
1 cup sour cream
Pimiento strips

1. Cook fresh green beans in boiling, salted water until tender. If using frozen green beans, cook according to package directions. Add water chestnuts. Heat thoroughly.
2. In another saucepan, sauté onion in butter until transparent. Add sugar, seasoned salt, vinegar, pepper and sour cream. Heat thoroughly but do not boil.
3. Drain green beans. Pour into a serving bowl and top with sour cream mixture. Garnish with pimiento strips.

Serves 6 to 8

MARINATED GREEN BEANS

1 cup mayonnaise
½ cup whipping cream
1½ tablespoons garlic vinegar
1 tablespoon lemon juice
1½ tablespoons wine vinegar
1 tablespoon anchovy paste

⅓ cup finely chopped parsley
¼ cup chopped onion
3 16-ounce cans whole green beans, drained or 2 10-ounce packages frozen green beans, cooked and drained

1. Combine first 8 ingredients and mix well.
2. Pour mixture over beans and toss gently.
3. Marinate overnight.

Serves 8

GREEN VEGETABLE MEDLEY

2   10-ounce packages frozen
    green beans
2   10-ounce packages frozen lima
    beans
2   10-ounce packages frozen peas
    or 6 carrots, sliced
1   cup diced green bell pepper,
    optional

1   cup diced onion
¼   cup butter
8   ounces sour cream
8   ounces mayonnaise
    Salt and pepper to taste
    Grated Parmesan cheese

1. Cook vegetables, according to package directions. Drain.
2. Sauté bell pepper and onion in butter until tender.
3. Stir in sour cream, mayonnaise, salt and pepper. Mix thoroughly.
4. Top with Parmesan cheese. Serve immediately.

Serves 10 to 12

CHILE CHEESE GRITS

¾   cup white grits
3   cups water
¾   teaspoon salt
½   cup butter
½   pound Old English cheese,
    grated
1   teaspoon seasoned salt

½   teaspoon Worcestershire sauce
2   eggs, well beaten
1   4-ounce can chopped green
    chiles
    Paprika or cayenne pepper,
    optional

1. Preheat oven to 350°.
2. Bring water to a boil. Add grits and salt. Cook over low heat 2 to 5 minutes,
    stirring occasionally.
3. Add butter and cheese. Stir until melted. Add seasoned salt and Worcester-
    shire. Fold in eggs. Add chiles.
4. Pour into a buttered 1½-quart baking dish. Bake 1 hour.
5. Sprinkle with paprika or cayenne.

Serves 6 to 8

ONION BAKE

Wonderful served with brisket and a salad.

6	medium onions (approximately 2 pounds), peeled and thinly sliced	8	ounces Cheddar cheese, grated
2	tablespoons butter Salt and pepper to taste	35	Ritz crackers, crumbled
		1	4-ounce can chopped green chiles, optional

1. Preheat oven to 325°.
2. Place onion slices in a large saucepan with enough water to cover. Bring to a boil. Pour off water and repeat procedure twice.
3. Drain onions in a colander until dry. Return to saucepan. Add butter, salt and pepper.
4. Layer onions, cracker crumbs, cheese and chiles in a buttered 1½-quart baking dish.
5. Bake, covered, 30 minutes.

Serves 4 to 6

POTATO SKINS

4	large baking potatoes Butter, softened	Bacon, crisply cooked and crumbled
4	ounces Cheddar cheese, grated	Sour cream

1. Scrub potatoes. Pat dry. Rub skins with butter. Place on a cookie sheet in a 375° oven 1 hour. Remove from oven.
2. Cut potatoes in half. Scoop out pulp leaving a thin wall of potato inside the skin. Save potato for another use.
3. Spread insides of potato skins with butter.
4. Return to oven for 10 minutes.
5. Remove from oven and add equal portions of cheese to each skin. Place in oven another 5 to 7 minutes or until cheese melts. Add bacon and return to oven 1 minute.
6. Serve with sour cream.

Serves 4

MUSHROOM TIMBALE

Freshly-shelled and cooked English peas make a lovely garnish for this mushroom ring.

1 pound fresh mushrooms, washed and dried	2 tablespoons all-purpose flour
1 onion	1 cup half and half
4 tablespoons butter, divided	4 large eggs, separated
	Salt and pepper to taste

1. Chop mushrooms and onion. Sauté in 2 tablespoons butter 5 minutes. Drain well.
2. Make a white sauce of remaining 2 tablespoons butter, flour and milk.
3. Fold mushrooms and onion into sauce. Add lightly beaten egg yolks. Season with salt and pepper. Fold in stiffly beaten egg whites.
4. Pour into a well greased 1-quart ring mold. Place in a pan of boiling water. Bake at 350° for 1 hour.

A wonderful accompaniment to poultry or game.

Serves 6

※ Mushrooms should be stored in a paper bag rather than plastic.

CRISPY OVEN BAKED POTATOES

An easy family favorite!

3 cups corn flakes	2 large baking potatoes, peeled and sliced
3 tablespoons Parmesan cheese	¼ cup butter
1 teaspoon paprika	
¼ teaspoon garlic salt	

1. Preheat oven to 375°.
2. Process corn flakes, cheese and spices in blender.
3. Dip potatoes in butter, then corn flakes mixture to coat.
4. Place on a well greased baking sheet. Bake 20 to 25 minutes.

Serves 4 to 6

NIGHT BEFORE MASHED POTATOES

A great recipe to prepare in advance.

8 to 10 potatoes, peeled	Salt and pepper to taste
8 ounces cream cheese, softened	Butter
1 cup sour cream	Seasoned salt

1. Boil and drain potatoes.
2. Whip hot potatoes adding cream cheese and sour cream. Continue beating until fluffy and smooth. Add salt and pepper.
3. Place in a buttered 9 by 13-inch baking dish. Dot generously with butter and sprinkle with seasoned salt. Cover with foil and refrigerate. Potatoes can be frozen at this stage and thawed before baking. Bake, covered with foil, 15 minutes at 325°. Continue baking, uncovered, 20 minutes.

Serves 10 to 12

✳ A pinch of baking soda added to mashed potatoes will make them fluffier.

SWEET POTATO CRUNCH

These sweet potatoes maintain a crisp, crunchy texture when baked.

4 cups grated raw sweet potatoes	1 teaspoon grated lemon peel
½ teaspoon ground ginger	1 teaspoon cinnamon
½ teaspoon ground cloves	½ teaspoon salt
1 cup brown sugar, firmly packed	5 beaten eggs
¾ cup butter, melted	2 cups chopped pecans

1. Preheat oven to 325°.
2. Place grated potatoes on a tea towel and wring out excess moisture.
3. Combine all ingredients except pecans. Mix well.
4. Pour into a greased 1½-quart baking dish. Top with pecans.
5. Bake 40 to 45 minutes or until bubbly.

Serves 6 to 8

RICH SWEET POTATO PUDDING

A delicious accompaniment to turkey or quail.

1	29-ounce can sweet potatoes, drained and mashed
⅓	cup evaporated milk
¾	cup sugar
2	eggs
½	cup butter, softened
1	teaspoon vanilla extract

Topping:

1	cup light brown sugar
⅓	cup butter, melted
⅓	cup all-purpose flour
1	cup chopped pecans

1. Mix first 6 ingredients together.
2. Pour into a lightly greased 7 by 11-inch baking dish.
3. Mix together topping ingredients. Sprinkle on top of potato mixture.
4. Bake at 350° degrees for 35 minutes or until crusty on top.

Serves 8

※ To keep sweet potatoes from turning dark, place them in salted water immediately after peeling. (5 teaspoons salt to 1 quart water)

CHEESY SPINACH AND RICE

1	cup rice
¼	cup butter
2	small onions, finely chopped
2½	tablespoons all-purpose flour
2½	cups milk
1½	cups grated sharp Cheddar cheese,

1	10-ounce package frozen chopped spinach, thawed
½	cup grated sharp Cheddar cheese

1. Preheat oven to 350°.
2. Cook rice in boiling, salted water 5 minutes. Drain.
3. Combine all ingredients except ½ cup cheese. Place in a buttered 2-quart baking dish.
4. Bake 1 hour.
5. Sprinkle with remaining cheese during the last 5 minutes of baking.

Serves 4 to 6

LEMONY SPINACH

2   10-ounce packages frozen
     chopped spinach
8   ounces cream cheese, softened
     Juice of ½ lemon
     Grated rind of 1 medium
     lemon

¼   cup butter, softened
     Salt and pepper to taste
     Bread crumbs, optional

1. Preheat oven to 350°.
2. Cook spinach according to package directions. Drain well.
3. Mix in cream cheese, lemon juice, lemon rind, butter, salt and pepper.
4. Place in a buttered 1-quart baking dish. Sprinkle with bread crumbs, if desired.
5. Bake 25 minutes.

Serves 4 to 6

※ Soften cream cheese by removing foil wrapper and heating in the microwave on low power 1 minute.

SPINACH AND ARTICHOKES
A Collection Classic

½   cup chopped green onions,
     tops included
½   cup butter
2   10-ounce packages frozen
     chopped spinach, cooked
     and drained

2   8-ounce cans artichoke hearts,
     drained
2   cups sour cream
     Salt and pepper to taste
½   cup grated Parmesan cheese

1. Preheat oven to 350°.
2. Sauté onions in butter. Fold in spinach, artichoke hearts and sour cream. Add salt and pepper.
3. Pour into 2-quart baking dish and sprinkle with cheese.
4. Bake 20 to 30 minutes.

Serves 4 to 6

SPINACH SOUFFLÉ

1   10-ounce package frozen,
      chopped spinach
1   tablespoon chopped onion
¼   cup butter
¼   cup all-purpose flour

1   cup milk
1   cup grated American cheese
1   teaspoon salt
⅛   teaspoon pepper
4   eggs, separated

1. Preheat oven to 350°.
2. Cook spinach according to package directions. Drain.
3. Sauté onion in butter until transparent. Stir in flour and add milk. Cook until thickened.
4. Remove from heat and add cheeses, spinach and seasonings.
5. Beat egg whites until they form stiff peaks. Beat egg yolks until they are thick and lemon colored. Stir yolks into spinach mixture. Fold in egg whites.
6. Pour into a well buttered 8-inch soufflé dish. Bake 45 minutes or until soufflé is set.

Variation I:
Broccoli Soufflé:
Substitute 1½ cups broccoli for spinach. Omit American cheese and sprinkle top of souf-flé lightly with Parmesan cheese.

Variation II:
Chicken Soufflé:
Substitute 1½ cups finely chopped chicken for spinach.

Variation III:
Cheese Soufflé:
Omit spinach.

Variation IV:
Corn Soufflé:
Add 1 tablespoon chopped green bell pepper and 1 cup cream style corn. Omit spinach

Serves 6

HEARTY CHEESE SPINACH SOUFFLÉ

2   10-ounce packages frozen, chopped spinach
½   pound Cheddar cheese, grated
1   pound cottage cheese
¼   cup butter, melted
2   eggs, separated
2   tablespoons all-purpose flour
½   teaspoon baking powder

1. Preheat oven to 350°.
2. Cook spinach according to package directions. Drain.
3. Mix together Cheddar cheese, cottage cheese, butter, spinach and egg yolks. Stir in flour and baking powder. Beat egg whites until stiff. Fold in gently.
4. Pour into a buttered 2-quart soufflé dish. Bake 1 hour.

Serves 6 to 8

HEARTY YELLOW SQUASH BAKE

10 to 12 medium yellow squash
1   medium onion, chopped
10   pieces of bacon, crisply cooked and crumbled
2   hard-cooked eggs, chopped
2 to 3 tablespoons Worcestershire sauce
1½ cups crushed cracker crumbs
Dash Tabasco sauce
½   cup butter, melted
8   ounces Velveeta cheese, cubed
Salt and pepper to taste
1   egg

1. Preheat oven to 350°.
2. Cook squash in small amount of boiling water until tender. Drain well.
3. Mash squash. Combine squash with remaining ingredients.
4. Pour into a 2-quart glass baking dish. Bake 30 minutes or until top is golden.

Serves 6 to 8

HARVEST BAKED SQUASH

A hearty side dish for a fall meal.

1 large red delicious apple, cut into ¼-inch cubes	1 tablespoon maple syrup
¾ cup raisins	1 teaspoon cinnamon
½ cup butter	¼ teaspoon ground cloves
4 tablespoons dark brown sugar	2 medium acorn squash
	1 teaspoon vegetable oil

1. Preheat oven to 400°.
2. Mix apple with raisins.
3. Melt butter. Add sugar and stir to dissolve. Add maple syrup, cinnamon and cloves. Stir until blended. Pour over apple mixture and mix well.
4. Slice squash lengthwise. Scoop out seeds and strings. Puncture cavity 20 times with a fork, being careful not to pierce skin. Rub oil over inside surface of squash. Fill cavity with apple mixture.
5. Cover with foil. Bake 1 hour.

This can be prepared a day in advance.

Serves 4

FAVORITE SQUASH AND CHEESE

3 pounds yellow squash, sliced	¼ cup butter
1 large onion, coarsely chopped	2 tablespoons cornstarch
½ cup butter	1 cup half and half
2½ cups crushed Ritz crackers	½ pound Velveeta cheese, cubed

1. Preheat oven to 350°.
2. Boil squash and onion in small amount of salted water until tender. Drain. While squash is cooking, prepare topping.
3. Melt ½ cup butter in skillet. Sauté crushed crackers in butter until crisp and brown. Set aside.
4. Make a white sauce using ¼ cup butter, cornstarch and half and half. Add cheese. Stir until melted and sauce is smooth.
5. Arrange squash in a 9 by 13-inch glass baking dish. Pour sauce over squash. Top with cracker topping. Bake 25 minutes or until hot and bubbly.

Serves 10 to 12

SUMMER SQUASH

A light and delicate taste that appeals to those who do not usually like squash.

3	pounds yellow squash	2	teaspoons salt
½	cup butter	1	teaspoon pepper
3	eggs, beaten	½	cup chopped onion
2	tablespoons cornstarch	3	tablespoons sugar
1	5-ounce can evaporated milk		

1. Preheat oven to 425°.
2. Wash and slice squash. Place in a large pot. Add a small amount of water. Boil squash until just tender. Drain well.
3. Slightly mash squash and mix with remaining ingredients.
4. Pour into a well buttered 3-quart glass baking dish.
5. Bake 30 minutes or until set.

This can be baked and served in individual ramekins.

Serves 8

ZUCCHINI MAISON

6	medium zucchini, sliced	2	ripe tomatoes, thinly sliced
¼	cup thinly sliced onion		Salt
4	tablespoons olive oil		Pepper
2	tablespoons chopped parsley	¼ to ½	cup Parmesan cheese

1. Cook squash in boiling salted water until tender. Drain.
2. Sauté onion in olive oil. Add parsley and remove from heat.
3. In a 1½-quart buttered baking dish, layer zucchini, tomatoes and onions. Sprinkle with salt, pepper and cheese. Repeat layers.
4. Bake 20 minutes at 375°.

Serves 6 to 8

SQUASH AND CARROT SAUTÉ

This colorful, delicate mixture goes nicely with veal, chicken or pork.

6 medium zucchini, grated	6 tablespoons butter
3 medium carrots, grated	1 clove garlic, minced
3 medium yellow crookneck squash, grated	Salt and pepper to taste
	Parmesan cheese

1. Place grated zucchini on a tea towel and wring out excess moisture.
2. Melt butter in a large Dutch oven. Add garlic. Cook 1 minute over low heat. Add vegetables.
3. Cook, stirring occasionally, for 10 minutes. Add salt and pepper. Sprinkle with Parmesan cheese.

Serves 10

❋ When cooking peas, carrots, cabbage, turnips or onions, add a teaspoon of sugar for every 3 cups water used. This improves the flavor.

CARROT ZUCCHINI TOMATO BAKE

3 cups sliced carrots	1 teaspoon salt
¾ cup boiling water	1 cup shredded Cheddar cheese, divided
3 small zucchini, sliced	
12 cherry tomatoes, peeled	2 tablespoons butter
1½ cups milk	Dash cayenne pepper
2 tablespoons cornstarch	½ cup slivered almonds

1. Cook carrots 5 minutes in boiling salted water.
2. Layer zucchini, carrots and tomatoes in a 12 by 8 by 2-inch baking dish.
3. In a saucepan, stir cornstarch into milk. Add ½ cup cheese, butter, salt and cayenne. Cook until smooth and thickened.
4. Pour over vegetables. Sprinkle with remaining cheese and almonds.
5. Bake 30 minutes at 375°.

Serves 6

RASPBERRY CARROTS

A delicate hint of raspberry makes this dish special.

4 to 5 carrots, thinly sliced
¼ cup butter
½ cup water
Pinch salt

2 to 4 teaspoons raspberry vinegar
2 teaspoons brown sugar
Chopped parsley

1. In a large, covered saucepan, simmer carrots in butter, water and salt until tender.
2. Add raspberry vinegar and sugar. Cook, uncovered, another 1 to 2 minutes.
3. Garnish with chopped parsley.

Serves 3 to 4

LEMON CARROTS WITH DILL

½ small onion, minced
1½ pounds carrots, peeled and sliced
4 tablespoons butter, divided
½ cup water

½ teaspoon salt
1 teaspoon sugar
1 tablespoon lemon juice
1 teaspoon dill
Pinch white pepper

1. Sauté onion and carrots in 2 tablespoons butter until onion is transparent.
2. Add water and salt. Simmer 10 minutes. Pour off liquid. Set aside.
3. In a small saucepan, melt remaining butter. Add sugar, lemon juice, dill and white pepper.
4. Toss carrots in butter mixture. Heat thoroughly and serve.

Serves 6 to 8

SNAPPY CARROTS

4½ cups sliced carrots
½ cup mayonnaise
2 tablespoons chopped onion
2 tablespoons prepared
    horseradish

¼ teaspoon salt
    Dash white pepper
¼ cup crushed saltine crackers
    (7)
2 teaspoons butter, melted

1. Cook carrots in a small amount of salted water until tender.
2. Drain and place carrots in a lightly greased 1½ quart baking dish.
3. Combine mayonnaise, onion, horseradish, salt and pepper. Stir into carrots.
4. Mix crushed crackers with butter. Sprinkle on carrots.
5. Bake 30 minutes at 350°.

This may be prepared ahead of time.

Serves 4 to 6

GLAZED CARROTS

2 pounds carrots, peeled and
    sliced
¼ cup butter, melted
⅓ cup brown sugar
⅓ cup granulated sugar

¼ cup orange juice
1 teaspoon cinnamon
1 teaspoon whole allspice
1 teaspoon vanilla extract

1. Cook carrots in salted water 5 minutes. Drain.
2. Combine butter, sugars, orange juice and spices in a 1-quart glass baking dish.
3. Mix carrots into butter mixture. Bake in a 350° oven approximately 15 to 20 minutes.

Serves 8 to 10

PECAN RICE

¾ pound sliced fresh mushrooms
½ cup shallots, minced
⅔ cup butter
1⅓ cups uncooked brown rice
1 teaspoon dried thyme
   Salt and pepper to taste

1 cup chopped pecans, toasted
4 cups chicken broth
   Whole toasted pecans or
     toasted walnut halves
   Parsley

1. Preheat oven to 375°.
2. In a Dutch oven, sauté mushrooms and shallots in butter 5 to 7 minutes or until golden.
3. Stir in rice. Cook, stirring with wooden spoon, approximately 3 minutes or until rice is hot.
4. Season with thyme, salt and pepper. Stir in 1 cup chopped nuts and chicken broth. Heat to boiling. Remove from heat.
5. Cover and bake approximately 1½ hours or until liquid is absorbed and rice is tender. Garnish with nuts and chopped parsley.

Substitute walnuts for pecans if desired.

Serves 8

※ Before using almonds or pecans as a garnish, sauté in butter.

RED PEPPER RICE

Serve as an accompaniment to barbequed chicken or brisket.

1 cup white rice
½ cup butter
1 12-ounce can chicken broth

1 10¾-ounce can onion soup
¼ teaspoon cayenne pepper
3 tablespoons Parmesan cheese

1. Preheat oven to 350°.
2. Brown rice in melted butter over medium heat. Add remaining ingredients. Pour into a 9 by 13 by 2-inch baking dish.
3. Cover. Bake 1 hour.

Serves 6

BROWN RICE

1 medium onion, finely chopped
¾ cup long grain rice
⅓ cup butter
1 10¾-ounce can beef bouillon

½ can water
½ to 1 teaspoon salt, optional
Parsley

1. Preheat oven to 350°.
2. Sauté onion and lightly brown rice in butter.
3. Pour bouillon and water into a 1½-quart baking dish. Add onion, rice and salt to mixture.
4. Cover and cook 45 to 60 minutes or until liquid is absorbed. Remove cover the last 10 minutes.
5. Garnish with fresh parsley and serve.

Variations:
For a different taste try adding any or all of the following:

½ cup sautéed mushrooms
½ cup sautéed sliced almonds
½ cup white raisins
½ cup butter cooked slowly until it turns deep golden brown. Pour over cooked rice.

Serves 6

RIPE TOMATO PIE

1 9-inch pie crust, baked
4 large tomatoes, peeled and sliced
2 tablespoons finely chopped onion

Salt and pepper to taste
¼ teaspoon basil
1 teaspoon sugar
1 cup grated Cheddar cheese
¼ cup mayonnaise

1. Preheat oven to 350°.
2. Layer tomatoes in pie crust. Sprinkle with onion and spices. Sprinkle sugar over spices.
3. Mix together cheese and mayonnaise. Spread over top of tomatoes.
4. Bake 20 minutes.

Serves 6 to 8

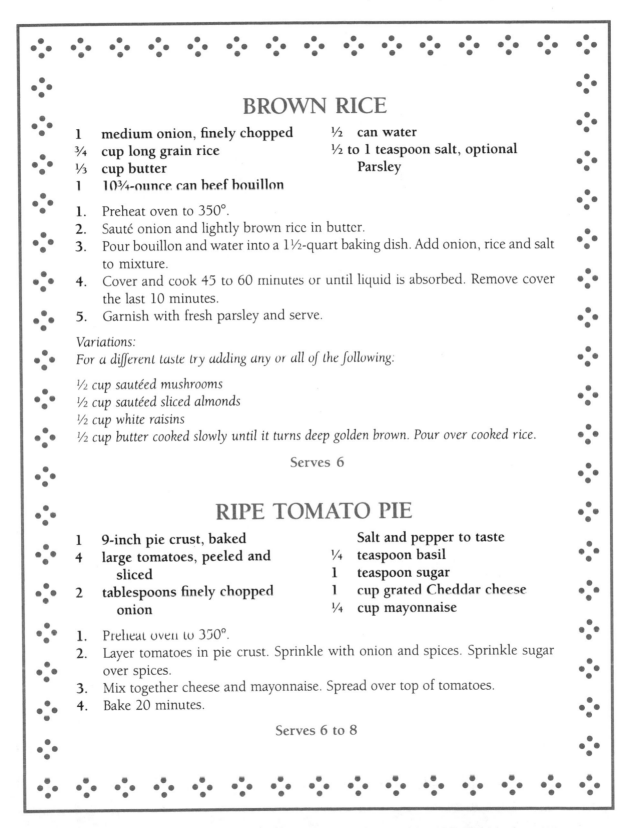

OKRA AND TOMATOES
A Collection Classic

1	pound okra	1	teaspoon salt
1	tablespoon bacon drippings	¼	teaspoon pepper
1	large onion, chopped	2	dashes cayenne pepper
2	large tomatoes, peeled, cored and chopped	½	teaspoon sugar

1. Rinse okra. Dry well. Remove tops and slice pods crosswise in ¼ -inch pieces.
2. Heat bacon drippings in a skillet. Sauté okra 10 to 15 minutes, stirring occasionally, until it begins to look dry and loses its ropy texture.
3. Stir in onions. Cook until onions are transparent.
4. Add tomatoes and seasonings. Lower heat and continue cooking several minutes.

Serves 4

EGGPLANT AND TOMATO MEDLEY

1	large eggplant	14 to 16	saltines, crushed
1	10-ounce can tomatoes and green chiles, slightly drained	1	cup grated, sharp Cheddar cheese

1. Preheat oven to 350°.
2. Peel and slice eggplant. Cover with boiling water. Cook approximately 8 to 10 minutes or until tender. Drain well on paper towels.
3. Mash eggplant. Stir in saltines, ¾ cup cheese and tomatoes. Mix well.
4. Put eggplant mixture in well greased 1-quart baking dish. Sprinkle with remaining cheese.
5. Bake 30 minutes.

For a milder flavor, substitute one drained 14½-ounce can tomatoes for the tomatoes and green chiles.

Serves 6

CURRIED BAKED TOMATOES

4	medium, ripe tomatoes	½	teaspoon curry powder
½	cup sour cream	¼ to ½	teaspoon salt
½	cup mayonnaise		

1. Preheat oven to 350°.
2. Cut each tomato in half.
3. Mix sour cream, mayonnaise, curry powder and salt until well blended.
4. Top each tomato with a portion of sour cream mixture.
5. Place tomatoes in a shallow, buttered baking pan. Bake approximately 20 minutes or until thoroughly heated. Do not overbake. Serve hot.

Variation I:
Add shredded Cheddar or Swiss cheese to topping mixture or chopped chives and crisp bacon.

Variation II:
Parmesan cheese, fine bread crumbs and chives mixed make a good topping.

Serves 8

BUTCH'S SAVORY RANCH BEANS

A backyard barbecue favorite!

2	medium white onions, chopped	1	15-ounce can Ranch Style beans
2	large, green bell peppers, chopped	1	pound Velveeta cheese, cubed
½	cup butter	½	cup ketchup
2	15-ounce cans pork and beans	½	cup Worcestershire sauce
		1	tablespoon garlic salt

1. Sauté onion and bell pepper in butter. Stir in remaining ingredients and pour in bean pot.
2. Bake 1 hour at 350°. Do not stir before serving.

Serves 8 to 10

TEXAS CAVIAR

Start the year right with these good-luck peas.

1	16-ounce package frozen black-eyed peas	2	bay leaves
1	tablespoon salt	3	green bell peppers, chopped
1	clove garlic, split	2	tablespoons cider or wine vinegar
½	cup vegetable oil		Pepper to taste
3	medium onions, chopped		

1. Cook peas according to package directions. Drain.
2. Combine all ingredients.
3. Marinate in refrigerator 2 to 3 days.
4. Heat or serve cold as an appetizer with corn chips.

Serves 8 to 10

HOT CURRIED FRUIT

1	29-ounce can cling peach halves	5	maraschino cherries, halved
1	15¼-ounce can pineapple slices	⅓	cup butter
1	29-ounce can pear halves	¾	cup light brown sugar
		4	teaspoons curry powder
			Sliced bananas, optional

1. Preheat oven to 350°.
2. Drain fruit. Pat individual pieces of fruit, with paper towels, until thoroughly dry.
3. Arrange fruit in a 1½-quart baking dish.
4. Melt butter. Add brown sugar and curry. Spoon over fruit and bake 25 minutes.

This can be made a day ahead, refrigerated and then baked.

Serves 10 to 12

SHERRIED BAKED FRUIT

Elegant for buffet dinner parties, large or small.

2 20-ounce cans chunk pineapple	2 15-ounce jars spiced apple rings
1 29-ounce can sliced freestone peaches	½ cup butter
1 17-ounce can apricots, sliced	4 tablespoons all-purpose flour
1 16-ounce can pitted Bing cherries or blueberries	1 cup brown sugar
	¼ cup sherry

1. Preheat oven to 350°.
2. Drain fruit. Arrange in layers in a 3-quart baking dish.
3. Melt butter. Add flour and stir until well blended. Add brown sugar and sherry. Cook until thick.
4. Pour over fruit.
5. Bake 30 minutes.

Serves 20

BANANA BEIGNETS

Great for brunch!

4 bananas, sliced	1 tablespoon sugar
1½ cups all-purpose flour	2 eggs, beaten
2 rounded teaspoons baking powder	Vegetable oil
½ teaspoon salt	

1. Mix dry ingredients and form a well in the center. Pour eggs into well and blend. Add a small amount of milk if mixture is too thick.
2. Dip banana pieces into batter. Fry bananas in 2 inches of hot oil until golden brown. Drain well on paper towels. Serve at once.

Serves 6

BISCUITS, BREADS, MUFFINS AND ROLLS

Breads

There are many recipes for bread. Different types of bread correspond to the ingredients and method of preparation involved in the baking process. Classic bread preparation usually involves the use of yeast and the necessity of kneading in conjunction with timed periods between steps. Quick breads do not use yeast, so they do not require kneading. They provide a short-cut alternative for cooks with less time for preparation. Of course, there is always sourdough bread for those who enjoy old-time baking. Listed below are the different kinds and varieties of flour and leavening agents used in making bread.

Flour

1. **All-purpose flour**—A basic multi-purpose flour that is usually a blend of hard and soft wheats, with the bran and wheat germ removed

2. **Whole wheat flour**—This flour contains all of the grain. The wheat germ is perishable, so wheat flour must be used quickly or stored in the freezer so that it does not become rancid.

3. **Self-rising flour**—Contains leavening and salt; it may not be used in bread recipes using yeast. When used in quick bread recipes, the salt, soda and baking powder are omitted.

4. **Cake flour**—This flour is made from soft wheat and is whiter with a finer texture than all-purpose flour. It is used in delicate cake recipes.

5. **Combinations**—Whole wheat, or graham flour, rye and buckwheat flours, bran, cornmeal and oatmeal may be used in combination with all-purpose flour for special bread recipes. Whole grain flours and meals are never sifted, but stirred lightly to mix, and then measured.

Leavenings

Leavenings are ingredients that form gas bubbles; specifically, carbon dioxide when combined with liquid and other ingredients. Examples of physical leavenings are steam and air. The gas, air or steam expands when dough is heated. Leavening agents include yeast, baking powder and soda.

1. **Yeast**—Yeast is a tiny plant organism that produces carbon dioxide when combined with other ingredients. Temperature and moisture combine to promote its growth. Yeast comes in two varieties: active dry yeast and compressed cake yeast.

2. **Baking powder**—Available in several varieties; all baking powders contain three basic ingredients: soda, some sort of acid and cornstarch or flour. Gas bubbles form when baking powder is combined with liquid and the batter is heated.

3. **Baking soda**—Releases gas when combined with acidic ingredients such as buttermilk, sour milk, vinegar or lemon juice.

Basic Ingredients of Yeast Bread

1. **Yeast**—Makes dough rise and gives baked products a light texture. The amount of yeast depends on the length of time the dough must rise. A small amount of yeast requires a longer rising time.

2. **Flour**—Wheat flour is best for bread making because of the gluten content of wheat. Gluten makes dough elastic so that it creates a framework to trap gas bubbles which form when yeast is activated. Flour from most grains, such as whole wheat, rye, rice and soy have a lower protein content than white flour. Therefore, it should be mixed with some white flour in order to maximize the action of the gluten.

3. **Liquid**—Water and milk are the most frequently used liquids to dissolve dry yeast. When liquid is used to dissolve dry yeast, it should be warmed to 105° to 115° F. A candy thermometer serves as a handy guide for checking the temperature of liquids. If compressed yeast is used, water need only be about 90° F. When water is used as the liquid, bread has a coarser texture and a crisper crust. When milk is used to dissolve yeast, bread has a finer texture as well as added nutritional value. If milk is used to dissolve yeast, the pan must first be rinsed to prevent sticking.

4. **Sweeteners**—Sugar, honey and molasses are examples of sugars that yeast feeds on to produce the gas that causes dough to rise.

5. **Salt**—It controls the growth of yeast and adds flavor.

6. **Fat**—Butter and other fats help tenderize the dough.

7. **Eggs**—They provide added nutrition as well as producing a firmer, richer loaf.

8. **Other ingredients**—Herbs, spices, nuts and fruits add variety and flavor. These extra ingredients will slow the rising process; use sparingly.

Proofing the Yeast

Proofing the yeast insures that it is active. If the yeast is not active, all that's lost is a little liquid and sweetener rather than a whole bread recipe. Pour the yeast over ½ cup of warm (100°–115°) liquid from recipe. Add 2 teaspoons of sweetener from recipe. After 5 to 8 minutes the mixture will bubble and foam indicating active yeast. Add to recipe as directed.

Kneading

Kneading develops the gluten in bread and evenly distributes air pockets which are expanded in dough by action of the yeast.

Bread should be kneaded for the first time after the ingredients have been well mixed. Form a ball of dough and place on a lightly floured surface. Work with the heel of the hand as it is the coolest part of the hand and will not increase the temperature of the dough. Flatten dough into a circle approximately one inch thick. Fold the top one-third of the dough toward you. Press down on the doubled-over dough, pushing away from you. Repeat this folding and kneading until dough feels smooth and elastic.

After the dough has risen to double in bulk, it should be kneaded a second time. Divide the dough into the number of loaves specified. Knead each section approximately three minutes. The dough is ready to be placed in a prepared baking pan.

Rising

After kneading, form dough into a ball. Place in a lightly greased bowl and turn to coat dough. (This will prevent a crust from forming on the dough as it rises). To determine what size bowl to use when making bread, use the following method. Pour water to equal the volume of dough into a bowl. Pour the same again into the bowl. The water should fit into the bowl with space left over. Cover the bowl with a damp, warm towel. Place in a warm, draft-free place to rise for 1 to 1½ hours, or until doubled in bulk.

After dough has risen, punch down using your fist. Turn out onto a floured surface and cover with a damp towel. Let it rest approximately 10 minutes to allow the gluten to relax. Knead dough briefly before shaping according to recipe directions.

During second rising, follow same procedure and put dough in a warm, draft-free place to rise. The length of time it takes to rise is determined by the temperature of the room or the place where it is rising. An unheated oven, with the light on, is an ideal rising place.

Working with Bread Dough

※ Be sure to differentiate dry cup measure from liquid cup measure.

※ Stir flour lightly before measuring.

※ All utensils and ingredients should be at room temperature. Mixing bowls can be warmed by rinsing with hot water.

※ Butter or shortening should be melted and cooled before it is added to other ingredients.

※ Sugar and salt should be dissolved in warm liquid.

※ The temperature of the liquid added to yeast is of utmost importance. If the liquid is too hot, it may kill the yeast. If it is too cool, the yeast may not dissolve completely, causing the dough to be sticky and difficult to handle. It may also interfere with the rising process.

※ Quick breads or bread in which baking powder or baking soda is used must be handled quickly. The production of carbon dioxide bubbles begins immediately when liquid is added. Batter or dough that is allowed to stand before baking will not rise as well as batter that is prepared and baked immediately.

※ To test if dough has been kneaded enough, press two fingers into the dough. If dough springs back, it is ready. Go on to next step.

※ To test if dough has risen enough, press two fingers into dough. If dough does not spring back, it has risen enough.

※ To make bread rise more quickly, add double the amount of yeast called for in the recipe. Proceed according to recipe directions.

※ Test bread for doneness by tapping on the top. If loaves sound hollow, they are done.

※ Prepare pans for baking by greasing with oil, solid shortening or non-stick vegetable spray.

※ To make loaves crusty, brush the top and sides with an egg white diluted with 1 tablespoon of water five minutes before the end of baking.

※ To brown biscuits and rolls, brush tops with slightly beaten egg white, egg yolk or whole beaten eggs.

※ To add additional decoration to bread loaves, sprinkle tops with caraway, sesame or poppy seeds after brushing with butter or egg coating.

※ Glazed or frosted breads may be decorated with candied fruits that have been cut and placed in patterns and designs. Nut halves may also be used to decorate fancy breads and cakes.

※ It is easiest to cut fresh, slightly warm bread with a hot serrated knife using a gentle sawing motion. This will enable the bread to retain its shape.

Etcetera

Bread crumbs—Save left over bread crusts and heels of bread to toast and process in the blender or food processor. Always store crumbs in an airtight container or freeze to prevent drying.

Bread cups—Cut bread slices with a large, round cookie cutter. Press bread rounds into muffin tins and bake at 375° until browned. Watch closely to avoid burning.

Bread fingers—To make bread fingers, slice hot dog buns in half crosswise and then slice in quarters lengthwise. Brush with butter and sprinkle with garlic and herbs and then brown quickly in the oven.

Garlic bread—Preheat oven to 425°. To ½ cup melted butter add ¼ teaspoon oregano, ¼ teaspoon basil, 1 teaspoon garlic salt and stir well. Slice a loaf of French bread and brush each piece with the butter mixture. Wrap the loaf in foil and heat 10 to 15 minutes.

Croutons—Dice 2 cups of stale bread, preferably sourdough or French. Stir in ¼ cup olive oil that is flavored with crushed garlic. Bake cubes in the oven, stirring until brown. Drain on paper towels and store in an airtight container until needed.

Muffins

※ Muffin batter should be stirred only enough to moisten the ingredients. Batter will appear lumpy.

※ For lighter muffins, place the greased muffin tin into the preheated oven for a minute or two before pouring in the batter.

※ Removing muffins from the tin while slightly warm will prevent sogginess.

Biscuits and Rolls

※ Shape and freeze unbaked yeast rolls on a cookie sheet. Package frozen dough in plastic bags and freeze. When ready to use, remove, allow dough to rise in a pan and bake.

※ If dough is kneaded after mixing ingredients for baking powder biscuits, the texture is improved.

Pancakes and Waffles

※ Never sift pancake, biscuit or cake mix.

※ Pancakes and waffles brown more quickly if a pinch of sugar is added to the batter.

※ Always add partially frozen rather than thawed berries, to pancake batter or bread mixtures. This prevents bleeding in cooking.

※ Give a favorite waffle batter new interest by adding chopped pecans, crumbled bacon or grated cheese.

FAMILY YEAST BREAD

A hearty, sweet treat that family and guests will love!

1 package active dry yeast	7 tablespoons sugar
1¼ cups warm water	1 egg, beaten
7 tablespoons vegetable shortening, melted	4 to 4½ cups all-purpose flour
	1¼ teaspoons salt

1. Soften yeast in warm water.
2. Add shortening, sugar, egg, 2 cups flour and salt. Beat until smooth. Stir in remaining flour.
3. Cover. Let it rise in a warm place 1 hour or until doubled in bulk.
4. Press dough into a greased 9 by 13 by 2-inch metal pan. Bake 1 hour at 300°.

Cut in squares and serve hot with butter.

Serves 12

※ Put 4 to 6 bay leaves in flour canister to keep bugs out.

WHEAT LOAVES

Great holiday gift for friends and neighbors.

½ cup sugar	1½ teaspoons salt
2 cups lukewarm water	2 cups whole wheat flour
1 package active dry yeast	5 cups all-purpose flour
2 eggs, lightly beaten	2 tablespoons butter
⅓ cup vegetable oil	

1. In a large mixing bowl, dissolve sugar in water. Stir in yeast. Let it stand in a warm place 20 minutes.
2. Add eggs, oil, salt and whole wheat flour. Add white flour until dough is smooth. Let it rise until doubled in bulk.
3. Turn dough onto a floured board. Knead until elastic. Sprinkle with extra flour if needed.
4. Divide dough into thirds and shape into loaves. Place in 3 greased 9 by 5 by 3-inch loaf pans. Let it rise until nearly doubled in bulk.
5. Bake 10 minutes at 400°. Lower heat to 375° and bake 25 minutes.
6. Turn out loaves to cool on a wire rack. Brush tops with butter.

Yields 3 loaves

HONEY WHOLE WHEAT BREAD

Absolutely delicious!

4 cups whole wheat flour, divided	2 packages active dry yeast
½ cup instant nonfat dry milk	3 cups water
1 tablespoon salt	¾ to 1 cup honey
¼ cup wheat germ, optional	2 tablespoons oil
	4 to 4½ cups unbleached flour

1. Combine 3 cups whole wheat flour, dry milk, salt, yeast and wheat germ in a large bowl.
2. Heat water, honey and oil until warm (105°–115°).
3. Pour liquid over flour mixture. Blend at low speed for 1 minute with a mixer, then at medium speed for 2 minutes.
4. Stir in, by hand, the remaining whole wheat flour and unbleached flour.
5. Turn dough onto a floured surface and knead approximately 5 minutes, or until dough is smooth and elastic. Place dough in a greased bowl. Cover. Let it rise 1 hour or until doubled in bulk.
6. Punch dough down and divide in half. Shape each part into a loaf by rolling dough out to a 14 by 7-inch rectangle. Starting with the narrow edge, roll up dough and put into greased and floured 9 by 5 by 3-inch bread pans.
7. Cover and let them rise 1 hour or until doubled in bulk. Bake 40 to 45 minutes at 375°. Remove from bread pans after 5 minutes. Cool on a rack.

Yields 2 loaves

ANADAMA BREAD

½ cup cornmeal	½ cup molasses
1 cup cold water	2 teaspoons salt
1 package active dry yeast	3 cups whole wheat flour
1½ cups boiling water	2½ to 3 cups sifted unbleached white flour
3 tablespoons butter	

1. Mix cornmeal with ¾ of the cold water. Soften yeast in remaining cold water.
2. Add cornmeal to boiling water and stir over low heat until mixture boils.
3. Add butter, molasses and salt. Cool to lukewarm.
4. Combine yeast with cornmeal mixture. Add whole wheat flour and enough white flour to form a firm, non-sticky dough.

5. Turn dough into a greased bowl. Grease the surface and cover with a towel. Let dough rise in a warm place until doubled in bulk.
6. Turn out on a floured surface and knead until smooth and elastic. Shape into loaves.
7. Place in greased 9 by 5 by 3-inch loaf pans or on greased cookie sheets. Brush with oil. Cover and let dough rise until doubled in bulk.
8. Bake 15 minutes at 400°. Lower oven temperature to 375°. Bake approximately 35 additional minutes.

Yields 2 loaves

DILL BREAD

Dill bread makes delicious sandwiches with a favorite tuna or chicken salad; also, divine ham sandwiches.

1 package active dry yeast
¼ cup warm water
1 cup small curd creamed cottage cheese, heated to lukewarm
2 tablespoons sugar
2 teaspoons dill weed

3 tablespoons minced onion, lightly browned in 1 tablespoon butter
1 teaspoon salt
¼ teaspoon baking soda
1 egg
2¼ to 2½ cups all-purpose flour

1. Soften yeast in water.
2. Combine in mixing bowl with all ingredients, except flour.
3. Add flour gradually, stirring after each addition, until dough has a smooth, elastic texture and can be handled without sticking.
4. Knead well and let it rise in a greased and covered bowl in a warm place approximately 1¼ hours or until doubled in bulk.
5. Punch down dough. Remove dough from bowl and place in a well greased 9 by 5 by 3-inch loaf pan.
6. Let it rise approximately 45 minutes or until just above edge of pan.
7. Bake 35 to 45 minutes at 350°.
8. Brush top with butter.

Yields 1 loaf

CHEESE BREAD

Makes superior hamburger buns.

1 teaspoon sugar	1 cup boiling water
¼ cup water	1 egg, beaten
1 package active dry yeast	3½ to 4 cups all-purpose flour
2 teaspoons salt	2½ cups grated Cheddar cheese
¼ cup sugar	

1. Dissolve sugar in ¼ cup warm water. Add yeast and set aside.
2. Add salt and sugar to 1 cup boiling water. Stir to dissolve. Cool. Add beaten egg.
3. Combine yeast and egg mixture. Add flour and cheese. Beat until well blended.
4. Turn onto a floured board and knead until dough is elastic.
5. Place in a buttered bowl, cover and let it rise approximately 1¼ hours.
6. When doubled in bulk, shape into 2 loaves and place in buttered 9 by 5 by 3-inch loaf pans to rise again until doubled in bulk.
7. Bake 1 hour at 300°.
8. When golden brown, remove from oven and brush with melted butter.
9. To make buns, roll dough out on a floured board to ¼-inch thickness. Cut into 3-inch rounds.
10. Butter tops of half the rounds and place second round on top.
11. Let rise on greased cookie sheet until doubled in bulk.
12. Bake 20 to 25 minutes at 300°. Remove from oven and butter tops.

Yields 2 loaves or 6 to 8 buns

REDEEMER BREAD

¾ cup vegetable oil	2 packages active dry yeast
¾ cup sugar	½ cup lukewarm water
1 tablespoon salt	2 eggs
1 cup bran cereal	6½ cups all-purpose flour
2 cups boiling water	

1. Combine oil, sugar, salt and cereal in a large mixing bowl. Pour boiling water over mixture. Cool.

2. Soften yeast in lukewarm water.

3. When bran mixture has cooled to lukewarm, add eggs, softened yeast and flour. Mix well. Knead 8 to 10 minutes sprinkling in extra flour as needed to prevent dough from being sticky.

4. Place in a greased bowl. Let it rise approximately 1¼ hours or until doubled in bulk.

5. Punch down. Knead 2 minutes. Shape into loaves or rolls. For large loaves, bake in 9 by 5 by 3-inch loaf pans. For small loaves, bake in 7½ by 3½ by 2½-inch loaf pans. Let dough rise, in greased pans, approximately 45 minutes or until doubled in bulk.

6. Bake approximately 30 minutes at 350° for loaves. Bake approximately 12 to 15 minutes for rolls.

Yields 2 large loaves
3 small loaves
1 dozen rolls

MOLASSES RYE BREAD

2 packages active dry yeast	¼ cup vegetable oil
2 cups lukewarm water, divided	2 teaspoons salt
½ cup molasses	2 cups rye flour
¼ cup brown sugar	5 to 6 cups all-purpose flour

1. Dissolve yeast in ¼ cup water. Set aside.

2. Combine molasses, sugar, oil, salt and remaining water. Add dissolved yeast. Stir in rye flour. Add white flour to make soft dough.

3. Knead 10 to 15 minutes on floured surface.

4. Let it rise in large bowl 1½ to 2 hours or until doubled in bulk. Punch down.

5. Form into 2 large loaves. Place in 2 greased 9 by 5 by 3-inch pans. Let it rise approximately 1 hour or until doubled in bulk.

6. Bake approximately 45 minutes at 325°. Loaf tops may be brushed with butter half way through baking time. When bread is done, it will have a hollow sound when tapped.

Yields 2 loaves

BRAIDED ONION BREAD

Great to serve with any casserole and a fruit salad.

1 package active dry yeast	*Filling:*
¼ cup warm water	¼ cup butter, melted
4 cups all-purpose flour, unsifted	1 cup finely chopped onion
¼ cup sugar	1 tablespoon grated Parmesan cheese
1½ teaspoons salt	1 tablespoon sesame or poppy seeds
½ cup hot water	1 teaspoon garlic salt
½ cup milk	1 teaspoon paprika
¼ cup butter, softened	
1 egg	

1. Dissolve yeast in warm water. Add 2 cups flour, sugar, salt, hot water, milk, butter and egg. Blend until moistened. Beat 2 minutes at medium speed.
2. Stir in remaining flour by hand. Cover and let it rise approximately 1 hour or until doubled in bulk.
3. Combine all filling ingredients.
4. Punch down dough. Knead on floured surface until dough is not sticky. Roll out to an 18 by 12-inch rectangle. Spread filling ingredients over dough.
5. Cut rectangle into three 18 by 4-inch strips. On a greased cookie sheet, braid strips. Cover and let it rise again 1 hour.
6. Bake 35 minutes at 350°.

Serves approximately 10

SOURDOUGH STARTER

| 1 | envelope active dry yeast | 2 | cups all-purpose flour |
| 2 | cups warm water | 1 | small potato, halved |

1. Combine all ingredients in a 1½ quart glass or earthenware bowl.
2. Cover with cheesecloth. Leave in warm room 48 hours. Stir 2 to 3 times. (Mixture will ferment, bubble and acquire a slightly sour smell.)
3. To use, stir and remove desired amount. To remaining starter, add equal parts flour and water, (e.g. 2 cups water and 2 cups flour). Stir and allow to stand a few hours at room temperature until mixture bubbles. Cover and refrigerate.

By replenishing starter, it will last indefinitely. Never add anything but flour and water to starter.

Yields 3 cups

SOURDOUGH BISCUITS

1	cup whole wheat flour	½	teaspoon salt
1	cup all-purpose flour	½	cup butter
1	tablespoon sugar	2	cups sourdough starter
2	teaspoons baking powder		

1. Mix together flours, sugar, baking powder and salt.
2. With pastry blender, cut in butter.
3. Stir in sourdough starter.
4. Turn dough onto floured board. Knead lightly, working in more flour if too sticky.
5. Roll dough ½-inch thick. Cut and place on lightly oiled pan. Let it rise in a warm place ½ hour.
6. Bake 20 to 25 minutes at 425° until lightly browned.

Biscuits can be made using all white flour. Reduce starter to 1⅔ cups.

Yields approximately 22 biscuits

SOURDOUGH PANCAKES

1	cup sourdough starter	2	tablespoons sugar
2	cups warm water	2	tablespoons vegetable oil
2¼	cups all-purpose flour	⅓	cup milk
2	eggs	1	teaspoon baking soda

1. Mix together sourdough starter, water and flour.
2. Cover bowl and allow to stand at room temperature overnight.
3. Whisk in eggs, sugar, oil, milk and baking soda.
4. Let batter stand 10 minutes.
5. Using hotter griddle than usual, make pancakes.

Yields 4½ cups batter, about 22 pancakes

SOURDOUGH FRENCH BREAD

1	package active dry yeast	5	cups all-purpose flour, divided
1	cup warm water	2	teaspoons salt
2	tablespoons sugar		Cornmeal
1½	cups sourdough starter		

1. In a large mixing bowl, sprinkle yeast over warm water. Let it dissolve for 5 minutes.
2. Stir in sugar and sourdough starter.
3. Gradually add 4 cups of flour mixed with salt.
4. Cover bowl with damp towel. Let it rise 1 to 1½ hours in a warm place.
5. Turn dough onto floured board. Work in about 1 cup more flour until dough is no longer sticky. Knead about 5 minutes, or until dough is satiny.
6. Shape dough into 1 large round or 2 oval loaves.
7. Set on cookie sheet sprinkled with cornmeal. Let it rise in warm place 1 to 1½ hours.
8. Place shallow pan of water on lower shelf of oven. Preheat to 400°.
9. Make diagonal slashes in bread, preferably with razor blade so dough does not fall.
10. Bake 40 to 50 minutes. Set on rack to cool.

Serves 6 to 8

SOURDOUGH CORNBREAD

1 cup sourdough starter	¼ cup butter, melted
1½ cups evaporated milk	1 teaspoon salt
1½ cups yellow cornmeal	½ teaspoon soda
2 eggs, beaten	

1. Mix together starter, milk, cornmeal and eggs. Stir thoroughly.
2. Stir in butter, salt and soda.
3. Pour into a hot, greased 9-inch iron skillet.
4. Bake 20 to 30 minutes at 450°.

Yields 8 pieces

RICH DINNER ROLLS

1 cup milk, scalded	2 eggs
¼ cup sugar	4½ cups all-purpose flour, divided
1 teaspoon salt	½ cup flour for board
¼ cup butter	Butter, melted
2 packages active dry yeast, softened in ½ cup very warm water	

1. Combine scalded milk, sugar, salt and butter in large mixing bowl. Cool to lukewarm.
2. Add softened yeast, eggs and 2 cups flour. Beat until smooth.
3. Stir in 2½ cups flour.
4. Turn out dough onto a lightly floured board. Knead 5 minutes.
5. Place dough in a greased bowl, turning to grease top of dough.
6. Cover with damp cloth. Let it rise 45 to 60 minutes in a warm place until doubled in bulk.
7. Punch down. Turn out onto lightly floured board.
8. For Parker House shape, roll dough to ¼-inch thick. Cut with biscuit cutter.
9. Brush dough with melted butter. Place on lightly greased cookie sheet, folding dough in half, and brush top with butter.
10. Let them rise 10 to 15 minutes.
11. Bake 7 to 10 minutes at 400°.
12. Rolls may be brushed with butter again when removed from oven.

Yields 4 dozen

GRANDMOTHER'S ROLLS

1	teaspoon sugar	1	teaspoon salt
¼	cup very warm water	½	cup sugar
1	package active dry yeast	3	eggs, beaten
½	cup butter, melted	4½	cups all-purpose flour
1	cup lukewarm milk	¼	cup butter, melted

1. Dissolve 1 teaspoon sugar in water and add yeast. Set mixture aside in a warm place.
2. Mix ½ cup butter, milk, salt, sugar and eggs together in a large bowl. Add 2 cups flour and yeast. Add 2½ cups additional flour. Stir until dough is thick and a little sticky.
3. Set in a warm place. Cover with a cloth. Let dough rise 2 hours (it may not rise very high). Stir dough down with a wooden spoon.
4. Cover dough and again set in a warm place for an additional ½ hour.
5. Separate dough and roll into balls, using 2 tablespoons of dough per ball. Dip in butter. Place 3 balls in each cupcake tin for cloverleaf rolls, or place 2 balls in each tin for pull-apart rolls.
6. Set rolls in a warm place. Let rise 1½ hours.
7. Bake rolls at 375° for 10 minutes.

Yields approximately 20 rolls

CHEESY SPOON BREAD

2	cups milk	2	eggs
½	cup yellow cornmeal	4	ounces medium-sharp Cheddar
1	tablespoon butter		cheese, grated
¾	teaspoon salt		

1. Preheat oven to 375°.
2. Scald milk in saucepan. Do not boil. Slowly stir in cornmeal, cooking until slightly thickened. Add butter and salt.
3. Remove from heat. Beat eggs and gradually add cornmeal mixture, beating to keep smooth. Add grated cheese.
4. Pour into a greased 1½-quart casserole. Bake 40 minutes.

Serves 6

MONKEY BREAD

2	packages active dry yeast	1	cup boiling water
1	cup warm water	2	eggs, beaten
1	cup vegetable shortening	2	cups whole wheat flour
1½	teaspoons salt	4	cups all-purpose flour
¾	cup sugar	¾	cup melted butter

1. Dissolve yeast in water.
2. Mix together shortening, salt, sugar and boiling water. Add eggs and yeast mixture. Beat well.
3. Add flour and let dough rise until doubled in bulk.
4. Divide into thirds. Roll out each third ¼-inch thick onto a floured surface.
5. Cut dough into odd sizes and dip each piece in melted butter. Place pieces in a 9 by 5 by 3-inch loaf pan, next to each other. Make 2 layers and let rise again.
6. Bake 20 to 30 minutes at 350°. If a glass pan is used, decrease temperature by 25°.

Variation I:
Dip dough pieces first in butter, then in a cinnamon and sugar mixture before baking.

Variation II:
For a dinner bread, dip dough in butter then in Parmesan cheese.

Yields 3 loaves

BUTTER ROLLS

1 cup butter	2 eggs, beaten
½ cup sugar	1 package active dry yeast
½ teaspoon salt	4 cups all-purpose flour, or
1 cup milk	unbleached flour

1. Melt butter. Add sugar, salt and milk. Heat to 105° to 115°.
2. Add eggs, yeast and flour. Mix well.
3. Turn into greased bowl, cover and refrigerate overnight.
4. Divide dough into fourths. Roll into 10-inch circles. Cut each circle into 10 to 12 pie-shaped wedges. Roll from big end to small.
5. Place shaped crescents on cookie sheets that have been lightly sprayed with non-stick vegetable cooking spray.
6. Cover. Let them rise 2 to 3 hours.
7. Bake 10 to 12 minutes at 350° or until lightly browned.

Freezes

Yields approximately 4 dozen rolls

EARLY TEXAS CORNBREAD

1 cup cornmeal	1 cup buttermilk
½ cup all-purpose flour	¼ cup sweet milk
1 teaspoon salt	1 egg, beaten
2 tablespoons sugar	¼ cup vegetable oil
1 teaspoon baking powder	¼ cup bacon grease
½ teaspoon baking soda	

1. Preheat oven to 375°.
2. Heat oil and bacon grease in a 10-inch skillet in oven until hot.
3. Combine all dry ingredients and mix well.
4. Combine buttermilk, milk and egg. Add to dry ingredients and mix until moistened.
5. Remove skillet from oven. Pour cornbread batter into hot grease.
6. Bake 15 to 20 minutes or until golden brown on top.

Yields 12 pieces

CORNBREAD WITH CHILES

2   eggs, beaten
8   ounces sour cream
1   16-ounce can creamed corn
½   cup vegetable oil
½   cup Cheddar cheese
1   4-ounce can green chiles, diced
3   tablespoons chopped onion

3   tablespoons chopped green
      bell pepper
1½ cups cornmeal
2   teaspoons baking powder
1   teaspoon salt
½   cup grated Cheddar cheese

1. Preheat oven to 350°.
2. Mix eggs, sour cream, creamed corn, oil, ½ cup cheese, chiles, onion and bell pepper.
3. Mix dry ingredients and add quickly to sour cream mixture.
4. Pour into greased 9-inch skillet or cake pan and top with cheese.
5. Bake 45 minutes. Let cool slightly before cutting or removing from pan.

Freezes

Serves 8

TEXAS HUSH PUPPIES

Always a favorite in the South. For a true central Texas flavor, add chopped jalapeños to taste.

2   cups all-purpose flour
1   cup yellow cornmeal
2 to 3 teaspoons baking powder
⅓   cup sugar
¼   teaspoon garlic salt

2   eggs, beaten
¾   cup milk
1   onion, grated
    Vegetable oil
    Jalapeños, optional

1. Mix dry ingredients.
2. Add eggs to milk.
3. Add to dry ingredients enough milk mixture to bind. Add onion.
4. Shape into small balls.
5. Deep fry in oil until golden brown.

Yields 3 to 4 dozen

SPICY, CHEESE OLIVE BREAD

Makes soup and salad a meal!

1 16-ounce loaf unsliced French bread	½ cup finely chopped black olives
½ cup butter, softened	½ teaspoon garlic powder
¼ cup mayonnaise	1 teaspoon onion powder
2 cups shredded mozzarella cheese	

1. Preheat oven to 350°.
2. Cut bread in half lengthwise.
3. Combine butter and mayonnaise. Stir in remaining ingredients.
4. Spread mixture on both sides of cut bread.
5. Place on baking sheet, side by side. Bake 10 minutes or until cheese melts.

Freezes

Serves 6 to 8

PAPRIKA BREAD

½ cup butter	2 teaspoons celery seed
2 teaspoons paprika	Loaf unsliced bread

1. Mix together butter, paprika, and celery seed.
2. Slice bread in 1¼-inch slices. Do not cut entirely through bottom crust.
3. Spread generously with butter mixture.
4. Wrap in foil and chill overnight.
5. Unwrap and heat 15 to 20 minutes at 350°. Slices will stand apart and be slightly brown and crisp on the edges.

Serves 8

FRENCH BREAD CALIENTE

1	loaf French bread	¾	cup Parmesan cheese
½	cup butter, softened		1 to 2 teaspoons Tabasco sauce

1. Slice French bread into 1-inch thick slices, or half lengthwise, then quarter.
2. Combine butter, Parmesan cheese and Tabasco. Spread on top of slices, using all the mixture.
3. Bake at 325° approximately 20 to 30 minutes, or until heated throughout and browned on top.

Freezes

Serves 12 to 15

PEANUT BUTTER STICKS

Children and adults will love these!

1	loaf white sandwich bread	1	teaspoon garlic salt
1	12-ounce jar peanut butter	1	teaspoon paprika
1	cup vegetable oil	1	teaspoon Tabasco sauce

1. Preheat oven to 300°.
2. Trim bread crusts. Cut each slice of bread into 6 strips.
3. Toast strips and crusts in oven until very dry and lightly browned.
4. Melt peanut butter, spices and oil together and cool.
5. Dip toasted strips of bread into peanut butter mixture, a few at a time. Roll strips in bread crumbs made from crusts.
6. Store in a cookie tin.

These freeze nicely. Consider omitting garlic and Tabasco if you are making them for children.

Freezes

Yields 150 sticks

BANANA BRAN MUFFINS

1 cup milk	½ teaspoon baking soda
1 cup bran cereal	1 egg
1 cup whole wheat flour or all-purpose flour	¼ cup vegetable oil
4 teaspoons baking powder	¼ cup honey
½ teaspoon salt	2 ripe bananas, mashed

1. Preheat oven to 400°.
2. Pour milk over bran cereal and let soften 5 minutes.
3. Combine flour, baking powder, salt and soda.
4. Add egg, oil and honey to cereal mixture and mix well. Stir in bananas. Add flour mixture, stirring only to moisten.
5. Pour mixture into 12 greased muffin cups. Bake 20 to 25 minutes.

Freezes

Yields 12 muffins

MELT IN YOUR MOUTH MUFFINS

1 cup butter, softened	2 cups self-rising flour
8 ounces sour cream	

1. Preheat oven to 400°.
2. Cream ingredients.
3. Fill greased miniature muffin pans with batter.
4. Bake 18 to 20 minutes. Serve warm from the oven.

Yields 15 to 20 miniature muffins

APPLESAUCE MUFFINS OR BREAD

Combine:
½   cup applesauce
1   cup sugar
½   cup vegetable oil
2   eggs
3   tablespoons milk
1   cup raisins

Add to this mixture:
2   cups all-purpose flour
1   teaspoon baking soda
½   teaspoon baking powder
½   teaspoon cinnamon
¼   teaspoon salt
¼   teaspoon allspice
½   teaspoon nutmeg
½   cup pecans, chopped

Topping:
¼   cup pecans, chopped
½   cup brown sugar
½   teaspoon cinnamon

1. Preheat oven to 350° or 400°.
2. Combine applesauce, sugar, oil, eggs, milk and raisins.
3. Sift together flour, baking soda, baking powder, cinnamon, salt, allspice and nutmeg.
4. Stir flour into applesauce mixture and mix well. Add pecans.
5. Pour into greased loaf pan or muffin tins.
6. Combine pecans, brown sugar and cinnamon. Sprinkle over batter.
7. Bake 1 hour at 350° for a loaf or 20 minutes at 400° for muffins.

Freezes

Yields 1 loaf or 12 muffins

BLUEBERRY YOGURT MUFFINS

1½ cups whole wheat flour, stirred
½ cup all-purpose flour, sifted
2 teaspoons baking powder
1 teaspoon baking soda
¼ teaspoon salt
⅓ cup brown sugar

1 cup vanilla yogurt
2 eggs, beaten
½ cup butter, melted
2 cups fresh or frozen blueberries

1. Preheat oven to 400°.
2. Combine sifted flours, baking powder, soda, salt and brown sugar.
3. Add yogurt, eggs and butter. Stir until flour is moistened. Fold in blueberries.
4. Spoon into greased muffin tins or use paper liners.
5. Bake 20 to 25 minutes.

Variation:
Use 1½ cups all-purpose flour and ¼ cup whole wheat flour.

Yields 18

CHERRY MUFFINS

¼ cup butter
½ cup granulated sugar
½ cup brown sugar
2 eggs, well beaten
1 cup less 2 tablespoons all-purpose flour
¼ teaspoon baking powder

2 tablespoons maraschino cherry juice
½ cup finely ground pecans
2 egg whites, stiffly beaten
2 6-ounce bottles maraschino cherries
Finely sifted powdered sugar

1. Preheat oven to 400°.
2. Combine and mix all ingredients except egg whites and cherries.
3. Fold egg whites into batter.
4. Pour batter into paper-lined miniature muffin tins.
5. Place ½ cherry in the center of each muffin. Bake 10 minutes.
6. Dust warm muffins with powdered sugar.

Yields 3½ to 4 dozen

※ For lighter muffins, put greased muffin tins into the oven for a few minutes before adding the batter.

RASPBERRY BREAD

Miniature muffins can be made from this recipe and are wonderful for a brunch or luncheon.

3 cups all-purpose flour	1 20-ounce package frozen raspberries, thawed and juice reserved
2 cups sugar	
3 teaspoons cinnamon	
1 teaspoon baking soda	4 eggs, beaten
1 teaspoon salt	1 cup vegetable oil

1. Preheat oven to 350°.
2. Mix flour, sugar, cinnamon, soda and salt together. Make a well in the center.
3. Mash raspberries well. Add eggs and oil. Combine with flour mixture. Mix well. If batter appears too dry, add reserved juice or ¼ to ⅓ cup milk.
4. Pour into 2 greased and floured 9 by 5 by 3-inch loaf pans.
5. Bake 1 hour. Let loaves cool completely before wrapping.

Strawberries are a delicious substitute for raspberries. Serve with fruit butter.

Yields 2 loaves

PECAN BREAD

½ cup all-purpose flour	½ cup butter
½ teaspoon baking powder	2 teaspoons vanilla extract
⅛ teaspoon salt	½ cup plus 2 tablespoons sugar
2 cups pecans, finely chopped	2 eggs, beaten until thick

1. Preheat oven to 325°.
2. Combine flour, baking powder and salt. Mix with nuts and set aside.
3. Cream butter and vanilla. Gradually add sugar. Beat until fluffy, after each addition. Add eggs, beating thoroughly. Add dry ingredients and mix well.
4. Pour batter into two 5½ by 3-inch pans, greased on bottoms only. Bake 55 to 60 minutes.
5. Cool on a rack 15 minutes before removing from pans. Cool bread completely before slicing.

Yields 2 loaves

CARROT BREAD

This bread is good served hot or cold. Spread with butter it makes a great breakfast or snack.

⅔	cup vegetable oil	½	teaspoon salt
1	cup sugar	½	teaspoon baking powder
2	eggs	1	teaspoon cinnamon
1½	cups all-purpose flour	1	teaspoon nutmeg
1	cup grated carrots	¾	cup pecans, chopped

1. Preheat oven to 350°.
2. Combine all ingredients and stir until moistened.
3. Pour into 2 greased and floured 5¾ by 3 by 2¼-inch loaf pans. Bake 40 to 60 minutes.

Yields 2 loaves

PUMPKIN BREAD

4	eggs	1	16-ounce can pumpkin
2	cups sugar	1	teaspoon salt
1	cup brown sugar	1	teaspoon baking powder
1	cup vegetable oil	2	teaspoons baking soda
⅔	cup brandy	1	tablespoon pumpkin pie spice
3½	cups all-purpose flour	1	cup chopped pecans

1. Preheat oven to 350°.
2. Cream eggs, sugar, brown sugar and oil until light and fluffy. Add remaining ingredients, except pecans and beat well. Stir in pecans.
3. Bake in 3 greased 7 by 3 by 2-inch loaf pans for 45 minutes.

Yields 3 loaves

BANANA BREAD

		Topping:	
1	cup butter	6	tablespoons butter
1½	cups sugar	10	tablespoons brown sugar
2	eggs	5	tablespoons milk
4	ripe bananas, mashed		Chopped pecans, optional
1	teaspoon vanilla extract		
4	tablespoons buttermilk		
2	cups all-purpose flour		
1½	teaspoons baking soda		
1	teaspoon salt		

1. Preheat oven to 350°.
2. Cream butter and sugar. Beat eggs and add to sugar mixture. Add bananas, vanilla and buttermilk.
3. Sift together flour, soda and salt. Add to banana mixture. Beat well.
4. Pour into 2 greased and floured 9 by 5 by 3-inch loaf pans.
5. Bake 45 to 50 minutes or until bread pulls away from sides of pan. Cool.
6. To prepare topping, melt butter in saucepan. Add sugar and milk. Cook until syrupy.
7. Remove from heat and add chopped pecans. Pour over bread and place under broiler 5 minutes.

Yields 2 loaves

※ Over-ripe bananas may be peeled and mashed, mixed with a small amount of lemon juice, and frozen in measured amounts. These are handy for making bread, cake or muffins. (Thaw before using.)

PEAR BREAD

½ cup butter
1 cup sugar
2 eggs
1 teaspoon vanilla extract
1½ cups all-purpose flour
1 teaspoon baking powder
½ teaspoon soda
½ teaspoon cinnamon

¼ teaspoon salt
1 tablespoon purchased grated
   orange rind
⅓ cup orange juice
1½ cups bran flakes
1¼ cups finely chopped, unpeeled
   pears
½ cup chopped pecans

1. Cream butter, sugar, eggs and vanilla until light and fluffy.
2. Stir in flour, baking powder, soda, cinnamon, salt, orange rind, and orange juice.
3. Fold in bran flakes, pears and pecans.
4. Spray 2 small loaf pans with non-stick vegetable spray. Pour batter into pans and bake 50 to 60 minutes at 350°.

Freezes

※ When peeling oranges, first place them in a hot oven for a brief time. There will be no white fiber on the orange when it is peeled.

COZY'S GINGERBREAD

2 eggs, beaten
1 cup buttermilk
1 pound brown sugar
2 cups all-purpose flour
¾ cup butter

1 teaspoon baking soda
1 teaspoon ginger
2 teaspoons cinnamon
1 teaspoon nutmeg

1. Preheat oven to 350°.
2. Add eggs to buttermilk. Blend and set aside.
3. Combine brown sugar and flour. Cut in butter. Reserve 1 cup of mixture for later use. To remainder of sugar mixture add baking soda, ginger, cinnamon and nutmeg. Stir in buttermilk mixture just until all ingredients are moist.

4. Pour batter into a 9 by 13-inch greased and floured metal baking pan. Sprinkle reserved cup of sugar mixture over top of batter.
5. Bake 35 to 45 minutes.

Serve with mounds of freshly whipped cream.

Freezes

Serves 24

※ Brown sugar will stay moist if an apple is placed in the package.

CINNAMON QUICKIES

These are a special treat that even the youngest child can help prepare. The measurements are not specific as they vary according to how thoroughly the rolls are dipped into butter and rolled in the cinnamon and sugar mixture. However, this is no problem. Adjust the amounts as needed.

2 loaves thin white sandwich bread	Butter, melted
	Cinnamon
16 ounces cream cheese	Sugar

1. Cut crusts off bread. Flatten bread with a rolling pin.
2. Spread each piece with a light layer of cream cheese.
3. Roll slices of bread tightly. Cut rolls into quarters.
4. Prepare a mixture of cinnamon and sugar. Dip each roll into melted butter, then roll in the cinnamon and sugar mixture.
5. Place rolls on a cookie sheet and freeze. When rolls are frozen, store in plastic baggies.
6. When ready to serve, place rolls on a cookie sheet. Bake at 350° until rolls are bubbly and puffy.

Serve with sour cream and strawberry preserves for dipping.

Serves 12 to 15

EASY COFFEE CAKE

3 10-ounce cans biscuit dough	2 teaspoons cinnamon
1 cup butter, melted	1 cup chopped pecans
1½ cups brown sugar, packed	

1. Preheat oven to 350°.
2. Grease bundt pan.
3. Quarter all biscuits, set aside.
4. Mix together melted butter, brown sugar, cinnamon and pecans.
5. Place half the biscuits on bottom of bundt pan. Pour half the sugar mixture over biscuits. Repeat layering process until all is used, ending with the sugar mixture on top.
6. Bake 40 to 45 minutes. After baking, wait 5 minutes before turning cake out onto a serving dish.

Variation:
Any leftover rolls may be halved, dipped into butter, then a cinnamon and sugar mixture and baked on a cookie sheet for 10 minutes at 350°. A quick, tasty good morning treat.

Serves 24 to 30

APPLE NUT COFFEE CAKE

	Topping:
½ cup butter	½ cup nuts
1 cup sugar	½ cup brown sugar
2 eggs	1 teaspoon cinnamon
1 teaspoon vanilla extract	2 tablespoons butter, melted
2 cups all-purpose flour	
1 teaspoon baking powder	
1 teaspoon baking soda	
½ teaspoon salt	
1 cup sour cream	
2 cups finely chopped apples	

1. Preheat oven to 350°.
2. Cream butter and sugar. Add eggs and vanilla. Beat well.
3. Sift flour, baking soda, baking powder and salt. Add to butter mixture alternately with sour cream. Fold in apples.
4. Spread in a greased 9 by 13-inch baking pan.
5. Combine nuts, brown sugar, cinnamon and butter. Sprinkle over batter.
6. Bake 30 to 40 minutes.

Serves 18 to 24

CHEESE DELIGHTS

Delicious with morning coffee.

¼ **pound sharp Cheddar cheese,**
   grated
½ **cup butter**
2 **tablespoons brown sugar**
1½ **cups all-purpose flour**

½ **teaspoon baking powder**
   Dash salt
   Raspberry jam

1. Preheat oven to 350°.
2. Cream cheese, butter and sugar. Mix in flour, baking powder and salt. Mixture will be crumbly.
3. Place half the mixture in the bottom of a greased 9 by 9-inch baking pan. Cover generously with jam. Sprinkle remaining mixture on top.
4. Bake 20 to 30 minutes or until slightly browned. Cut in squares.

Freezes

Yields 15 to 20 squares

NUT ROLLS

Dough:
½   cup milk
1   package active dry yeast
6   cups all-purpose flour
3   tablespoons sugar
½   teaspoon salt
2   cups butter
4   eggs
½   cup butter, melted

Filling:
2   cups sugar
1   teaspoon cinnamon
¼   cup butter, melted
1   cup evaporated milk
½   cup water
2   pounds ground walnuts or
    pecans
3   egg whites, beaten

1. To make dough, heat milk to lukewarm and add yeast. Dissolve and set aside.
2. Mix flour, sugar and salt in a bowl. Cut in butter until mixture is the consistency of oatmeal.
3. Beat eggs. Add to flour mixture and mix well. Add yeast mixture to flour mixture. Mix and knead like bread dough. Set aside. Dough does not need to rise.
4. To make filling, in a saucepan combine sugar and cinnamon. Add butter, evaporated milk and water. Stir and cook over low heat until mixture comes to a rolling boil. Boil 2 or 3 minutes. Add nuts and cook several minutes, stirring constantly.
5. Add egg whites and mix thoroughly. Set aside to cool.
6. Divide dough and nut mixture into 6 portions.
7. Sprinkle sugar on work surface. Roll dough into thin rectangles, as long as a cookie sheet. Brush dough with melted butter. Spread a thin layer of nut filling on dough.
8. Roll jelly-roll fashion. Place seam side down on a greased cookie sheet.
9. Bake 35 to 40 minutes at 350° or until the roll is golden. Do not overbake. Brush with butter when done. Place on a rack to cool.

Yields 6 rolls (12" x 3"), about 24 slices per roll

FESTIVE ISLAND TOAST

Delicious served with pecan butter, maple or coconut syrup.

8	slices fine white bread	½	cup fine sugar
	Butter	¾	cup chopped pecans
2	teaspoons vanilla extract	¾	cup chopped coconut
2	eggs		

1. Toast bread medium-light on both sides. Trim crusts if desired.
2. Butter toast and place on a cookie sheet. Set aside.
3. Add vanilla and sugar to slightly beaten eggs. Mix well.
4. Add chopped pecans and coconut. Spoon this mixture onto toast and spread to edges.
5. Bake 15 minutes at 350°. Cut in half and serve.

Yields 16 pieces

✳ Maple syrup may be warmed in the bottle by removing the cap. Heat on high 25 to 30 seconds in a microwave oven.

WHIPPED CREAM PANCAKES

A delightful variation of a traditional favorite using packaged biscuit mix.

4	eggs, at room temperature, separated	¼	cup whole milk or whipping cream
¼	cup packaged biscuit mix	¼	teaspoon vanilla extract
1	tablespoon sugar		

1. Preheat griddle.
2. Beat egg whites until stiff but not dry.
3. Combine and mix all remaining ingredients.
4. Stir half of egg whites into mixture. Fold remaining whites in gently.
5. Cook pancakes using ¼ cup batter per pancake.

Do not stack pancakes to serve as they will quickly flatten.

Yields 6 pancakes

GERMAN PANCAKES

Filling:

4 tablespoons sour cream or softened cream cheese	2 tablespoons butter
1 tablespoon plus 1 teaspoon powdered sugar	4 eggs
1 medium peach or ½ cup fresh blueberries, strawberries or stewed apples	½ cup all-purpose flour
	½ cup milk
	½ teaspoon salt

1. To make filling, combine sour cream, powdered sugar and fruit. Set aside.
2. Preheat oven to 550°.
3. Melt butter in an iron skillet and coat the entire surface of the skillet.
4. Beat eggs until frothy.
5. Using a whisk, add flour to mix and beat until batter is smooth. Gradually add milk and salt.
6. Pour batter into heated iron skillet. Place on upper rack of the oven.
7. As edges of the pancake rise above the skillet, approximately 4 minutes, lower the temperature to 500°.
8. Cook 2 to 3 more minutes until center is done and slightly puffy.
9. Remove from oven and slide pancake out of skillet, face up, onto a platter.
10. Pour filling near one edge and roll up pancake. Sift powdered sugar over the top. Slice into serving portions and serve immediately.

Serves 4 as a side dish or 2 as a meal

BANANA COCONUT PANCAKES

A special weekend breakfast.

2   bananas, very ripe
1½ teaspoons fresh lemon juice
1   cup milk
2   eggs, separated
3   tablespoons butter, melted
1¼ cups all-purpose flour
2   tablespoons sugar
2   teaspoons baking powder
¼   teaspoon salt
⅔   cup grated, toasted coconut,
     divided

Mango sauce:
⅓   cup sugar
1   large ripe mango, peeled and
     pitted
1½ tablespoons lemon juice

1. Place bananas and lemon juice in blender or food processor. Blend until smooth. Add milk, egg yolks, butter. Blend.
2. In a small bowl, sift together flour, sugar, baking powder and salt. Combine with banana mixture.
3. Beat egg whites until stiff. Fold egg whites and ½ cup toasted coconut into batter.
4. Cook pancakes and sprinkle with toasted coconut.
5. To make mango sauce, blend sugar, mango and lemon juice.

Pancakes may be served with mango sauce, maple or coconut syrup.

Serves 4 to 6

PUMPKIN ROLL

3 eggs
1 cup sugar
⅔ cup canned pumpkin
1 teaspoon lemon juice
¾ cup all-purpose flour
2 teaspoons cinnamon
1 teaspoon baking powder
½ teaspoon salt
1 teaspoon ginger
1 teaspoon nutmeg

Filling:

1¼ cups powdered sugar, reserve
  ¼ cup for towel
8 ounces cream cheese, softened
¼ cup butter, softened
½ teaspoon vanilla extract

1. Preheat oven to 375°.
2. Beat eggs 5 minutes at high speed, until fluffy.
3. Gradually add sugar. Stir in pumpkin and lemon juice.
4. Combine flour, cinnamon, baking powder, salt, ginger and nutmeg. Add to pumpkin mixture and blend.
5. Spoon onto jelly roll pan that has been greased and lined with greased wax paper.
6. Bake 15 minutes. Turn out on dish towel sprinkled with ¼ cup powdered sugar. Peel off wax paper from bottom of cake. Trim edges of roll just to cut off crusty part.
7. Roll up cake and towel jelly-roll fashion. Cool.
8. Combine all filling ingredients. Mix well.
9. When cake is cool, unroll and spread filling over entire jelly roll. Roll again. Place seam side down. Sprinkle with powdered sugar. Chill.

Serves 6 to 8

DESSERTS AND SWEETS
Sugars

The South is known for its delicious desserts and breads. These are sweetened with honey, sugar, syrup, and molasses, and each varies in consistency and composition. The following information may answer your questions regarding substituting, accurate measuring and storing.

Types of Sugar

1. **Granulated sugar**—Granulated sugar is available in regular, which is uniform in granulation, and extra-fine, which has smaller crystals. Extra-fine sugar, the result of additional processing, is used when quick mixing is important, as in a fine-textured cake. It is possible to make your own by processing regular granulated sugar in a blender or food processor.

2. **Powdered Sugar**—Powdered sugar is granulated sugar that has been crushed and screened. The number of X's on the box indicate the degree of fineness. The fine powdered is 4X; the very fine powdered is 6X; and the extremely fine powdered is 10X. Powdered sugar should be measured like flour. Sift it first, being careful not to pack when measuring. Level off with a knife.

3. **Brown sugar**—Brown sugar is a less refined beet or cane sugar and is either light or dark. It contains more moisture than granulated sugar and should be stored in air-tight containers. This keeps it soft and moist. It is possible to soften hardened brown sugar by putting it into an air-tight container and placing a bread or apple slice in the container. A crisp lettuce leaf may also be used. Another method calls for placing the package in a low oven (250°) for 10 minutes. Press out lumps with a spoon or roll with a rolling pin. To measure brown sugar, press or pack it into a measuring spoon or cup for accuracy.

Liquid Sugars

Honey, molasses and syrup are composed of 20 to 30% water. They have a very distinct flavor and vary in their ability to sweeten. Their greater moisture content must be taken into account. It is a good idea to grease the measuring container first before measuring.

1. **Corn syrup or honey**—These may be substituted for one-half the amount of sugar called for, but the liquid in the recipe must be decreased by one-fourth.

2. **Molasses**—Unsulphured molasses is manufactured from the juice of ripened cane. Sulphured molasses is a by-product of the sugar making process. Blackstrap molasses is a waste product. Molasses should replace no more than one-half the amount of sugar in a recipe. However, in baking, one cup molasses may be substituted for every cup of sugar. For each cup, ½ teaspoon soda must be added and any baking powder called for must be omitted. Reduce the liquid by one-fourth cup for each cup of sugar used in the recipe.

3. **Cane syrup**—It is made from sugar cane that has been boiled down to the consistency of syrup. It is substituted like molasses.

4. **Sorghum syrup**—This syrup comes from coarse Sorghum grass. The grass is processed into juice which is boiled until it becomes syrup. It is substituted like molasses.

5. **Liquid Brown**—This is a much more concentrated, liquid form of brown sugar and substituting it for regular brown sugar is not recommended.

Chocolate

Chocolate, derived from ground, roasted and shelled cocoa beans, ranges from bitter to sweet in flavor. There are several types of chocolate available for baking.

1. **Cocoa Powder**—The solid substance that remains after the cocoa butter has been removed from chocolate.

2. **Liquid Chocolate**—Different from chocolate syrup in that it may or may not be sweetened when purchased. It may be substituted in recipes calling for cocoa powder or unsweetened chocolate. It is usually packaged in one ounce packets. A packet equals one square of unsweetened or one-fourth cup of cocoa powder.

3. **Chocolate morsels**—A convenient form of chocolate. When used as a substitute for other forms of chocolate, it must be melted first to ensure proper blending.

Storing Chocolate

Chocolate must be stored in a cool, dry place with a moderate temperature (60° to 78°) and approximately 50% humidity. It can be refrigerated but does become brittle and hard. Chocolate should be allowed to reach room temperature before using. Airtight wrapping will keep it from absorbing odors in the refrigerator and will prevent moisture from forming when it is removed from the refrigerator.

Chocolate has a high content of cocoa butter. When stored at temperatures that fluctuate between hot and cold, it may develop a gray film called "bloom", which is caused by cocoa butter rising to the surface. Though unattractive, this does not affect the taste. Melting will eliminate the film so do not hesitate to use it.

Melting Chocolate

While melting, chocolate may harden or tighten if the smallest amount of moisture is present in the melting pan. This can be corrected by adding one teaspoon of solid vegetable shortening for each ounce of chocolate and blending well.

1. **Top of Stove Method**—A heavy saucepan can be used to melt chocolate over low heat if it is combined with fat or liquid. When melting it alone, avoid scorching by using a small bowl in hot water or by using a double boiler.

2. **Oven Method**—Baking chocolate can also be melted by placing it on a piece of aluminum foil, in its own wrapper, in the oven while it is preheating.

3. **Microwave Method**—To melt a six ounce package of morsels, place it in a two-cup glass measuring cup. Microwave on high for one minute. Stir with a dry spoon. Microwave for one additional minute on high. Remove and stir until chocolate is smooth. For a twelve ounce package, use a four cup measure and microwave on high for two minutes. Stir. Microwave on high one more minute.

Melt two chocolate squares at a time uncovered on medium (50%) three to four minutes. Stir after two and one-half minutes and continue microwaving. Stir.

Nuts and Fruit

Pecans

Pecans are a southern favorite used in everything from salads and vegetables to desserts. If you are fortunate enough to have your own pecan tree, you may be interested in the following tips. Try soaking whole nuts in salted water overnight before shelling. This keeps the pecans from breaking into tiny pieces during the shelling process. They should never be stored at room temperature. Storage by refrigerator is possible for up to three months if they are shelled. To store for a longer period of time, freeze in plastic containers or screw top glass jars.

Almonds

Almonds have a delightful flavor but must be blanched first after shelling. One method of blanching calls for covering the shelled nut with boiling water, then cooling. The skin then slips off. The other method calls for placing shelled almonds in a saucepan and covering with cold water. Bring to a boil. Remove from the heat, drain, and rinse with cold water. Drain again and remove the outer skin.

Coconut

Fresh coconut is a treat and removing the meat from the shell is not difficult. First, drain the milk and place the coconut in an oven until hot to touch. Remove and tap all over with a hammer, giving one hard knock at the end to crack open. Remove shell, peel off brown skin and cool before grating or grinding. Dry and store in jars.

Dates

Dates are good for baking; also, stuffed dates are wonderful and easily made by removing the stones and stuffing with fondant, nut meats, marshmallows, seedless raisins, coconut, or preserved ginger and cherries chopped together. Close dates after stuffing. Brush with beaten egg white, roll in colored coconut, colored sugar or chopped nuts.

Raisins

Raisins are excellent for baking and are used frequently in recipes. They are distributed more easily in batters if heated first. Chopped dates or prunes may be substituted if raisins are not available.

Prunes

Prunes are stuffed by first steaming them for fifteen minutes or until soft and plump. Remove the pits from the prunes and stuff with the filling of your choice. The same procedure can be used with figs; however, slit the sides of the figs to stuff with fillings.

Candy

It is best to use a large pot when making candy. Butter the pot to a depth of two inches to prevent boiling over. Cover for the first three minutes of boiling to prevent the formation of crystals. When making hard candies, remove pot from heat and allow to cool for two minutes before pouring.

It is wise not to make candy in hot, humid weather as it will become sticky and sugary. If the candy should become sugary, add a small amount of water and bring to a boil.

Sugar, Syrup and Candy Cooking Tests

Stage of Hardness	Range of Temperature	Stage Determination Test (Cold Water Test)	Uses
Thread	223°–234° F (106°–112° C)	Syrup forms a 2-inch soft ball	Cooked icings and syrups
Soft ball	234°–240° F (112°–116° C)	Syrup forms a soft ball, but it does not hold its shape	Fondant, fudge and penuche

Stage of Hardness	Range of Temperature	Stage Determination Test (Cold Water Test)	Uses
Firm ball	242°–248° F (117°–120° C)	Syrup forms a firm ball that holds its shape unless pressed	Caramels
Hard ball	250°–268° F (121°–131° C)	Syrup forms a hard ball that holds its shape, yet is pliable	Divinity, popcorn balls, marshmallows, nougat and saltwater taffy
Soft crack	270°–290° F (132°–143° C)	Syrup separates into threads that are hard, but not brittle	Butterscotch and taffies
Hard crack	300°–310° F (149°–154° C)	Syrup separates into hard and brittle threads	Brittle glace
Clear liquid	320° F (160° C)	Thick clear liquid, sugar liquifies	Barley sugar
Caramel	338°–350° F (170°–177° C)	Thick brown liquid (at this stage, do not drop into cold water)	Flavoring and color

Cakes

Cake Batter

The key to a good cake is in the batter. Try adding vanilla to the creamed butter and sugar, even though most recipe instructions say to add it last. The butter will absorb the flavor better. It is always best to allow butter, cream cheese and eggs to reach room temperature before using. Shortening should be soft (room temperature) so that when beaten with sugar it will resemble whipped cream. If soda is used in the recipe, it should be added at this point, as should the spices.

Dry ingredients are the mainstay of any cake. It is best to use cake flour for all cakes as it produces larger, more velvety cakes with a more uniform texture. Put dry ingredients into a bowl and mix thoroughly with a whisk. This takes the place of sifting. Raisins, dates and berries will not settle to the bottom if coated with flour first.

Preparing Cake Pans

A good cook knows that no cake will be a success if half of it remains in the cake pan. To avoid this, grease or oil the bottom and sides of the pan and dust with flour. A large kitchen salt shaker is wonderful for this purpose. If the cake is chocolate, use cocoa, rather than flour, for dusting. Be sure to tilt the pan back and forth until all sides are evenly coated. Invert the pan over the sink and tap to dislodge loose flour. A tip that truly makes removing a cake from the pan a breeze is to cover the bottom of the pan with wax paper cut to fit. The cake will easily lift out. To keep cakes from cracking while cooking, add one envelope of unflavored gelatin to the dry ingredients of the cake batter. It will not affect the flavor or moistness of the cake.

Ingredients and Pan Size Chart

If a recipe calls for:	You may use:
1 or 2 eggs with 1 to 2 cups of flour	a 8 x 8-inch pan or two 8-inch round layer pans
2 eggs with 2½ cups flour	a 9 x 9 or 10 x 10-inch pan or two 9-inch round layer pans
4 eggs with 2 to 3 cups flour	a 9 x 13 or 10 x 12-inch pan or two 9-inch round layer pans or three 8-inch round layer pans
6 egg whites and 2½ cups flour	a 10 x 14-inch pan or three 9-inch round layer pans
8 or more egg whites with 2½ cups flour	a 10 x 14-inch pan

Interchangeable Pan Sizes

If a recipe calls for:	Substitute:
2 8-inch layers	2 thin 8″ x 8″ x 2″ squares or 18 to 24 2½-inch cupcakes
3 8-inch layers	2 9″ x 9″ x 2″ squares
2 9-inch layers	2 x 8″ x 8″ x 2″ squares or 3 thin 8-inch layers or 1 15″ x 10″ x 1″ rectangle or 30 2½-inch cupcakes
1 8″ x 8″ x 2″ square	1 9-inch layer
2 8″ x 8″ x 2″ squares	2 9-inch layers or 1 13″ x 9″ x 2″ rectangle
1 9″ x 9″ x 2″ square	2 thin 8-inch layers
2 9″ x 9″ x 2″ squares	3 8-inch layers
1 13″ x 9″ x 2″ rectangle	2 9-inch layers or 2 8″ x 8″ x 2″ squares
1 12″ x 8″ x 2″ rectangle	2 8-inch layers
1 9″ x 5″ x 3″ loaf	1 9″ x 9″ x 2″ square or 24 to 30 2½-inch cupcakes
1 8″ x 4″ x 3″ loaf	1 8″ x 8″ x 2″ square
1 9″ x 3½″ tube	2 9-inch layers or 24 to 30 2½-inch cupcakes
1 10″ x 4″ tube	2 9″ x 5″ x 3″ loafs or 1 13″ x 9″ x 2″ rectangle or 2 15″ x 10″ x 1″ rectangles

Pouring Batter

For a prettier cake, fill the cake pans about ⅔ full and spread the batter into corners and to the sides, leaving a slight hollow in the center. After pouring batter into the pan, hit the pan on the counter to prevent air holes in the finished cake. (Angel food cake is an exception)

Test for Doneness

The cake is ready when it springs back if lightly pressed in the center. It will shrink slightly from the sides of the pan. Also, if a toothpick comes out clean when inserted in the middle, it is done.

Removing from Pan

The cake should be placed on a wire rack for 5 to 10 minutes to cool after it comes from the oven. After cooling period, loosen the sides with a knife or small metal spatula and invert cake on the wire rack to finish cooling. (Be sure the cake cools in the pan for the recommended time and no longer (as this makes it tough).

Cutting the Cake

If you are cutting a cake while it is still hot, try using a thread instead of a knife. If the cake has cooled, dip a knife into water before cutting each slice. A nutmeg grater will remove burnt edges. If brownies (or cake) stick to the bottom of the pan, place the pan on a wet tea towel for several minutes. It will loosen the brownies. Place half an apple in the storage container with the cake to keep it fresh.

Icing

If icing will not thicken, beat it in strong sunlight or near an open oven door or in a double boiler over boiling water. Add a pinch of salt to the sugar (before adding to the icing) to prevent graining. (Try using leftover egg whites, beaten stiff, with a small glass of tart jelly for cake icing.)

When using powdered sugar as a topping, place a lace doily over the top of the unfrosted cake. Sprinkle powdered sugar over the doily and then remove it carefully so that the lace design on the cake is not disturbed. Powdered sugar or icing should not be applied until cake is thoroughly cooled. A little flour dusted on the cake before frosting will keep icing from running.

Frosting Hints and Ideas
Party Cupcake Cones

Fill flat-bottomed ice cream cones half-full of cake batter. Place cones in muffin tins. Bake according to cake package directions. Cool cones. Frost and decorate.

To frost cupcakes quickly, dip the top of each into soft frosting, twirl and turn right side up.

When frosting a layer cake, place two pieces of wax paper about five inches wide on the plate (covering it). Place the cake on top of this and frost. When done, pull out the wax paper. The plate will be clean with no frosting drips to clean up!

Cookies
Preparation

Cookies are easy and fun to make and there are as many favorite recipes as there are cooks. Keep these tips in mind to make preparation easier.

When making rich butter cookies, combine dry ingredients thoroughly with creamed mixture so that the dough will not be crumbly. For recipes that require chopped raisins and marshmallows, save time by cutting with scissors. As with pie dough, chill cookie dough ten minutes in the refrigerator to reduce the amount of flour needed when rolling it out. (Excess flour makes cookies tough.) Using powdered sugar instead of flour when rolling out also prevents toughness. (Cookies will taste sweeter.) For thin rolled cookies, roll dough directly onto a greased and floured cookie sheet. Cut into shapes and remove excess dough between them.

Storage

Crisp cookies must be kept in air tight containers, but if they do become soft they may be placed in a 300° oven for five minutes to restore crispness. Keep soft cookies soft by placing a slice of bread in the container.

Baking

Baking sheets without sides will allow cookies to bake evenly and quickly. The sheets should be shiny and should clear the sides of the oven by at least two inches for good heat circulation and even baking. Cool baking sheets before placing unbaked cookies on them. When using baking paper (as in jelly rolls or on cookie sheets), do not butter the pan or the paper.

Sometimes cookies, especially thin ones, become hard or stick to the cookie sheet. Reheat them quickly and allow to cool for a minute before removing them.

Variations

To create an attractive top on "dropped" cookies, press top of cookie with a fork dipped in confectioners sugar. To create waffle pattern, press a second time in the opposite direction.

Pies

Pie Crusts

Combine ingredients for crust and chill dough for ten minutes in the refrigerator. This reduces the amount of flour needed when rolling crust. (Excess flour toughens crust.)

Too much moisture in the dough will make the crust tough and cause the pie to steam rather than bake. Handle dough as little as possible after adding water, and use a pastry cloth and stockinet covered rolling pin when rolling the crust. Besides creating a tender, flaky crust, you will use less flour and fewer strokes.

Pastry may be rolled between two sheets of wax paper. Peel off the top paper and flip the bottom into the pie pan, removing the paper. When placing a crust in the pan, be sure it covers the surface smoothly. If air is trapped beneath the surface, it can push the crust out of shape when baking. For a two crust pie, fold the top crust over the lower crust before crimping it. This will keep the juices in the pie.

To prevent a soggy bottom crust, brush surface with well beaten egg white before adding the filling and cool pie on a rack after baking. When baking a pie shell, place another pie pan on top of crust to prevent "bubbling" of the crust. Bubbling may also be prevented by pricking crust all over with a fork.

Fruit Pies

Fruit pies are especially tempting during the summer months when fresh fruit is at its peak. To save time when cooking the fruit, add sugar after the cornstarch (or flour) has been added to the hot juice.

A few pieces of large macaroni inserted through the top crust or drinking straws (cut into short pieces) placed in the slits of the crust will prevent juices from running out and will allow steam to escape. (If the juice does run over in the oven, shake salt on it. This causes it to burn to a crisp so it is easily removed.)

Custard Pies

There are many types of custard pies ranging from pumpkin to refrigerator. Custard pies may be baked and frozen or may be made ahead and frozen unbaked. A frozen 8-inch pie will bake in one hour at 400° F. When baking a custard pie that has not been frozen, bake at a high temperature for ten minutes; then finish baking at a lower temperature. This prevents a soggy crust. A layer of marshmallow placed in the bottom of a pumpkin pie before the filling makes an excellent topping because the marshmallows rise to the top. Always remove a pie from the refrigerator 20 minutes before serving to remove the chill from the crust.

Crumb Crust Chart

	Crumbs	Sugar	Butter
Graham Crackers (18)	1½ cups	¼ cup	½ cup
Vanilla Wafers (38)	1¼ cups		⅓ cup
Ginger Snaps (24)	1¼ cups		⅓ cup
Chocolate Wafers	1¼ cups		⅓ cup

Mix ingredients well and press into a 9-inch pie plate. Bake approximately 10 minutes at 375°.

NEVER FAIL PIE SHELL

1 cup all-purpose flour	**⅓ cup shortening**
½ teaspoon salt	**3 tablespoons cold water**

1. Sift flour and salt together.
2. Cut in shortening with pastry blender until mixture resembles small peas.
3. Sprinkle water over mixture while tossing lightly with a fork until particles stick together.
4. Form into a smooth ball. Wrap in wax paper and chill.
5. Lightly roll pastry into a circle 1-inch larger than pie plate.
   Lift into pie plate, pat out air, fold edges under and crimp.
6. Prick crust thoroughly.
7. Bake approximately 12 minutes at 450° or until golden brown. Cool and fill.

Yields 1 8 or 9-inch crust

Decorative Pie Crusts

Meringues

Meringue will not shrink if spread on the pie so that it touches the crust on each side. Bake meringue in a moderate oven. Cool baked meringue slowly away from drafts. "Tears" form if meringue is cooled too quickly.

MERINGUE

For a perfect non-weeping meringue:

3	egg whites	3	tablespoons sugar
¼	teaspoon cream of tartar	½	teaspoon vanilla extract
½	teaspoon baking powder, optional		

1. Beat eggs with cream of tartar until foamy. Add ½ teaspoon baking powder if extra high meringue is desired.
2. Gradually add sugar until peaks are stiff and glossy.
3. Spread meringue on pie and seal all edges.
4. Bake 8 to 10 minutes, or until lightly browned, at 400°.
5. Cool away from drafts.

General Tips

❋ Pie crust will stay together better if one tablespoon lemon juice is added to the crust as it is mixed.

❋ To avoid tough pie pastries, do not use all butter.

❋ To measure shortening, fill the cup with water less the amount desired. Add the shortening then pour out the water.

❋ To keep a pie from being soggy, do not pour the filling into the pastry shell until just before baking.

❋ Brushing the top pie crust with milk before baking will make it brown and glossy.

❋ There is a difference in pie pans. Shiny metal pans do not bake bottom crusts well. Use aluminum pans with a dull finish or heat proof glass pie plates. When baking fruit pies, place a sheet of aluminum foil directly under pie plate on the bottom of the oven to catch the drippings from the pie.

Fruit Desserts

Try these ideas for refreshing and satisfying summer desserts. Sprinkle strawberries with sugar and pour a small amount of brandy or orange juice over them. Chill for three or four hours. Pour pink champagne over the strawberries and garnish with mint before serving.

Place lime sherbet in the center of honeydew melon halves. Honeydew is wonderful filled with strawberries and fresh pineapple. A sauce of beaten vanilla ice cream and brandy poured over all makes it really special. Or simply serve melon with crystallized ginger or powdered ginger sprinkled on top.

FILLED RUSSIAN TEA CAKE

The cake layers can be frozen and filled when ready to serve. Filling and cake can be made ahead and assembled a day before serving.

10 egg whites
Pinch of salt
1 teaspoon cream of tartar
4 egg yolks
1½ cups sugar
1 cup all-purpose flour, sifted twice
1 teaspoon vanilla extract

Filling:

5 egg yolks
1½ cups evaporated milk
¾ cup sugar
1 envelope unflavored gelatin
¼ cup cold water
2 cups whipping cream

1. Preheat oven to 325°.
2. Beat egg whites until frothy. Add salt and cream of tartar. Beat until stiff peaks form.
3. In another bowl, beat yolks until lemon colored. Add sugar and beat until creamy.
4. Fold in half the egg whites and all the flour. Fold in remaining egg whites. Add vanilla.
5. Pour into ungreased tube pan. Bake 70 minutes at 325°.
6. Remove cake from oven. As cake cools, make filling.
7. Beat egg yolks until light and set aside.
8. Heat milk in top of double boiler. Add egg yolks and sugar. Cook, stirring constantly until thickened enough to coat a spoon.

9. Dissolve gelatin in cold water and add to hot custard.
10. Refrigerate just until cool.
11. Whip cream until stiff. Fold into cold custard.
12. Slice cooled cake into 3 layers. Spread filling between layers and all over cake. Refrigerate.

A beautiful dessert garnished with strawberries.

Serves 16

SWEDISH CAKE ROLL

5   eggs, separated
¾   cup powdered sugar
2   heaping tablespoons all-purpose flour
2   heaping tablespoons cocoa
1½ tablespoons vanilla extract

Whipped Cream:
1   cup whipping cream
¼   cup powered sugar
1   teaspoon vanilla extract

Frosting:
6   tablespoons cocoa
2   cups powdered sugar
¼   cup butter
½   teaspoon vanilla extract
¼   cup milk, divided
¼   cup chopped pecans, optional

1. Preheat oven to 350°.
2. Beat egg yolks until lemon colored. Gradually add powdered sugar. Beat until dissolved.
3. Sift together flour and cocoa. Add to egg yolk mixture. Stir in vanilla.
4. Beat egg whites to form stiff peaks. Fold into batter.
5. Bake in a greased and floured 11 by 16-inch jelly roll pan 20 minutes.
6. Turn hot cake out on a dish towel. Sprinkle with powdered sugar. Roll in dish towel and cool.
7. When cool, unroll. Spread with whipped cream and roll again.
8. To make frosting, combine cocoa and sugar. Cream butter.
9. Add cocoa and sugar mixture alternately with milk to butter and mix well. Add vanilla. Beat until light and fluffy.
10. Frost cake roll. Sprinkle with pecans. Refrigerate until ready to serve.

Serves 10 to 12

FILLED CHOCOLATE CAKE

Cake:

2	cups all-purpose flour
1	teaspoon baking soda
½	cup butter
½	cup vegetable oil
3	squares unsweetened chocolate
2	cups sugar
2	eggs, beaten
½	cup sour milk (1½ teaspoons vinegar added to ½ cup milk)
1	teaspoon vanilla extract

Filling:

1	5.3-ounce can evaporated milk
¾	cup sugar
¼	cup water
1	egg, beaten
¼	cup raisins
1	teaspoon vanilla extract
½	cup chopped walnuts or pecans
½	cup chilled whipping cream

Frosting:

1	6-ounce package semi-sweet chocolate morsels
½	cup sour cream
	Dash salt

1. Preheat oven to 350°.
2. Sift flour with soda into a large bowl.
3. In a small saucepan, combine butter, oil and chocolate. Cook over low heat to melt chocolate. Stir in 1 cup water. Cool mixture 15 minutes.
4. To flour mixture, add sugar, eggs, sour milk and vanilla. Mix well by hand. Stir in chocolate mixture.
5. Pour batter into 2 greased and floured 8-inch square or round pans.
6. Bake 30 to 35 minutes. Remove and cool in pans 5 minutes before turning out on racks. Cool completely.
7. To make filling, combine milk, sugar and water in a saucepan. Cook until hot and sugar is dissolved. Add a little of the hot mixture to egg. Stir egg into hot mixture and continue to cook over low heat until thick. Add raisins, nuts and vanilla. Cool completely.
8. Whip cream until stiff.
9. Place cake layer, top side down, on serving plate. Spread with filling. Top with whipped cream. Place other layer on top.
10. To make frosting, melt chocolate in top of a double boiler. Remove from heat. Stir in sour cream and salt.
11. Beat until smooth. Let stand 5 minutes before spreading on cake.
12. Refrigerate. Remove cake from refrigerator 20 to 25 minutes before serving.

Serves 12

WINE CAKE WITH JAM AND CREAM

This cake can be baked ahead, wrapped airtight and frozen.

6	cups whipping cream	½	cup raspberry jam
1	cup sugar	½	cup apricot jam
2	9-inch layers white cake	2	cups sliced almonds
¾	cup white wine (not too dry)		

1. Whip cream until soft peaks form. Slowly add sugar and beat until cream is stiff.
2. Split each cake layer in half, making 4 layers.
3. Place 1 layer on serving plate (be sure plate can be placed in the freezer for 6 to 8 hours without damaging it).
4. Sprinkle layer with wine, spread with raspberry jam and whipped cream. Add next layer, sprinkle with wine, spread with apricot jam and whipped cream. Add third layer, sprinkle with wine, spread with whipped cream, and sprinkle with ½ cup almonds. Add last layer, repeating process.
5. Frost top and sides with remaining whipped cream and sprinkle with remaining almonds.
6. Freeze cake. After cream on top and sides is firm, cover with plastic wrap. Place in refrigerator approximately ½ hour before serving to soften. Cut into thin slices.

Serves 12

CLASSIC ANGEL FOOD CAKE

1¼ cups cake flour, sifted
½   cup sugar
1½ cups egg whites, at room
      temperature, (approximately
      12 large eggs)

¼   teaspoon salt
1¼ teaspoons cream of tartar
1   teaspoon vanilla extract
¼   teaspoon almond extract
1⅓ cups sugar

1. Preheat oven to 375°.
2. Sift flour and ½ cup sugar 4 times.
3. Combine egg whites, salt, cream of tartar and flavorings. Beat until soft peaks form.
4. Add 1⅓ cups sugar, sprinkling in ⅓ cup at a time. Beat until well blended after each addition.
5. Sift in flour mixture in 4 additions. Fold in with 15 strokes after each addition.
6. Pour into tube pan. Use a knife to cut through batter several times to eliminate air bubbles.
7. Bake 35 to 40 minutes.

Frost with Cream Almond Frosting.

Serves 12 to 16

CHOCOLATE ANGEL FOOD CAKE WITH MOCHA FROSTING

Cake:
1 cup all-purpose flour
½ cup cocoa
2 cups sugar
1½ cups egg whites
    (approximately 12 eggs), at
    room temperature
2 teaspoons cream of tartar
2 teaspoons vanilla extract

Mocha Frosting:
2 tablespoons cocoa
3 cups powdered sugar
½ cup butter
1 egg yolk
2 tablespoons strong coffee
2 teaspoons vanilla extract
2 teaspoons half and half,
    optional
½ cup chopped walnuts or
    pecans

1. Sift flour and cocoa 3 times. Sift sugar 3 times.
2. Beat egg whites. When frothy, add cream of tartar. When whites form soft peaks, add sugar and beat until stiff.
3. Gently fold in cocoa and flour mixture. Add vanilla.
4. Pour into an ungreased angel food cake pan. Bake 40 to 50 minutes at 325°.
5. Invert cake pan on a rack. Cool completely before removing and frosting.
6. To make frosting, beat together first 6 frosting ingredients. Add vanilla. If frosting is too thick to spread, gradually add cream until desired consistency is reached. Stir in chopped nuts. Frost.

Serves 10

THREE FLAVOR POUND CAKE

This is a delicious, moist cake that can be prepared ahead and frozen.

½   cup shortening
1   cup butter
3   cups sugar
5   eggs
3½ cups all-purpose flour
½   teaspoon baking powder
1   cup milk
1   teaspoon rum flavoring
1   teaspoon coconut flavoring

Glaze:

¼   cup plus 1 tablespoon water
1   cup sugar
½   teaspoon almond extract

1. Preheat oven to 300°.
2. Cream together shortening, butter and sugar. Add eggs, beating well.
3. Sift together flour and baking powder.
4. Add dry ingredients and milk, alternately to butter mixture, beginning and ending with flour.
5. Add rum and coconut flavoring. Pour into greased and floured bundt pan.
6. Bake 1½ to 1¾ hours. DO NOT OPEN THE DOOR.
7. Shortly before cake is removed from oven, bring water and sugar to a rolling boil. Remove from heat and add almond flavoring.
8. Pour over hot cake and let stand until cool. Remove from pan.

Serves 16 to 18

Freezes

COCONUT POUND CAKE

1½ cups butter
2½ cups sugar
5 eggs
2 teaspoons coconut flavoring
3 cups all-purpose flour
½ teaspoon salt
1 teaspoon baking powder
1 cup milk
1⅓ cups flaked coconut

Glaze:
2 cups sugar
1 cup water
¼ cup light corn syrup
2 tablespoons coconut flavoring
3 tablespoons butter

1. Cream butter and sugar. Add eggs 1 at a time, beating well after each addition.
2. Add coconut flavoring.
3. Sift together flour, salt and baking powder. Add milk and flour alternately to butter mixture. Fold in coconut.
4. Pour into greased and floured tube or bundt pan. Place in cold oven.
5. Heat oven to 350°. Bake 1¼ to 1½ hours.
6. To make glaze, bring all ingredients, except flavoring, to a boil. Cook 5 minutes.
7. Add coconut flavoring. Cool.
8. Pour glaze over hot cake in pan. Let stand until completely cold. Run spatula around pan sides and tube to remove. Cake must be cold before removing from pan or it will fall apart.

Serves 16

GERMAN CHOCOLATE POUND CAKE

3 cups sugar
1 cup vegetable shortening
4 eggs
2 teaspoons vanilla extract
2 teaspoons butter flavor
1 cup buttermilk

3 cups sifted all-purpose flour
½ teaspoon baking soda
1 teaspoon salt
1 package German's sweet
   chocolate, melted

1. Preheat oven to 300°.
2. Cream sugar and shortening.
3. Add eggs, flavorings and buttermilk.
4. Sift together flour, soda and salt. Add to shortening mixture and beat well.
5. Add chocolate. Mix well.
6. Bake in a greased and floured bundt pan 1½ to 2 hours.

Cake can be prepared ahead and frozen.

Serves 12 to 15

APRICOT BRANDY POUND CAKE

Delicious served with vanilla ice cream or strawberries and whipped cream.

1 cup butter
3 cups sugar
6 eggs
3 cups all-purpose flour
½ teaspoon soda
½ teaspoon salt
1 cup sour cream

½ teaspoon rum or rum flavoring
½ teaspoon almond flavoring
½ teaspoon lemon flavoring
1 teaspoon orange flavoring
1 teaspoon vanilla extract
½ cup apricot brandy

1. Preheat oven to 350°.
2. Cream butter and sugar. Add eggs 1 at a time, beating well after each addition.
3. Sift together flour, soda and salt.
4. Add dry ingredients alternately with sour cream. Add flavorings and apricot brandy.
5. Bake in a greased and floured bundt pan, or tube pan that DOES NOT COME APART. Bake 60 to 70 minutes.

Serves 16 to 18

POUND CAKE

Cream, sour cream, or cream cheese—whichever version you choose, you will have a hit!

Pound Cake Base

1 cup butter
3 cups sugar
6 eggs
3 cups cake flour, sifted

Cream variation:

1 cup whipping cream
1 tablespoon almond extract

Sour Cream variation:

1 cup sour cream
½ teaspoon vanilla extract
½ teaspoon lemon flavoring
¼ teaspoon nutmeg
¼ teaspoon salt

Cream Cheese variation:

½ cup additional butter
8 ounces cream cheese, softened
2 teaspoons lemon flavoring
1 teaspoon butter flavoring
¼ teaspoon salt

1. Preheat oven to 325°.
2. Cream butter and sugar until light and fluffy.
3. Add eggs, 1 at a time, beating well after each addition.
4. Depending on variation chosen, add whipping cream, sour cream or cream cheese alternately with flour.
5. Add flavorings for chosen variation and beat well.
6. Pour batter into greased and floured 10-inch tube or bundt pan.
7. Bake 1½ hours or until cake springs back when touched.

When testing similar recipes for this book, we usually found a favorite very quickly. When it came to pound cakes we had a different situation! Each was similar and yet each was unique in the variation of flavorings. Try all three, we think you will have three favorites.

Serves 12 to 15

KENTUCKY CAKE

1   package yellow cake mix
1   4-ounce package vanilla
    instant pudding
4   eggs
¾   cup cold coffee
½   cup vegetable oil
¼   cup Kahlua or Amaretto

Glaze:
½   cup butter
½   cup sugar
½   cup coffee
¼   cup Kahlua or Amaretto

1. Preheat oven to 350°.
2. Combine all cake ingredients and beat according to cake mix package directions.
3. Pour batter into greased, not floured, tube pan.
4. Bake 40 to 45 minutes.
5. Combine all glaze ingredients and bring to boil. Boil slowly 4 to 5 minutes.
6. Remove cake from oven and cool slightly. Remove from pan.
7. Poke holes in cake surface. Spoon glaze over cake until absorbed.

This cake is delicious served with whipped cream.

Freezes

Serves 12 to 14

BUTTERNUT CAKE

1 cup butter
½ cup vegetable shortening
3 cups sugar
1 tablespoon Vanilla Butter and Nut Flavoring
6 eggs
3¼ cups all-purpose flour
1 teaspoon salt
1 small can evaporated milk, add water to make 1 cup

Butternut frosting:
1 cup brown sugar
½ cup milk
2 tablespoons butter
1 teaspoon Vanilla Butter and Nut Flavoring
Powdered sugar

1. Do not preheat oven.
2. Cream butter, shortening and sugar. Add flavoring and beat well. Add eggs 1 at a time, beating well after each addition.
3. Sift flour and salt together. Add flour and milk alternately to butter mixture.
4. Pour batter into a greased but not floured bundt pan. Place in a cold oven. Bake 1 hour and 45 minutes in a 300° oven. Do not open door until cake is done.
5. To make frosting, mix brown sugar, milk and butter in a saucepan. Boil 5 minutes. Remove from heat. Beat well with an electric mixer until cool.
6. Add Vanilla Butter and Nut Flavoring. Add enough powdered sugar to reach spreading consistency. Mix well. Frost cooled cake.

Serves 15

COCONUT CAKE

Do not expect this delicious treat to last long! The aging time is worth the wait.

2¼ cups all-purpose flour
1½ cups sugar
3   teaspoons baking powder
1   teaspoon salt
½   cup vegetable shortening
1   cup milk
2   eggs
1½ teaspoons vanilla extract

Frosting:

2   6-ounce packages frozen coconut
1   cup sour cream
2   cups sugar

1. Preheat oven to 350°.
2. Sift together flour, sugar, baking powder and salt.
3. Combine flour, shortening and milk. Beat 2 minutes at medium speed.
4. Add eggs and vanilla. Beat 2 additional minutes.
5. Bake in 2 greased and floured, round 9-inch cake pans 30 minutes.
6. Let stand 5 minutes after removing from oven. Turn out on wax paper.
7. Prepare frosting by combining coconut, sour cream and sugar in saucepan. Boil and stir 10 minutes.
8. Split each cake layer in half.
9. Spoon hot icing between each of 4 layers. Frost top and sides.
10. Refrigerate 3 days before serving.

Serves 12

PIÑA COLADA CAKE

3 cups all-purpose flour
1 teaspoon baking soda
1 teaspoon salt
1 teaspoon cinnamon
2 cups sugar
3 eggs
1½ cups vegetable oil
1 tablespoon vanilla extract

2 cups ripe mashed bananas (approximately 4 large bananas)
1 15-ounce can crushed pineapple, drained
1 cup chopped walnuts or pecans

1. Preheat oven to 350°.
2. Sift together flour, soda, salt and cinnamon.
3. Cream together sugar, eggs and oil.
4. Combine egg mixture and dry ingredients.
5. Add vanilla, bananas, pineapple and nuts.
6. Pour into greased and floured bundt pan. Bake 1 hour and 15 minutes.

Serves 16 to 18

FRESH APPLE CAKE

1 cup vegetable oil
2 cups sugar
2 eggs
2½ cups all-purpose flour
2 teaspoons baking powder
1 teaspoon baking soda
1 teaspoon cinnamon
1 teaspoon salt

1 teaspoon vanilla extract
3 cups peeled, diced apples
1 cup pecans or walnuts, chopped
½ cup flaked coconut
1 12-ounce package butterscotch morsels

1. Preheat oven to 350°.
2. Combine oil, sugar, eggs and dry ingredients. Beat until smooth. Add vanilla.
3. Fold in apples, nuts and coconut.
4. Pour into greased tube pan. Sprinkle butterscotch morsels over top of cake. Bake 55 minutes.

This cannot be frozen, but stays moist for several days.

Serves 16

STRAWBERRY CAKE

A family birthday favorite.

1 10-ounce package frozen
   strawberries, thawed
1 box white cake mix, (without
   pudding)
1 3-ounce box strawberry
   gelatin
½ cup vegetable oil
¼ cup water
3 eggs

Frosting:
½ cup butter
1 pound powdered sugar
1 teaspoon vanilla extract

1. Preheat oven to 350°.
2. Reserve ½ cup strawberry juice for frosting.
3. Combine cake mix, gelatin, oil, water, eggs and strawberries. Beat until well blended.
4. Pour batter into 3 greased and floured 8-inch round pans. Bake 30 to 35 minutes. Cool.
5. Frost cake with frosting made of butter, powdered sugar, reserved strawberry juice and vanilla.

Serves 12

PINEAPPLE CAKE WITH CREAM CHEESE GINGER FROSTING

2 cups all-purpose flour	
1 cup sugar	
1 cup brown sugar	
2 teaspoons baking soda	
2 eggs, beaten	
1 20-ounce can crushed	
pineapple, undrained	
1 cup nuts, chopped	

Frosting:

3 ounces cream cheese
¼ cup butter, softened
1 teaspoon vanilla extract
2 cups powdered sugar
½ teaspoon ground ginger

1. Preheat oven to 350°.
2. Mix together flour, sugar, brown sugar and soda.
3. Add eggs and pineapple. Mix well by hand. Stir in chopped nuts.
4. Spread batter into an ungreased 9 by 13-inch glass baking dish. Bake 45 to 50 minutes.
5. To make frosting, beat together cream cheese, butter and vanilla. Gradually add powdered sugar and ginger. Beat until mixture is smooth.
6. Spread on cooled cake.

Serves 12

FRUIT PRESERVE CAKE

1 teaspoon baking soda	2 cups sugar
1 cup buttermilk	4 eggs, well beaten
3 cups cake flour	⅔ cup cherry preserves
½ teaspoon allspice	⅔ cup apricot preserves
½ teaspoon cinnamon	⅔ cup pineapple preserves
½ teaspoon nutmeg	½ teaspoon vanilla extract
¾ cup butter	1 cup pecans

1. Preheat oven to 325°.
2. Mix soda with buttermilk. Set aside.
3. Sift remaining dry ingredients with flour.
4. Cream butter and sugar. Add eggs and beat well.
5. Add flour alternately with milk to butter mixture. Beat well after each addition.
6. Stir in preserves, nuts, and vanilla.
7. Bake in a greased and floured bundt pan 85 to 90 minutes.

Serves 10 to 12

FIG PRESERVE CAKE

½ cup milk
1 teaspoon vinegar
½ cup butter
1 cup sugar
3 eggs
2 cups all-purpose flour
1 teaspoon baking soda

1 teaspoon cinnamon
½ teaspoon allspice
½ teaspoon nutmeg
⅛ teaspoon cloves
1 pint fig preserves
1 cup chopped pecans
1 tablespoon peanut butter

1. Combine milk and vinegar. Let stand while mixing other ingredients.
2. Cream butter, sugar and eggs until light and fluffy.
3. Combine flour with remaining dry ingredients.
4. Add flour mixture alternately with milk to butter mixture. Beat well after each addition.
5. Mash figs with a fork.
6. Add preserves, pecans and peanut butter to batter. Mix well.
7. Pour into a greased and floured bundt pan. Bake 1 hour at 325°.

Serves 12 to 15

HOLIDAY FRUIT CAKE

1 pound chopped dates
8 ounces candied pineapple, chopped
8 ounces candied cherries, chopped
3½ cups pecan pieces

1 cup all-purpose flour
1 cup sugar
1 teaspoon baking powder
½ teaspoon salt
4 eggs, beaten
1 teaspoon vanilla extract

1. Preheat oven to 325°.
2. Combine chopped fruit and nuts. Add dry ingredients
3. To fruit mixture add eggs and vanilla. Mix well.
4. Pour into 2 greased and floured 9 by 5 by 3-inch loaf pans.
5. Bake 1 hour.

Yields 2 large loaves

AUSTIN'S BEST CHEESECAKE

Crust:

1½ cups finely ground graham crackers
¼ cup sugar
6 tablespoons butter, melted

Filling:

2 pounds cream cheese, softened
2 cups sugar
2 cups sour cream
2 tablespoons vanilla extract
6 eggs

1. Preheat oven to 375°.
2. Combine crust ingredients and mix well.
3. Press firmly into greased and floured 10 by 3-inch spring form pan.
4. Bake crust 6 to 9 minutes, or until edges are brown. Cool.
5. Reduce temperature to 350°.
6. With electric mixer, blend together cream cheese, sugar, vanilla, sour cream and eggs. Beat until creamy.
7. Pour batter into a prebaked crust.
8. Bake 1 hour. Turn off heat and open oven door slightly. Leave in oven 1 additional hour. Cool and refrigerate before serving.

Serves 12

FROZEN MOCHA CHEESECAKE

1¼ cups chocolate wafer cookie
    crumbs
¼ cup sugar
¼ cup butter, melted
8 ounces cream cheese, softened
1 14-ounce can sweetened
    condensed milk

⅔ cup chocolate syrup
2 tablespoons instant coffee
1 teaspoon hot water
1 cup whipping cream, whipped

1. In a small bowl, combine crumbs, sugar and butter.
2. Pat crumb mixture on the bottom and sides of a 9-inch spring form pan. Chill.
3. In a large bowl, beat cream cheese until fluffy. Add condensed milk and chocolate syrup.
4. In a small bowl, dissolve coffee and hot water. Add to condensed milk mixture. Mix well and fold in whipped cream. Pour over crust.
5. Cover and freeze 6 hours or until firm. Garnish top with cookie crumbs or chocolate shavings.

Serves 10 to 12

NUTTY DEVIL'S CAKE

Topping:

1 cup all-purpose flour	½ cup sugar
2 teaspoons baking powder	½ cup brown sugar
¾ cup sugar	2 tablespoons cocoa
¼ teaspoon salt	1 cup boiling water
½ cup milk	
2 tablespoons butter	
1 teaspoon vanilla extract	
1 ounce unsweetened baking chocolate, melted	
½ cup finely chopped nuts	

1. Preheat oven to 350°.
2. Sift dry ingredients together.
3. Combine dry ingredients with milk, butter and vanilla. Add chocolate. Stir well.
4. Pour into a greased 8 by 8 by 2-inch metal pan.
5. Combine sugar, brown sugar and cocoa. Sprinkle mixture evenly over cake batter. Pour boiling water over all.
6. Bake 30 minutes.

Serve warm with whipped cream or vanilla ice cream.

Serves 6 to 8

CHOCOLATE FROSTED RUM CAKE

Cake:

1   box white cake mix with butter added
½   cup orange juice
2   tablespoons white rum
2   teaspoons grated orange rind
8   tablespoons white rum
½ to 1 cup chopped walnuts

Filling:

2   teaspoons unflavored gelatin
2   tablespoons hot water
2   cups whipping cream
½   cup powdered sugar
⅓   cup white rum

Chocolate Frosting:

4   ounces unsweetened baking chocolate
1   cup sugar
2   tablespoons hot water
2   eggs
6   tablespoons butter, room temperature
2 to 4 tablespoons white rum

1. Preheat oven to 350°.
2. Mix cake according to package directions, substituting orange juice and 2 tablespoons rum for water. Add orange rind.
3. Pour into 2 greased and floured 9-inch cake pans. Bake according to package directions.
4. Remove and cool. When cool, split cake into 4 layers. Sprinkle each layer with 2 tablespoons rum and walnuts.
5. To make filling, dissolve gelatin in water and cool slightly.
6. Beat cream with sugar until stiff. Gradually beat in rum. Add gelatin slowly, beating until stiff.
7. Spread 3 layers with filling and stack.
8. To make frosting, melt chocolate in top of a double boiler over hot water.
9. Remove from heat. Beat in sugar and hot water.
10. Beat in eggs 1 at a time.
11. Beat in butter. Add rum, a tablespoon at a time, until smooth.
12. Place frosting in refrigerator and cool thoroughly before frosting cake.

Serves 12

GERMAN CHOCOLATE CAKE WITH MOCHA PECAN FROSTING

A nutty chocolate frosting gives this traditional favorite a different taste.

Cake:
1	cup butter, softened
2	cups sugar
4	eggs, separated
1	teaspoon baking soda
1	cup buttermilk, divided
4	ounces sweet chocolate, melted
2	teaspoons vanilla extract
2½	cups cake flour

Frosting:
½	cup butter, softened
3	cups powdered sugar
3	tablespoons cocoa
2	teaspoons vanilla extract
5	tablespoons strong black coffee
	Whipping cream
2	cups chopped pecans

1. Preheat oven to 350°.
2. Grease and flour three 9-inch round cake pans or a 9 by 13-inch pan.
3. Cream together butter and sugar. Add egg yolks. Mix well.
4. Combine soda and 2 tablespoons buttermilk.
5. Melt chocolate. Add vanilla. Combine chocolate with buttermilk mixture. Blend well.
6. Add butter mixture to chocolate mixture. Blend well.
7. Sift cake flour, then measure. Add cake flour and buttermilk alternately to batter.
8. Beat egg whites to form soft peaks. Fold into batter.
9. Bake in 3 layers 30 minutes or in a 9 by 13-inch pan 45 minutes. Cool and frost.
10. To make frosting, cream butter, powdered sugar, cocoa, vanilla and coffee. Thin with whipping cream to spreading consistency. Stir in pecans.

Serves 16

※ Cake layers are easily removed from the pans if the hot pans are placed on a damp cloth as soon as they come out of the oven.

CARAMEL TURTLE CAKE

1 pound caramels
1 box German chocolate cake
  mix
½ cup vegetable oil
½ cup butter, melted
1½ cups water
1 14-ounce can sweetened
  condensed milk, divided
1 cup chopped pecans

Frosting:
½ cup butter
½ cup evaporated milk
⅓ cup cocoa
1 16-ounce box powdered sugar
1 teaspoon vanilla extract

1. Preheat oven to 350°.
2. Mix cake mix, oil, butter, water and half the sweetened condensed milk until well blended.
3. Pour half the batter into a greased 9 by 13 by 2-inch cake pan. Bake 20 to 30 minutes.
4. Unwrap caramels. In a double boiler melt caramels and remaining sweetened condensed milk. (Melting takes approximately 20 minutes, so begin when cake is put in oven.) Pour over warm cake layer. Sprinkle with chopped pecans.
5. Pour remaining batter on top and bake again for 30 to 40 minutes.
6. To make frosting bring butter, evaporated milk and cocoa to a boil. Add powdered sugar and vanilla. Beat until smooth.
7. Spread warm frosting on warm cake.

Serves 12 to 15

LOTTIE LEE'S CAKE

A perfect cake for the lunch box.

3	eggs	*Broiler Icing:*	
1	cup sugar	½	cup butter
1	teaspoon vanilla extract	1	cup sugar
1	cup all-purpose flour	¼	cup milk
1	teaspoon baking powder	¾	cup chopped pecans
½	cup milk	¾	cup flaked coconut
2	tablespoons butter		

1. Preheat oven to 350°.
2. Scald milk with butter. Set aside.
3. Beat eggs. Gradually add sugar and beat until thick. Add vanilla.
4. Sift together flour and baking powder. Add to egg mixture.
5. Add scalded milk to first mixture.
6. Pour batter into a greased and floured 13 by 9 by 2-inch pan. Bake 20 minutes.
7. While cake bakes, make icing by combining butter, sugar, milk, pecans and coconut.
8. Cook over medium heat, until mixture slowly bubbles. Cook approximately 15 minutes, or until thick, stirring occasionally.
9. Pour icing over cake. Place under broiler 3 to 5 minutes or until coconut is lightly toasted and icing is bubbly.

Serves 12 to 15

CHESS CAKE

First Layer:
1 box butter flavor, yellow cake mix
1 teaspoon vanilla extract
½ cup butter
2 eggs

Second Layer:
1 box powdered sugar
2 eggs
1 teaspoon vanilla extract
8 ounces cream cheese

1. Preheat oven to 350°.
2. Combine first layer ingredients and mix well. Spread in a greased 9 by 13 by 2-inch glass baking dish.
3. Mix ingredients for second layer. Spread over first layer.
4. Bake 35 to 40 minutes.

Yields 24 pieces

BUTTERY CHOCOLATE PECAN CUPCAKES

A great dessert to take on a picnic.

4 squares unsweetened chocolate
1 cup butter
¼ teaspoon butter flavoring
1½ cups chopped pecans
1¾ cups sugar
1 cup all-purpose flour
4 large eggs
1 teaspoon vanilla extract

1. Preheat oven to 325°.
2. Melt chocolate and butter. Add butter flavoring and pecans. Stir mixture to coat pecans.
3. Combine sugar, flour, eggs and vanilla. Mix only until blended. Do not beat.
4. Add chocolate and nut mixture and again mix carefully without beating.
5. Pour into paper lined muffin tins. Bake 30 to 35 minutes.

Yields 18 cupcakes

BANANA BIRTHDAY CAKE
A Collection Classic

1 cup butter, room temperature
3 cups sugar
4 eggs
6 very ripe bananas, mashed
2 teaspoons baking soda
½ cup sour cream
3 cups sifted all-purpose flour

Butter Frosting:
½ cup butter, room temperature
3 cups sifted powdered sugar
3 to 4 tablespoons whipping cream
1 teaspoon vanilla extract

1. Preheat oven to 325°.
2. Cream together butter and sugar.
3. Add eggs one at a time, beating thoroughly after each addition.
4. Beat in bananas.
5. Mix baking soda and sour cream. Add to banana mixture.
6. Add flour. Mix well.
7. Bake in 3 greased and floured 8-inch cake pans 25 to 35 minutes. When cool, frost layers with butter frosting.
8. To make frosting, cream together butter and powdered sugar.
9. Add cream and vanilla. Mix well.

Serves 12 to 14

COOKIE CUTTER CAKES

Cake:
1½ cups sugar
½ cup butter
¼ cup vegetable shortening
½ cup milk
3 eggs
1 teaspoon vanilla extract
1½ cups all-purpose flour

Icing:
6 cups powdered sugar
⅓ cup light corn syrup
3 tablespoons butter
½ cup water
1 teaspoon vanilla extract
Assorted food coloring

1. Preheat oven to 350°.
2. Combine all cake ingredients except flour. Beat 2 minutes at medium speed. Add flour. Beat 2 additional minutes. Pour batter into a greased and floured 9 by 13-inch baking pan.
3. Bake 25 to 35 minutes. Remove from oven. Cool. Freeze 30 minutes before cutting. Cut with 2-inch metal cookie cutters.
4. Store in freezer until ready to frost.
5. To prepare frosting, combine all ingredients except food coloring. Blend well. Add 1 to 2 tablespoons additional water if too thick. Color icing as desired.
6. Spoon icing over cakes. Place cakes on cooling racks to allow icing to set.

Yields 13 to 14 cookies

CAKE FROSTINGS
Chocolate Frosting

This will generously frost a 3 layer cake.

¾	cup cocoa	1	teaspoon vanilla extract
4	cups powdered sugar	½	cup milk
½	cup butter		

1. Mix cocoa and sugar together.
2. Cream ½ the cocoa mixture with butter. Blend in vanilla and ¼ cup milk.
3. Add remaining cocoa sugar mixture and remaining milk.
4. Refrigerate and cool before frosting cake.

Chocolate Morsel Frosting

This is enough icing for two 8-inch square cakes or two 9-inch round cakes. It is very easy to make and has a very rich taste.

1	6-ounce package semi-sweet chocolate morsels	½	cup sour cream
			Dash salt

1. Melt chocolate morsels in top of double boiler over hot water.
2. Remove pan from hot water and stir in sour cream and salt.
3. With a wooden spoon, beat until smooth. Cool 5 minutes.

Chocolate Rum Frosting

A delicious frosting to use on a favorite 2 layer white or yellow cake. This is especially good if cake layers are split and spread with whipped cream flavored with sugar and rum.

4	squares unsweetened chocolate	2 to 4	tablespoons rum
2	eggs	2	tablespoons hot water
6	tablespoons butter, softened		

1. Melt chocolate in top of a double boiler over hot water.
2. Beat in eggs, 1 at a time, beating well after each addition.
3. Beat in butter. Add rum, 2 tablespoons at a time, until frosting is smooth. Add hot water if consistency is too thick.

Sour Cream Coconut Frosting

This is wonderful as a filling or frosting for a favorite yellow cake.

1½ cups powdered sugar
16 ounces sour cream
16 ounces coconut

1 tablespoon vanilla extract

1. In a saucepan, combine sugar, sour cream and coconut. Boil and stir 10 minutes.
2. Remove and stir in vanilla.
3. Slice cake layers and cover each one with a thin layer of frosting. Stack layers and frost top and sides.
4. Refrigerate 1 to 3 days before serving.

Custard Frosting

This is especially good on angel food or pound cake.

2 cups whipping cream
½ cup sugar

1 can sweetened condensed milk
Juice of 3 lemons

1. Whip cream and add sugar. Fold in condensed milk.
2. Stir in lemon juice.
3. Frost cake and place in freezer. Remove cake from freezer 10 to 15 minutes before serving.

Berry Cream Frosting

Use this delicious topping for a favorite angel food cake.

1 16-ounce package frozen strawberries or raspberries
1½ cups whipping cream

1 cup sour cream
1 cup powdered sugar
½ teaspoon vanilla extract

1. Drain fruit.
2. Beat whipping cream until stiff.
3. Mix sour cream, sugar and vanilla until well blended. Fold mixture into whipped cream.
4. Fold berries into cream.
5. Chill.

Orange Nut Sauce

This is delicious served over slices of angel food, sponge or pound cake.

1   cup sugar
1   cup orange juice
    Grated rind of 1 orange
8   egg yolks, beaten
    Pinch salt

1   cup whipping cream, whipped
1   cup chopped almonds or
    pecans

1. Mix together sugar, orange juice and orange rind. Place in a double boiler. Add egg yolks and salt. Cook over medium-high heat until thickened.
2. Add whipped cream and nuts to orange mixture.
3. Cool and refrigerate until ready to serve.

Yields 4 cups

Cream Almond Frosting

10 egg yolks
10 tablespoons sugar
2   tablespoons cornstarch
2½ cups half and half

1   teaspoon vanilla extract
1   cup blanched, slivered
    almonds

1. Blend together egg yolks, sugar and cornstarch.
2. Heat cream. When hot (do not boil), pour portion of cream into egg and sugar mixture.
3. Pour back into remaining cream. Cook in double boiler until thickened. Frosting should be the consistency of mayonnaise. Cool.
4. Add vanilla and nuts. Keep refrigerated.

Yields 3 cups

CHOCOLATE ANGEL PIE

A rich and delicious treat for all chocolate lovers.

1   baked 10-inch pie shell

Meringue:

2   egg whites
½   teaspoon vinegar
    Dash salt
¼   teaspoon cinnamon
½   cup sugar

Chocolate layers:

1   cup semi-sweet chocolate
      morsels, melted
2   egg yolks, lightly beaten
¼   cup water
½   cup sugar
½   teaspoon cinnamon
2   cups whipping cream, whipped

Topping:

1   cup whipping cream
½   cup powdered sugar
½   teaspoon vanilla extract
    Shaved chocolate or chocolate
      curls

1. To make meringue, beat egg whites with vinegar, salt and cinnamon until soft peaks form. Add sugar, beating until stiff glossy peaks form.
2. Spread on bottom and sides of baked pie shell. Bake 18 minutes at 325° or until lightly browned. Cool.
3. To make chocolate layers, melt chocolate morsels. Add egg yolks and water.
4. Spread 1 tablespoon of mixture over cooled meringue layer. Cool remainder of chocolate.
5. Combine sugar and cinnamon with whipping cream. Beat until firm. Spread half the mixture over chocolate layer in pie shell.
6. Combine remainder of whipped cream with remainder of cooled chocolate.
7. Spread over whipped cream in pie shell.
8. Chill at least 4 hours.
9. To make topping, combine whipping cream with powdered sugar and vanilla. Whip until firm. Spread on pie and top with shaved chocolate or chocolate curls.

Serves 8 to 10

MUD PIE

1	package chocolate wafers	3	tablespoons butter
½	cup melted butter	2	teaspoons vanilla extract
2	pints mocha ice cream	2	tablespoons sugar
⅓	cup cocoa	2	1-ounce squares unsweetened
⅔	cup sugar		chocolate
1⅓	cups whipping cream, divided		

1. Preheat oven to 375°.
2. Crush wafers. Add melted butter. Mix well with a fork and press into a 9-inch pie plate. Bake 10 minutes. Cool completely.
3. Spread ice cream carefully onto crust. Freeze 1½ hours, or until solid.
4. In a saucepan, cook cocoa, sugar, ⅓ cup cream and butter until mixture is smooth and boils. Stir in 1 teaspoon vanilla. Cool but do not let mixture get too hard to pour.
5. Pour sauce over frozen ice cream base. Freeze at least 1½ hours.
6. Before serving, whip remaining cream with remaining 2 tablespoons sugar until soft peaks form. Add remaining vanilla and spread over pie. Garnish with bitter chocolate shavings.

Serves 10

GERMAN CHOCOLATE PIE

2 ounces German's baking chocolate
¼ cup butter
¾ cup sugar
Pinch salt
½ cup light corn syrup
3 eggs
¼ cup milk
1½ tablespoons cornstarch
1 teaspoon vanilla extract
½ cup chopped pecans
¼ cup coconut
1 9-inch unbaked pie shell

1. Preheat oven to 375°.
2. Melt chocolate in a double boiler.
3. Add butter, sugar, salt and corn syrup. Stir until dissolved. Cool.
4. Beat eggs. Add milk and cornstarch. Mix well.
5. Add egg mixture to chocolate mixture. Stir in vanilla, pecans and coconut. Pour into pie shell.
6. Bake approximately 35 to 45 minutes or until filling is set.

Serves 8

BUTTERSCOTCH CUSTARD PIE

1 cup brown sugar
½ teaspoon salt
2 tablespoons butter
½ cup all-purpose flour
2 cups milk
3 egg yolks
½ teaspoon vanilla extract
½ cup chopped pecans
1 9-inch pie crust, baked
1 cup whipping cream

1. Combine brown sugar, salt, butter and flour in top of a double boiler. Cook until butter has melted and brown sugar has started to dissolve. Slowly add milk. Stir and cook until all sugar has dissolved
2. Beat egg yolks until light. Add a little hot milk mixture to eggs. Slowly add eggs to milk and cook, stirring constantly, until thick.
3. Add vanilla to custard. Add pecans.
4. Pour into baked pie crust. Chill several hours before serving. Top with whipped cream that has been sweetened with a little sugar.

Serves 8

CARAMEL COFFEE ICE CREAM PIE

Crust:

1 egg white
¼ teaspoon salt
¼ cup sugar
1½ cups chopped walnuts

Filling:

1 quart coffee ice cream, softened
1 quart vanilla ice cream, softened

Caramel Sauce:

2 tablespoons butter
½ cup brown sugar, firmly packed
¼ cup half and half
2 tablespoons chopped walnuts
½ teaspoon vanilla extract

1. Preheat oven to 400°.
2. Beat egg white with salt until stiff. Beat in sugar, 1 tablespoon at a time, to form stiff peaks. Fold in walnuts.
3. Spread mixture evenly over bottom, sides and slightly onto the rim of a buttered 9-inch pie plate.
4. Bake 10 minutes. Cool.
5. Combine softened ice creams and fill pie crust. Freeze until serving time.
6. To make caramel sauce, melt butter over medium heat. Add brown sugar. Remove from heat. Very slowly stir in cream. Return to heat 1 minute, stirring constantly. Stir in walnuts and vanilla.

Before serving, spoon caramel sauce over pie. Sauce may be used warm or cold.

Serves 6 to 8

BOURBON PIE

Pie Crust:

1   package chocolate wafer
    cookies
⅓ to ½ cup butter, melted

Filling:

6   egg yolks
1   scant cup sugar
1   envelope unflavored gelatin
½   cup cold water
2   cups whipping cream
½   cup bourbon

1. To make crust, crush cookies and add melted butter. Press into 10-inch pie plate.
2. Beat egg yolks with sugar until lemon colored and thick.
3. Put gelatin in top of double boiler and soak in cold water. Dissolve gelatin over hot water, stirring until thoroughly melted.
4. Slowly add gelatin to egg mixture. Cool thoroughly.
5. Whip cream and fold into egg mixture. Set this bowl in a bowl of ice water and very slowly fold in bourbon.
6. Stir mixture over ice until it begins to set. It is very important that the mixture thicken a little before it is poured into the pie crust. Pour filling into pie shell and chill until firm.
7. Garnish with shaved chocolate or crushed cookie crumbs on top.

Serves 8

BAVARIAN CREAM PIE

Chocolate Crumb Crust:
1½ cups chocolate cookie wafer
    crumbs
½ cup butter, melted

Filling:
3 egg yolks
½ cup sugar
¼ teaspoon salt
1 cup milk, scalded
1 tablespoon unflavored gelatin
    softened in ¼ cup cold water
1 teaspoon vanilla extract
3 egg whites, stiffly beaten
1 cup whipping cream, whipped

1. To make crust, blend chocolate cookie crumbs with melted butter. Press into a 10-inch pie plate. Chill.
2. Combine egg yolks, sugar and salt in top of double boiler. Slowly add scalded milk. Cook, stirring constantly in double boiler until mixture coats a spoon. Remove from heat.
3. Add softened gelatin and stir until dissolved.
4. Cool to room temperature. Fold in vanilla, egg whites and whipped cream.
5. Pour into crust. Chill 3 hours.

Serves 8

SUMMER FRUIT PIE

Crust:
¼ cup butter
¼ cup sugar
1 egg yolk
1 cup all-purpose flour

Filling:
¾ cup quartered strawberries
¾ cup sliced green grapes
¾ cup sliced bananas
¾ cup sliced peaches
¾ cup chunk pineapple, drained

Glaze:
¾ cup orange juice
¼ cup sugar
1½ to 2 tablespoons cornstarch
1 teaspoon grated lemon rind

Kiwi fruit

1. Cream butter, sugar and egg yolk. Stir in flour until crumbly. Gently press into a 9-inch pie plate.
2. Bake 8 minutes at 400° or until edges are brown. Cool completely.
3. Combine orange juice, sugar, cornstarch and lemon rind. Cook over medium heat until mixture thickens and boils. Cool.
4. Combine prepared fruits. Mix with glaze. Pour into baked pie shell. Refrigerate until thoroughly chilled.
5. Garnish top of pie with sliced kiwi fruit.

Serves 8

COOL LEMON PIE

2 cups crushed vanilla wafers	Juice of 3 lemons
5 tablespoons butter, melted	Grated lemon rind to taste
1 can sweetened condensed milk	3 egg whites
3 egg yolks	¼ teaspoon cream of tartar
	½ cup sugar

1. Preheat oven to 350°.
2. Combine vanilla wafer crumbs with melted butter. Press firmly into a 9-inch pie plate.
3. Combine sweetened condensed milk, egg yolks, lemon juice and lemon rind. Pour into prepared crust.
4. Beat egg whites just until fluffy and add ¼ teaspoon cream of tartar. Beat until stiff and slowly add sugar.
5. Spread over lemon filling and bake 5 minutes. Reduce heat to 275°. Bake until meringue is brown. Cool.

Serves 6 to 8

PECAN PIE

2 tablespoons all-purpose flour	1 tablespoon vanilla extract
2 tablespoons butter	Pinch salt
2 eggs, beaten	1 cup pecans
½ cup sugar	1 9-inch pie shell
1 cup corn syrup	

1. Preheat oven to 350°.
2. Blend flour and butter together. Add eggs and sugar. Mix well. Add corn syrup, vanilla, salt and pecans.
3. Pour into pie crust. Bake 10 minutes. Reduce heat to 250°. Bake approximately 1¼ to 1½ hours.

Serves 8

FRESH STRAWBERRY PIE

Peaches, blueberries, plums or other fresh fruits are wonderful in this pie.

1 cup water	2 pints fresh strawberries, rinsed and sliced
½ cup water	Red food coloring, optional
1⅓ cups sugar	1 9-inch baked, cooled pie shell
7 tablespoons all-purpose flour	1 cup whipping cream, sweetened and whipped
½ pint strawberries, mashed	
2 tablespoons lemon juice	

1. Heat 1 cup water in a saucepan.
2. In a bowl, mix ½ cup water, sugar and flour. Add this mixture to water heated in saucepan. Stir constantly over medium heat approximately 5 minutes or until mixture begins to thicken and becomes clear instead of cloudy.
3. Remove from heat. Add mashed strawberries, lemon juice and a few drops of food coloring. Cool 30 minutes. Add sliced strawberries.
4. Pour into pie shell. Refrigerate 3 to 4 hours.

Top with whipped cream before serving.

Serves 6

SCOTCH APPLE PIE

A crunchy, rich apple dessert.

3 large tart apples	1 cup brown sugar
½ cup sugar	1 cup all-purpose flour
Juice of 1 lemon	½ cup butter, softened

1. Preheat oven to 300°.
2. Peel and slice apples. Arrange in a 9-inch pie plate.
3. Mix granulated sugar with lemon juice. Cover apples with mixture.
4. Combine brown sugar and flour. Cut in butter until mixture is crumbly. Sprinkle mixture over apples.
5. Bake 25 minutes.

Serve with ice cream or whipped cream.

Serves 8

CHERRY CREAM CHEESE PIE

A delicious dessert that is easy to prepare.

Crust:
1 cup all-purpose flour
½ cup chopped nuts
¼ cup brown sugar
½ cup butter, softened

Cream cheese filling:
8 ounces cream cheese
½ teaspoon almond extract
1 cup powdered sugar

Cherry filling:
1 cup whipping cream
1 tablespoon sugar
1 21-ounce can cherry pie filling

1. Preheat oven to 350°.
2. Combine flour, nuts, brown sugar and butter. Mix well. Bake in a 13 by 9 by 2-inch pan 15 to 20 minutes, stirring once. Reserve ½ cup crumb mixture.
3. Press baked crumbs into a 9-inch pie plate. Chill.
4. Beat cream cheese, extract and powdered sugar until light and fluffy. Spread over crumb crust.
5. For cherry filling, whip cream and sugar together. Fold in cherry pie filling. Spoon cherry filling over cream cheese filling and sprinkle reserved crumbs on top.
6. Chill at least 2 hours before serving.

Serves 6 to 8

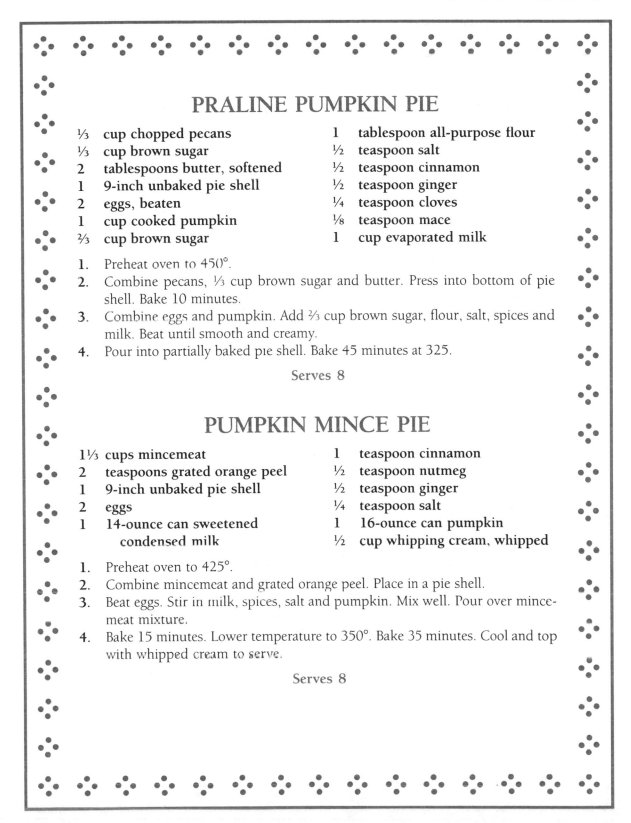

PRALINE PUMPKIN PIE

⅓ cup chopped pecans
⅓ cup brown sugar
2 tablespoons butter, softened
1 9-inch unbaked pie shell
2 eggs, beaten
1 cup cooked pumpkin
⅔ cup brown sugar

1 tablespoon all-purpose flour
½ teaspoon salt
½ teaspoon cinnamon
½ teaspoon ginger
¼ teaspoon cloves
⅛ teaspoon mace
1 cup evaporated milk

1. Preheat oven to 450°.
2. Combine pecans, ⅓ cup brown sugar and butter. Press into bottom of pie shell. Bake 10 minutes.
3. Combine eggs and pumpkin. Add ⅔ cup brown sugar, flour, salt, spices and milk. Beat until smooth and creamy.
4. Pour into partially baked pie shell. Bake 45 minutes at 325.

Serves 8

PUMPKIN MINCE PIE

1⅓ cups mincemeat
2 teaspoons grated orange peel
1 9-inch unbaked pie shell
2 eggs
1 14-ounce can sweetened
    condensed milk

1 teaspoon cinnamon
½ teaspoon nutmeg
½ teaspoon ginger
¼ teaspoon salt
1 16-ounce can pumpkin
½ cup whipping cream, whipped

1. Preheat oven to 425°.
2. Combine mincemeat and grated orange peel. Place in a pie shell.
3. Beat eggs. Stir in milk, spices, salt and pumpkin. Mix well. Pour over mincemeat mixture.
4. Bake 15 minutes. Lower temperature to 350°. Bake 35 minutes. Cool and top with whipped cream to serve.

Serves 8

WHITE CHOCOLATE AND RUM MOUSSE

Chocoholics will relish this. Garnish with fresh raspberries and mint.

6	ounces white chocolate	1	cup whipping cream, whipped
⅓	cup milk, heated	1	tablespoon white rum,
2	large egg whites		optional
	Pinch cream of tartar		

1. Put chocolate and milk in double boiler. Melt over moderate heat. Remove and cool to room temperature.
2. Beat egg whites with cream of tartar until stiff. Gently fold whites into chocolate mixture.
3. Fold in whipped cream and rum. Spoon into individual ramekins or a 1-quart soufflé dish.
4. Refrigerate.

Serves 8

KEY LIME MOUSSE

1	tablespoon unflavored gelatin	¼	cup water
1	cup sugar	1	teaspoon grated lime peel
¼	teaspoon salt	1	cup whipping cream
4	eggs, separated		Green food coloring
½	cup lime juice		

1. Mix first 3 ingredients and set aside.
2. In a saucepan, combine egg yolks, lime juice and water. Add gelatin mixture and cook until mixture boils, stirring constantly. When boiling, remove from heat. Add lime peel and enough food coloring to make mousse pale green. Chill, stirring occasionally. Do not let mixture get too cold and start to jell.
3. Beat egg whites until stiff. Beat whipping cream. Fold ½ cup cream into gelatin mixture. Fold in egg whites. Pour in glasses and refrigerate.
4. Top with remaining whipped cream and a thin slice of lime.

Serves 8 to 10

LEMON MOUSSE WITH RASPBERRY SAUCE

1   envelope unflavored gelatin
2   tablespoons white wine
⅓   cup lemon juice
1½ tablespoons grated lemon rind
3   eggs, separated
½   cup sugar, divided
1   cup whipping cream, whipped

Sauce:

1   10-ounce package frozen
    raspberries, thawed and
    drained (reserve juice)
2   tablespoons sugar
1   tablespoon lemon juice
1   tablespoon kirsch
    Whole fresh raspberries,
    optional

1. In the top of a double boiler, sprinkle gelatin over white wine to soften. Add lemon juice and grated lemon rind.
2. Stir over simmering water until gelatin is dissolved. Remove from heat.
3. In another bowl, beat egg yolks with 3 tablespoon sugar until mixture is lemon-colored. Slowly add gelatin mixture and stir.
4. Beat egg whites until foamy. Add remaining sugar and beat until meringue holds soft peaks.
5. Add whipped cream to egg yolk mixture. Gently fold in meringue.
6. Spoon mixture into individual serving dishes or 1 large serving dish.
7. Chill mousse at least 2 hours.
8. To make sauce, place remaining ingredients (except whole raspberries) in a blender or food processor and purée.
9. Strain purée to remove seeds. Add enough reserved raspberry juice to thin slightly.
10. To serve, spoon raspberry sauce over individual servings of mousse. Garnish with whole raspberries.

Serves 6 to 8

SATIN SIN MOUSSE

1 cup whipping cream, chilled
1 pound semi-sweet chocolate, broken into small pieces
¼ cup unsalted butter, cut into 4 pieces
⅓ cup strong coffee, room temperature
2 large egg yolks
⅓ cup Crème Grand Marnier, Kahlua or Tia Maria
4 large egg whites, at room temperature
4 tablespoons sugar

Custard sauce:

7 large egg yolks, beaten
½ cup sugar
1 cup milk
1 cup half and half
1¼ teaspoons vanilla extract

1. Beat cream until stiff peaks form. Refrigerate.
2. Melt chocolate with butter and coffee in top of double boiler. Transfer mixture to a large bowl.
3. Combine egg yolks and Creme Grand Marnier. Gradually whisk into chocolate mixture.
4. Beat egg whites until soft peaks form. Add sugar, 1 tablespoon at a time, beating constantly until stiff peaks form. Fold egg whites into chocolate mixture.
5. Fold whipped cream into chocolate mixture. Pour mousse into a glass dish at least 3-inches deep. Cover with plastic wrap and glass cover. Refrigerate overnight.
6. To make sauce, combine egg yolks and sugar in a heavy saucepan. Gradually stir in milk and half and half. Cook over low heat, stirring constantly until mixture coats a metal spoon.
7. Remove from heat and place in pan of cool water 1 or 2 minutes. Stir in vanilla.
8. Pour in a bowl. Refrigerate overnight.

9. To serve, pour ¼ to ⅓ cup custard sauce onto each dinner plate. Tilt plate to cover with sauce.

10. Dip large serving spoon into hot water. Dip spoon into mousse to make oval-shaped scoop. Place scoop, rounded side up, on sauce in plate. Use 2 per serving. Serve immediately.

Serves 6 to 8

FROZEN MAPLE MOUSSE

4 egg yolks	2 cups whipping cream, well chilled
⅛ teaspoon salt	½ cup walnuts or pecans, finely chopped
1 cup pure maple syrup	
1 teaspoon vanilla extract	

1. To make custard, beat egg yolks with salt in top of double boiler until thickened. Do not cook at this point. Set aside.

2. Bring maple syrup to a slow boil. Reduce heat and simmer 10 minutes. Add hot syrup to yolks in a thin stream, beating constantly. Set over simmering water and cook. Beat constantly with a wire whisk until thick enough to coat a metal spoon (approximately 5 minutes).

3. Remove from heat and stir in vanilla.

4. Refrigerate 15 minutes or until cool.

5. Whip cream until soft peaks form. Fold ⅓ into custard. Pour mixture over remaining whipped cream and fold.

6. Pour mousse into a 1-quart charlotte mold or soufflé dish. Smooth the top with a spatula and sprinkle with ¼ cup nuts. Freeze 8 hours or until firm.

7. To serve in a mold, set frozen mousse in refrigerator for about ½ hour to temper.

8. To unmold, run a small knife around edge of mold to loosen mousse. Dip quickly in warm water and turn out on serving plate. Should surface ruffle, smooth with a metal spatula. Sprinkle top with remaining nuts. Cut in wedges as a cake.

Serves 6 to 8

SWEDISH ALMOND CREAM

1	envelope unflavored gelatin	¾	cup sugar
¼	cup cold water	2	cups whipping cream, whipped
2	cups sour cream	½	teaspoon almond extract

1. Stir gelatin into cold water. Heat until gelatin is dissolved.
2. Add gelatin to sour cream. Stir in sugar. Fold in whipped cream. Add almond extract. Stir well.
3. Pour into parfait glasses or mold. Chill overnight.

Serve with sliced fresh fruit.

Serves 8

CHOCOLATE CHARLOTTE

8	ounces sweet baking chocolate	2	cups whipping cream
24	marshmallows	⅓	cup powdered sugar
4	eggs, separated	1	tablespoon vanilla extract
2	dozen lady fingers		

1. Heat chocolate and marshmallows in double boiler until melted. Add 4 beaten egg yolks. Cook 3 minutes longer, stirring. Cool.
2. Beat egg whites and fold into cooled chocolate mixture.
3. Line a 2-quart soufflé dish with wax paper. Line bottom and sides of dish with split lady fingers. Pour chocolate over lady fingers until dish is full.
4. Refrigerate 3 hours or overnight.

Invert on a serving dish and cover with whipped cream, sweetened with powdered sugar and vanilla, or serve whipped cream on the side.

Serves 8 to 10

BAKED CUSTARD

4   eggs
    Pinch salt
½   cup sugar

¾   teaspoon vanilla extract
1   cup whipping cream
1   cup whole milk

1. Preheat oven to 300°.
2. Beat eggs until light and fluffy. Add salt, sugar and vanilla. Mix well.
3. Add whipping cream and milk. Mix well.
4. Pour into a 1-quart baking dish. Place dish in a pan of hot water. Bake 1½ hours.

Serves 4

BAKED LEMON CUSTARD

2   tablespoons butter
1½   cups sugar
⅓   cup all-purpose flour
¼   teaspoon salt

½   cup fresh lemon juice
3   eggs, separated
1¼ cups milk

1. Preheat oven to 375°.
2. Combine butter, sugar, flour, salt and lemon juice.
3. Mix egg yolks and milk. Add to flour mixture.
4. Fold in stiffly beaten egg whites.
5. Pour into custard cups or baking dish. Place in a pan of water and bake 45 minutes.

Custard is best served warm from the oven. Can be chilled and served with raspberry or strawberry sauce.

Serves 6

CHOCOLATE COCONUT CUSTARD

6 tablespoons flaked coconut
½ cup semi-sweet chocolate
  morsels
1⅔ cups evaporated milk
1 cup water

4 eggs
½ cup sugar
½ teaspoon salt
1 teaspoon vanilla extract

1. Preheat oven to 350°.
2. Place 1 tablespoon coconut in bottom of six, 6-ounce custard cups.
3. Combine chocolate, milk and water in saucepan. Stir mixture over low heat until chocolate melts.
4. Beat eggs, sugar, salt and vanilla together until well blended. Slowly pour into chocolate mixture, stirring constantly. Beat until well blended.
5. Pour mixture into custard cups. Place cups in a pan 2½-inches deep. Pour hot water around cups .
6. Bake 30 to 40 minutes. Cool and refrigerate.

Serves 6

ESSEL'S CHOCOLATE PUDDING

1⅓ cups sugar
½ cup all-purpose flour
6 tablespoons cocoa
¼ teaspoon salt
2⅔ cups milk

3 eggs, separated
1 tablespoon butter, melted
2 teaspoons vanilla extract
6 tablespoons sugar

1. In top of double boiler, combine sugar, flour, cocoa and salt.
2. Slowly add milk and stir.
3. Beat egg yolks and butter together. Stir into first mixture.
4. Cook over slowly boiling water 15 minutes, stirring constantly. Add vanilla. Cool.
5. Beat egg whites and 6 tablespoons sugar until stiff peaks form.
6. Fold egg whites into cooled chocolate mixture.
7. Spoon into parfait glasses or custard cups.

Serve chilled with dollops of whipped cream.

Serves 6

SHERBET MACAROON DELIGHT

1 dozen soft coconut macaroons
1 cup whipping cream, whipped

3 pints sherbet, 1 each, raspberry, orange and lime, softened
Fresh mint

1. Bake macaroons 10 minutes at 300°. Break into small pieces. Cool.
2. Fold macaroons into whipped cream.
3. Completely line a loaf pan with foil. Spread 1 pint of orange sherbet in loaf pan. Spread layers of whipped cream mixture, raspberry sherbet, whipped cream mixture, and lime sherbet. Freeze overnight.
4. Unmold and remove foil. Slice and garnish with fresh mint.

Serves 10 to 12

ORANGE CREAM SHERBET

2½ cups sugar
Pinch salt
Juice of 1 lemon
3 cups orange juice

3 cups whole milk
2 cups whipping cream
1 cup half and half

1. Stir sugar and salt into lemon and orange juice.
2. Add milk, whipping cream and half and half.
3. Freeze in ice cream freezer.

Yields 1 gallon

GRAPEFRUIT SORBET

A wonderful way to use delicious sweet Texas grapefruit.

8 large Texas Ruby Red grapefruit, peeled and sectioned	2 cups sugar 4 cups water

1. Remove all peeling and seeds from grapefruit. Section.
2. Place grapefruit sections in a glass dish or stainless steel pan.
3. Combine sugar and water. Simmer over low heat until all sugar is dissolved. Cool.
4. Pour syrup over sections and freeze.
5. Before serving, place sorbet in food processor with steel blade. Blend quickly.
6. Scoop mixture into balls. Return to freezer to firm and hold shape until ready to serve.

Serves 6 to 8

BEST HOMEMADE VANILLA ICE CREAM

An old family favorite!

4 large eggs, slightly beaten 3 cups whole milk, chilled 2 cups sugar ½ teaspoon salt 1 13½-ounce can evaporated milk, chilled 1 tablespoon vanilla extract	*Optional:* 1½ to 2 cups fresh peaches, peeled and sliced ½ cup sugar

1. Whisk eggs, milk and sugar together in a large, heavy saucepan. Cook over low heat until mixture thickens.
2. Remove from heat when mixture begins to coat a metal spoon. Cool.
3. Add salt, evaporated milk and vanilla. Freeze in ice cream freezer.
4. If adding fresh peaches and sugar, add to mixture before freezing.

Yields 1 gallon

PEPPERMINT ICE CREAM SANDWICHES

Chocolate dipped and easy to make. The perfect dessert for informal dinners and children's parties.

½ gallon peppermint ice cream, slightly softened

2 boxes chocolate wafers

1 12-ounce package semi-sweet chocolate morsels

1. Spread 2 tablespoons softened ice cream between 2 wafers, making a sandwich. Work quickly, returning completed sandwiches to freezer. Freeze overnight.
2. Melt chocolate chips in double boiler.
3. Working with 2 or 3 sandwiches at a time, dip half the sandwich into melted chocolate. Place on wax paper lined cookie sheet. Return to freezer until solid.
4. Store in plastic bags until ready to serve.

Yields 36 to 40 sandwiches

FROZEN FRUIT POPS

A refreshing fruity treat that kids and adults will love.

Simple Syrup:

1 cup sugar

1 cup water

1 16-ounce package frozen strawberries

1 10-ounce package frozen strawberries

1 20-ounce can crushed pineapple, undrained

2 bananas, sliced

1 17-ounce can apricot halves, drained and chopped

1. Boil sugar and water together until sugar is dissolved. Cool.
2. Thaw strawberries until mushy. Mash.
3. Combine all fruits with syrup. Pour into muffin tins lined with cupcake papers or 5-ounce drinking cups. Add popsicle sticks if desired. Freeze.

Yields 26 to 30 pops

SWEDISH FRUIT DESSERT

½ pound seedless white raisins
½ pound dried apricots
½ pound pitted prunes
3 quarts liquid, reserved from canned fruits and water used to soak fruits
2 slices lemon
2 slices orange

2 apples, sliced and cored
4 tablespoons tapioca,(slightly more if thicker dessert is desired)
1 stick cinnamon
1 cup sugar
8 to 10 canned plums
1 cup sliced canned peaches

1. Rinse raisins, apricots and prunes. Add enough water to cover. Soak overnight.
2. Drain fruit, reserving liquid.
3. To 3 quarts liquid, add lemon, orange and apple slices, tapioca, cinnamon and sugar. Bring mixture to a boil. Lower heat. Simmer 30 to 45 minutes or until apples are soft.
4. Remove from heat. Add plums and peaches. Allow fruit to stand 2 to 4 hours before serving.
5. Fruit may be served warm or cold in compotes with whipped cream or over ice cream. Delicious served over pound cake.

Fruit will keep 2 weeks refrigerated.

Serves 6 to 8

ROYAL CHERRIES

2 cans Royal Ann Cherries, pitted
Dark rum

½ cup butter
1 cup brown sugar

1. Drain cherries and cover with dark rum.
2. Melt butter. Add brown sugar. Add part of the rum from the cherries, until desired taste is reached. Add cherries.
3. Warm and serve over ice cream.

Serves 4

RASPBERRY SAUCE

A versatile sauce to be served warm or cold.

10 ounces frozen raspberries, with juice

1 12-ounce jar raspberry jam

½ cup sugar

2 to 3 tablespoons cornstarch

1. Place all ingredients into a saucepan. Cook over low to medium heat, stirring constantly until mixture is smooth and thick. Press through a strainer for a smooth, clear liquid.

Sauce can be served warm or cold. It can be stored in the refrigerator for 1 month.

Serve with Fruit and Cream Meringue Squares, over Homemade Vanilla Ice Cream, Baked Lemon Custard, fresh sliced fruit or with cold lemon or chocolate mousse.

Yields 3 cups

PEACHES AMARETTO

Simply delicious! Wonderful served over vanilla ice cream.

4 cups peeled, sliced peaches

½ cup amaretto

½ cup sour cream

⅓ cup brown sugar

1. Layer peaches in 1½-quart baking dish.
2. Pour liqueur over peaches.
3. Spread sour cream over peaches.
4. Sprinkle brown sugar, evenly, over all.
5. Broil until mixture is thoroughly heated and sugar melts.
6. Serve immediately.

Yields approximately 4 cups

FLAMING CHERRIES JUBILEE

An elegant dessert that is quick and easy.

1	16-ounce can pitted Bing cherries or 1 pound frozen cherries and ½ cup water	1	teaspoon brandy or rum, optional
¾	cup currant jelly	½	cup brandy or rum
1	tablespoon grated orange rind		Ice cream

1. Poach cherries in liquid from can or water approximately 10 minutes. Drain.
2. Melt jelly in a chafing dish over medium heat. Add cherries, rind and 1 teaspoon brandy. Stir gently.
3. Pour over individual bowls of homemade vanilla ice cream.
4. To flame topping, add ½ cup heated brandy to cherries before pouring over ice cream. Do not stir! Pour mixture over large bowl of ice cream and light to flame.

Yields approximately 3 cups

BAVARIAN APPLE TORTE

½	cup butter	1	egg
⅓	cup sugar	½	teaspoon vanilla extract
¼	teaspoon vanilla extract	⅓	cup sugar
1	cup all-purpose flour	½	teaspoon cinnamon
8	ounces cream cheese, softened	4	cups peeled and sliced apples
¼	cup sugar	¼	cup slivered almonds

1. Preheat oven to 450°.
2. Cream butter, sugar and vanilla. Blend in flour. Press into bottom and sides of an 11-inch removable ring torte pan. Chill.
3. Combine cream cheese and sugar. Mix well. Add egg and vanilla. Pour into crust lined pan. Chill.
4. Combine sugar and cinnamon. Toss with sliced apples. Spoon over cheese layer. Sprinkle with almonds.
5. Bake 10 minutes. Reduce heat to 400°. Bake 25 minutes.
6. Cool before removing rim of pan.

Serves 8 to 12

BANANAS MARGUERITE

A creamy rich dessert that is delicious and easy.

2 tablespoons butter	½ cup whipping cream
4 firm bananas, ripe but not too soft	¼ teaspoon vanilla extract
1½ teaspoons sugar	3 ounces cream cheese, softened

1. Preheat oven to 375°.
2. In a hot oven, melt butter in a 1½-quart baking dish.
3. Slice bananas lengthwise and place in baking dish.
4. Beat together sugar, cream, vanilla and cream cheese. Pour over bananas.
5. Bake 20 minutes.
6. Garnish with raspberries, blueberries or strawberries dusted with powdered sugar.

Serves 6 to 8

ALMOND TART

1½ cups all-purpose flour	1½ cups sliced almonds
1½ tablespoons sugar	1⅛ cups sugar
¾ cup butter, softened	1⅛ cups whipping cream
1½ tablespoons water	1½ teaspoons orange liqueur
¾ teaspoon vanilla extract	¼ teaspoon almond extract
¼ teaspoon almond extract	⅛ teaspoon salt

1. To make crust, combine flour and sugar. Cut in butter until mixture resembles corn meal.
2. Add water, vanilla and almond extract. Mix well.
3. Press dough into tart pan and chill 1 hour.
4. Heat oven to 400°. Line dough with wax paper and fill with rice. Bake 7 minutes. Remove rice and bake 3 to 10 minutes or until crust is golden. Cool.
5. To make filling, mix together almonds, sugar, whipping cream, orange liqueur, almond extract and salt. Set aside 15 minutes.
6. Pour mixture into crust. Bake at 400° for 30 to 40 minutes or until mixture is set and golden.

Serves 8 to 10

PEACH COBBLER

Crust:
⅔ cup vegetable shortening
2 cups sifted all-purpose flour
1 teaspoon salt
7 tablespoons cold water

Filling:
1½ tablespoons cornstarch
½ cup sugar
½ teaspoon salt
1 cup juice from fruit
1 tablespoon butter
¼ teaspoon vanilla extract (or combination vanilla and almond extract)
4 cups fresh, peeled, sliced peaches
Butter
Sugar

1. To make crust, cut shortening into flour and salt until mixture resembles corn meal.
2. Carefully stir in water until all flour is moistened.
3. Roll dough to fit a 1½-quart rectangular glass baking dish. Fit pastry into dish. Use remaining dough to make a lattice top.
4. Combine cornstarch, sugar, salt and fruit juice in saucepan. Cook, stirring over medium-high heat until mixture begins to boil. Cook 2 more minutes.
5. Remove from heat. Add butter and flavoring. Stir in fruit.
6. Pour into unbaked pastry. Cover with lattice crust. Dot top with butter and sprinkle with sugar.
7. Bake 10 minutes at 400°. Lower heat to 350° and bake 45 minutes.

Blackberries or dewberries can be substituted for peaches.

Serves 6 to 8

APPLE BREAD PUDDING WITH VANILLA SAUCE

1	loaf French bread cut into 2 by 2-inch pieces, or 1 loaf white bread, 2 days old and slightly dried out
1	quart milk, heated
3	eggs
2	cups sugar
½	teaspoon cinnamon
2	tablespoons vanilla extract
3	tablespoons butter
1	cup raisins
¾	cup chopped pecans
3	apples, peeled and diced

Vanilla Sauce:

⅓	cup sugar
1	tablespoon cornstarch
1	cup boiling water
1	tablespoon butter
	Pinch salt
1	teaspoon vanilla extract

1. Preheat oven to 350°.
2. Place bread and milk in a large bowl. Soak bread 10 minutes.
3. Mix together eggs, sugar, cinnamon, vanilla, butter, raisins, pecans and apples. Stir into bread and milk.
4. Pour into a 3-quart buttered baking dish. Bake 45 minutes. Serve warm with cold vanilla sauce.
5. To make vanilla sauce, stir sugar and cornstarch together. Gradually add boiling water. Add butter and salt. Cook until mixture thickens.
6. Remove from heat. Stir and add vanilla. Cool.

Serves 10 to 12

CLASSIC APPLE CRISP

Serve with whipped cream or ice cream.

4 or 5 apples
2   tablespoons butter
½   teaspoon cinnamon

Topping:
¾   cup sugar
1   cup all-purpose flour
½   cup butter

1. Preheat oven to 300°.
2. Peel and slice apples very thin. Place in a buttered 9 by 13 by 2-inch baking dish. Dot with 2 tablespoons butter and sprinkle with cinnamon.
3. For topping, mix together sugar and flour. Cut in ½ cup butter until mixture resembles corn meal.
4. Press mixture firmly and evenly on top of apples.
5. Bake 45 minutes.

Best served warm. Can be topped with whipped cream mixed with ¼ teaspoon ginger or vanilla ice cream.

Serves 6 to 8

EASY PLUM PASTRIES

So simple and so good!

1   cup butter
1   cup sugar
2   egg yolks
2   cups all-purpose flour

1   cup chopped nuts
1   cup plum jam
    Powdered sugar

1. Preheat oven to 325°.
2. Cream butter and sugar. Fold in egg yolks, flour and nuts. Divide mixture in half and press half on the bottom of a 8 by 8-inch pan.
3. Top with jam and sprinkle remaining pastry mixture on top.
4. Bake approximately 1 hour (30 minutes on the bottom rack and 30 minutes on the top rack.)
5. Cool. Sprinkle with powdered sugar before slicing.

Serves 10 to 12

BLUEBERRY CREAM CHEESE CRUMBLE

18 graham crackers, or 22 to 30
     vanilla wafers, crushed
½   cup powdered sugar
½   cup butter, melted
2   eggs
¾   cup sugar

8   ounces cream cheese, softened
1   12-ounce can blueberry or
     strawberry pie filling
   Juice of ½ lemon
   Whipped cream

1. Preheat oven to 350°.
2. Combine crumbs, powdered sugar and butter. Pat crumb mixture into a 9 by
    13 by 1-inch metal baking pan.
3. Beat eggs, sugar and cream cheese until smooth. Spread over crumb crust.
4. Bake 25 minutes.
5. Mix pie filling and lemon juice. Pour over baked mixture and refrigerate
    overnight.
6. Cut into squares and top each serving with whipped cream.

Serves 6 to 8

FRUIT AND CREAM MERINGUE SQUARES

An easy and impressive dessert.

Meringue:

1½ cups sugar	1 cup whipping cream
½ teaspoon cream of tartar	1 pint fresh strawberries, peaches, raspberries, or kiwi fruit, sliced
¼ teaspoon salt	
5 egg whites at room temperature	

1. Preheat oven to 450°.
2. Sift together sugar, cream of tartar and salt.
3. Beat egg whites until stiff. Add sugar mixture, a spoonful at a time, and beat 15 minutes or until sugar is dissolved.
4. Pour into 8 by 8 by 2-inch pan. Place in oven and turn off heat. Leave in oven 6 hours or overnight.
5. Spread with whipped cream 3 hours before serving. Chill.
6. Top with fruit and cut in squares to serve. Garnish with chocolate shavings or fruit slices.

Serves 6 to 8

MINT DAZZLER

A colorful and festive dessert that can be made several days in advance.

4 tablespoons butter, melted	1 8-ounce package miniature marshmallows
1¼ cups vanilla wafer crumbs	1½ cups whipping cream, whipped
½ cup butter	½ cup crushed peppermint stick candy
½ cup sifted powdered sugar	
3 eggs, slightly beaten	
3 squares unsweetened chocolate, melted	

1. Combine 4 tablespoons butter and wafer crumbs. Press into the bottom of a 9-inch spring form pan. Set aside.
2. Cream together ½ cup butter and powdered sugar. Add eggs and melted chocolate. Beat until light and fluffy.
3. Spoon over crust and set in freezer.

4. Gently fold marshmallows into whipped cream and spread over chocolate layer.
5. Sprinkle with crushed candy. Return to freezer.
6. Remove from freezer 10 to 15 minutes before slicing.

This can be frozen for days before serving.

Serves 10 to 12

KAHLUA CRUNCH

Crust:

1   **cup graham cracker crumbs**
½   **cup coconut**
⅓   **cup butter, melted**
¼   **cup brown sugar**

Filling:

1¼   **cups butter, softened**
1   **cup sugar**
1   **square unsweetened chocolate, melted**
1   **teaspoon vanilla extract**
2   **teaspoons Kahlua**
2   **eggs**
1   **cup unblanched almonds, roasted and chopped**
1   **cup whipping cream, whipped**

1. Preheat oven to 350°.
2. To make crust, combine graham cracker crumbs, coconut, melted butter and brown sugar. Press into a 9-inch pie plate. Bake 10 minutes. Cool.
3. Break crust into small pieces.
4. Sprinkle crust into 12 cupcake liners in muffin pan.
5. Beat butter. Gradually add sugar, chocolate, vanilla and Kahlua.
6. Add 1 egg. Beat. Add other egg and beat 5 minutes.
7. Spoon filling into cupcake liners.
8. Sprinkle almonds on each.
9. Top with whipped cream.
10. Chill in refrigerator for several hours. These can be frozen, thawed slightly and served.

Serves 12

BRANDY SNAPS

This is a very special, rich cookie. Elegant to serve with coffee, after dinner or at tea.

Cookie:
½   cup all-purpose flour
⅓   cup sugar
½   teaspoon ginger
¼   cup butter
¼   cup molasses
1   teaspoon brandy or apricot
     brandy or vanilla extract

Hard Sauce:
¾   cup butter, softened
1½   cups powdered sugar
2   tablespoons brandy or apricot
     brandy or vanilla extract

1. Preheat oven to 325°.
2. Sift together flour, sugar and ginger.
3. Melt butter and molasses together.
4. Beat flour mixture and brandy into butter and molasses.
5. Drop ½ teaspoonfuls of batter on a greased and floured cookie sheet. Place dough far apart as it will spread. Bake approximately 10 cookies at a time.
6. Bake 10 to 12 minutes. Cool 1 minute.
7. Wrap each cookie (smooth side in) around a wooden spoon handle to form "logs". If cookies become too brittle, return to oven for a few minutes.
8. After cookies are shaped and cooled, mix hard sauce. Using a pastry tube, fill each cookie with sauce. Fill just before serving to keep cookie crisp.

Yields 30

FROSTED GINGER COOKIES

A pleasant combination of spices makes this cookie a hit. The frosting is a must!

¼ cup vegetable shortening
½ cup sugar
1 egg
½ cup molasses
1 teaspoon baking soda, dissolved in 1 teaspoon hot water
2 cups sifted all-purpose flour
½ teaspoon salt
1 teaspoon ginger
½ teaspoon nutmeg
½ teaspoon cloves
½ teaspoon cinnamon

Frosting:
1¼ cups powdered sugar
2 tablespoons butter, softened
1 teaspoon vanilla extract
Milk

1. Cream together shortening, sugar, egg and molasses.
2. Dissolve soda in hot water. Stir into shortening mixture.
3. In another bowl, sift together flour, salt, ginger, nutmeg, cloves and cinnamon. Stir into shortening mixture. Mix until dough is well blended. Chill overnight.
4. Drop by rounded teaspoons about 2-inches apart on a lightly greased cookie sheet.
5. Bake 7 to 8 minutes at 400°. Cookies should spring back when touched.
6. Remove cookies from oven and frost while still warm.
7. To prepare frosting blend together powdered sugar, butter and vanilla. Slowly add milk until frosting is a stiff spreading consistency. The frosting will melt a little on warm cookies.

Yields 3 dozen 2-inch cookies

CHOCOLATE DELIGHTS

2	cups sifted all-purpose flour	2	cups sugar
2	teaspoons baking powder	4	eggs
½	teaspoon salt	½	cup pecans, chopped
¼	cup butter		Powdered sugar
4	1-ounce squares chocolate		

1. Sift together flour, baking powder and salt. Set aside.
2. Melt butter and chocolate. Allow mixture to cool slightly.
3. Blend in sugar. Stir in eggs, 1 at a time.
4. Add flour mixture and nuts. Blend thoroughly.
5. Chill dough.
6. Shape dough into balls, using 1 tablespoon dough for each cookie.
6. Roll balls in powdered sugar. Place on a greased cookie sheet.
7. Bake 18 to 20 minutes at 300°.

Yields 5 dozen

BRICKLE CHOCOLATE CHIP COOKIES

2	cups all-purpose flour	¾	cup firmly packed brown sugar
½	cup quick cooking oats	1	teaspoon vanilla extract
1	teaspoon baking soda	2	eggs
1	teaspoon salt	1	12-ounce package chocolate morsels
1	cup shortening		
¾	cup sugar	6	tablespoons Bits O' Brickle

1. Preheat oven to 375°.
2. In a small bowl, combine flour, oats, soda and salt. Set aside.
3. In a large bowl, combine shortening, sugar, brown sugar and vanilla. Beat until creamy.
4. Beat in eggs. Gradually add flour mixture. Mix well.
5. Stir in chocolate morsels and Bits O' Brickle.
6. Drop by rounded teaspoonfuls onto an ungreased cookie sheet. Bake 8 to 10 minutes.

Freezes

Yields 100 2-inch cookies

MIMI WURZBACH'S BINGHAM COOKIES

Cinnamon makes this crisp cookie a favorite.

2 cups butter	1 tablespoon baking powder
1 pound brown sugar	1 tablespoon cinnamon
2 eggs	4 cups chopped pecans
4 cups all-purpose flour	

1. Preheat oven to 350°.
2. Cream butter and brown sugar, adding sugar gradually.
3. Add eggs, 1 at a time, beating well after each addition.
4. Sift flour with cinnamon and baking powder. Add flour mixture gradually to creamed mixture. Stir in pecans.
5. Shape into rolls on wax paper, twisting ends of paper to tighten. Rolls should be about 2-inches in diameter.
6. Wrap in foil and chill.
7. Slice thin (⅛ to ¼-inch thick). Bake 8 to 10 minutes. Dough may be frozen and used as needed.

Yields 10 dozen

CHOCOLATE KISS COOKIES

The familiar taste of a sand tart with the added treat of chocolate.

1 cup butter, softened	1 cup finely chopped pecans
½ cup sugar	40 chocolate kisses
1½ teaspoons vanilla extract	Powdered sugar
2 cups all-purpose flour	

1. Preheat oven to 375°.
2. Cream together butter, sugar and vanilla. Add flour and nuts. Mix well.
3. Chill dough 20 minutes. Shape approximately 1 teaspoon dough around each kiss.
4. Bake on an ungreased cookie sheet 12 to 18 minutes. Do not brown. Cool slightly. Roll in powdered sugar.

Yields 40 cookies

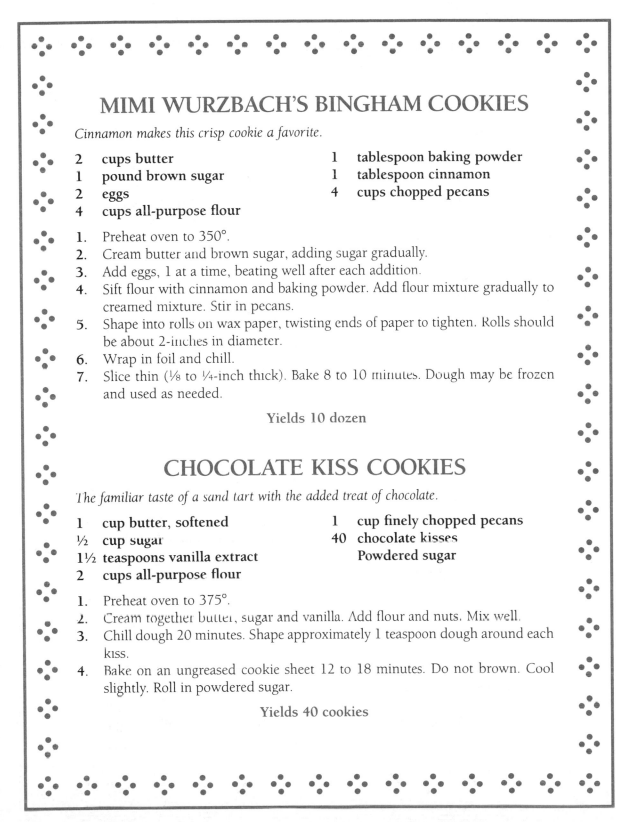

OUR FAVORITE COOKIES

1	cup butter	1	cup crushed cornflakes
1	cup sugar	½	cup shredded coconut
1	cup brown sugar	½	cup chopped walnuts or
1	egg		pecans
1	cup vegetable oil	3½	cups sifted all-purpose flour
1	teaspoon vanilla extract	1	teaspoon baking soda
1	cup regular rolled oats	1	teaspoon salt

1. Preheat oven to 325°.
2. Cream butter and sugars until light and fluffy.
3. Add egg, oil and vanilla. Mix well.
4. Add oats, cornflakes, coconut and nuts. Stir well.
5. Add flour, soda and salt. Stir until well blended.
6. Drop by teaspoonfuls on ungreased cookie sheets. Flatten with fork dipped in water.
7. Bake 15 minutes.

Freezes

Yields 8 dozen

ALMOND COOKIES

½	cup almonds, unskinned	1	egg white
½	cup sugar	⅔	cup whole wheat flour
½	cup unsalted butter	¼	teaspoon ground ginger
1	teaspoon vanilla extract		
	Grated peel of ½ lemon		

1. Spread almonds in a baking pan. Toast in a 350° oven 10 minutes, stirring several times.
2. Remove from oven. Cool and grind to a powder. Be very careful not to grind almonds too long or almonds will turn to almond butter.
3. Cream sugar and butter. Add vanilla and lemon peel. Beat in egg white.
4. Combine flour, ginger and almonds. Mix into batter. Beat until smooth.
5. Drop from a teaspoon onto an ungreased cookie sheet, about 1-inch apart.
6. Bake at 375° approximately 10 minutes or until brown around the edges.

Yields 40 small cookies

SURVIVAL COOKIES

These are great for camping trips, travel and kids. They will keep well for a month unrefrigerated.

1 egg	½ teaspoon baking soda
¼ cup apricot juice	1 teaspoon ginger
¾ cup vegetable shortening	1 teaspoon allspice
1½ cups firmly packed brown sugar	1 teaspoon cloves
1 cup whole wheat flour	2 teaspoons cinnamon
½ cup powdered milk	2 cups rolled oats
1 teaspoon salt	1 cup wheat germ
	1 cup chopped dates
	1 cup chopped nuts

1. Preheat oven to 325°.
2. Beat together egg, juice, shortening and brown sugar.
3. Sift together flour, powdered milk, salt, soda and spices. Add to first mixture.
4. Stir in oats, wheat germ, dates and nuts.
5. Drop by teaspoonfuls onto a greased cookie sheet.
6. Bake 15 minutes. Bake longer if a crisper cookie is preferred. Remove and cool on a wire rack.

Yields 4 dozen

BROWN SUGAR PECAN COOKIES

2 cups butter	2 teaspoons vanilla extract
16 ounces brown sugar	5 to 6 cups all-purpose flour
1 egg	1 cup pecans, coarsely broken

1. Preheat oven to 350°.
2. Cream together butter and sugar. Add egg and vanilla.
3. Add flour to mixture until an electric mixer cannot mix it. Fold in pecans.
4. Shape dough into three 2½-inch rolls. Wrap rolls in wax paper. Chill overnight in refrigerator.
5. Cut into thin slices and place on a lightly greased cookie sheet.
6. Bake 12 to 15 minutes or until slightly brown. Store in a tightly covered cookie tin.

Freezes

Yields 200 cookies

MOLASSES COOKIES

This dough will keep two weeks in refrigerator.

1	cup sugar	1	teaspoon baking soda
1	cup shortening	1	teaspoon salt
1	cup dark molasses	2	teaspoons cinnamon
2	eggs	1	teaspoon ginger
4	cups sifted all-purpose flour	¼	cup sugar

1. Preheat oven to 350°.
2. Cream together sugar and shortening until fluffy. Add molasses and eggs. Mix well.
3. Sift together flour, soda, salt, cinnamon and ginger. Add to shortening mixture.
4. Dip fingers into ¼ cup sugar. Pinch off a small amount of dough. Roll to the size and shape of a walnut. Dip ball in sugar. Place balls on a greased cookie sheet approximately 3 inches apart.
5. Bake 12 to 15 minutes.

Freezes well.

Yields 4 dozen

LEMON THINS

1	cup butter	3	cups all-purpose flour
1¼	cups sugar	½	teaspoon baking soda
1	egg	½	teaspoon cream of tartar
1 to 2 teaspoons lemon extract		Extra sugar	

1. Preheat oven to 325°.
2. Cream butter and sugar until fluffy.
3. Add egg and lemon extract. Beat well.
4. Add flour, soda and cream of tartar. Mix well.
5. Chill dough. Roll into balls the size of a walnut. Flatten with a fork. Sprinkle with sugar and bake 15 to 20 minutes.

Yields 8 dozen

OATMEAL COOKIES

¾ cup vegetable shortening
1   cup packed brown sugar
½ cup sugar
1   egg
¼ cup water
1   teaspoon vanilla extract

1   cup all-purpose flour, sifted
1   teaspoon salt
½ teaspoon baking soda
3   cups rolled oats
1   cup raisins, optional
¾ cup chopped pecans

1. Beat shortening, sugar, egg, water and vanilla until creamy.
2. Sift together flour, salt and soda. Add to creamed mixture. Blend.
3. Stir in oats, raisins and nuts.
4. Drop dough by spoonfuls onto greased cookie sheets.
5. Bake 12 to 15 minutes at 350°.

Yields 5 dozen

BEST BROWNIES

1   cup butter
½ cup cocoa
4   eggs
2   cups sugar
1½ cups all-purpose flour

Dash salt
1   teaspoon vanilla extract
1   cup chocolate morsels,
    optional
1   cup chopped pecans, optional

1. Preheat oven to 350°.
2. Melt butter. Dissolve cocoa in butter and set aside.
3. Beat eggs and sugar together until light and fluffy.
4. Beat in flour, salt and vanilla.
5. Add cocoa and butter to flour mixture. At this point, add optional ingredients.
6. Bake in a greased and floured 9 by 13-inch metal pan for 30 to 40 minutes. Bake 30 minutes for chewy brownies or 40 minutes for cake-like brownies.

Freezes

Variation:
For a truly decadent dessert, top brownie squares with vanilla ice cream and hot fudge sauce.

Yields 24 to 36 squares

3 D BROWNIES

This brownie is a perfect chocolate taste treat for luncheons or teas. Absolutely delicious!

4	squares unsweetened chocolate
1	cup butter
2	cups sugar
4	eggs, lightly beaten
1	cup all-purpose flour
1	teaspoon vanilla extract
½	teaspoon salt
1	cup chopped nuts

First Icing Layer:

3	cups powdered sugar
2	tablespoons butter
	Cream or milk

Second Icing Layer:

4	squares semi-sweet chocolate, melted
4	tablespoons butter

1. Preheat oven to 325°.
2. Melt unsweetened chocolate and butter.
3. Add sugar and eggs. Mix well.
4. Add flour, vanilla, salt and nuts. Mix well and pour into a greased 9 by 13 by 2-inch metal pan.
5. Bake 25 to 30 minutes. Cool.
6. First Icing Layer: Mix together powdered sugar, butter and enough milk to make icing a spreadable consistency. Ice brownies with this mixture.
7. When first layer of icing is set, melt chocolate with butter and cover first layer with chocolate icing.
8. Freeze or refrigerate. Before serving, cut into squares. Serve at room temperature.

Yields 24 to 36 squares

CHOCOLATE CREAM CHEESE BROWNIES

First Layer:
½ cup butter
1 box chocolate cake mix
1 egg, beaten
1 cup pecans

Second Layer:
8 ounces cream cheese
1 16-ounce box powdered sugar
2 eggs

1. Preheat oven to 350°.
2. First Layer: Melt butter in a 9 by 13 by 2-inch metal pan. Sprinkle cake mix over butter. Add egg and pecans. Stir ingredients together and pat down.
3. Second Layer: Cream together cream cheese, sugar and eggs.
4. Spread over chocolate mixture.
5. Bake 45 minutes. Cut while still warm.

Yields 24 to 36 bars

PECAN TOFFEE BARS

12 to 15 whole graham crackers
1 cup butter, melted
1 cup dark brown sugar

1 12-ounce package semi-sweet or milk chocolate morsels
1 cup chopped pecans

1. Preheat oven to 400°.
2. Line a cookie sheet with foil. Cover foil with whole graham crackers.
3. Simmer butter and brown sugar 3 minutes and pour quickly over graham crackers.
4. Bake 5 minutes.
5. Remove from oven and sprinkle chocolate morsels and pecans over crackers.
6. Refrigerate. Break into pieces of "toffee" when hardened.

Yields 35 to 45 pieces

PECAN SQUARES

2 tablespoons butter
1 cup brown sugar
5 tablespoons all-purpose flour
⅛ teaspoon baking soda
1 cup chopped pecans

2 eggs
1 teaspoon vanilla extract
Pecan halves
Powdered sugar

1. Preheat oven to 350°.
2. Melt butter in an 8 by 8-inch pan.
3. Mix together brown sugar, flour, soda and pecans.
4. Beat eggs and vanilla. Add to sugar mixture. Stir well.
5. Pour batter over butter, but do not stir.
6. Place pecan halves on top of mixture.
7. Bake 20 to 25 minutes. Cool. Cut into squares and sprinkle with powdered sugar.

Yields 16 2-inch squares

COCONUT ALMOND SQUARES

¾ cup butter
3 tablespoons sugar
1½ cups all-purpose flour
2¼ cups brown sugar
3 egg yolks, beaten

1 cup chopped almonds
¾ cup shredded coconut
3 egg whites, stiffly beaten
Powdered sugar

1. Preheat oven to 375°.
2. Cream butter and sugar until light and fluffy.
3. Stir in flour.
4. Pat mixture into a greased 9 by 13-inch pan. Bake 15 minutes or until lightly browned.
5. Combine brown sugar and beaten egg yolks. Blend well. Add almonds and coconut.
6. Fold in beaten egg whites.
7. Pour over crust and return to oven for 20 to 25 minutes. Cool. Cut into 1-inch squares and dust with powdered sugar.

Yields 35 squares

ICED LEMON SQUARES

The best of the tried and true lemon squares with a delicious icing.

2	cups all-purpose flour
1	cup butter
½	cup powdered sugar
4	eggs
4	tablespoons lemon juice
2	teaspoons grated lemon rind
2	cups sugar
4	tablespoons all-purpose flour
1	teaspoon baking powder

Icing:

¾	cup powdered sugar
1½	teaspoons vanilla extract
2	tablespoons butter, softened
1	tablespoon milk

1. Preheat oven to 350°.
2. Cream together flour, butter and powdered sugar. Press evenly into an ungreased 16 by 11-inch jelly roll pan. Bake 20 minutes.
3. Beat together eggs, lemon juice, lemon rind, sugar, flour and baking powder.
4. Pour this mixture over baked first layer. Return to oven. Bake 25 minutes. Cool.
5. Combine ingredients for icing and beat until smooth. Spread on lemon squares.

Yields 3 dozen squares

ENGLISH TOFFEE BARS

1   cup butter
1   cup firmly packed brown sugar
1   egg yolk
1   cup sifted all-purpose flour

1   teaspoon vanilla extract
6   ⅝-ounce chocolate bars
½   cup finely chopped pecans

1. Preheat oven to 325°.
2. Cream butter until fluffy. Add brown sugar and egg yolk, mixing well after each addition. Add flour and vanilla. Continue to beat until well mixed.
3. Grease a 17 by 12 by ½-inch jelly roll pan. Turn dough onto pan. Spread with a spatula.
4. Bake 25 minutes or until edges are crisp and brown.
5. Remove pan from oven and place chocolate bars on top. Spread melted chocolate evenly over cookie. Sprinkle with nuts. Cut into squares while warm.

Yields 30 to 45 squares

NO BAKE PEANUT BUTTER SQUARES

This is a favorite! It will remind you of peanut butter cups.

1½   cups graham cracker crumbs
1½   cups peanut butter, smooth or crunchy
¾   cup butter, melted

1   16-ounce box powdered sugar
6   ounces semi-sweet chocolate morsels

1. In a large bowl, combine graham cracker crumbs, peanut butter and butter.
2. Slowly add powdered sugar and stir until well mixed. Press into a 9 by 12-inch pan.
3. Melt chocolate morsels and spread over peanut butter mixture.
4. Refrigerate only until the chocolate is firm. Cookies should be brought to room temperature before cutting.

This recipe can be successfully made in a large food processor.

Yields 24 to 36 bars

APRICOT OAT BARS

Apricot is delicious but any flavored jam may be used in these cookies.

1½ cups sifted all-purpose flour
1   teaspoon baking powder
¼   teaspoon salt
1½ cups quick cooking oats

1   cup brown sugar
¾   cup butter
¾   cup apricot jam

1. Preheat oven to 375°.
2. Sift together flour, baking powder and salt.
3. Stir oats and brown sugar into flour mixture.
4. Cut in butter until crumbly.
5. Pat ⅔ cup crumb mixture into an 11 by 7 by 1½-inch pan. Spread with jam and sprinkle remaining crumbs on top.
6. Bake 35 minutes or until brown. Cool before cutting.

Yields 12 to 16 bars

WHOLE WHEAT PICNIC BARS

¾   cup vegetable oil
2¼ cups brown sugar, packed
4   eggs, well beaten
2½ cups sifted whole wheat flour
¾   teaspoon salt
1   tablespoon baking powder

1   6-ounce package chocolate
     morsels
¾   cup raisins, optional
¾   cup quick cooking oats
1   cup chopped nuts

1. Preheat oven to 350°.
2. Combine oil and sugar. Add eggs and beat until smooth.
3. Sift together flour, salt and baking powder. Stir into oil mixture.
4. Add chocolate morsels, raisins, oats and nuts. Mix well.
5. Bake in a greased 9 by 13 by 2-inch baking dish 25 minutes. Cool. Cut into bars.

Yields 24 to 30 bars

WHOOPIE PIES

Cookies:

½ cup butter
1 cup sugar
1 egg
1 cup milk
1 teaspoon vanilla extract

2 cups all-purpose flour
1½ teaspoons soda
½ cup cocoa
Pinch salt

1. Preheat oven to 425°.
2. Mix all ingredients well.
3. Drop by teaspoonfuls on ungreased cookie sheet.
4. Bake 6 to 7 minutes. Cool.

Filling:

⅓ cup evaporated milk
⅔ cup shortening
¾ cup powdered sugar
1 teaspoon vanilla extract
Pinch salt

One of the following:

1 cup raspberry jam
1 cup peanut butter
2 tablespoons cocoa
½ to 1 teaspoon peppermint
    extract and 3 drops red food
    coloring

1. Mix first 5 ingredients. Let stand ½ hour.
2. Beat until fluffy.
3. Fold in optional ingredient.
4. Spread filling between 2 cookies.

Yields 3 dozen

COOKIES AND CREAM SQUARES

Fun for a child's birthday.

24 cream filled chocolate cookies, crushed	1 5.5-ounce can chocolate syrup
½ gallon vanilla ice cream, softened	1 12-ounce container frozen whipped topping

1. Arrange crushed cookies in bottom of 9 by 13-inch glass baking dish. Spread ice cream over cookies. Pour syrup over ice cream and top with whipped topping.
2. Freeze 12 hours. Cut into squares to serve.

These will keep several weeks in the freezer.

Variations:
Use peppermint ice cream and place crushed peppermints on top. Other flavors of ice cream may be used and garnished with any number of toppings.

Serves 15

VALENTINE COOKIES

These are great for a celebration, served with milk or hot tea.

2½ cups sifted all-purpose flour	2 teaspoons vanilla extract
¼ teaspoon baking powder	½ cup sifted powdered sugar
½ teaspoon salt	2 tablespoons milk
1 cup vegetable shortening	Raspberry jam

1. Sift flour, baking powder and salt.
2. Cream shortening, vanilla and sugar until light and fluffy.
3. Stir in flour mixture and milk.
4. Refrigerate until dough is easy to handle. Preheat oven to 350°.
5. On a lightly floured surface, roll dough ¼-inch thick. Cut into bite-size, heart shapes with cookie cutter. Place 1-inch apart on an ungreased cookie sheet.
6. Bake 12 to 15 minutes. Cool.
7. Place 1 teaspoon jam in centers of flat side of cookies. Press 2 cookies together, puffed sides out and flat sides together.

Yields 2 dozen

SWEDISH ALMOND SPRITZ COOKIES

Different from most spritz recipes in that no eggs are used. These go very well with poached pears or dessert fruit compotes.

2 cups butter	1 teaspoon almond extract
1 cup sugar	4¼ cups all-purpose flour
1 teaspoon vanilla extract	

1. Preheat oven to 400°.
2. Mix butter, sugar and flavorings thoroughly.
3. Work in flour.
4. Press dough through cookie press.
5. Bake on an ungreased cookie sheet 7 to 10 minutes. Do not brown.

Decorate with small pieces of candied cherries or colored sugar sprinkles if desired.

Freezes

Yields 6 dozen

SUGAR COOKIE CUT OUTS

An absolute hit when served at the opening of the Junior League sponsored Austin Ronald McDonald House.

¾ cup butter	2½ cups all-purpose flour
1 cup sugar	1 teaspoon baking powder
2 eggs	1 teaspoon salt
1 teaspoon vanilla extract	

1. Cream first 4 ingredients together until light and fluffy.
2. Add flour, baking powder and salt. Beat well.
3. Chill dough 1 hour.
4. Roll dough ⅛-inch thick. Cut into desired shapes.
5. Bake on ungreased cookie sheets 6 to 8 minutes at 400°.

Yields approximately 5 dozen

When rolling cookie dough, use powdered sugar instead of flour. (Cookies will not be tough.)

LOU NEFF'S SAND TARTS
A Collection Classic

2 cups butter (do not substitute), at room temperature
¾ cup sifted powdered sugar
4 cups sifted all-purpose flour

1 tablespoon cold water
1½ teaspoons vanilla extract
2 cups chopped pecans
Sifted powdered sugar

1. Cream butter and sugar.
2. Add flour and water. Blend well.
3. Stir in vanilla and pecans.
4. Roll into small balls and place on ungreased cookie sheets.
5. Bake at 325° for 20 minutes or until brown.
6. Roll in powdered sugar while still warm.

Published previously in *House and Garden Magazine* as part of a description of Neff family Christmas traditions.

Freezes

Yields 16 dozen

CHOCOLATE COVERED BUTTER COOKIES
A Collection Classic

The favorite of our testers.

½   cup butter, at room
      temperature
½   cup brown sugar
1   egg yolk, beaten
1   cup sifted all-purpose flour
½   teaspoon vanilla extract
1   8-ounce Hershey brand milk
      chocolate bar

½   8-ounce Hershey brand dark
      chocolate bar
1   4-ounce Baker's brand
      German's chocolate bar
½   cup broken pecan pieces

1. Cream butter and brown sugar. Add egg yolk, flour and vanilla. Mix well.
2. Spread on ungreased jelly roll pan approximately ¼-inch thick. Bake at 350°
    for 15 minutes.
3. Melt chocolate in top of double boiler.
4. When cookie is done, spread on chocolate while both are warm.
5. Sprinkle with pecans. Place in freezer.
6. When frozen, break into pieces with point of knife.

Best when served shortly after removing from freezer.

Freezes

Yields 4 dozen

ALMOND BUTTER TOFFEE

2   cups butter
2½ cups sugar
¼   teaspoon cream of tartar
2   cups slivered almonds

1   12-ounce package chocolate
      morsels
1   cup chopped pecans

1. Melt butter in a saucepan.
2. Add sugar. Raise heat. Stir constantly until mixture bubbles around edges of pan.
3. Add cream of tartar and almonds. Stir constantly until mixture turns a caramel color.
4. Pour onto 2 buttered cookie sheets, spreading thin.
5. Pour chocolate chips on top of toffee. The heat from the toffee will melt chocolate. As chocolate melts, spread with a knife.
6. Sprinkle with pecans.
7. Refrigerate until chocolate is hard and candy cooled. Break into pieces.

Yields 40 pieces

CHOCOLATE TRUFFLES

3 tablespoons unsalted butter
⅔ cup whipping cream
1 tablespoon sugar
6 ounces semi-sweet baking chocolate
2 tablespoons flavoring: vanilla, brandy or rum, optional

Choice of coating for truffles:
Cocoa powder
Chocolate sprinkles
Powdered sugar
Finely chopped nuts

1. Heat butter, cream and sugar until very hot, either in microwave or over hot water.
2. Remove from heat and stir in chocolate until melted. Mix well.
3. Add flavoring and cool.
4. Refrigerate until firm.
5. Form into 1-inch balls. Place balls on wax paper lined cookie sheet. Return to refrigerator. Chill approximately 1 hour or until firm.
6. Roll truffles in desired coating and store in refrigerator. Bring to room temperature before serving.

Yields 30 truffles

FABULOUS FUDGE

4 cups sugar	4 tablespoons white corn syrup
4 heaping tablespoons cocoa	2 cups half and half
Dash salt	2 teaspoons vanilla extract
½ cup butter	

1. Combine all ingredients except vanilla. Using a wooden spoon, stir constantly over medium heat until mixture reaches soft ball stage (234°–240°).
2. Remove from heat and place pan in cool water.
3. Add vanilla and beat until gloss is gone. Be careful not to overbeat because candy quickly turns to sugar.
4. Pour into a buttered 9 by 13-inch glass dish.

Yields 48 1-inch squares

CHOCOLATE COVERED PECAN CARAMELS

1¼ cups sugar	Dash salt
¾ cup butter	2 cups whipping cream, divided
1 cup plus 2 tablespoons brown sugar	4 cups pecans
	½ teaspoon vanilla extract
1 cup dark corn syrup	30 ounces milk chocolate

1. Combine sugars, butter, corn syrup, salt and half the cream. Bring to a boil. Add remaining cream.
2. Cook over low heat until mixture reaches soft ball stage (234°–240°).
3. Add pecans and vanilla.
4. Pour into a well buttered 9 by 13-inch pan.
5. Cool and cut into squares.
6. Melt chocolate in double boiler. Cool to tepid. (Warm chocolate will melt candy.)
7. Dip squares and place on wax paper. Store in closed container.

Variation:
To make turtles undercook mixture a bit. Roll into a ball, place on wax paper in refrigerator before dipping.

Yields 75 pieces

KENTUCKY COLONELS

½ cup butter
1 pound powdered sugar, sifted
½ cup chopped nuts, soaked
    overnight in 6 tablespoons
    bourbon

5 ounces bitter chocolate
⅓ cup paraffin

1. Cream butter and sugar well. Add bourbon and nuts.
2. Shape into 1-inch balls.
3. Chill in refrigerator until firm.
4. Melt chocolate over hot water, in double boiler. Add melted paraffin. Blend well.
5. Place each ball on a toothpick and dip in chocolate.
6. Allow chocolate to harden. Store in refrigerator.

Yields 70 pieces

KAHLUA BALLS

Good at holiday time when serving plates of cookies and candies

2 8-ounce packages chocolate
    wafer cookies, crushed
1 cup powdered sugar
2½ cups finely chopped pecans

⅓ cup light corn syrup
⅓ cup Kahlua
1 tablespoon vanilla extract

1. Mix cookie crumbs, powdered sugar and 1½ cups of pecans.
2. Add corn syrup, Kahlua and vanilla. Mix by hand until it is the consistency of cookie dough. If it is too dry, add corn syrup by tablespoonfuls until consistency is right. Be careful as mixture can quickly become too soft.
3. Grind remaining pecans to a powder.
4. Grease hands with butter and roll dough into balls, then roll in remaining pecans to coat.
5. Store in a candy tin with sheets of wax paper between layers. Keep in a cool dry place. These taste fresh for about a week.

Yields 3 dozen

PEANUT BRITTLE

1	cup light corn syrup	2	tablespoons butter
2	cups sugar	2	teaspoons vanilla extract
1	pound (2¼ cups) raw peanuts	2	teaspoons baking soda

1. Turn 3 large cookie sheets upside down. Use these as a work surface for pulling candy. Butter and lightly sprinkle salt onto cookie sheets.
2. Cook corn syrup, sugar and peanuts over high heat in a large, heavy saucepan, stirring constantly until peanuts turn a medium brown color.
3. Remove from heat. Add butter and vanilla. Stir well.
4. Add soda and barely blend.
5. Quickly pour onto cookie sheets, ⅓ of mixture per sheet.
6. Allow to stand until edges of candy can be lifted with a buttered knife edge and pulled. Begin pulling almost immediately so brittle does not harden. Work each sheet of candy, working toward the middle always gently pulling up and out. Pull until very thin. Candy will pull out past the edge of the cookie sheet.
7. Let it cool completely, break into large pieces. Store in air tight container.

Yields 3 pounds

PICKLES, PRESERVES AND RELISHES

Pickling and Preserving Food

In past generations, preserving food was necessary to preserve life. Women who were responsible for canning the bounty of farm and garden, worked long, hard hours to ensure certain foods would be available year round for their families.

In most modern homes, preserving and canning food is done for pleasure and self-satisfaction. Quantities no longer have to be on a production-line scale and can easily be handled in today's kitchen. Home canned foods are a treat for family members and wonderful gifts for friends.

Basic Equipment

A few pieces of basic, inexpensive equipment, in addition to regular kitchen utensils, make it possible to successfully prepare all of the recipes in the following chapter.

1. Water Bath Canner—A large kettle with a cover deep enough to permit water to cover jars at least one inch over the top and a little extra space for boiling; canner must have a rack to hold jars ½-inch above bottom of canner.
2. Wide Mouth Jar Funnel for packing foods in jars.
3. Long Handled Fork
4. Ladle
5. Tongs
6. Jar Lifter
7. Liquid Measuring Cup
8. A selection of tempered Mason Jars, Lids and Screw Bands.

Hint: A gift appreciated by any cook is a new water bath canner filled with the above listed equipment and favorite jam, jelly and pickle recipes!

Getting Started

Select firm, fresh, ripe, young fruits or vegetables. Wash them thoroughly but do not soak. Soaking causes loss of flavor and nutrients. Be sure to cut away any bruised or damaged parts of the food before preparing. Use the freshest spices available. When vinegar is called for, use a pickling strength with 4 to 6% acidity.

Wash jars, rings and lids in hot, soapy water and rinse. Place clean jars in a large pot and cover with water. Bring to a boil and boil 5 minutes. Let the jars remain in the hot water until ready to pack. Jar lids and rings should be placed in a small pan, covered with boiling water and allowed to remain in hot water until ready to use.

Methods of Canning

Open Kettle—This method involves cooking the food product and pouring it into sterilized jars. The jars are then sealed and stored. Because this method does not supply the amount of heat needed to sterilize, it is only used with foods that can be cooked with sufficient sugar or vinegar to keep them from spoiling. Foods such as jams, jellies, relishes and pickles are canned by this method.

Cold Pack—Sometimes referred to as "raw pack" means that the jars are filled with unheated or raw food and then covered with a boiling liquid. The filled jars are then processed either in a water-bath or a steam-pressure canner.

Hot Pack—Refers to food that is cooked for a short time and then packed into hot jars. The food is then processed immediately.

Methods of Processing

Steam-Pressure Method—A method of processing foods at a temperature higher than that of boiling water; a steam pressure canner is the only kitchen equipment that supplies enough heat to destroy the spoilage organisms in certain foods. Low-acid foods have to be processed by this method.

Boiling Water Bath—A method of processing foods at a temperature of 212° F; this method is recommended only for processing fruits, tomatoes and other foods high in acid. Enough heat is supplied to destroy the organisms which cause spoiling in acidic foods. Only enough jars should be prepared to fill the container at one time. Jars of food should be placed on the rack in the container. There must be space between and under the jars to allow the free circulation of boiling water. When processing time is complete, jars are removed immediately and placed on a thick cloth to cool.

Helpful Hints

❋ Carefully read and follow the directions that come with Mason jars and lids.

❋ Always clean the top of the jar or threads with a damp cloth before putting on the lid. Food particles or liquid on the jar rim can cause improper sealing.

❋ The ring or band should be screwed on securely but not too tightly which could cause the can lid to buckle.

❋ Always use jars and lids specifically manufactured for canning. Do not re-use lids.

ROSY PEACH BANANA JAM

3¼ cups mashed peaches (about 2 pounds)
1 cup mashed banana (about 3 medium)
½ cup coarsely chopped maraschino cherries

2 tablespoons lemon juice
1 1¾-ounce package powdered fruit pectin
6 cups sugar

1. Combine peaches, banana, cherries, lemon juice and fruit pectin in a large heavy kettle. Stir well.
2. Place over high heat and bring to a boil, stirring constantly.
3. Quickly stir in sugar. Bring to a boil. Boil 1 minute or until mixture reaches 220° on a candy thermometer (stir constantly).
4. Remove from heat. Skim off foam with a metal spoon.
5. Quickly ladle jam into hot sterilized jars. Seal.
6. Process in boiling water bath 5 minutes.

Variation:
½ cup mashed strawberries can be substituted for cherries. When using cherries, juice can be used to make Maraschino Honey Jelly.

Yields 7 half pints

MARASCHINO HONEY JELLY

A favorite for the honey lover.

3　cups honey
1　cup maraschino cherry juice

6　ounces liquid fruit pectin

1. Combine honey and cherry juice in a large saucepan. Mix well.
2. Place over high heat and bring to a boil, stirring constantly.
3. Immediately stir in pectin and bring to a full rolling boil. Boil 1 minute, stirring constantly.
4. Remove from heat. Skim off foam with a metal spoon. Pour quickly into jars or glasses. Seal.

Yields 5 half pints

JALAPEÑO PEPPER JELLY

Jalapeño jelly spread over a block of cream cheese and served with crackers is a quick, delicious appetizer or snack.

¼ to ½ cup chopped fresh jalapeño pepper
1　cup chopped green bell pepper
1½ cups apple cider
1　cup apple cider vinegar

6½ cups sugar
6　ounces liquid pectin
　Green food coloring, optional

1. Bring all ingredients, except pectin and food coloring to a hard rolling boil.
2. Boil 1 minute. Remove from heat. Let stand 5 minutes.
3. Add pectin and stir well.
4. Strain if clear jelly is desired. Food coloring may be added sparingly for a bright green color.
5. Pour into hot, sterilized jars. Seal.

Use caution when working with fresh jalapeños. Wearing rubber gloves is a good idea. Be careful not to rub eyes or face until hands are carefully washed.

Yields 4 pints

PEAR MARMALADE

4   cups mashed ripe Bartlett
      pears (6 medium)
1   15¼-ounce can crushed
      pineapple, drained
2 to 4 cups sugar (depending on
      desired sweetness)

1   9-ounce jar maraschino
      cherries, quartered
Juice of 1 lemon

1. Combine all ingredients in a large kettle. Let stand until sugar melts.
2. Cook over low heat, stirring occasionally until thick.
3. Ladle into jars. Seal with paraffin.

Yields 9 half pints

FIG CONSERVE

2   pounds figs
1   cup diced pineapple
    Sugar

½   cup almonds or walnuts,
      coarsely chopped

1. Wash and stem figs. Slice if desired.
2. Add pineapple and juice if desired.
3. Measure or weigh fruit. Add an equal amount of sugar.
4. Place fruit and sugar in a heavy kettle. Cook over medium heat, stirring occasionally, until mixture is thick. Be careful not to scorch.
5. Add nuts just before removing from heat.
6. Ladle into jars. Seal.

Yields 2 pints

HOLIDAY CRANBERRY JAM

2 cups fresh or frozen
    cranberries
1 medium orange, peeled
½ cup water
1 10-ounce package frozen
    strawberries, thawed and
    crushed

3 cups sugar
½ bottle liquid pectin

1. Finely chop or grind cranberries.
2. Grind or chop orange very fine.
3. In a medium saucepan, combine fruits, water and sugar. Mix well.
4. Cook over low heat 2 minutes, stirring constantly. Raise heat to high and bring mixture to a full rolling boil. Boil hard exactly 1 minute, stirring constantly.
5. Remove from heat and stir in pectin.
6. Skim and alternately stir 4 or 5 minutes.
7. Ladle into jars. Seal.

Yields 3 pints

Cranberries can be frozen in original plastic bags.

CRANBERRY WINE JELLY

7 cups sugar
¼ teaspoon ground cloves
¼ teaspoon ground cinnamon

3 cups cranberry juice cocktail
1 cup port wine
1 box (2 packages) Certo

1. Combine sugar, spices and cranberry juice in large kettle. Bring to a hard, rolling boil. Boil 1 minute.
2. Remove from heat. Stir in wine and pectin. Stir and skim until jelly is clear.
3. Pour into hot sterilized jars. Seal. Jelly may be sealed with paraffin.

Great on a hot biscuit, as a glaze for meats or as a center in muffins.

Yields 7 six ounce jars

FAYE HARRIS' PEACH PRESERVES
A Collection Classic

1   pound sugar to each pound of peaches

1. Peel and slice peaches.
2. In a large kettle, arrange peaches and sugar in layers, adding 4 to 5 peach kernels. Let stand overnight.
3. Bring peaches to a boil, stirring gently. Simmer 4 to 5 hours until transparent, skimming foam occasionally.
4. Pack in sterilized jars and seal.

½ bushel of peaches yields approximately 8 quart jars

DILLED CARROTS

1   pound carrots

SEASONINGS AND SPICES TO ADD TO EACH JAR:
½ to 1 tablespoon salt
½   teaspoon sugar
1   large clove garlic
1   teaspoon dill seed
⅛   teaspoon red pepper

LIQUID FOR PICKLING:
1½ cups boiling water
1½ cups boiling vinegar

1. Peel and cut carrots into ⅛ to ¼-inch strips the length of pint Mason jars.
2. Add seasonings and spices to 3 hot, sterilized pint Mason jars.
3. Quickly pack carrot strips into jars.
4. Combine boiling water and vinegar. Pour over carrots. Seal jars.
5. Process in boiling water bath 15 minutes.

Best eaten after 3 to 4 days. Refrigerated dilled carrots are best!

Yields 3 pints

FIG PRESERVES
A Collection Classic

1 gallon figs, cut into small pieces	1 cup light corn syrup
8 cups sugar	3 lemons, thinly sliced

1. Combine all ingredients and cook until thick.
2. Pour into sterilized jars and seal with paraffin.

Yields 8 pints

PICKLED PEACHES

6 16-ounce cans cling peach halves	3 sticks cinnamon
¾ cup packed brown sugar	1 tablespoon whole cloves
½ cup cider vinegar	Extra whole cloves

1. Drain syrup from peaches. Reserve syrup from 2¼ cans.
2. Combine syrup, sugar, vinegar and spices in a saucepan. Bring to a boil. Lower heat. Simmer 5 minutes.
3. Stick 1 whole clove in each peach half.
4. Place peaches in hot sterilized jars. Pour simmered syrup mixture over peaches.
5. Seal immediately. Process in boiling water bath 15 minutes.

Yields 4 quarts

PEAR RELISH

Excellent with meats.

12	pears, peeled and pared	1	teaspoon celery salt
6	sweet red bell peppers (green if desired)	2 to 3	hot peppers
		3½	cups vinegar
4	medium onions	1	tablespoon cornstarch
3	cups sugar		

1. Coarsely grind or chop pears, peppers and onions. Place in a large kettle.
2. Add remaining ingredients. Cook, stirring occasionally, over medium heat 20 minutes.
3. Add cornstarch mixed with 2 tablespoons water. Cook 10 additional minutes.
4. Ladle into hot sterilized jars. Seal.

Yields 8 pints

EASY CORN RELISH

½	cup sugar	1	17-ounce can corn, drained
½	teaspoon salt	2	tablespoons diced green bell pepper
½	teaspoon celery seed		
¼	teaspoon dry mustard	1	4-ounce jar diced pimientos
⅛	teaspoon white pepper	1	tablespoon instant minced onion
½	cup cider vinegar		

1. Combine sugar, salt, celery seed, mustard, pepper and vinegar in a saucepan.
2. Bring to a boil. Boil 2 minutes. Remove from heat.
3. Stir in corn, bell pepper, pimientos and onion. Cool.
4. Pour into pint jar. Cover tightly. Refrigerate 3 days before serving.

Will keep refrigerated 1 month

Yields 1 pint

OLD-TIME ICE BOX PICKLES

1 cup vinegar	7 cups sliced, unpeeled
1 cup sugar	cucumbers
1 tablespoon celery seed	1 cup thinly sliced onion
1 tablespoon salt	

1. Combine vinegar, sugar, celery seed and salt. Refrigerate until cold.
2. Combine vinegar mixture with cucumbers and onion. Let stand, covered, overnight at room temperature.
3. Store in jars in refrigerator up to 2 months.

Yields 2 quarts

GREEN TOMATO RELISH

1 gallon green tomatoes (16 to 18)	2½ cups vinegar
3 large red bell peppers	1 cup water
3 large green bell peppers	3½ cups sugar
6 onions	1 tablespoon whole mixed
½ cup salt	pickling spice, wrapped in cheesecloth and tied

1. Chop tomatoes, peppers and onions in a food processor. Add salt.
2. Refrigerate in a glass bowl overnight.
3. Drain liquid. Place vegetables in a large kettle.
4. Add remaining ingredients. Bring to a boil while stirring. Simmer 30 minutes. Remove spice bag.
5. Ladle into hot sterilized jars. Process in boiling water bath 5 minutes.

Yields 6 pints

QUICK REFRIGERATOR PICKLES

1	quart dill pickles, drained	2	cloves garlic
1	onion, sliced	2	cups sugar
1	teaspoon celery seed	1	cup vinegar
1	teaspoon mustard seed		

1. Slice pickles in strips or rounds.
2. In a glass or china bowl, combine onion, celery seed, mustard seed, garlic and pickles.
3. Combine sugar and vinegar. Bring to a boil.
4. Pour boiling vinegar over pickles. Cool.
5. Place in desired glass container. Refrigerate 1 day before eating.

Keeps 1 month in refrigerator.

Yields 1 quart

SWEET HOT PICKLES

1	gallon hamburger dill slices	1 to 2 ounces Tabasco sauce	
5	pounds granulated sugar	½	jar chopped garlic

1. Drain juice from pickles. Pat with paper towels until dry.
2. Combine sugar, Tabasco and garlic. Layer with pickles in gallon jar. Any remaining sugar mixture may be added the next day.
3. Screw lid tightly on jar and invert.
4. Leave jar on counter top 10 days. Turn once in the morning and again in the evening.
5. After 10 days, repack pickles in smaller sterilized jars. Keep refrigerated. (These pickles do not need to be sealed or processed.) Pickles are very crisp when refrigerated.

Yields 8 pints

SWEET BREAD AND BUTTER PICKLES

4	quarts sliced cucumbers	1	tablespoon mustard seed
½	cup salt	1	tablespoon ground ginger
	Ice cubes	1	teaspoon tumeric
1	quart pickling vinegar	½	teaspoon white wine vinegar
4	cups sugar	2	quarts sliced onions
1	tablespoon celery seed		

1. Mix cucumbers and salt in an enamel pan. Cover with ice cubes and refrigerate 3 hours.
2. Combine all remaining ingredients, except onion slices. Bring to a rolling boil. Lower heat and boil 10 minutes.
3. Drain cucumbers. Mix with onions. Add to hot vinegar mixture.
4. Bring to a boil, time and cook 5 minutes.
5. Pack in hot sterilized jars and seal at once. Let season several days. Chill before serving.

Yields approximately 6 quarts

POTPOURRI

This section contains the little extras that cooks and children enjoy making. There are many instructions and techniques for special recipes and projects. Cooking novelties, food gifts and crafts, rainy day entertainment and party ideas for children are some of the featured sections.

DECORATIVE FRILLS AND FLOURISHES

It is a challenge, as well as great fun, to decorate desserts, cookies and cakes for holidays or special occasions. Do not hesitate to try any of these techniques. They are simple and with a little experimentation and practice, any cook can create a "masterpiece". This section provides the essential recipes and instructions that make the attempt much easier. It includes a grand set of instructions and drawings for making a holiday candy house and other holiday treats.

Brilliantine

Add interest to your baked goodies with this colorful edible glitter.

2   tablespoons gum Arabic   Paste color, if desired
⅓ to ½ cup water

1. In a saucepan, combine Arabic, water and a dot of color.
2. Over medium heat, cook, stirring constantly until Arabic dissolves.
3. Strain through cloth.
4. Brush mixture on foil and place in a 350° oven.
5. Close door one minute. Open door and turn off heat. A crackling noise will occur when mixture dries and crystals form. If mixture does not dry, turn oven on and off periodically until mixture dries and crackling stops.
6. Shake glitter off foil.
7. Sift through strainer for fine sparkling dust.

Colored Coconut

Place loosely packed coconut in a large jar. Add a few drops of food coloring. Add several drops of water to vary intensity of color. Seal jar and shake until coconut is evenly colored.

Colored Sugar

1 cup granulated sugar   Liquid food coloring

1. Place sugar in a glass jar.
2. Add desired number of drops for color intensity.
3. Place lid on jar and shake to evenly distribute color.

A gift idea: Carefully layer different colors of sugar in an attractive glass jar.

Marzipan

Marzipan is a dough-like confection made with a base of almond paste. It can be molded into decorative shapes and colored to adorn other desserts or served by itself. Sometimes it is rolled like pie crust and draped over cakes as a covering, with the edges trimmed.

Marzipan Recipe

2 8-ounce packages almond   ¼ cup light corn syrup
   paste   3¾ cups extra fine sugar
1 7-ounce jar marshmallow   Liquid food coloring
   cream   Extra sugar

1. Crumble almond paste into a bowl.
2. Add marshmallow cream and corn syrup. Blend well.
3. Add sugar and mix well. Dough should be stiff. Add more sugar if necessary.
4. Knead marzipan dough until sugar is absorbed and the dough is smooth and pliable.
5. Pinch off pieces to mold fruits or other shapes.
6. Place pieces on wax paper and allow to dry several hours.
7. With a brush, paint shapes with liquid food coloring diluted with water.
8. Roll in sugar for a frosted effect, if desired.

Marvelous Baked Meringues

Meringue may be used to create fanciful shapes or forms. These melt-in-your-mouth decorative desserts may be filled with creams, custards, fresh fruits and berries.

When making meringue, be sure that the whisk, beaters and bowl are dry and free of any trace of grease. A balloon whisk creates the greatest volume. A hand-held rotary beater produces the next greatest volume. An electric mixer creates the least volume but saves time.

Basic Meringue Recipe

1 cup egg whites, at room temperature	1 teaspoon vanilla extract or ½ teaspoon almond extract
½ teaspoon cream of tartar	2 cups extra fine sugar
¼ teaspoon salt	

1. Beat egg whites until frothy.
2. Add cream of tartar, salt and vanilla. Beat until soft peaks form. Add sugar, 1 tablespoon at a time, continually beating until stiff peaks form.
3. Preheat oven to 225°. Bake piped and molded meringues 2 to 3 hours. (Meringue may be baked at 250° to 275° for 1 to 1½ hours.) When baking meringue never set the oven higher than 275° as a higher temperature may cause the sugar to caramelize.

Variation:
Chocolate meringue may be made by adding 2 ounces of grated sweet chocolate to Basic Meringue Recipe.

❈ Granulated sugar that has been processed in a blender until finely ground may be substituted for extra fine sugar.

❈ Always pipe meringue onto a foil-lined pan or cookie sheet.

❈ When constructing meringue forms or containers, use meringue as glue or smooth icing.

❈ Although instructions call for baking meringue, it is actually dried in the oven rather than baked. After baking, allow meringue to cool thoroughly before gently removing from foil.

❈ Baked meringues may be stored 4 to 6 weeks in an airtight container.

❈ Meringues may be lightly dusted with cocoa for added color.

❈ Melted chocolate may be used to bond individual pieces of meringue together when creating fanciful meringues.

Meringue Rosettes

Divide Basic Meringue recipe into 3 bowls. Color and flavor these with desired extracts. Place a large star tip on each pastry bag. Fill bags with different colored and flavored meringue. Pipe large rosettes on foil lined cookie sheets. Bake 2 to 3 hours at 225°. Cool completely. Store flavors separately in airtight containers.

Yields 4 to 6 dozen

Coconut Meringue Nests

Fill a pastry bag with Basic Meringue Recipe. Using a star tip, form a base by piping a circle the desired diameter of the nest on a foil-lined cookie sheet. Fill circle with a piped coil. Build the sides by piping coils to desired height. Sprinkle with colored or toasted shredded coconut. Bake approximately 2 hours at 250°. For Easter, fill with jelly beans. Use as a bowl for desserts throughout the year.

Meringue Baskets

A large meringue basket or several individual baskets make lovely containers for sliced and sweetened fruit or berries.

Place a large round tip on a pastry bag. Fill bag with Basic Meringue recipe. Form a base by piping a circle the desired diameter of the base on a foil-lined cookie sheet. Fill circle with a piped coil. Build sides by piping coils to desired height. With a flat spatula, ice sides of baskets with meringue to cover coils and produce a smooth surface. Fill another pastry bag with meringue and use a smaller decorative tip to pipe an edge at the base and top of the basket. Bake 2 to 3 hours at 225°. Cool thoroughly and gently remove baskets. These may also be frozen. After thawing, place baskets in a warm oven for 5 minutes.

Yields 1 large or 6 individual baskets

CHOCOLATE GARNISHES

Chocolate decorations are easy to make and add an elaborate touch to desserts. Use a double boiler to melt chocolate over hot, but never boiling water. Melt chocolate carefully as heat can alter the texture. Try not to touch chocolate as the warmth of your hands will melt the chocolate. Use tweezers, wooden picks or kitchen implements to handle decorations.

Chocolate Cut Outs

Pour melted chocolate and spread as evenly as possible onto parchment or wax paper. Cool chocolate until firm, but not hard. To make shapes, use small cookie cutters or cut shapes with a sharp knife. Chill chocolate decorations in refrigerator until ready to use.

Piped Chocolate Decorations

Chocolate Piping Glaze

3   ounces semi-sweet chocolate   1   tablespoon water
    or ½ cup semi-sweet   ¼   cup light corn syrup
    chocolate morsels

1. In the top of a double boiler, over hot but not boiling water, melt chocolate pieces, corn syrup and water. Stir frequently until chocolate reaches a smooth consistency.
2. Remove from heat and cool 5 minutes before using as piping.
3. Pour melted chocolate into a pastry bag.
4. Through a small opening in the bag, pipe chocolate onto parchment or wax paper. Create desired letters, numbers or designs.
5. Allow chocolate to cool. Carefully remove decorations and chill in refrigerator until ready to use.

Chocolate glaze may be piped onto a smooth, iced surface and feathered.

Chocolate Curls

Pour melted chocolate and spread as evenly as possible onto parchment or wax paper. Before chocolate becomes too hard, shave chocolate surface with a swivel-bladed vegetable parer. For long, thin curls, use a sharp, thin knife.

Chocolate curls can also be made from a solid block of chocolate. Let chocolate stand in a warm place for 15 minutes. Carefully draw knife or parer across chocolate to produce curls. When using a knife, dip it into hot water for easier shaving. Continue dipping the knife in hot water during the process. Place curls in refrigerator until ready to use.

Chocolate Leaves

Select small, stiff leaves from any non-poisonous plant. Melt chocolate in a double boiler. With a small pastry brush, paint a thin coat of chocolate on the undersides of leaves. Apply a second coat to produce a firm decoration. If chocolate becomes too thick during the painting process, carefully rewarm chocolate over hot water. After chocolate has set, peel off the leaves and chill chocolate leaves in refrigerator until ready to use.

Chocolate Containers

A variety of chocolate containers may be formed by coating paper or foil baking cups with melted chocolate. For every 8 ounces of chocolate, add 1 tablespoon vegetable oil to the melted chocolate and blend thoroughly. Pour enough melted chocolate into the cup and thoroughly coat bottom and sides. Briefly chill to set the chocolate, then repeat the process. When the chocolate has set after the second coating, remove the exterior foil or paper cup. Store, separated and covered, in the refrigerator until ready to fill.

These chocolate dessert cups are best when filled with chilled mousse or puddings. Accent with a dollop of whipped cream and chocolate shavings.

Chocolate dessert cups may also be used to serve liqueurs that are complementary to chocolate. Before serving, place cups in a new foil wrapper to serve as a coaster.

Chocolate Sprinkles

Chill a block of chocolate until hard. Using a chilled knife, shave chocolate onto wax paper. Chop shavings to make sprinkles.

PIPED ICING DECORATIONS

Practice Makes Perfect

Practice is the key to successful cake and cookie decoration. Purchased cookies and cakes provide great experimental models. This will save time and alleviate the anxiety of ruining a special recipe. Purchased samples are especially practical for children who want to learn icing decoration.

Necessary Tools

Decorating Tips—These are the cone-shaped tips with different designs on the points that make patterns for decoration. They may be purchased in basic plastic kits at the grocery store or fancy professional sets with as many as fifty tips. Some basic tips are:

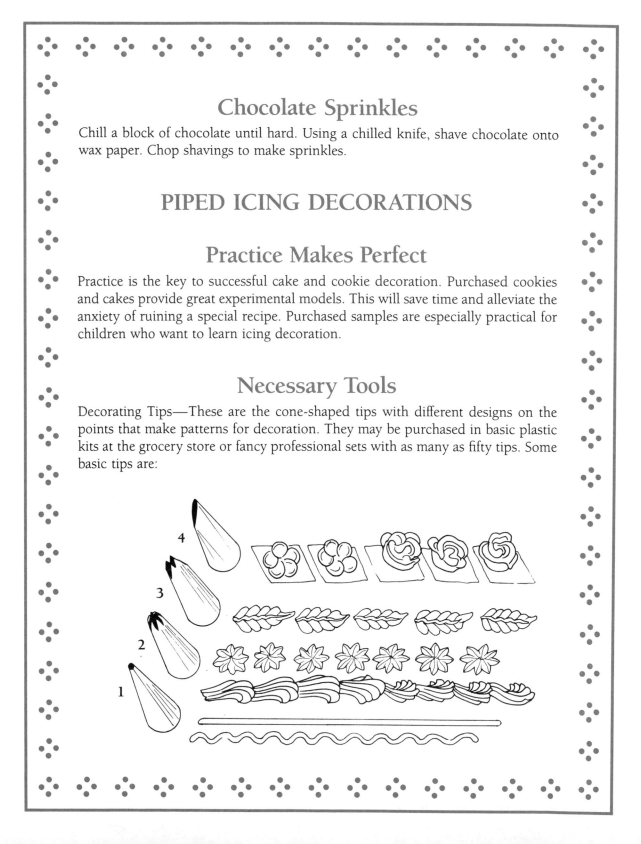

1. **Writing Tip:**
    fine line, script,
    numbers and outlines

2. **Star Tip:**
    rosettes, shell and
    scored boarders

3. **Leaf Tip:**
    ruffled leaves and
    boarders

4. **Petal Tip:**
    wide flat edge for
    petals, bows, roses
    and rosebuds

Most decorating sets will have detailed instructions for assembly and use.

Pastry Bag or Cones—This is the container that holds the decorative icing and attaches to the decorative tips to pipe the icing through the tip.

If you do not have a decorating set or kit, make a simple cone from paper by either of these two methods.

A. Paper envelope method:
  1. Place decorative icing in a bottom corner of a large paper envelope.
  2. Seal the envelope and roll excess paper toward the icing, creating a pastry tube effect.
  3. Carefully cut a tiny hole at the tip of the corner. Gently squeeze icing from the bag.

This is a good emergency substitute for a pastry bag and may be used for piping simple designs or lettering.

B. Paper cone method:
1. Cut a large square of wax or parchment paper (at least 12-inches square).
2. Fold in half diagonally, then cut along fold to create two triangles.
3. Using one triangle, lift point C and place on point B, curling edge of point C under. While holding these two points together, wrap point A around entire cone, meeting points C and B. Adjust point A, by lifting up to ensure a tightly closed opening at cone tip.
4. Fold points inside cone and staple to hold securely.
5. Fill cone two-thirds full with icing. Fold top over twice so icing cannot escape through the top.
6. Cut off tip allowing for an opening of approximately ¹⁄₁₆-inch. Hold bag with both hand and squeeze.

Experiment before decorating. Even pressure will produce a smooth attractive decoration.

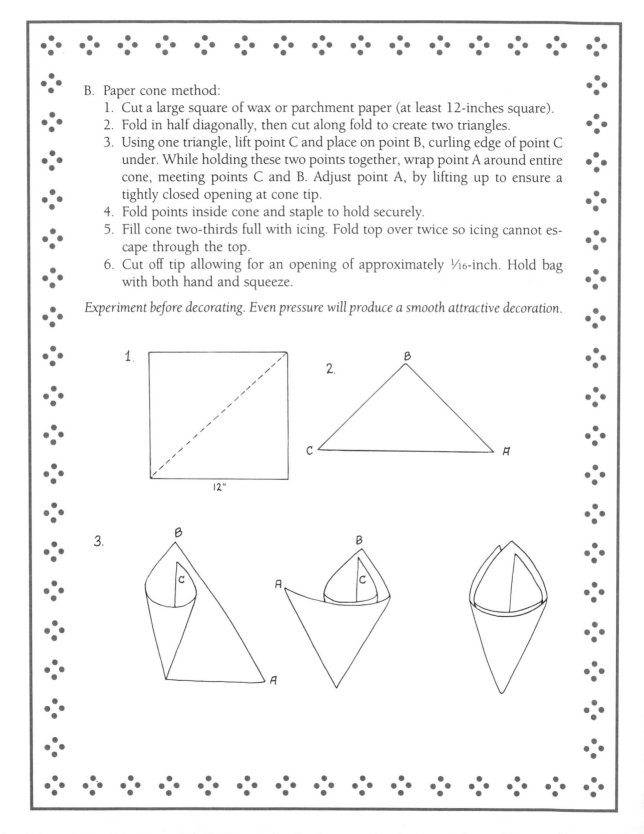

4.

5.

Food Coloring Chart

Apricot . . . . 5 parts lemon yellow, 2 parts pink
Aqua . . . . 3 parts royal blue, 1 part leaf green
Bright Red . . . . 1 part lemon yellow, 5 parts red-red
Brown . . . . 4 parts lemon yellow, 3 parts pink, 1 part leaf green
Burgundy . . . . 5 parts pink, 1 part royal blue
Coral . . . . 2 parts lemon yellow, 3 parts pink
Egg Yellow . . . . 8 parts lemon yellow, 1 part Christmas red
Golden Yellow . . . . 6 parts lemon yellow, 1 part Christmas red
Lavender . . . . 2 parts pink, 1 part royal blue
Lilac . . . . 3 parts pink, 1 part royal blue
Lime . . . . 3 parts lemon yellow, 1 part leaf green
Mint . . . . 1 part lemon yellow, 1 part royal blue, 1 part leaf green
Peach . . . . 4 parts lemon yellow, 2 parts pink
Purple . . . . 2 parts Christmas red, 2 parts royal blue
Rust . . . . 1 part lemon yellow, 3 parts Christmas red, 2 parts royal blue
Sky Blue . . . . 5 parts royal blue, 1 part leaf green
Strawberry . . . . 2 parts lemon yellow, 5 parts Christmas red
Turquoise . . . . 4 parts royal blue, 1 part leaf green

DECORATIVE ICINGS

Bakery Icing

½   cup water
1½ teaspoon butter flavoring
1   teaspoon vanilla extract
1½ cups shortening
¼   teaspoon salt
½ to 1 teaspoon meringue powder
     (commercial product)

2 to 4 tablespoons all-purpose
     flour
2   pounds sifted powdered sugar,
     divided

1. Combine all ingredients except 1 pound sugar, adding dry ingredients to liquid.
2. Mix well. Add remaining sugar and beat until smooth.

Butter Icing I

½   cup butter
2   cups powdered sugar, sifted

1   egg white

1. Cream butter.
2. Gradually add sugar to butter.
3. Add unbeaten egg white and beat thoroughly.

Butter Icing II

4   tablespoons butter
2   cups powdered sugar, sifted

Flavoring
Milk

1. Cream butter until soft and smooth.
2. Slowly add powdered sugar, mixing thoroughly.
3. Add flavoring and milk, one drop at a time until desired consistency is reached.

Flavor and color variations:
   ※ ¼ teaspoon vanilla
   ※ ½ ounce melted chocolate
   ※ Coffee, instead of milk, for mocha icing
   ※ Yolk of one egg to produce yellow icing
   ※ Food colorings

Canned Icing—Prepared vanilla frosting may be used for decorative icing. If it becomes soft while decorating, refrigerate until it acquires a stiff consistency. These icings may be colored with liquid or paste food coloring.

Icing Mixes—Prepared vanilla frosting mixes may be used for decorative icing. Follow package directions, but reduce water by 4 teaspoons to make a stiffer consistency which is better for decorative icing. These icings may be colored with liquid or paste food coloring. If liquid food coloring is used, reduce water by the amount of liquid coloring used.

Royal Icing—This icing is a favorite of many cooks. It is easy to prepare and versatile. Royal Icing adds a grand flourish to any cookie or cake.

✳ Royal icing dries quickly. To prevent a crust from forming, cover icing, while not being used.

✳ Icing may be covered tightly and stored in the refrigerator several days. While the original texture will not be completely restored, it will be satisfactory for touch-ups.

✳ Add a few drops of water if icing is too thick or add extra powdered sugar if icing is too thin. Beat a few minutes to mix thoroughly.

✳ Add a few drops of any flavoring. Some favorites are mint, cinnamon, and lemon.

✳ One tablespoon of corn syrup may be added to icing to create a shiny effect.

✳ Royal icing will not dry satisfactorily in high humidity. Do not attempt to use this recipe on humid days.

✳ When making Royal icing all utensils must be free from grease and oil.

✳ Paste food colorings are preferred as they will not alter the consistency of the icing.

✳ Royal icing makes an excellent "glue" for building cookie houses.

✳ Royal icing is used for painting cookies (royal icing paint).

Royal Icing Recipe

3   egg whites (room temperature)   4   cups powdered sugar
½   teaspoon cream of tartar

1. In a large mixing bowl, combine egg whites and cream of tartar. With an electric mixer, beat on medium until mixture is frothy.
2. Gradually add powdered sugar. Mix well. Add flavorings, colorings or corn syrup. Beat on high speed 8 to 10 minutes.

Yields 2½ cups

Royal Icing Paint

Royal icing paint is made by thinning royal icing with water. Determine the number of decorating colors needed. Divide royal icing into one container for each color. Slowly add water until icing is the consistency of egg whites. Lift a spoonful of icing out of container and hold spoon approximately 6 inches above container. Drizzle icing back into the container. Icing should be reabsorbed and the surface smooth after approximately 10 seconds. Thin with more water if necessary. Color Royal Icing Paint, using only paste food coloring (liquid food coloring will thin mixture).

Using a pastry tube, pipe an outline around cookie or other dessert with unthinned Royal Icing. Fill outlined surface with Royal Icing Paint. Paint may be applied by spooning, piping or painting icing onto the surface.

Combining different decorative techniques adds interest to dessert decorations. Use the feathering technique described in this chapter to draw with or move Royal Icing Paint around an iced surface.

Stencils

Stenciled decorations may be used on any smoothed, iced surface. After baked item has cooled, outline surface with unthinned Royal Icing. Fill center with Royal Icing Paint and allow paint to dry. Choose or make simple stencil designs with sharp, clear edges. Securely place stencil on iced surface and paint with colored Royal Icing Paint. When removing stencil, lift carefully to avoid disturbing the design.

Feathering

This decorative technique may be used on any cake or cookie with a smooth glazed icing. Chocolate or a contrasting colored icing paint is piped onto the surface of the smooth glazed icing while it is still wet. The contrasting piped icing may either be applied in concentric circles or parallel lines. Quickly draw a pointed metal skewer, a wooden pick or a hat pin through the contrasting piped icing to create the feathered effect. Each time the pick is pulled through the contrasting piped icing, wipe the point to remove any excess icing so the design will be sharp. Working quickly is the secret to creating this feathered effect; so fill the piping tubes before applying the smooth glazed surface icing. Experiment and create different patterns by alternately pulling the pick in different directions. You may work from the center outward to the edges or vice versa.

COOKIES AND DECORATIVE EXTRAS

Gingerbread Cookies

This dough may be chilled or used immediately.

1 cup shortening	5 cups all-purpose flour
1 cup sugar	1½ teaspoons baking soda
½ teaspoon salt	1 tablespoon ground ginger
1 egg	1 teaspoon cinnamon
1 cup molasses	1 teaspoon ground cloves
2 tablespoons vinegar	

1. Cream together shortening, sugar and salt. Add eggs, molasses and vinegar. Mix well.
2. Add dry ingredients.
3. Roll out on a lightly floured surface. Cut with floured cutter.
4. Place on lightly greased baking sheet. Bake at 375° until lightly browned.

Yields 25 gingerbread men

Sugar Cookies

⅔ cup shortening	4 cups all-purpose flour
1½ cups sugar	2½ teaspoons baking powder
2 eggs	½ teaspoon salt
1 teaspoon vanilla extract	½ cup milk

1. Cream together shortening, sugar, eggs and vanilla. Beat until light and fluffy.
2. Mix in dry ingredients, alternately with milk.
3. Drop from spoon onto ungreased cookie sheet.
4. Bake at 375° until done. Watch carefully, do not let cookies brown.

Variation I:
To make chocolate dough, add 4-ounces melted, unsweetened chocolate to shortening mixture.

Variation II:
To make butterscotch dough, substitute 2 cups packed brown sugar for granulated sugar.

Yields 10 dozen

Egg Yolk Paint

Egg Yolk Paint—This simple recipe may be brushed on unbaked cookies to create bright and colorful cookies.

1	egg yolk	Paste food coloring
¼	teaspoon water	Inexpensive paint brush

1. Mix egg yolk with water. Add desired coloring.
2. Keep paint covered when not using, as it will dry out.
3. Brush paint onto unbaked cookies. If paint becomes too thick, add a few drops of water.
4. Bake until cookies are just done. Do not let them brown.

Variation:
For a cracked, antique texture, bake cookie until almost done. Remove from oven. Paint with egg yolk paint. Return to oven and bake until done.

Shiny Cookie Glaze

The addition of glycerine makes this icing glossy.

3	cups powdered sugar, sifted	¾	teaspoon glycerine
¼	cup warm water	¼	teaspoon flavoring
1	tablespoon corn syrup		Food coloring

1. Add syrup to warm water and stir until dissolved. Add remaining ingredients.

Edible Glue for Cookies

1	cup sifted powdered sugar	Food coloring, optional
1	tablespoon hot milk or hot water	

1. Dissolve sugar in hot liquid. Blend thoroughly.
2. Brush glue on tops of cookies. Immediately decorate with colored sugar, coconut, nuts, non-pareils, and small or broken pieces of candy. Be creative!

Gingerbread Man Glaze

Piping gel (commercial product)   **Egg white**

1. In a small bowl, combine equal parts of piping gel and egg white.
2. Brush mixture onto baked and cooked gingerbread cookies. Allow to dry.

This makes the finished cookie shiny.

HOLIDAY CANDY HOUSE

This whimsical creation makes a delightful addition to your holiday decorations or a unique gift for family or friends. This craft project requires no special talent, only enthusiasm and imagination. Its creation can fascinate and involve the entire family from preschoolers to grandparents. If properly cared for, your candy house will last at least 3 holiday seasons.

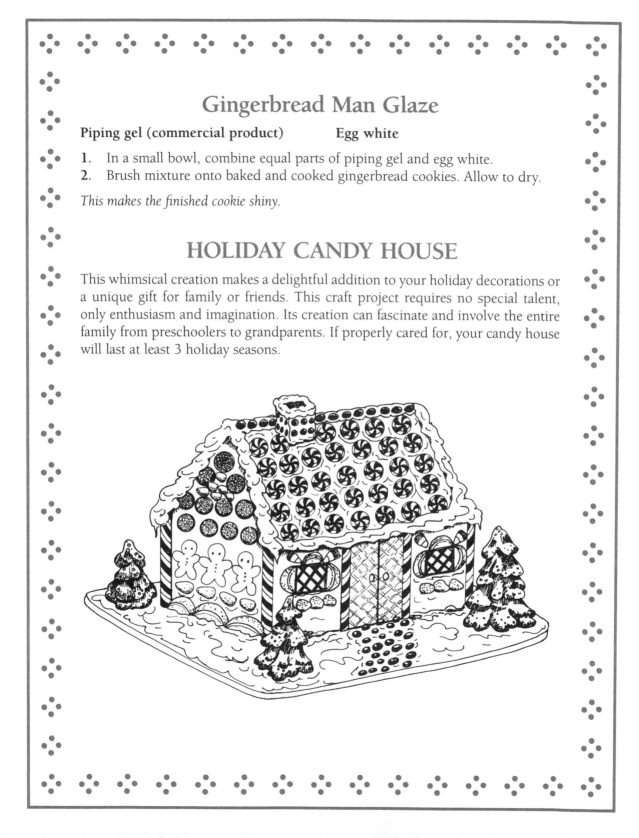

Framework:
Sturdy Cardboard Box (9" x 6" x 6") for House
Extra Cardboard for Roof and Chimney
Board or Flattened Cardboard Box for Base
Stained Balsa Strips for Windows
Cellophane for Windows
Tape
Cotton for Chimney
Glue Gun
Cutting Blade

Assembly

1. Cut open the box, flatten and cut out windows and roof peak.

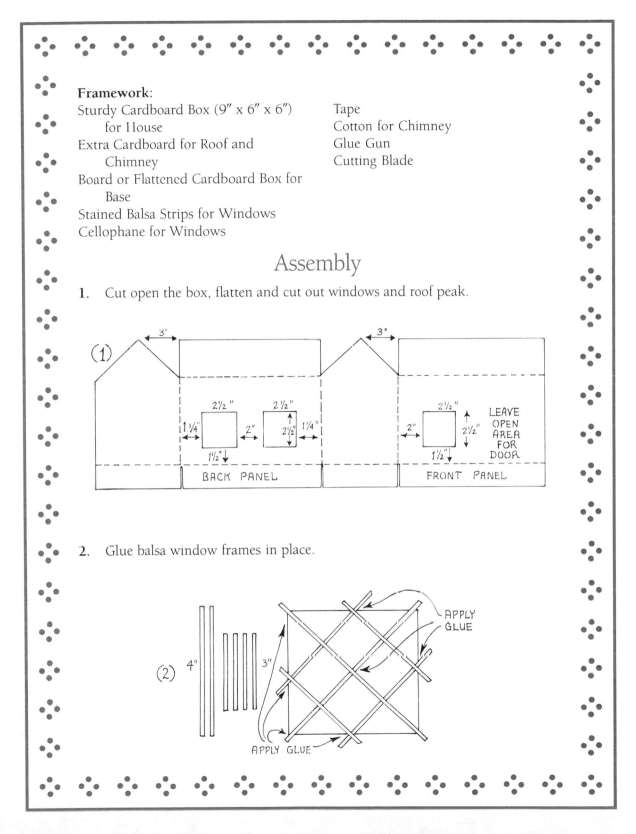

2. Glue balsa window frames in place.

3. Design, color and cut out window pictures. Use Christmas cards and coloring books for inspiration.
4. Tape window pictures and cellophane in place.

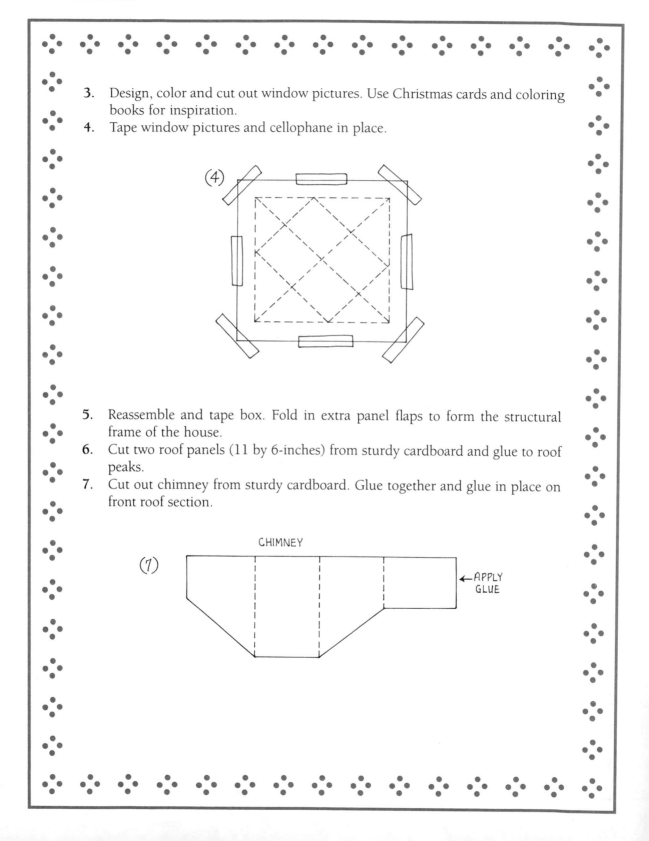

5. Reassemble and tape box. Fold in extra panel flaps to form the structural frame of the house.
6. Cut two roof panels (11 by 6-inches) from sturdy cardboard and glue to roof peaks.
7. Cut out chimney from sturdy cardboard. Glue together and glue in place on front roof section.

CHIMNEY

(7)

←APPLY GLUE

8. Wrap base in non-absorbent paper.
9. Assemble the framework using hot glue gun. Glue frame to the base (tape side up) allowing enough room at front of the house for walkway.

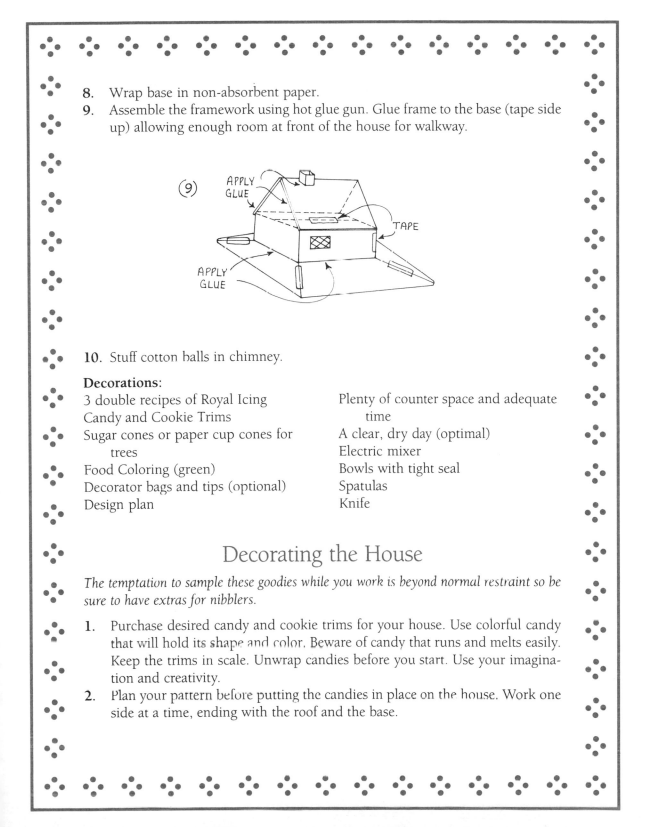

10. Stuff cotton balls in chimney.

Decorations:

3 double recipes of Royal Icing
Candy and Cookie Trims
Sugar cones or paper cup cones for trees
Food Coloring (green)
Decorator bags and tips (optional)
Design plan

Plenty of counter space and adequate time
A clear, dry day (optimal)
Electric mixer
Bowls with tight seal
Spatulas
Knife

Decorating the House

The temptation to sample these goodies while you work is beyond normal restraint so be sure to have extras for nibblers.

1. Purchase desired candy and cookie trims for your house. Use colorful candy that will hold its shape and color. Beware of candy that runs and melts easily. Keep the trims in scale. Unwrap candies before you start. Use your imagination and creativity.
2. Plan your pattern before putting the candies in place on the house. Work one side at a time, ending with the roof and the base.

3. **Suggested trims:**

Chocolate non-pareils	Candy canes
Gum drops	Life savers
JuJu bees	Licorice ropes
Sour balls	Licorice sticks
Orange slices	Red hots
Fruit slices	Marshmallows
Candy corn	Sugar cubes
Jelly beans	Sugar Wafers
Starlight mints	Prepared gingerbread men
Watermelon mints	cookies
Peppermint sticks	Sugar grahams
M and M's	Frosted shredded wheat
Pastel mints	Black licorice drops

4. Decorate the framework with icing and trims. Complete one side at a time ending with roof and base. Icing will set rather quickly. Note: For special finishing, use decorator tips.

5. To make trees, add dark green food coloring to leftover icing. Use sugar cones or paper cup cones for tree frames. Start at the bottom and work around the cone using stokes of a spatula or a #16 decorator tip to create "branches". Decorate trees with small non-pareils. Allow trees to dry thoroughly, overnight, before "gluing" in place with icing.

Storage

With tender loving care, this candy house will last for several holiday seasons.

Seal in 1 or 2 dark, plastic bags, safe from sunlight and little critters (including the 2-legged variety!).

Store in a cool, dry place such as a closet.

For added protection, you may spray your house with clear, non-yellowing spray such as acrylic or polyurethane. Do not use shellac.

Tasting is not recommended though candy is edible.

May this "vision of sugarplums" bring joy to your home!

Stained Glass

Add a festive touch to holiday cookies, gingerbread houses or churches with this architectural embellishment.

When baking gingerbread panels, place dough on foil that has been heavily misted with vegetable cooking spray. Cut out desired windows. Bake panels until almost done. Fill holes with multi-colored crushed Lifesavers. Complete baking. After gingerbread has cooled, remove foil from back of panel.

Miniature Candy Houses

These small versions can be made by using sugar wafers or graham crackers to construct the houses. Pieces may be glued together with Royal Icing. Candy decoration is also attached in this way. This is a wonderful holiday project for children.

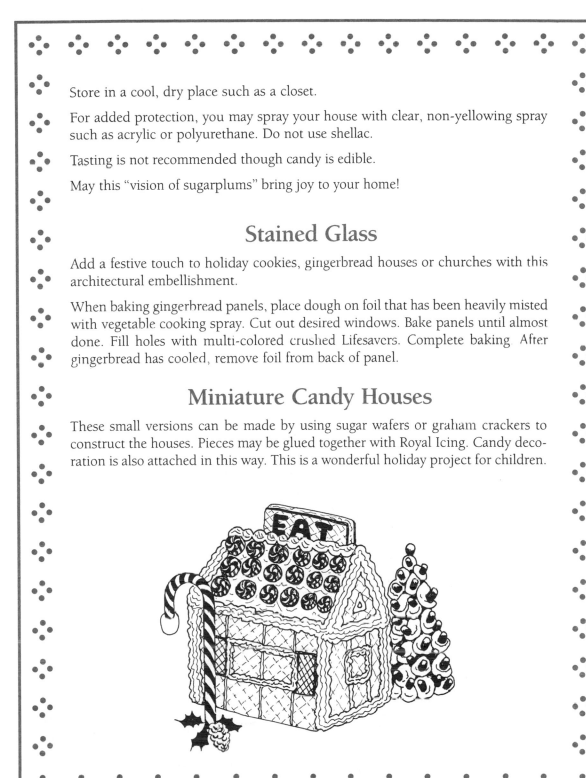

Caramel Candy Brick House
and Accessories

This candy house is constructed with caramel candy bricks and marshmallow mortar. Use a cardboard form as the structure for the house. This variation uses snipped marshmallows to form the roof, make a wreath above the door, and miniature marshmallows to make "snowdrifts" at the base of the house. Snowmen and women are made by joining whole marshmallows with toothpicks, accenting noses and eyes with cloves and gumdrop pieces. Marshmallow pine trees are made by gluing snipped pieces to a paper cone then sprinkling with colored sugar. Marshmallow reindeer are made by joining large and small marshmallows together with toothpicks using gumdrops for hooves.

Cookie/Candy Boxes

Cookie/candy boxes can be constructed and cemented with Royal Icing, then decorated with candy pieces. You may also construct and decorate a lid if desired. The boxes may be filled with M and M's or other non-sticky candies. This is an easy and fun holiday activity for children.

Peppermint Stick Baskets

Make peppermint stick baskets or boxes gluing (with Royal Icing) around straight sided containers, such as dip cartons and butter tubs. Finish by tying brightly colored ribbon around peppermint sticks. Fill with wrapped pieces of candy.

Gumdrop House, Wreath, Trees and Animals

Whole and snipped colored gumdrops may be used to construct many holiday creations, using styrofoam forms and toothpicks, accented with ribbon and holly.

GIFTS FROM THE KITCHEN

LONGHORN CARAMEL CORN

Air popped corn is best to use for this recipe. Remove all unpopped corn kernels.

1	cup butter	½	teaspoon soda
2	cups brown sugar	1	teaspoon vanilla extract
½	cup light corn syrup	6	quarts popped corn
1	teaspoon salt		

1. Bring butter, brown sugar, corn syrup, and salt to a boil.
2. Boil gently, without stirring, 5 minutes.
3. Remove from heat. Stir in soda and vanilla.
4. Pour popcorn into large roasting pan.
5. Pour syrup over popcorn and toss.
6. Bake 1 hour at 250°, stirring every 15 minutes.
7. When cool, store in airtight container.

(High humidity makes this crispy light treat sticky and hard to chew.)

Yields 10 to 12 cups

ORANGE SUGARED PECANS

½	cup water	1	tablespoon orange juice
1	cup sugar	2	cups pecan halves
	Grated rind of 1 orange		

1. Bring water and sugar to a boil. Continue cooking until mixture reaches soft ball stage, 235°.
2. Remove syrup from heat. Cool 5 minutes.
3. Stir in orange rind and orange juice. Immediately stir in pecans.
4. Turn onto a cookie sheet lined with wax paper. Separate pieces.
5. Cool 2 to 3 hours. Store in an air tight container.

Yields 2 cups

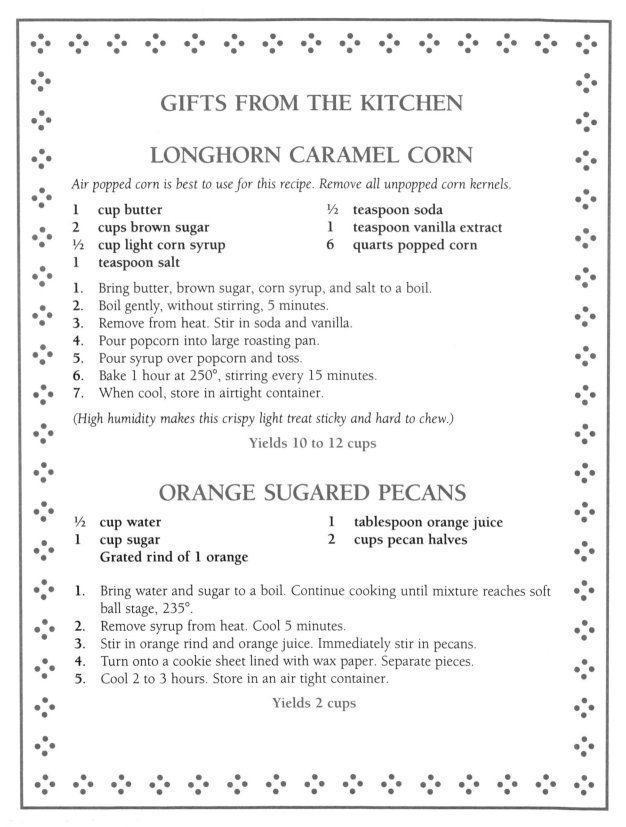

TOASTED PEPITA PECAN MIX

3 cups roasted pumpkin seeds
3 to 4 tablespoons butter, melted

2 cups whole pecans
Salt to taste

1. Preheat oven to 350°.
2. Spread pumpkin seeds on a jelly-roll pan.
3. Dot with melted butter.
4. Bake 30 minutes, stirring every 10 minutes.
5. Add pecans and continue roasting an additional 30 minutes.
6. Salt to taste.
7. Cool on absorbent brown paper.
8. Store in a tightly covered container.

Variation I:
This makes a delicious, crunchy salad topping. Serve with iceberg lettuce and sliced carrots, lightly sprinkled with Parmesan cheese and ranch dressing.

Variation II:
For a sweet taste, break caramels into small pieces. Form balls, press on to the backs of some of the pecan pieces and roll in toasted pumpkin seeds.

Variation III:
Spicy pepitas can be made by adding garlic salt and cayenne pepper to taste.

Yields 5 cups

AMARETTO

3 cups sugar
2¼ cups water
Rind of 3 lemons, finely grated

1 quart vodka
3 tablespoons almond extract
2 tablespoons vanilla extract

1. Combine first 3 ingredients in a large pan. Bring mixture to a boil. Reduce heat. Simmer 5 minutes, stirring occasionally.
2. Add remaining ingredients. Stir well.
3. Store in airtight containers.

Yields approximately 2 quarts

POPCORN BALLS

5 quarts popped popcorn	½ teaspoon salt
2 cups sugar	½ teaspoon vinegar
1½ cups cold water	1 tablespoon vanilla
½ cup light corn syrup	

1. Put popped corn in a large mixing bowl. Discard unpopped or burned kernels of corn.
2. Combine sugar, corn syrup and water in a saucepan. Cook until mixture reaches a soft ball stage (238°).
3. Add salt and vinegar. Cook until mixture reaches a hard crack stage (290°).
4. Remove from heat and add vanilla. Stir well.
5. Slowly pour mixture over popcorn. Mix well with a wooden spoon.
6. Butter hands and shape popcorn into balls. Place balls on wax paper until cool. Wrap individual balls and store in an airtight container.

Yields approximately 20 balls

INSTANT HOT CHOCOLATE

½ cup powdered sugar	8 quarts powdered milk
1 6-ounce jar non-dairy creamer	2 pounds hot cocoa mix

1. Mix all ingredients. Store in a tightly sealed container.
2. To serve, stir 3 tablespoons (more or less if preferred) mix into 1 cup of boiling water. Top with marshmallows or freshly whipped cream.

INSTANT RUSSIAN TEA

1 cup powdered orange drink mix	1 teaspoon cinnamon
1 cup instant tea	1 teaspoon ground cloves
1 cup sugar	1 package unsweetened lemonade mix

1. Mix all ingredients well.
2. Store in a tightly sealed container.
3. To serve, stir 2 to 3 teaspoonsful (more or less if preferred) into 1 cup boiling water.

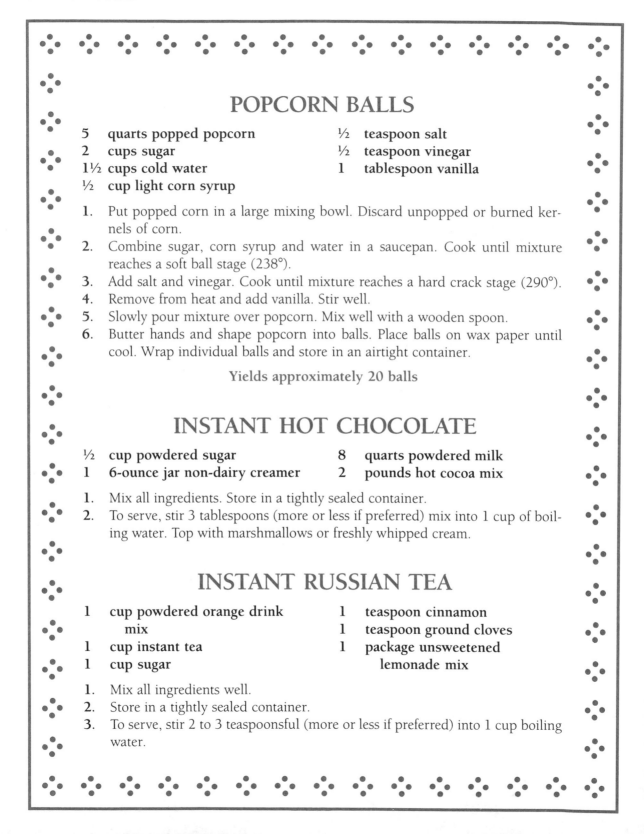

KAHLUA
A Collection Classic

3	cups sugar	
¼	cup Yuban instant coffee	
2	cups boiling water	

2   cups cognac
1   vanilla bean

1. Combine sugar and instant coffee. Stir in boiling water and mix until sugar and coffee dissolve.
2. Pour mixture into a glass container. Add Cognac and vanilla bean. Seal tightly and allow to stand in a dark place 3 to 4 weeks.

In small bottles this is a lovely gift. Serve over ice cream or use in desserts calling for coffee liqueur.

Yields approximately 1 quart

LOUISIANA CAJUN SEASONING

1   cup salt   ½   cup cayenne pepper
¾   cup garlic powder   ½   cup chili powder
¾   cup black pepper   ¼   cup cumin

Combine all ingredients. Store in an airtight container.

Yields 3¾ cups

For gifts, pour into small shakers, wrap in plastic wrap and tie with ribbons.

SEASONED SALT

1   cup salt   1   teaspoon curry powder
1   teaspoon dried thyme leaves   2   teaspoons dry mustard
1½   teaspoons crushed dried oregano   ½   teaspoon onion powder
     ¼   teaspoon dill, optional
½ to 1 teaspoon garlic powder

1. Combine all ingredients in food processor or blender. Mix well for a few seconds.
2. Store in a tightly covered jar or place in small jars and decorate with ribbon.

Yields approximately 1 cup

LAYERED CALICO BEAN SOUP

1 pound barley pearls	1 pound dried lentils
1 pound dried black beans	1 pound dried navy beans
1 pound dried black-eyed peas	1 pound dried pinto beans
1 pound dried Great Northern	1 pound dried red beans
Beans	1 pound dried split peas

1. In each jar, pour approximately ½-inch layer of each type bean creating a banded effect.
2. Seal jar and cover lid with calico fabric circles, tied with matching ribbon. Tie cooking instructions on ribbon or glue on jar.

Layered Calico Bean Soup Cooking Instructions

1 pint Calico Bean Soup Mix	1 16-ounce can tomatoes,
2 quarts water	undrained and chopped
1 pound ham, diced	1 10-ounce can tomatoes and
1 large onion, chopped	green chiles, undrained and
1 clove garlic, finely chopped	chopped
¾ teaspoon seasoned salt	

1. In a colander, rinse beans thoroughly. Place beans in a Dutch oven, cover generously with water and soak overnight.
2. Drain beans. Add water, ham, onion, garlic and salt. Cover and bring mixture to a boil. Reduce heat and simmer 1 ½ hours or until beans are tender.
3. Add tomatoes. Simmer an additional 30 minutes, stirring occasionally.

Yields 8 cups

LEMON BASIL VINEGAR

2   cups fresh lemon basil leaves   1   pint boiling cider vinegar

1. Rinse basil thoroughly and pat dry.
2. Place leaves in a wide-mouthed sterilized canning jar.
   Gently bruise leaves with a wooden spoon.
3. Add vinegar. Cool to room temperature.
4. Tightly seal jar and store 10 days to 2 weeks in a cool, but unrefrigerated place. The longer the vinegar stands, the more pungent the flavor. Gently shake jar daily.
5. When flavoring period is completed, strain vinegar through extra fine sieve or several layers of cheese cloth.
6. Using a funnel, if necessary, pour vinegar into a small-mouthed decorative bottle. Garnish with a fresh sprig of basil. Seal tightly.

Use other fresh herbs for varied flavors of vinegar.

RED AND GREEN CHILE PEPPER VINEGAR

2   cups small red chile peppers   1   quart boiling white wine
2   cups small green chile peppers   vinegar

1. Wash peppers and remove stems. Use caution when working with fresh peppers. It is wise to wear rubber gloves. Be careful not to rub eyes or face until hands are thoroughly washed.
2. Place peppers in a sterilized gallon jar.
3. Add vinegar. Cool to room temperature.
4. Tightly seal jar and store in refrigerator or cool dark place for 1 to 2 weeks. The longer the vinegar stands, the more pungent the flavor.

Experiment with the many varieties of hot, colorful peppers.
This vinegar makes a bright and festive gift when bottled in decorative jars.

WINE VINEGAR

1 pint red or white wine	1 clove garlic, minced
1 pint cider vinegar	Whole pepper corns

1. Combine all ingredients and mix well.
2. Pour into a sterilized canning jar.
3. Seal tightly and store several weeks in a cool dark place.
4. When flavoring period is completed, strain vinegar through an extra fine sieve or several layers of cheesecloth.
5. Pour through a funnel, if necessary, into small-mouthed decorative bottles. Seal tightly.

Yields 1 quart

BUTTERSCOTCH SAUCE

⅔ cup light corn syrup	¼ cup butter
1¼ cup brown sugar, firmly packed	¼ teaspoon salt
	1 6-ounce can evaporated milk

1. Boil mixture of first four ingredients until thickened. Cool.
2. Add milk.
3. Seal in an airtight container and refrigerate.

Serve over ice cream, puddings or cakes.

Yields 1 pint

HOT FUDGE SAUCE

½ cup sugar	¼ cup half and half
¼ cup cocoa	2 tablespoons butter
½ cup light corn syrup	½ teaspoon vanilla extract

1. In a saucepan, combine sugar and cocoa. Stir in corn syrup and half and half.
2. Stir over medium heat until mixture boils. Stir and simmer 3 minutes.
3. Stir in butter and vanilla.
4. Store in an airtight container and refrigerate.

Yields 1 cup

QUICK HOT FUDGE SAUCE

1 can sweetened condensed milk	1 cup sugar
	¼ cup butter
3 squares unsweetened chocolate	1 tablespoon vanilla extract

1. Place first 3 ingredients in the top of a double boiler. Stir over hot water until chocolate melts and sauce is smooth.
2. Add butter and vanilla. Stir until butter melts and sauce is well blended.
3. Store in an airtight container and refrigerate.

Yields 2 cups

VANILLA EXTRACT

5 vanilla beans	2 cups vodka or brandy

1. Break vanilla beans into 1-inch pieces.
2. Place beans in a jar. Pour liquor over beans and seal tightly.
3. Let mixture stand 2 to 3 months. Gently shake mixture several times a week.
4. Divide mixture into smaller decorative bottles. This thoughtful and special gift will be welcomed by any cook.

Yields 2 cups

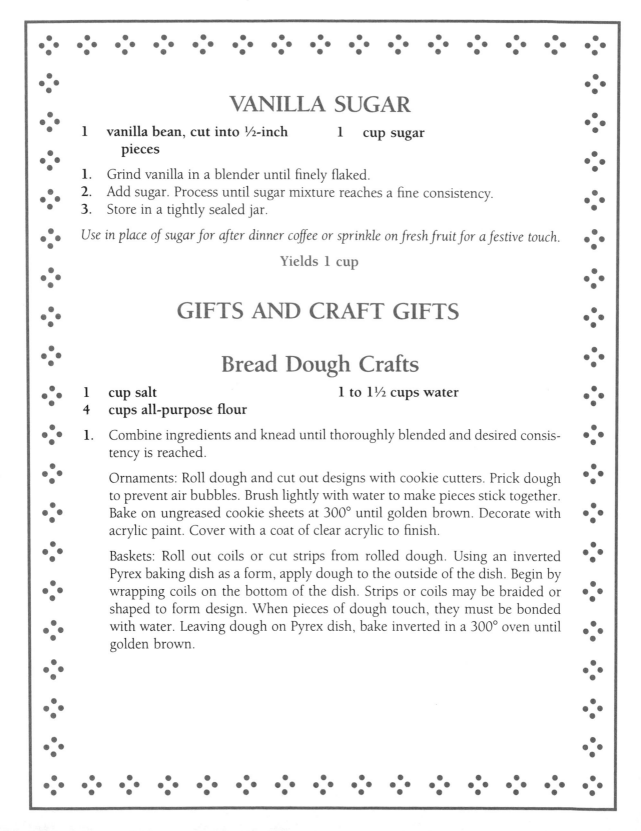

VANILLA SUGAR

1   vanilla bean, cut into ½-inch   1   cup sugar
     pieces

1. Grind vanilla in a blender until finely flaked.
2. Add sugar. Process until sugar mixture reaches a fine consistency.
3. Store in a tightly sealed jar.

Use in place of sugar for after dinner coffee or sprinkle on fresh fruit for a festive touch.

Yields 1 cup

GIFTS AND CRAFT GIFTS

Bread Dough Crafts

1   cup salt   1 to 1½ cups water
4   cups all-purpose flour

1. Combine ingredients and knead until thoroughly blended and desired consistency is reached.

Ornaments: Roll dough and cut out designs with cookie cutters. Prick dough to prevent air bubbles. Brush lightly with water to make pieces stick together. Bake on ungreased cookie sheets at 300° until golden brown. Decorate with acrylic paint. Cover with a coat of clear acrylic to finish.

Baskets: Roll out coils or cut strips from rolled dough. Using an inverted Pyrex baking dish as a form, apply dough to the outside of the dish. Begin by wrapping coils on the bottom of the dish. Strips or coils may be braided or shaped to form design. When pieces of dough touch, they must be bonded with water. Leaving dough on Pyrex dish, bake inverted in a 300° oven until golden brown.

Cookie Ornaments

1 pound baking soda
1 cup cornstarch

1¼ cups water
Cookie cutters

1. Mix baking soda, cornstarch and water. Cook and stir over medium heat. The mixture will form a ball similar to pie dough.
2. Remove from heat. Let cool a few minutes.
3. Roll out dough. Cut in desired shapes. Make a hole in each cookie ornament using a large toothpick.
4. Let dry overnight on a cookie sheet. (Do not bake them!)
5. Food coloring may be added to the dough. When cookies are dry, decorate with paint or magic markers.

Decorative Fruit Ornament

2 cups salt
⅔ cup water
1 cup cornstarch
½ cup water

Food coloring
Wire hooks
Artificial leaves
Wire

1. Mix together salt and ⅔ cup water. Heat, stirring constantly.
2. Remove from heat. Add a paste made of cornstarch and ½ cup water colored with food coloring. Stir together.
3. Mold into desired shapes. Place a hook into each ornament before it dries. Wire artificial leaves to hook.
4. Rough edges may be smoothed with water while fruits are still moist.

Peppermint Snowflakes

7 to 8 round peppermint candies
 Ice pick
3½-inch individual, fluted tart
  pans with removable
  bottoms
 Plastic drinking straws

1. Preheat oven to 325°.
2. Spray bottoms and sides of pan with non-stick vegetable spray.
3. Outline the bottom of tart pans with candy. Be sure to leave a hole in the center.
4. Place pans in oven 5 to 6 minutes or until candy begins to melt and cover the pan bottom. Watch closely as the calibration of ovens varies and candy may melt too quickly.
5. Remove pans from oven and immediately make a hole at the top of each wreath by inserting a short segment of a drinking straw. Before candy cools, insert an ice pick into the straw, loosen melted candy until the pan bottom is visible. Leave straw in place until ornament is removed from pan.
6. Allow to stand until pan is cool enough to handle. Push tart bottom up from pan. Gently scrap excess melted candy from edges. Carefully pry snowflake from bottom piece. Snip straw off flush with the opening.
7. Remove straw, tie with colorful ribbons and hang.

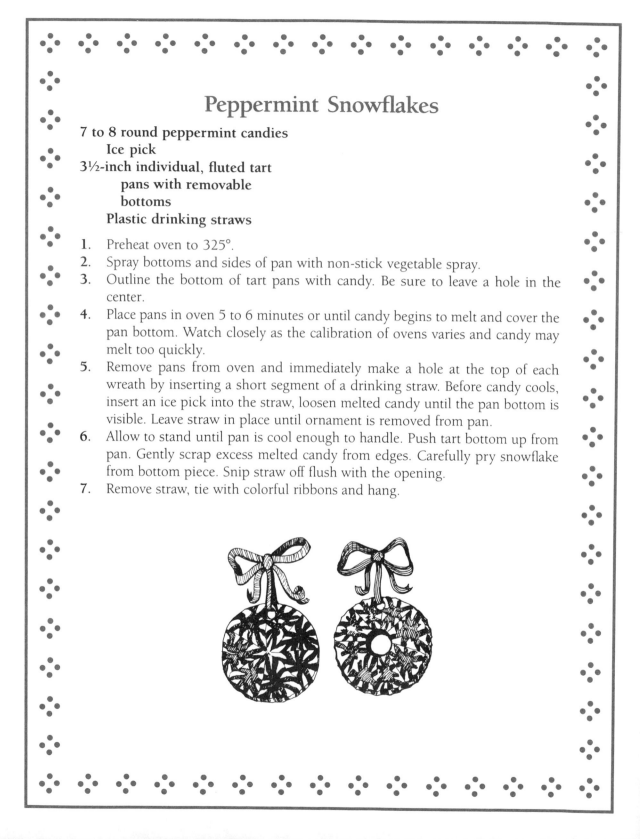

Variation: Candy Wreath

If desired, substitute other round, seasonal hard candies for peppermints. Follow above directions to step 4. Remove pan as candy flows into fluted edges but still retains a wreath shape. (Candy will continue to flow and fill the center after the pan is removed from the oven, so be sure to remove pan before the candy becomes too liquid). If candy has not melted enough, return pan to oven for additional melting. Complete steps 5 and 6.

Popcorn and Cranberry Wire Ornaments

Popcorn
Cranberries
Ribbons

Medium gauge wire
Wire cutters

1. String popcorn and cranberries on wire to desired lengths.
2. After stringing, shape into hearts, stars, Christmas trees, dove or other holiday shapes.
3. Leave enough wire to close ends by twisting.
4. Finish by attaching decorative bow hangars.

If popcorn breaks after completion of ornament, glue broken pieces around the wire.

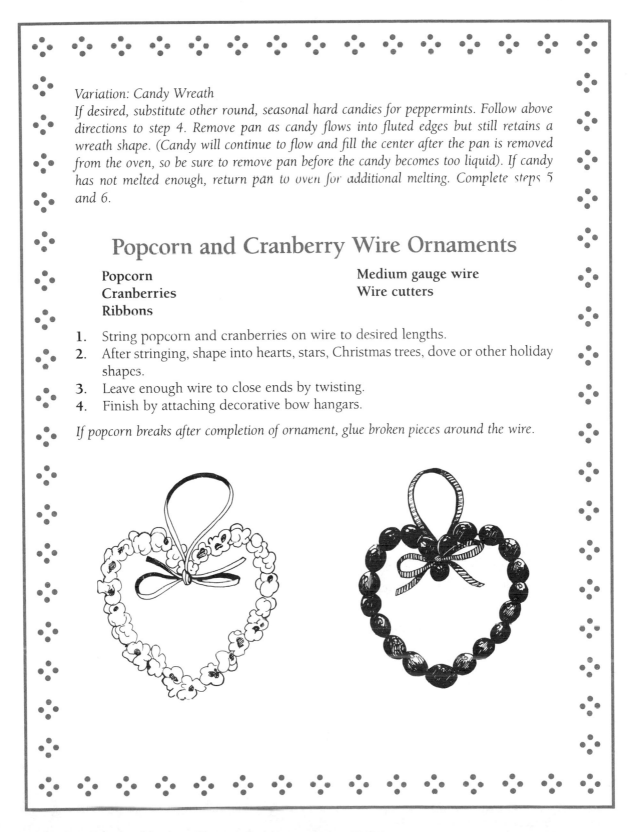

FAVORITE CHILDREN'S ACTIVITIES

These games and activities will provide hours of fun and entertainment for your child and will stimulate curiosity and creativity! With a little supervision and a lot of imagination, children can benefit from these invaluable learning experiences and realize a sense of accomplishment.

Crystal Garden

6   charcoal briquettes   4   tablespoons liquid bluing
6   clay pot fragments   4   tablespoons water
4   tablespoons non-iodized salt   Food coloring
1   tablespoon ammonia

1. Place charcoal and clay fragments in a shallow bowl.
2. Mix together salt, ammonia, bluing and water. Stir until salt is partially dissolved.
3. Pour mixture into the pan, making sure some salt falls over both charcoal and clay fragments.
4. Put several drops of different food coloring on various parts of the garden. Leave it undisturbed for several days and crystals will cover it in an interesting formation, growing and spreading daily.

Paint Containers

❋ Paper milk cartons, with tops removed, make good water or paint containers.

❋ Plastic mustard or ketchup containers make good paint dispensers. An aluminum nail in the top of each will keep paint fresh.

❋ Syrup pitchers also make good paint dispensers.

Finger Paint I

½ cup starch
1 quart boiling water
½ cup soap flakes
¼ cup talcum powder

Poster paint or finely ground
   colored chalk
Oil of clove

1. Soften starch in a small amount of cold water.
2. Over medium-low heat, add boiling water, stirring constantly until mixture bubbles.
3. Remove from heat, let it cool and add soap flakes and powder. Stir until well mixed.
4. Pour into containers, one for each color and stir in color pigment.
5. Add a few drops of oil of clove to prevent distressing odors.

Finger Paint II

1 cup liquid starch
6 cups water
½ cup soap chips

Food coloring
Oil of clove

1. Dissolve soap chips in water until lumps disappear.
2. Stir in starch.
3. Pour into containers, one for each color and stir in color pigment.
4. Add a few drops of oil of clove to prevent distressing odors.

Plastic Foam Paint

6 tablespoons plastic starch
1 cup dry detergent

Water
Powdered color for tinting

1. Mix starch and detergent with water.
2. Whip to the consistency of marshmallow cream.

Soap Paint

1 cup powdered detergent
4 tablespoons liquid starch

Tempera paint or finely
   crushed colored chalk

1. Beat detergent and starch with a rotary beater until peaks form.
2. Add coloring.

Tempera Paint for Glossy Surfaces

Liquid detergent or a few drops of glycerine mixed with tempera paint enables the paint to adhere to slick or shiny surfaces, such as aluminum foil or glass.

No-Cook Play Dough

1 cup salt	Water
1 cup all-purpose flour	Food coloring, if desired
1 tablespoon powdered alum	

1. Mix dry ingredients. Slowly add water and mix until desired consistency is reached.

Play Dough

1 cup all-purpose flour	1 tablespoon oil
½ cup salt	2 teaspoons cream of tartar
1 cup water	Food coloring

1. Combine all ingredients except food coloring.
2. Cook and stir over medium heat until mixture forms a ball. (approximately 3 minutes)
3. Remove from heat. At this point, dough can be divided and colored as desired.
4. Knead several minutes on wax paper until dough is smooth and workable.

Salt and Cornstarch Clay

1 cup salt	¾ cup water
½ cup cornstarch	

1. Combine all ingredients in a double boiler. Cook about two minutes, until mixture forms a glob or mass.
2. Place mass on wax paper until it cools enough to handle. Knead for three minutes.

Material can be wrapped in foil until time for use. It will keep several days, but must be kneaded again before using. This is a very hard clay.

Soda and Cornstarch Sculpture

1	cup cornstarch	1¼ cups cold water
2	cups baking soda	Food coloring

1. In a saucepan, add food coloring to water and combine with other ingredients.
2. Cook over medium heat, stirring constantly, about three to four minutes until mixture thickens to the consistency of mashed potatoes.
3. Cover with a damp cloth to cool.
4. Knead until smooth.
5. Keep clay covered with foil or place in a plastic bag to keep it pliable when not in use.

Clay may be rolled and cut into shapes or may be modeled into small shapes.

Salt and Flour Relief Mixture

3	parts salt	Water
1	part all-purpose flour	

1. Mix salt and flour with water for desired consistency.

Salt Beads

2	parts table salt	Water
1	part all-purpose flour	Food coloring or dry pigment

1. Mix salt, flour and water to a dough-like consistency.
2. Add coloring if desired.
3. Break off small pieces and form into beads.
4. Pierce each with a toothpick and allow to dry, then string.

Papier-Mâché

Shape form from chicken wire, cardboard tubes, boxes or balloons.

Newspaper or magazines	1 cup water
¼ cup wheat paste or Library	Wax paper
paste	Tempra paint and gesso, optional

1. Tear enough paper into small pieces to cover form.
2. Soak paper in warm water overnight.
3. Mix paste with water to a creamy consistency.
4. Add paste to paper and mix with hands.
5. Continue adding paste until mixture feels like clay and can be formed.
6. Papier-mâché is now ready to be applied to a form.
7. After sculpture is completed, dry on wire racks or wax paper for several days.
8. If sculpture is to be painted, gesso, dry and paint with tempera paint. Cover with clear acrylic to finish.

Silly Putty

¼   cup white glue (do not use school glue)   2   tablespoons starch

1. Mix glue and starch together. Allow to dry a bit until mixture is pliable. Store in an airtight container.

Soap Bubbles

1   part glycerine   2   parts water
1   part liquid detergent

1. Combine ingredients. Glycerin will make bubbles iridescent.

ENTERTAINING
WINE AND SPIRITS
Selection

A reputable wine merchant can assist with wine selection and offer suggestions for a particular menu. The character of the food with which it is to be served should determine the choice of wine. The standard of serving white wine with white meat and red wine with red or dark meat is always a safe rule to follow if in doubt. White wines are usually considered light and delicate and complement light and delicate entrées. Red wines are usually richer and more robust and complement richer, highly seasoned or heavier foods. Do not serve wine with acidic fruits, artichokes and asparagus, salads with vinegar dressings or extremely oily fish, as these foods do not complement wine. Of course, there are a few exceptions and personal preference and taste should be a primary consideration. Always sample the wine before serving to be confident that it is good and that there are no pieces of cork in the wine. If serving more than one wine with dinner, begin with light dry wines progressing to fuller, richer wine for the main course and ending with sweet wine or champagne. An easy way to remember the order of service when serving wine is white before red, dry before sweet, light before full-bodied and young before old.

Storage

It is not necessary to have a wine cellar to store and age wine properly. Simply follow a few rules to insure the correct atmosphere that enhances wine. Select a dark place away from any appliances that might distribute heat, moisture or vibration. Never store wine against an exterior wall. Try to find an area that maintains a relatively constant temperature. The ideal storage temperature is 55° to 60° F., but up to 75° F. is permissible as long as there are no extreme temperature fluctuations. However, wines stored between 70° to 75° F. will mature more quickly than wine stored at cooler temperatures. Also, wine stored in smaller bottles matures more quickly than wine in larger bottles.

Once an acceptable storage area has been selected, purchase a wine rack for storing bottles on their sides. Most wine merchants have inexpensive racks that store wine properly. Look for one that best suits your storage area and allows the wine to be in constant contact with the cork. The cork should always remain moist so that it does not dry out or shrink or allow air to enter the wine. The neck of the bottle should not be lower than the rest of the bottle. This prevents sediment from settling near the cork. Wine sealed with screw caps may be stored upright and is ready to be consumed when purchased.

Serving Wine

Red wine should be served at room temperature between 62° F. and 70° F. Red wines usually should not be chilled as this destroys the bouquet and flavor. However, in warm weather when room temperatures may be higher, it is permissible to chill red wine briefly. Open red wine at least twenty minutes to an hour before serving. Red wines that are eight to ten years old should be decanted so that sediment may be separated. Before decanting, stand the bottle at an angle, allowing the sediment to collect for a day. When ready to serve, carefully open the bottle without disturbing the sediment, and slowly pour into the decanter. Use an extra fine strainer or paper filter to pour the last portion of wine separating the residue. Some experts feel that decanting is entirely unnecessary and destroys the delicate bouquet of fine old wine. This faction advocates pouring directly from the bottle being careful to reserve the sediment in the bottle. Personal preference should determine your method of serving old wine.

White wine, Beaujolais, rosé, sparkling wine or champagne are served chilled and never decanted. Sparkling wines and champagne should be served at 40° F. The sweeter a wine, the colder it should be. Chilled corresponds to approximately 50° F., which takes two to three hours in a refrigerator or twenty minutes in an ice bucket.

Once a bottle of wine has been opened it is immediately exposed to the ravages of air. It is best to use left over red or white wine in cooking or to make wine vinegar. If you choose to do this, use the wine quickly as spoiled wine used in cooking is as bad as spoiled wine served at the table. Sparkling wines and champagne do not keep well. They should be consumed when opened.

There should never be more than three glasses at a table setting at once, one glass always reserved for water. Wine glasses are placed on the right side of the place setting and arranged in order of use. If two wine glasses are used, the larger glass should be used for red wine or the older red wine if two red wines are served. Wines should be poured for each course. A used wine glass should be removed after the course is completed. Never fill wine glasses more than one-half full. Only sherry, liqueurs and champagne glasses are filled two-thirds full. Wine should be served and replenished from the guest's right side.

Table Placement of Wine Glasses

There are many acceptable variations for placement of wine glasses other than this illustration which is the formal placement. Remember, the convenience of serving directs the placement of glassware.

1. Water glass
2. Wine glass
3. Wine glass

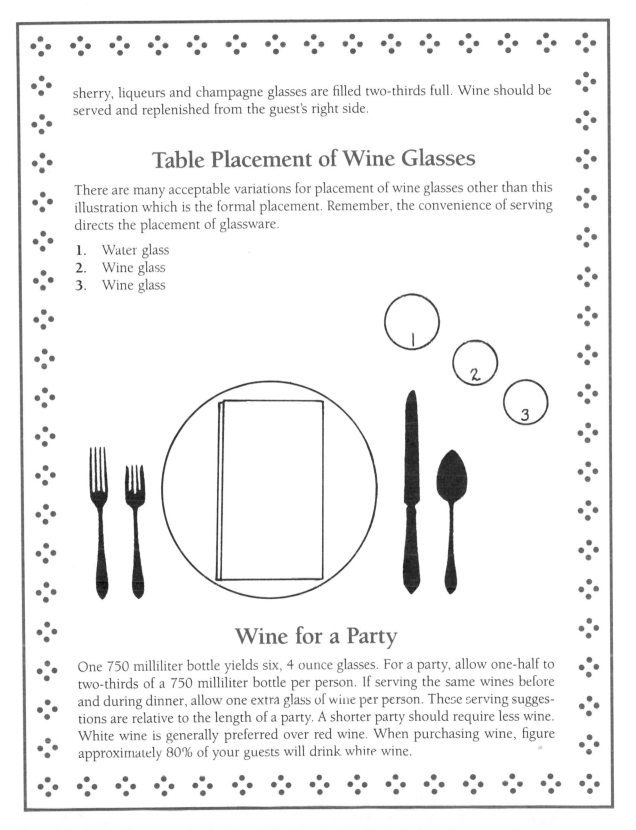

Wine for a Party

One 750 milliliter bottle yields six, 4 ounce glasses. For a party, allow one-half to two-thirds of a 750 milliliter bottle per person. If serving the same wines before and during dinner, allow one extra glass of wine per person. These serving suggestions are relative to the length of a party. A shorter party should require less wine. White wine is generally preferred over red wine. When purchasing wine, figure approximately 80% of your guests will drink white wine.

Ice

To chill wine for a party, allow twenty pounds of ice to chill two cases. Adding salt to ice will lower the temperature of the ice, chilling the wine more quickly. Remember red wine usually does not need to be chilled. When chilling wine or beer consider using the tub of your washing machine as a cooler. If you do this, do not salt the ice.

Cooking with Wine

The addition of wine in cooking can enhance a dish and give it character. This is particularly true for sauces, marinades and pan juices. Table wines and fortified wines are often called for in particular dishes. Fortified wines such as sherry, port, Madeira and brandy are used quite frequently. Because fortified wines have a greater alcoholic content, they are useful in many cooking processes. Restraint when cooking with wine is the key to ensuring the perfect blend of flavors to enhance a dish rather than overpower it.

* Rosé wine, if not too sweet, is an all-purpose substitute for either white wine or light red wine.

* Cooking wines are specifically formulated for that purpose, with salt added to them. They do not need refrigeration and are not for table consumption. Do not hesitate to use drinking wines for cooking.

* Use wine to de-glaze a pan.

* Wine can be used as cooking liquid for poaching.

* Some wine can be substituted for vinegar in salad dressings.

* Wine added to clear gelatin salads adds a special flavor.

* Burgundy or Chianti enhances beef dishes. Chablis complements poultry.

* Wine complements soups; Chablis for consommé or chicken or vegetable soups; sherry in onion soup; Burgundy or claret in beef stew or Minestrone.

Wine Bottle Sizes and Servings

Wine is sold in metric size bottles but the old terms are listed for reference and conversion. This chart is based on 3 to 3½-ounce servings for dinner wines and champagnes. Allow two to three glasses per guests during the evening. Allow 2 to 2 ½-ounce servings of dessert wine.

Bottle Size	Ounces	Dinner Wines (Servings)	Dessert Wines (Servings)
Split	6.4 to 6.5 oz.	2	2
Tenth or Half Bottle	12.8 to 13 oz.	4	4 to 6
Pint	16 oz.	5	5 to 7
Fifth (⅘ qt.)	25.6 to 26 oz.	8	8 to 12
750 MILLILITER BOTTLE (25.4 FL. OZ.) CORRESPONDS TO A FIFTH			
Quart	32 oz.	10	10 to 14
ONE LITER (33.8 FL. OZ.) CORRESPONDS TO A QUART			
Magnum	52 oz.	16	20 to 26
Half Gallon	64 oz.	20	20 to 30
1.75 LITER (59.2 FL. OZ.) CORRESPONDS TO HALF GALLON			
Jeroboam	104 oz.	34	41 to 52
Gallon	128 oz.	40	40 to 60
Rehoboam	156 oz.	52	62 to 78
Methuselah	208 oz.	69	83 to 104
Balthazar	416 oz.	138	166 to 208
Nebuchadnezzar	528 oz.	176	211 to 264

❋ ONE 750 MILLILITER BOTTLE (25.4 OZ.) SERVES SIX 4 OUNCE SERVINGS

❋ ONE 1 LITER BOTTLE (33.8 OZ.) SERVES EIGHT 4 OUNCE SERVINGS

❋ ONE 1.75 MILLILITER BOTTLE (59.2 OZ.) SERVES FOURTEEN 4 OUNCE SERVINGS

❋ ONE CASE CHAMPAGNE CONTAINS 72 SERVINGS

Wine Selection Guide

Appetizer Wines—usually served chilled with appetizers and cheese
    Dubonnet
    Madeira (dry)
    Lillet
    Port (dry)
    Sherry (dry)
    Vermouth (dry)
    Sparkling Wines or Champagne

Red Table Wines—served at room temperature (approximately 65° F.) with richer, heavier entrées
    Burgundy
    Chianti
    Claret

White Table Wines—served chilled, (approximately 50° F.) with light and delicate entrées
    Chablis (white Burgundy)
    Rhine Wine or Hock
    Graves (white Bordeaux)
    Sauternes
    Moselle
    Rosé or Blush

Sparkling Wines—served chilled, (approximately 50° F.) usually with dessert, but can be served with an appetizer or main course or alone
    Champagne
    Sparkling Burgundy

Dessert Wines—served chilled or cooled with desserts, usually sweeter and heavier than table wines

    Madeira (sweet, only slightly chilled)
    Muscatel
    Angelica
    Port (do not chill)
    Sherry (sweet)
    Sauternes
    Marsala
    Malaga
    Tokay
    Champagne
    Crème Sherry (do not chill)

❋ Chocolate and most wines do not blend well. If your dessert is chocolate and you wish to serve a dessert wine, select certain cabarnets or champagne.

Spirits

To determine the quantity of liquor to stock a bar for a party, first try to assess the drinking habits of your guests and always provide an alternative for non-drinking guests. A liquor merchant can be very helpful and usually unopened bottles can be returned, but always ask before purchasing. Naturally, a cocktail buffet for one hundred requires more liquor than cocktails and wine for a dinner party of eight, so it is important to carefully consider the kind of entertaining that best suits your personal considerations. When you have determined the kind of party to give, then consider if any rentals are necessary, such as glasses or tables. After this, decide if you need to hire a bar service. A bartender is extremely helpful in serving groups of thirty or more.

If it is necessary to hire a bar service, first decide whether drink orders should be taken by waiters and served or whether a central service bar, manned by bartenders should be set up. The waiter service bar may be set up in an out of the way area, as long as the waiter traffic does not interfere with any major aspect of the party such as guest entry or food service. A direct service bar should be conveniently located in an open area where congestion may be avoided. Always write down any special instructions for waiters and bartenders to address when they arrive, which should be at least forty-five minutes to one hour before the party. Brief bartenders on whether you want to use 1 or 1½-ounce portions per mixed drink or possibly what time to cut down the proportions. These considerations are more easily determined before the party begins.

If the party is more casual, a self-service bar may be set up. A self-service bar should be very simple and only provide the basics. This method of serving drinks requires careful planning and placement to avoid congestion and a massive mess. Location is the most important consideration of a self-service bar, because convenient access of many guests at one time is essential. Several large pitchers of water, mixers, stirrers, scoops or tongs and several large buckets of ice should be placed in different areas of the bar table. Lemons, limes and bar garnishes should be pre-cut and served in bowls. Mixers should be kept to the basics: soda, mineral water, tonic, ginger ale and cola. One person should be in charge of checking these supplies frequently and replenishing when necessary. When guests mix their own drinks, the hosts have no control over quantities served and for this reason the alternative of hiring a bartender might be preferable.

Serving Estimates

Wine and spirits are no longer sold in fifths (⅘ of a qt., 25.6 oz.) but metric bottles instead. The metric equivalent to a fifth is a 750 milliliter bottle which contains 25.4 fluid ounces. For a larger party it is more economical to purchase larger bottles.

Dinner drinks—estimate 2 to 3 drinks per person using a 1½-ounce portion of liquor per drink

Cocktail party—estimate 3 to 4 drinks per person using a 1½-ounce portion of liquor per drink

Bottle Sizes and Servings

One 750 milliliter bottle (25.4 oz.) serves sixteen 1½ ounce-portions.

One liter (33.8 fl. oz.) serves twenty-two 1½-ounce portions.

1.75 liter (59.2 fl. oz.) serves thirty-nine 1½-ounce portions.

Ice

Allow one pound of ice per person when serving mixed drinks.

Liqueur

Liqueurs are flavored spirits that have a higher percentage of alcohol than other spirits. Some contain up to 40 percent alcohol. They are made with a base of neutral alcohol or brandy with herb, seed or fruit added to saturate the base alcohol with flavor. Some liqueurs use whiskey as a base that dominates the flavor. Liqueurs are served in one to two ounce glasses. Coffee and liqueurs complement each other's flavor and are usually served together after a meal.

Basic Home Bar

Liquor

Bourbon	1 liter
Dark rum	1 750 milliliter bottle
Gin	1 liter
Light rum	1 liter
Scotch	2 liter
Tequila	1 liter
Vodka	2 liters (1 liter chilled)
Whiskey	1 liter

Fortified Wines

Cognac	1 750 milliliter bottle
Courvoisier	1 750 milliliter bottle
Crème sherry	1 750 milliliter bottle
Dry sherry	1 750 milliliter bottle
Dry Vermouth	1 750 milliliter bottle
Dubonnet	1 750 milliliter bottle
Port	1 750 milliliter bottle
Sweet Vermouth	1 750 milliliter bottle

Liqueurs

Amaretto	1 750 milliliter bottle
B & B	1 750 milliliter bottle
Cassis	1 750 milliliter bottle
Cointreau	1 750 milliliter bottle
Crème de Cacao	1 750 milliliter bottle
Crème de Menthe	1 750 milliliter bottle
Framboise	1 750 milliliter bottle
Grand Marnier	1 750 milliliter bottle
Grenadine	1 750 milliliter bottle
Kahlua	1 750 milliliter bottle
Tia Maria	1 750 milliliter bottle

Beer

Light	1 six pack
Dark	1 six pack
Imported	1 six pack

Wine

White	3 liter bottles
Red	3 liter bottles

Mixers

Club soda
Cola
Diet cola
Ginger ale
Mineral water
Orange juice
Sweet and sour mixes
Tomato juice
Tonic

Garnishes

Cherries
Cinnamon sticks
Cocktail onions
Lemons
Limes
Oranges

Seasonings

Cinnamon
Nutmeg
Pepper
Roses lime
Salt
Simple syrup
Tabasco sauce
Worcestershire sauce

Equipment

Bottle / can opener
Corkscrew
Cutting board
Jigger or shot glass
Ice scoops and tongs
Ice tubs or buckets
Pitchers
Sharp knives
Stirrers
Strainers

Supplies

Cloth towels
Glasses
Napkins
Paper towels
Straws
Toothpicks

GLASSWARE

For large parties rent glasses. They come in stacking racks and are sent back to the rental agency to be washed.

✺ If glasses are stacked while damp they will stick. If glasses do stick do not try to force them apart. Fill top glass with cold water and place stack of glasses in warm water. This should separate the glasses. Repeat for glasses in between top and bottom glasses that are still stuck.

All-Purpose Wine Glasses

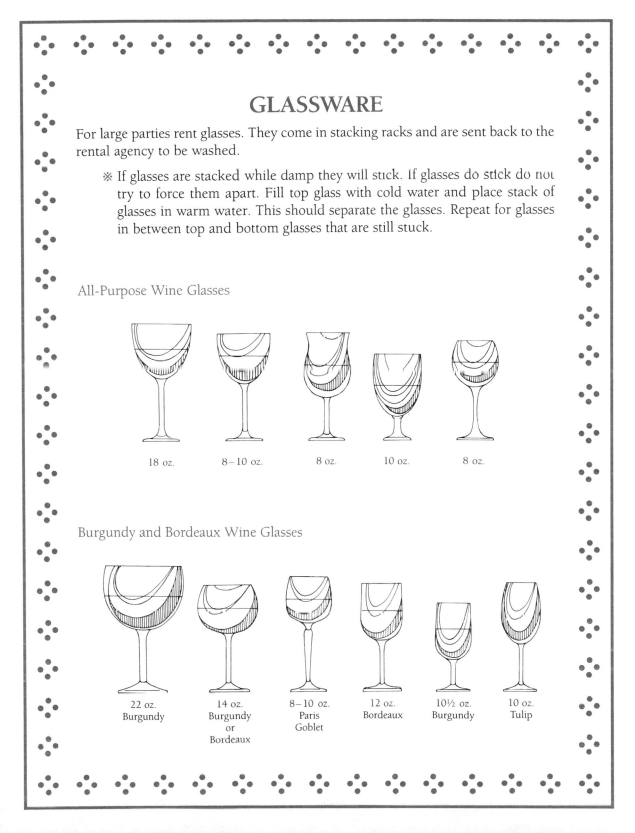

18 oz.   8–10 oz.   8 oz.   10 oz.   8 oz.

Burgundy and Bordeaux Wine Glasses

22 oz.
Burgundy

14 oz.
Burgundy
or
Bordeaux

8–10 oz.
Paris
Goblet

12 oz.
Bordeaux

10½ oz.
Burgundy

10 oz.
Tulip

Champagne Glasses

6–8 oz.
Flute

6–7 oz.
Tulip

3½ oz.
Saucer

4 oz.
Coupe

White Wine Glasses

8 oz.

8 oz.

4 oz.

Brandy or Sherry Glasses

4–5 oz.
Pipe-Stem
Sherry

4–5 oz.
Spanish
Brandy

6 oz.
Sherry

5 oz.
Brandy
Chimney

6–10 oz.
Classic
Brandy
Snifter

Beer Glasses

12 oz.
Pilsner

16 oz.
Mug

16 oz.
Stemmed Mug

Liquor and Mixed Drink Glasses

1½ oz.
Shot
or
Jigger

12 oz.
Cooler

8 oz.
Old fashioned

8 oz.
Stemmed
Old
Fashioned

10 oz.
Highball

10 oz.
Tumbler

13 oz.
Tumbler or
Old fashioned

19 oz.
Tumbler

19 oz.
Highball

Liqueur or Cordial Glasses

1 oz.

2 oz.

PLANNING AND PREPARATION

Planning and preparation are the most important factors in giving a successful party. Every last detail, from invitations to clean-up, should be dissected and examined so that nothing is left to chance. The first element in planning is to determine what kind of party and the date it is to be held. Space limitations will determine how many to invite. Check the calendar closely and try not to schedule the occasion so that it conflicts with a major event.

Invitations should be considered next. If the affair is small and casual, telephone invitations are fine. Make the calls a week or so before the date, with a follow up confirmation call. This follow up call is especially necessary for dinner or luncheon invitations. Larger parties need written invitations with clear details and a reply request sent two to three weeks ahead of time. "Reply requested", is a better gauge to determine the number of guests than "R. S. V. P.", which people do not always respond to. If dinner is to be served, specify exact times: cocktails at seven, dinner at 8. Also, give your guests good clues pertaining to dress, either through a theme or very direct instructions. Vary the guest list with people of different occupations, background and interests. Also, invite different groups of friends who are not acquainted or do not see each other frequently.

The menu should be appropriate for the kind of party to be given, with convenient preparation and easy service the prime considerations. Inventory of plates, utensils, glassware and necessary serving pieces should be coordinated with the menu to determine if any equipment rental will be necessary. Consider whether extra helpers are needed or if a catering service is a possibility. Mentally rehearse every aspect of the party, to pick up missed details and provide for them. Plan a time schedule down to the last minute. Prepare as much food ahead of time as possible and always consider reheating and cooling requirements in the time schedule. Preparatory cleaning of the house and utensils can be done early in the week, saving the finishing touches for the day of the party. Tables can be arranged days before and covered with plastic or tissue to prevent any dust from settling. Any major changes, such as moving furniture, should be done earlier in the week.

Decorations, candles, flowers and linen should be placed the last two days before the party. Lists should be amended and revised. On the day of the party, the list should be very minimal with only the last minute details left. Always allow ample relaxation time so that you can enjoy your own party.

Clearing and cleaning should be well-planned to create as little attention and fuss as possible. Detailed plans give the hostess peace of mind and confidence. If disasters occur, do not panic. Simply compensate and carry on as if nothing has happened.

Party Times

Coffee	10:00 a. m. to noon
Brunch	10:30 a. m. to 1 p. m.
Luncheon	Begins between noon and 1 p. m. and lasts 1½ to 2 hours
Tea	Begins at 4:00 to 4:30 p. m. and ends promptly at 5:30 p. m.
Cocktail	6:00 to 8:00 p. m., lasts 45 minutes to an hour
Dinner	Begins between 8:00 and 9:00 p. m. and lasts 3 to 3½ hours. May begin with cocktails at 7:00 or 7:30 p. m.

These times are guidelines to assist in party planning. However, any of these times may vary for tradition and convenience.

Working With a Caterer

A caterer can assist you as little or as much as you wish. Take recommendations from friends and ask for recommendations from the caterer. The caterer can arrange every last detail: menu, wines, kitchen help, and waiters or simply plan and prepare the food. A caterer may offer a price per plate or per person based on the kind of menu or occasion. If you plan to use the services of a caterer, contact him well in advance as good ones are booked early. More planning time will be needed for a large party. Once menu, price and services have been agreed upon, a detailed, written contract should be signed by both parties. It is then customary to give a caterer a deposit of up to 50%. All details should be agreed upon in writing so that there are no misunderstandings about what you provide and what the caterer provides. The more you ask the caterer to do, the greater the expense. Keep this in mind when planning. Ask a caterer if tips for the helpers are included in the fee and who will own the left-over liquor and food.

Help for Hire

Sometimes you may not need a full scale caterer, simply waiters or waitresses, bartenders, kitchen helpers, parking valets or coat checkers to assist with a party. Teenagers are good coat checkers, but any other party help should be trained professionals accustomed to handling many different kinds of entertaining. Consult friends and check references from agencies. Look for services or agencies that are bonded and insured for your protection. Liquor stores usually have lists of bartenders or can provide them if you purchase the liquor from them. Party services can provide most of the usual help required. Again, complete discussion of exact duties and services should be discussed and detailed in a written contract. Tipping is usually left to your discretion. If you are pleased and the service has been good, a tip is definitely expected if not already included in the fee. If you are not pleased the tip should be minimal. Some agencies add gratuity, others do not. Be aware of the policy. After the party, write down the names of your favorite helpers so that you may request them the next time you need help.

Staff Requirements

Bartenders

Full bar—1 bartender per 30 guests

Partial bar—1 bartender per 50 guests

Waiters

Formal dinner (continental service)—1 waiter per 4 guests

Formal seated buffet—1 waiter per 6 to 8 guests to set up and replenish buffet, serve wine, remove plates and glasses and serve dessert and coffee.

❋ For either kind of dinner it is helpful to have at least one kitchen helper in addition to waiters.

Large buffet—1 waiter per 25 guests

Cocktail party—1 waiter per every 35 guests

❋ Large parties of 50 or more require at least two or more kitchen helpers in addition to waiters and bartenders.

Kitchen help—Even though waiters or bartenders are not necessary for a party or dinner, at least one helper in the kitchen helps the event run more smoothly.

Rental Equipment List

China
Plates (10-inch)
Plates (9-inch)
Plates (6-inch)
Soup Bowls and Plates
Dessert Plates
Tea/Coffee Cups and Saucers
Coffee Pots or Urns
Teapots or Service
Sugar Bowls
Salt/Pepper
Pitchers (all sizes)
Glasses
Ashtrays
Butter Dishes

Serving Pieces
Serving Platter and Bowls
Tables and Chairs
Serving Tables
Coat Rack and Hangers
Tablecloths
Napkins
Ice Buckets and Coolers
Warming Trays
Chafing Dishes
Punch Bowl and Ladle
Tents
Covered Passages
Flooring/Runners or Carpeting

Decorations

Decorations, elaborate or simple, set the mood for an occasion and should be reflected throughout the entire house. Flowers, votive candles and special guest linen are simple touches that dress up every nook and cranny of a home, creating a party atmosphere. Personal style and creativity are expressed through decorating. Flowers, candles, balloons, baskets, ribbons and even party favors add flair and flourish to a party. The manner in which you decorate should complement the menu and style of the occasion. Decorations should enhance but never interfere with all practical aspects and logistics of the party. Use your imagination to create a memorable setting.

TABLE LINEN, STAINS AND NAPKIN FOLDS
Selection

The kind of table linen you select should reflect the formality and style with which you entertain. If you enjoy formal entertaining, begin to acquire and collect formal table linen and vice versa for more casual entertaining. It is handy to have at least one formal set and one casual set of table linen. Purchase the very best quality you can afford. Better quality linen is more durable and withstands frequent use and laundering. This is particularly true of fine damask cloths which are the accepted standard of formal entertaining. Fine damask actually improves with age and develops a soft patina and smooth texture with use.

Proper care of table linen and napkins is essential. Never starch linen. Heavy starching can harm the fibers of the fabric and cause premature fading of colored linen. Excessive bleach or sunlight will cause fibers of linen to rot. Do not iron in creases or folds. This causes permanent lines to form in the cloth. If you have adequate padding that does not react to heat, it is easiest to iron the table linen on the dining table. To store linen, do not wrap in tissue or plastic. Tissue contains acid, and will discolor linen and plastic does not allow evaporation and may cause mildew. Place in a dark, moisture free area to prevent yellowing. If you do not care for the yellowed, antique look and want to restore the linen to white, simply wash the cloth in plain hot water and damp dry at medium heat or allow to dry in bright sunlight. Linen tablecloths and napkins look best if pressed on the wrong side while slightly damp. Damp linen can be placed in the freezer, removed piece by piece and ironed. This process gives linen a starched, crisp look but retains a smooth soft texture. Lace tablecloths should be carefully laundered by hand to prevent tearing. All tablecloths should be laundered with mild soap. Embroidery or lace tablecloths should be ironed between two sheets. To prevent permanent creasing, do not stack damask linen when storing.

Determining the size of cloth to purchase depends upon the length of overhang preferred. A cloth that is too short looks awkward. The minimum length of overhang for a formal table is ten inches. A longer overhang is less critical on a smaller table. If using the dining table as a service table for a buffet, use an eighteen to twenty inch overhang for proper proportion. When a solid cloth is used under a lace or cutwork cloth, the top piece may have less overhang than the minimum because this treatment is primarily decorative. Once the best length of overhang has been determined, add that length to each of the four sides of the table top dimensions. Tablecloths are sold in standard dimensions. Select the standard size that fits your ideal measurement most closely. For a round table, double the overhang length and add to the diameter of the table top to determine the tablecloth size.

Table linen and napkins are available in many varieties. There are wrinkle and stain resistant blends of fabrics that make maintenance of table linen much easier than it once was. Despite convenient new features, table linen is subject to spills and stains by the nature of its use. Below are listed the most common types of stains and the most reliable remedies for removal.

Stains

Always try to remove stains before laundering, but do not disrupt an entire dinner because of a stain. Simply soak or rub the stain with a little water and go on with the meal. If you are confident that you can remove the stain, ignore it completely until the guests have gone. Always treat a stain before laundering, as hot water may sometimes permanently set a stain.

Wine—Pour cold water through stain until it disappears. If the stain is still present, pour club soda through it and rub gently, and launder immediately. If wine is spilled during a meal, try this quick fix for easier removal later: pour salt directly on the stain and let it remain until the table is cleared.

Tea and coffee—Rinse with cold water or pour boiling water through the stain if the fabric can tolerate this treatment. If the beverage contained cream, blot with a grease solvent before laundering.

Fruit juice—Blot stain with cold water, then launder. If the stain has dried, pour boiling water through the stain, then launder.

Dairy products—Rinse with cold water, then launder. If grease stains remain after rinsing, blot with a grease solvent.

Gravy or meat juices—Rinse in cold water, then rub with a mild soap. If grease stains remain, use a grease solvent or an enzyme presoak before laundering.

Jelly—Rinse in cold water, rub with mild soap, rinse and launder.

Butter, grease or oil—Place dry cloth under stain and rub with hot sudsy water. Then blot with a grease solvent and launder.

Tomato stains—Rinse with cold water. Use an enzyme presoak before laundering.

Scorching—Squeeze lemon juice on the scorch, sprinkle with salt, then dry in sunlight. Or rub with a cut onion, then rinse with cold water and launder.

Candlewax—First remove wax with blunt knife. Place cloth between two dry, clean towels and apply warm iron repeatedly. If wax stain is still visible, pour boiling water through the stain, blot with cleaning fluid and launder.

Lipstick and cosmetics—Rub stain with mild liquid soap and rinse. If stain is still visible, blot with cleaning fluid and launder.

Ink—Test the stain to see if it bleeds and runs when water is applied. If it bleeds or runs, continue to pour cold water through the stain until it disappears. If the stain is not affected by water, try cleaning fluid or a commercial ink remover which may be purchased at an office supply store.

Blood—Fresh blood stains should be rinsed immediately with cold water. Use an enzyme presoak for at least thirty minutes. Launder.

Mildew—Launder in hot water and dry in sunlight. If stain is still visible, blot with buttermilk, rinse and dry in sunlight.

Rust—Blot stain with commercial remover or mixture of lemon juice and salt, rinse with cold water and dry in sunlight.

Napkin Folds

Folded napkins add a fanciful and festive touch and there are many ways to fold them. We have selected twelve different folds listed in order of difficulty, beginning with the simplest. Always experiment before the party and select a fold most suitable to the occasion and table decor. Fold the napkins two or three days before the party. Place folded napkins on the table and cover with tissue or plastic. The larger the party, the more simple the fold should be. If you are serving buffet style with the napkins placed on the serving table, you must consider the amount of space available. Experiment with different size napkins to see which folds work best with different size linens. Regardless of the size, the napkin should be a square. A formal size napkin is 22 inches square. Folded napkins may be placed to the left, right, center, above or on the plate as well as in the glass.

KNOT

1. Open napkin and lay it flat.

3. Roll points from top to bottom.

2. Fold napkin into triangle with points at top.

4. Tie knot in center.

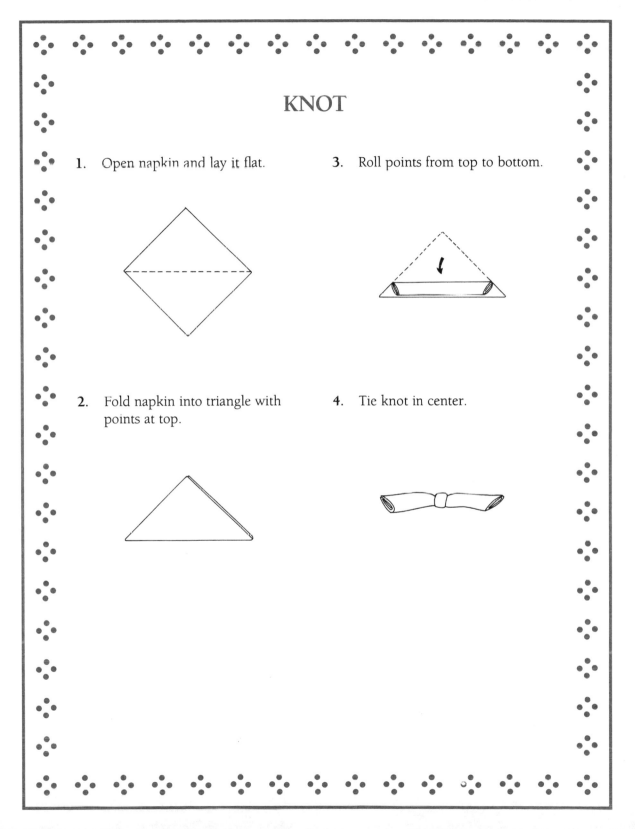

TIARA FOLD

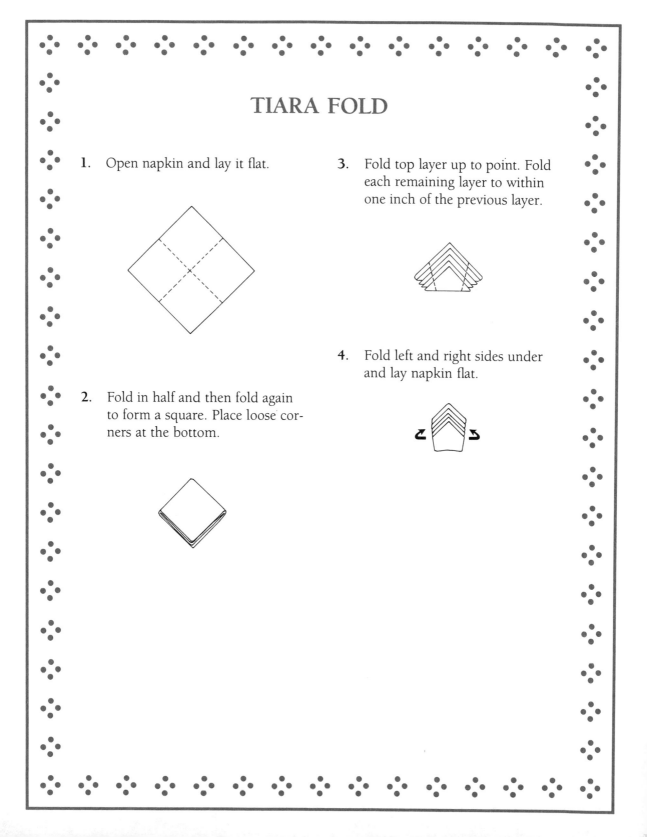

1. Open napkin and lay it flat.

2. Fold in half and then fold again to form a square. Place loose corners at the bottom.

3. Fold top layer up to point. Fold each remaining layer to within one inch of the previous layer.

4. Fold left and right sides under and lay napkin flat.

FAN IN A GOBLET

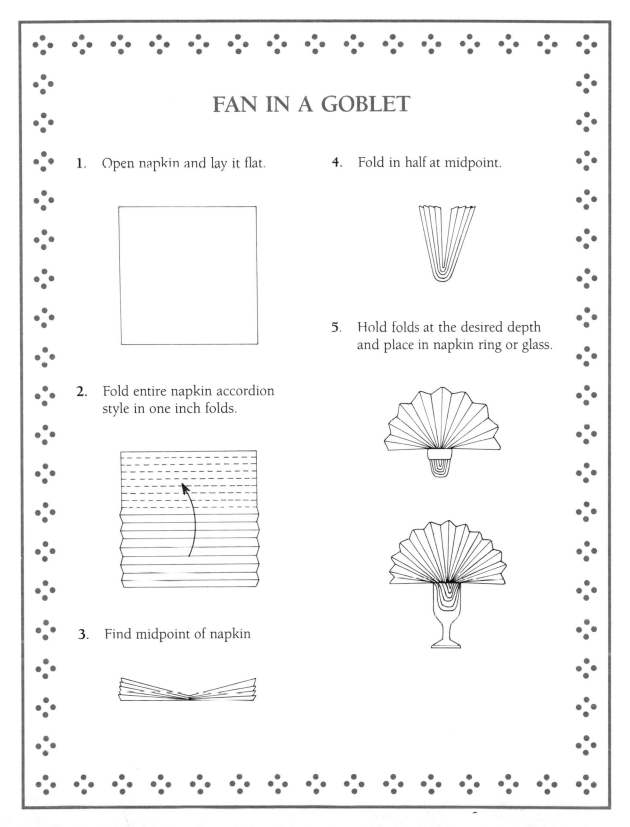

1. Open napkin and lay it flat.

4. Fold in half at midpoint.

5. Hold folds at the desired depth and place in napkin ring or glass.

2. Fold entire napkin accordion style in one inch folds.

3. Find midpoint of napkin

BUFFET POCKET

1. Open napkin and lay it flat.

4. Turn napkin over, fold side down.

2. Fold entire napkin in half with fold at bottom.

5. Fold left and right sides to center.

6. Fold in half and insert flatware.

3. Turn down top layer to bottom fold.

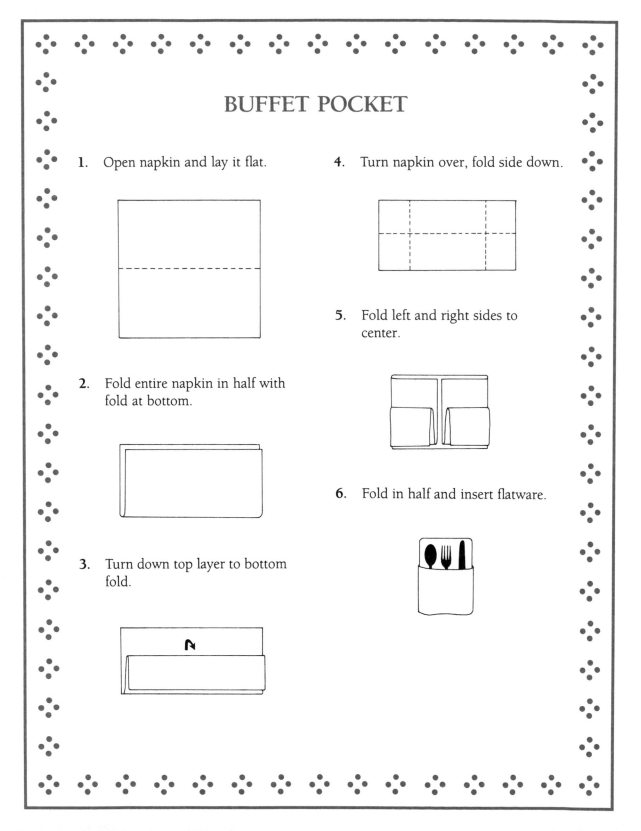

LACE NAPKIN FOLD

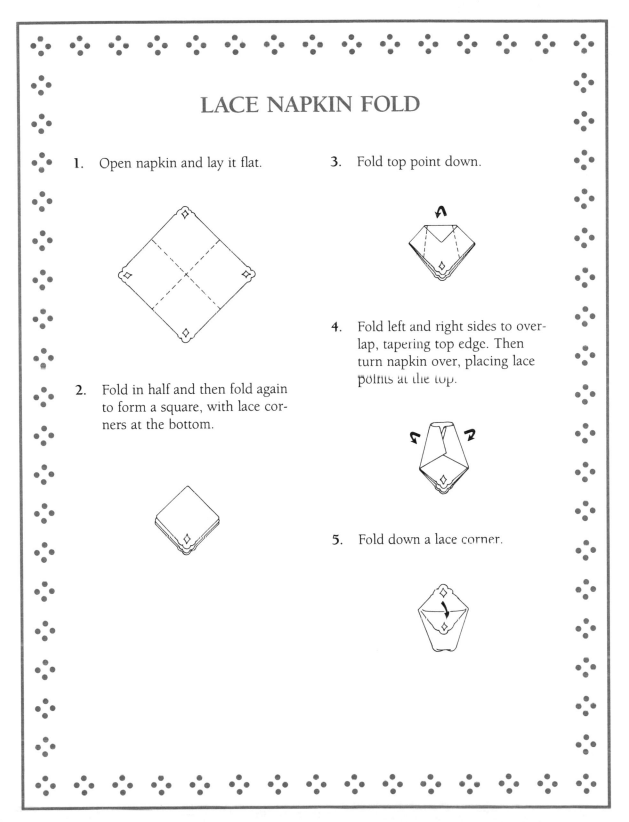

1. Open napkin and lay it flat.

2. Fold in half and then fold again to form a square, with lace corners at the bottom.

3. Fold top point down.

4. Fold left and right sides to overlap, tapering top edge. Then turn napkin over, placing lace points at the top.

5. Fold down a lace corner.

CLASSIC FOLD

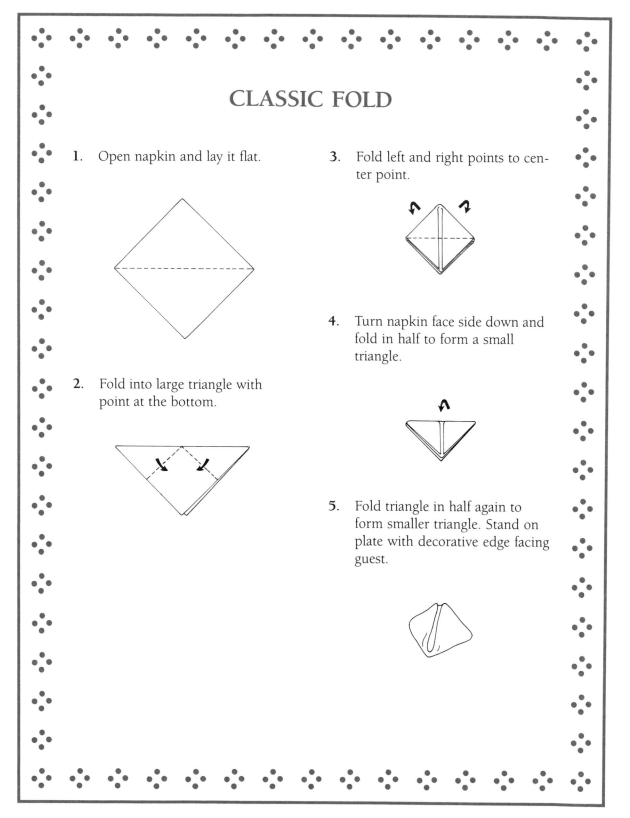

1. Open napkin and lay it flat.

2. Fold into large triangle with point at the bottom.

3. Fold left and right points to center point.

4. Turn napkin face side down and fold in half to form a small triangle.

5. Fold triangle in half again to form smaller triangle. Stand on plate with decorative edge facing guest.

FLAT POCKET FOLD

1. Open napkin and lay it flat.

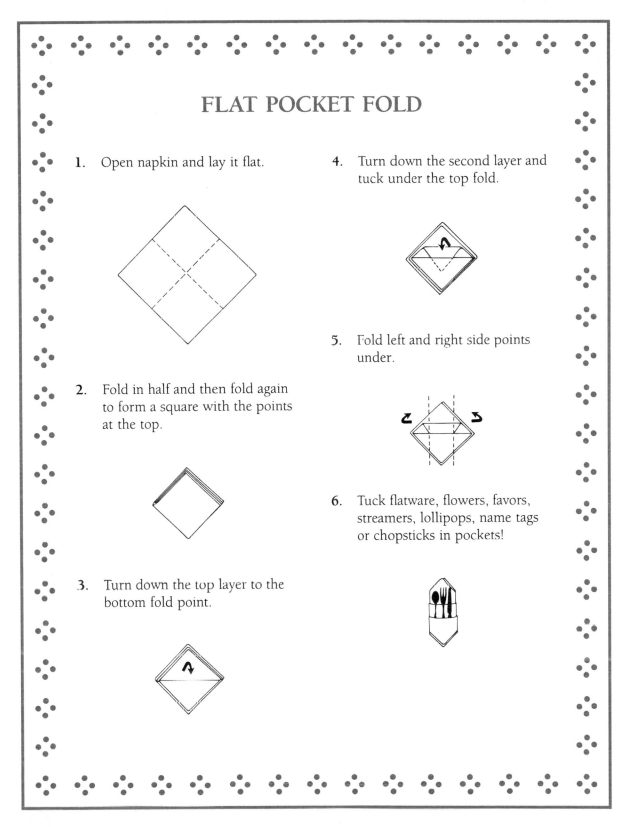

2. Fold in half and then fold again to form a square with the points at the top.

3. Turn down the top layer to the bottom fold point.

4. Turn down the second layer and tuck under the top fold.

5. Fold left and right side points under.

6. Tuck flatware, flowers, favors, streamers, lollipops, name tags or chopsticks in pockets!

BISHOP'S HAT OR FLEUR-DE-LIS

1. Open napkin and lay it flat.

4. Fold top point down to within one inch of bottom point.

2. Fold open napkin into triangle, center point down.

5. Fold same point up to edge. Fold left and right points under and overlap, tucking one inside the other.

3. Fold left and right points to center point to create a diamond.

6. Stand upright, leave as is or turn down points to form a fleur-de-lis.

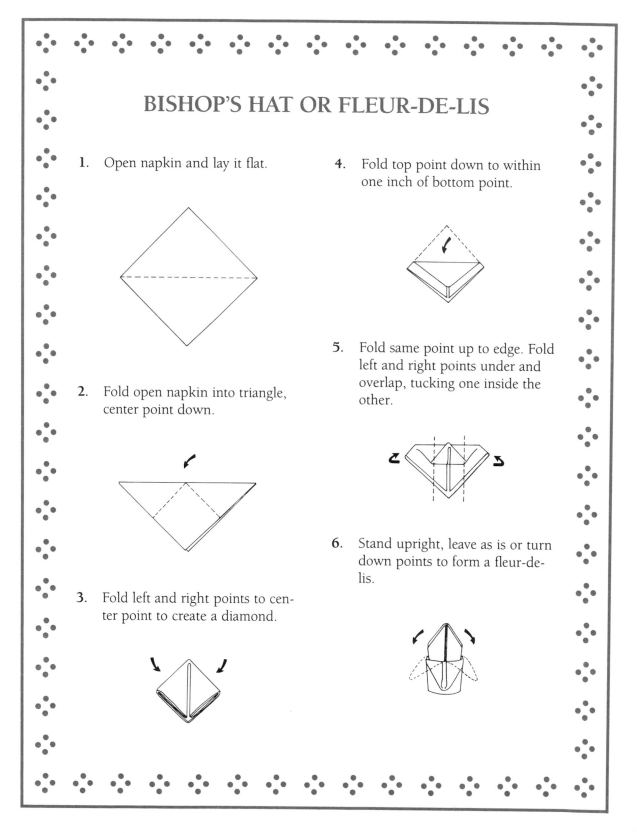

STANDING FAN

1. Open napkin and lay it flat.

2. Fold napkin in half vertically with the fold side on the right.

3. Beginning at the bottom, fold accordion style ⅔ way up.

4. Fold in half with pleats on outside.

5. Fold upper right corners into triangle, overlapping side fold by one inch. Tuck overlap under to create a base.

6. Stand upright and release pleats to form fan.

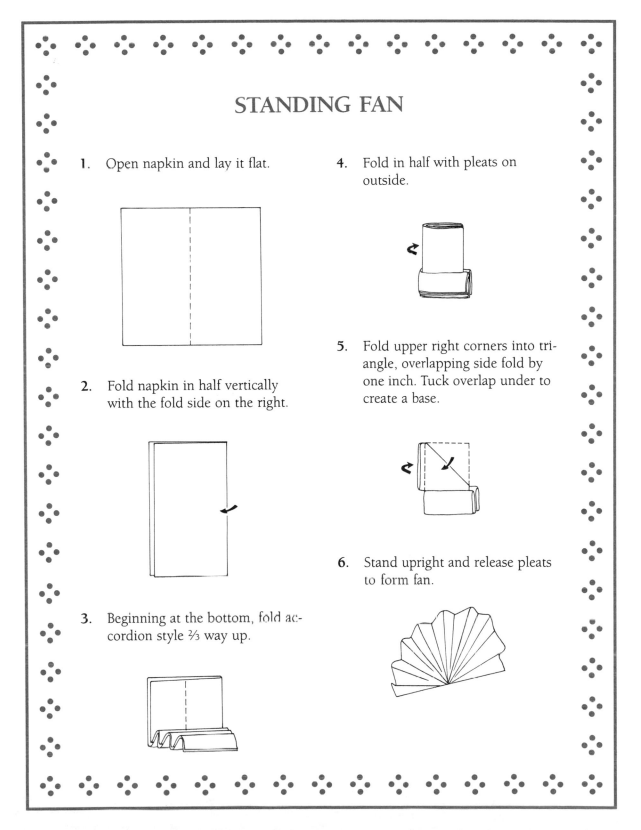

CLOWN'S HAT

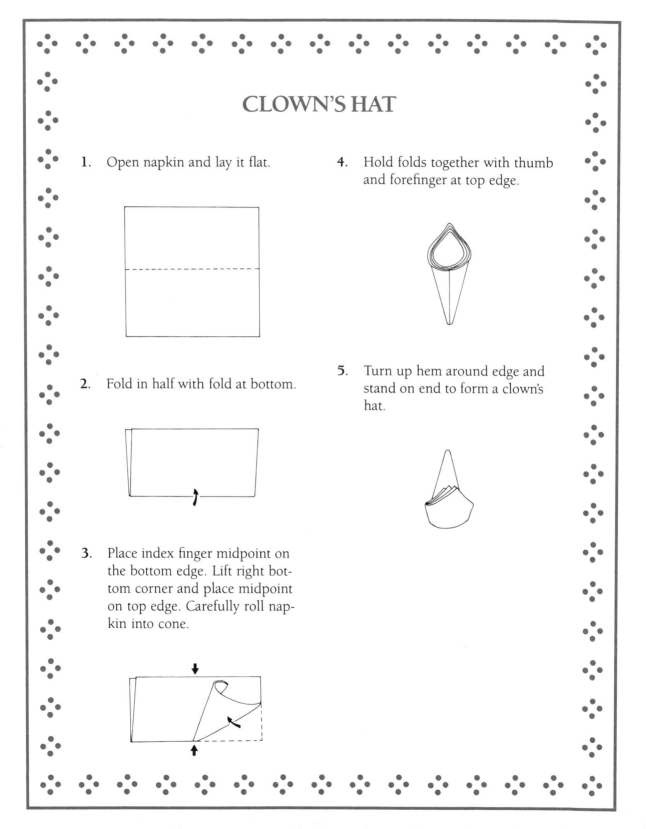

1. Open napkin and lay it flat.

2. Fold in half with fold at bottom.

3. Place index finger midpoint on the bottom edge. Lift right bottom corner and place midpoint on top edge. Carefully roll napkin into cone.

4. Hold folds together with thumb and forefinger at top edge.

5. Turn up hem around edge and stand on end to form a clown's hat.

BOAT WITH SAILS

1. Open napkin and lay it flat.

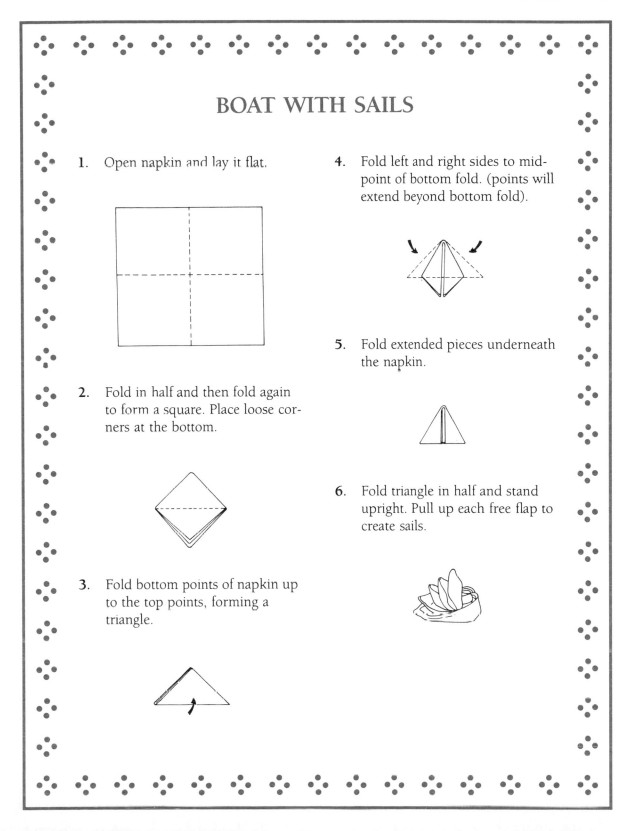

2. Fold in half and then fold again to form a square. Place loose corners at the bottom.

3. Fold bottom points of napkin up to the top points, forming a triangle.

4. Fold left and right sides to mid-point of bottom fold. (points will extend beyond bottom fold).

5. Fold extended pieces underneath the napkin.

6. Fold triangle in half and stand upright. Pull up each free flap to create sails.

ELF'S SLIPPER

1. Open napkin and lay it flat.

2. Fold napkin from bottom to top. Fold from bottom to top again.

3. Fold points A and B to meet in center.

4. Fold points C and D to meet in center.

5. Fold napkin with points C and D inside, creating an airplane effect. Lift corner flap of napkin up and forward.

6. Fold down point E. Wrap section around to front and tuck inside slot.

7. Curl toe. Adjust top of boot to create ruffled effect. Tie with ribbons and tuck candy canes, place cards, flowers or favors in folds.

STERLING SILVER

Many companies that manufacture silver bear the names of eighteenth and nineteenth century silversmiths who originated the trade in this country. Kirk, Wallace, Gorham, Towle, Rogers, Stief and Reed and Barton are a few of the companies originated by these silversmiths. These men revolutionized the silver flatware production process and invented better methods of reproducing intricate designs and patterns.

Etiquette still determines where silver should be placed, but the standard place setting consists of five pieces. It is interesting to collect old period pieces which enhance and add value to your silver service. Even though you may not use the pieces for their original purpose, you may fine them extremely versatile and handy.

| Salad Fork | Dinner Fork | Dinner Knife | Dessert Spoon | Teaspoon |

During the Victorian period, elaborate designs and the production of highly specialized serving pieces reached a level that has not been duplicated since. The standard place setting at the turn of the century consisted of twenty-five different knives, spoons and forks. Each piece of silver had a very specific use and strict etiquette of the period dictated when it should be used and where it should be placed.

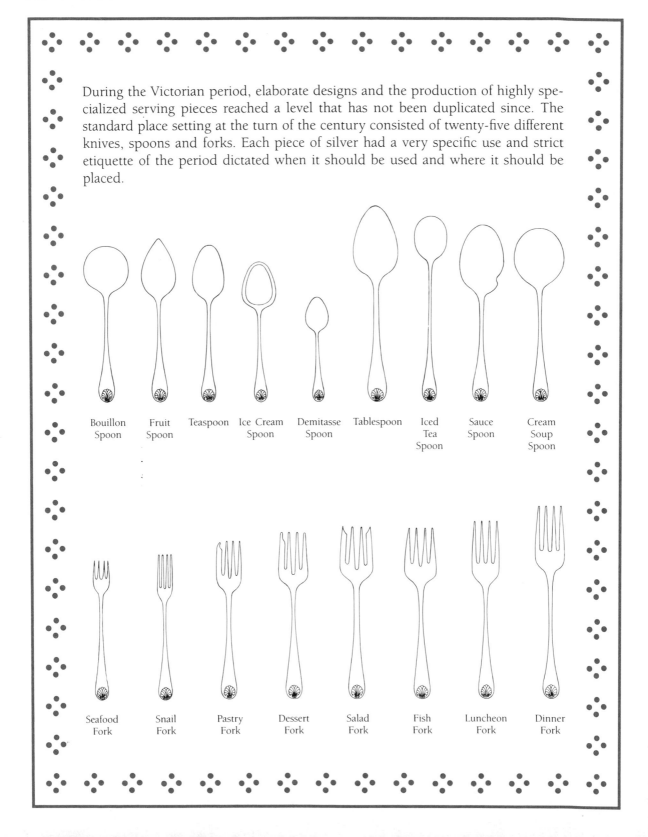

Bouillon Spoon Fruit Spoon Teaspoon Ice Cream Spoon Demitasse Spoon Tablespoon Iced Tea Spoon Sauce Spoon Cream Soup Spoon

Seafood Fork Snail Fork Pastry Fork Dessert Fork Salad Fork Fish Fork Luncheon Fork Dinner Fork

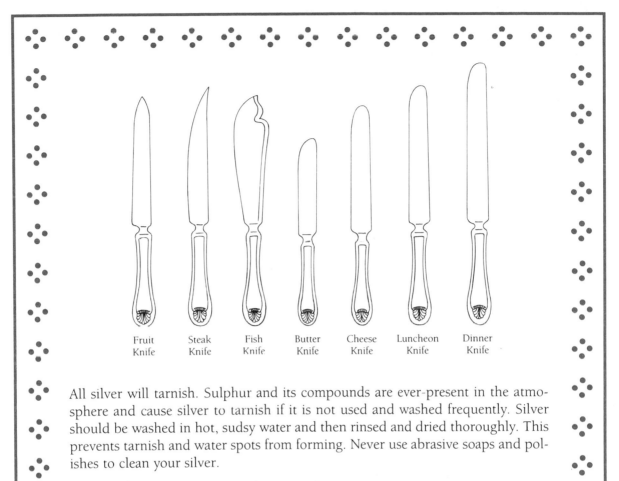

Fruit Knife · Steak Knife · Fish Knife · Butter Knife · Cheese Knife · Luncheon Knife · Dinner Knife

All silver will tarnish. Sulphur and its compounds are ever-present in the atmosphere and cause silver to tarnish if it is not used and washed frequently. Silver should be washed in hot, sudsy water and then rinsed and dried thoroughly. This prevents tarnish and water spots from forming. Never use abrasive soaps and polishes to clean your silver.

Sterling Silver Care

❋ Never wash silver with stainless steel.

❋ Never wash silver in a dishwasher.

❋ Dry silver with a soft cloth to prevent water spots.

❋ Camphor, alum or carbon paper will prevent tarnishing if kept with the silver.

❋ Pacific cloth will retard tarnishing.

❋ To retard tarnishing, store large pieces of silver in plastic wrap. Do not close with rubber bands.

❋ To avoid misplaced pieces, inventory silver to be used at a party.

❋ Empty sterling silver salt and pepper shakers before storing as salt will corrode the silver. Wash and dry shakers thoroughly.

TABLESETTING

The strict confines of precise etiquette once dictated the placement of silver, linen and china. Rules are not as rigid, but the practical basics of serving are still intact. We have presented the rules with illustrations of individual placesetting diagrams. Convenience and practicality are more important than any rule as long as all aspects work well together. The two examples of formal tablesettings we illustrate are both correct. Also illustrated, is the sequence of a four course meal. Exceptions and cutlery substitutions may vary, however, begin with the basic rule of forks to the left, spoons and knives to the right with handles placed one inch from the edge of the table. The cocktail fork, or small fish fork, is placed to the right with knife and spoons, and is the only exception to the rule. Silver is placed in order of service, working from the outside in toward the plate. The first flatware to be used will be the farthest from the plate on either side. The last flatware to be used will be closest to the plate. These are usually the dessert fork and spoon, unless they are placed nose to tail, horizontally above the dinner plate. A fruit knife may replace the dessert spoon when appropriate. The flatware, tines and bowls may be placed down or up, but should be consistent throughout all placement. Knife blades should always face the dinner plate. Butter knives are placed horizontally across the top of the bread plate, blades down, handle right. European custom sometimes places the butter knife to the right of the dinner knife. No more than three pieces of silver should be placed on either side of the dinner plate at one time. Any additional flatware required for the meal should be brought with course. Napkins may be placed to the left, right, above or on the plate, whichever is most convenient. Serving pieces are placed nose to tail in the center of the table next to the appropriate dish, unless dinner is served from a sideboard. The bread plate is placed to the left, above the forks on the same level as the water glass. A salad plate or service plate may be placed on top of the dinner plate and removed after it is used. Water and wine glasses are placed to the right of the dinner plate, above the dinner knife. Glasses are placed in order of use, the closest being the first to be used, moving in order of sequence outward to the last glass. There should never be more than three glasses present at a tablesetting. Wine glasses should not be filled ahead of time, but poured with the appropriate course and removed afterwards. Coffee cups and saucers should be brought during or after dessert. Empty cups and saucers are placed to the right of the guests, with a spoon placed on the saucer, but it is customary to serve coffee elsewhere allowing the table to be discreetly cleared.

Dinner guests are served from the left and plates are removed from the right. Beverages are served from the right.

Formal Placesetting

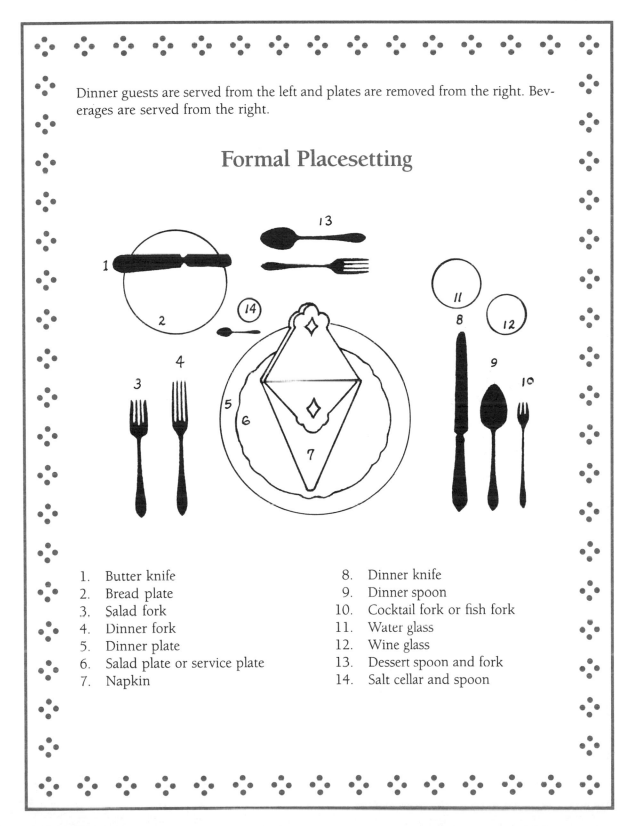

1. Butter knife	8. Dinner knife
2. Bread plate	9. Dinner spoon
3. Salad fork	10. Cocktail fork or fish fork
4. Dinner fork	11. Water glass
5. Dinner plate	12. Wine glass
6. Salad plate or service plate	13. Dessert spoon and fork
7. Napkin	14. Salt cellar and spoon

OR

Formal Placesetting

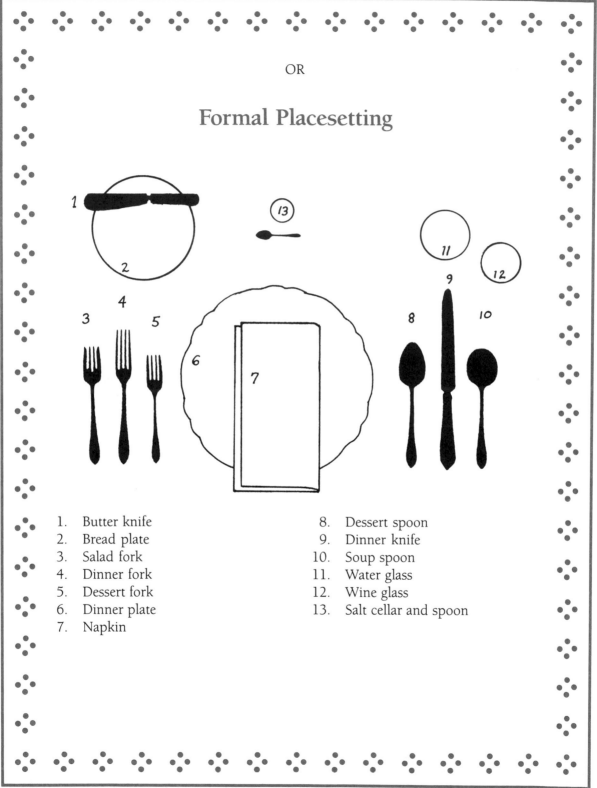

1. Butter knife
2. Bread plate
3. Salad fork
4. Dinner fork
5. Dessert fork
6. Dinner plate
7. Napkin

8. Dessert spoon
9. Dinner knife
10. Soup spoon
11. Water glass
12. Wine glass
13. Salt cellar and spoon

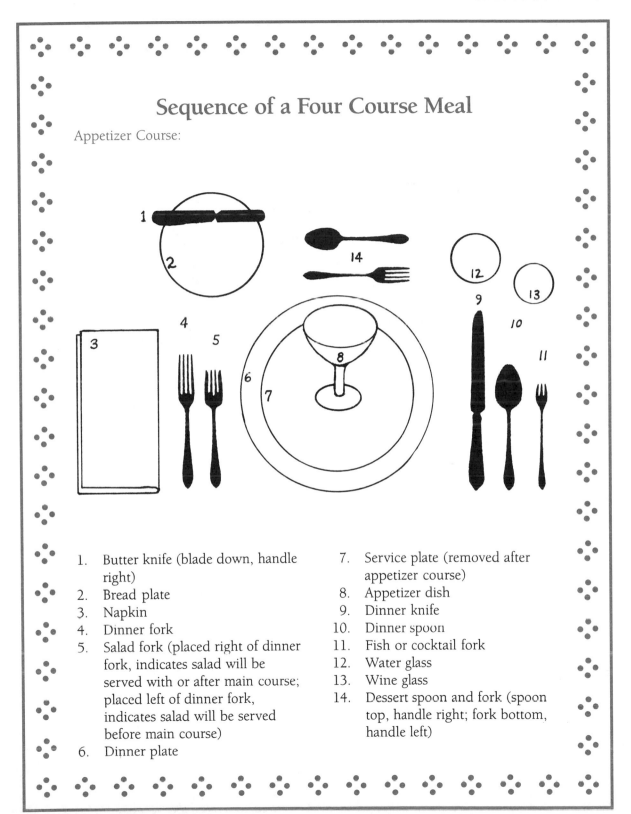

Sequence of a Four Course Meal

Appetizer Course:

1. Butter knife (blade down, handle right)
2. Bread plate
3. Napkin
4. Dinner fork
5. Salad fork (placed right of dinner fork, indicates salad will be served with or after main course; placed left of dinner fork, indicates salad will be served before main course)
6. Dinner plate
7. Service plate (removed after appetizer course)
8. Appetizer dish
9. Dinner knife
10. Dinner spoon
11. Fish or cocktail fork
12. Water glass
13. Wine glass
14. Dessert spoon and fork (spoon top, handle right; fork bottom, handle left)

Soup course:

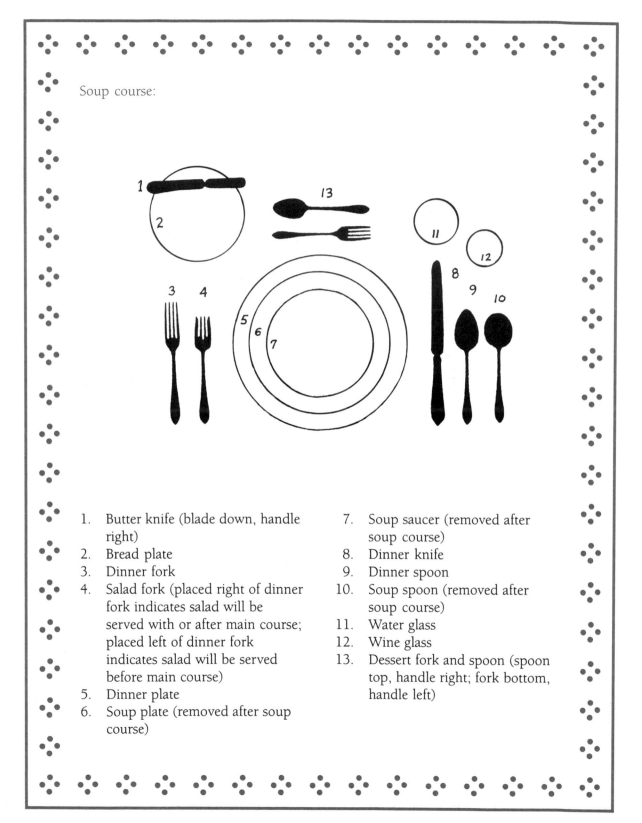

1. Butter knife (blade down, handle right)
2. Bread plate
3. Dinner fork
4. Salad fork (placed right of dinner fork indicates salad will be served with or after main course; placed left of dinner fork indicates salad will be served before main course)
5. Dinner plate
6. Soup plate (removed after soup course)
7. Soup saucer (removed after soup course)
8. Dinner knife
9. Dinner spoon
10. Soup spoon (removed after soup course)
11. Water glass
12. Wine glass
13. Dessert fork and spoon (spoon top, handle right; fork bottom, handle left)

Entrée or Main Course:

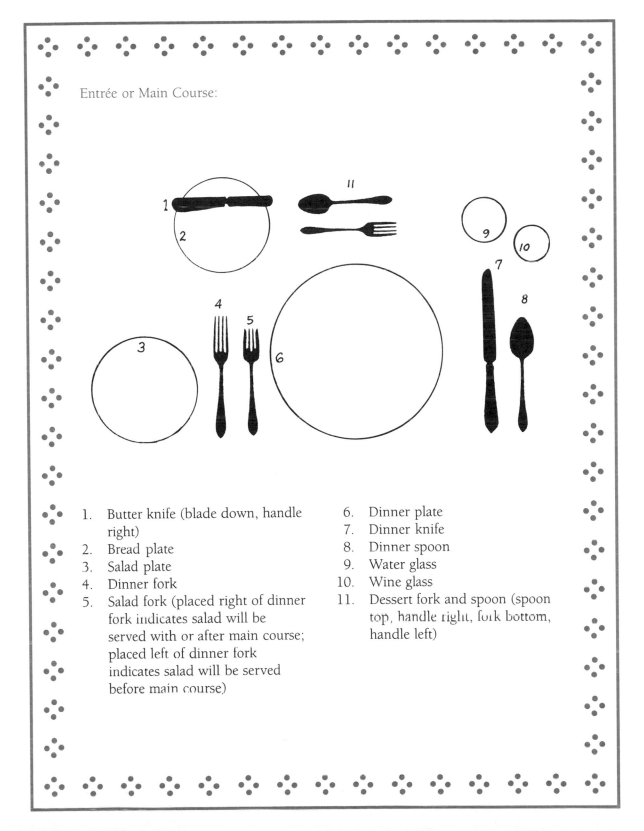

1. Butter knife (blade down, handle right)
2. Bread plate
3. Salad plate
4. Dinner fork
5. Salad fork (placed right of dinner fork indicates salad will be served with or after main course; placed left of dinner fork indicates salad will be served before main course)

6. Dinner plate
7. Dinner knife
8. Dinner spoon
9. Water glass
10. Wine glass
11. Dessert fork and spoon (spoon top, handle right, fork bottom, handle left)

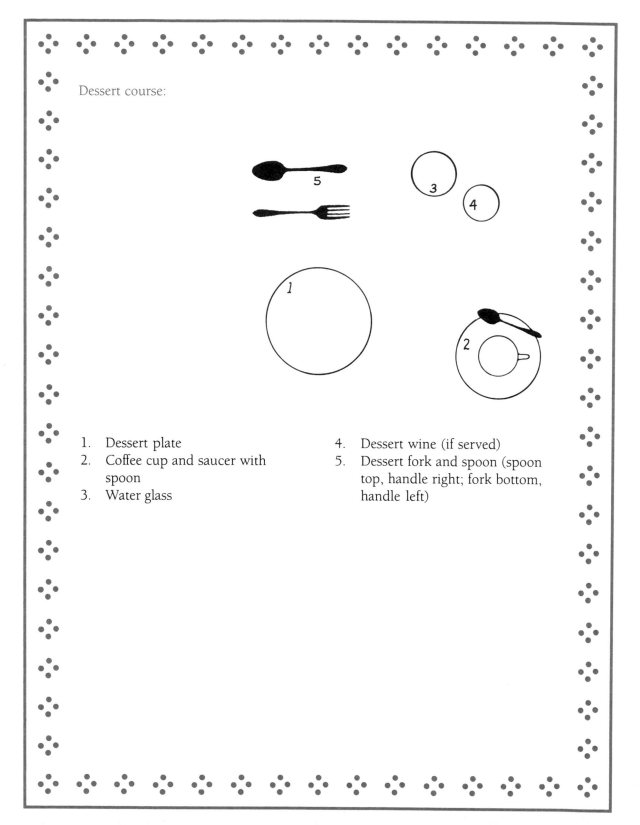

Dessert course:

1. Dessert plate
2. Coffee cup and saucer with spoon
3. Water glass
4. Dessert wine (if served)
5. Dessert fork and spoon (spoon top, handle right; fork bottom, handle left)

METHODS OF SERVING
Continental

Continental or formal service occurs when guests are served from platters by waiters. The guest of honor is served first or the female guest to the right of the host is served first, followed by all other female guests and the hostess. Then the male guests to the right of the hostess and all other gentlemen with the host last. This order of service is repeated for each course.

Family Style

In a family style meal, dinner plates are stacked in front of the head of the table. All serving dishes are placed at that end of the table and the host serves each plate and passes it to guests.

Country Style

All place settings are set and serving dishes are placed on the table. Each guest serves himself and passes the dish to the right.

Blue Plate

Portions are served in the kitchen and brought to the table before guests sit down.

Buffet

This versatile method of serving enables a hostess to serve a small dinner or large crowd with little help. A hostess may ask a few friends to help or she may engage professional kitchen help. Planning requires a step by step, mental dress rehearsal. Beverages, menu, traffic, serving, seating, clearing and cleaning should be carefully considered.

The number of guests that can be conveniently served is the first consideration. Decide whether the buffet will be a seated, lap or standing buffet. Foods that require a knife should only be served at a seated buffet or trays should be provided. If a large number of people are being served, then all items on the menu must be served on one plate, with the exception of dessert. To avoid a messy plate, avoid foods that run or melt. Portions should be offered in individual servings when possible and served with all the trimmings on them. Common sense and serving convenience should dictate menu selections. A buffet table requires that guests serve themselves in a logical sequence. Each dish should have a serving utensil next to it and portions should be pre-cut for individual servings.

Traffic is a key consideration for any buffet. Determine space limitations and compensate for them, if possible. If necessary, move furniture and store in garage to prevent congestion. Always serve beverages in an area separate from the food. Several serving and clearing stations are convenient for large buffets, if space permits. If the weather is agreeable, move outdoors, but do not rely on it. Be sure to have an alternate rain plan or date for outdoor occasions.

To simplify the clearing of dishes, formulate a plan in advance. If it is not a seated buffet, a trolley or tray should be clearly designated to guests so that plates may be returned and cleared from sight.

We have stressed that planning each aspect of a buffet is of prime consideration. Several diagrams are illustrated below to assist you with your planning.

Seated Buffet Served from a Sideboard

Glasses, napkins, silver, bread and condiments are placed at the dining table. After dinner is almost complete and ready to be cleared, the dinner buffet may be removed and replaced by a dessert buffet. Coffee or other beverages should be located at a smaller table and served to the guests by the host.

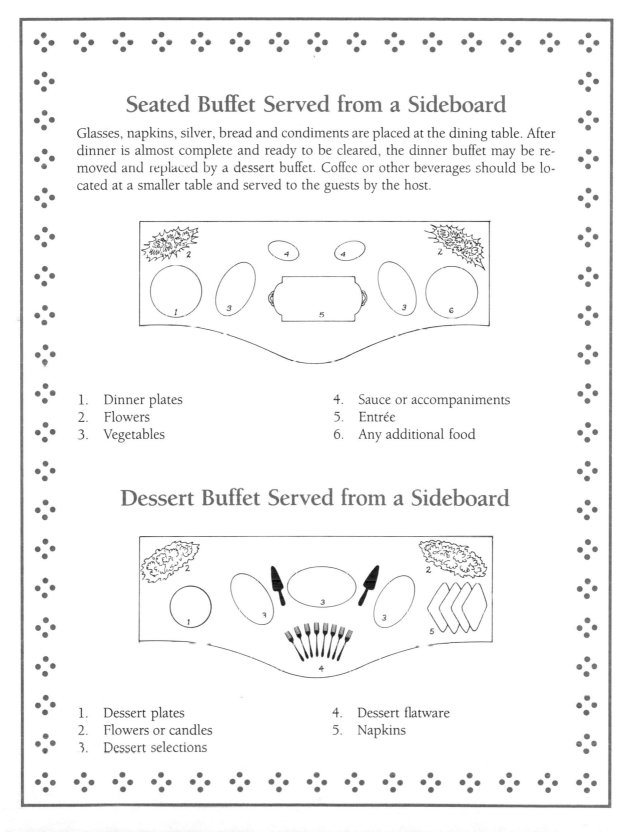

1. Dinner plates	4. Sauce or accompaniments
2. Flowers	5. Entrée
3. Vegetables	6. Any additional food

Dessert Buffet Served from a Sideboard

1. Dessert plates	4. Dessert flatware
2. Flowers or candles	5. Napkins
3. Dessert selections	

Central Buffet

This buffet is served from the dining table. Location of entry and exit determine where the beginning of the buffet should be placed. Dessert and coffee may be served from this table, but may be placed in another room for convenience. This allows the buffet table to be cleared while dessert is served elsewhere. Flatware is placed at the end of the table, or may be placed at the beginning according to preference. Always remember to have enough space beside serving dishes for guests to set their plates while serving.

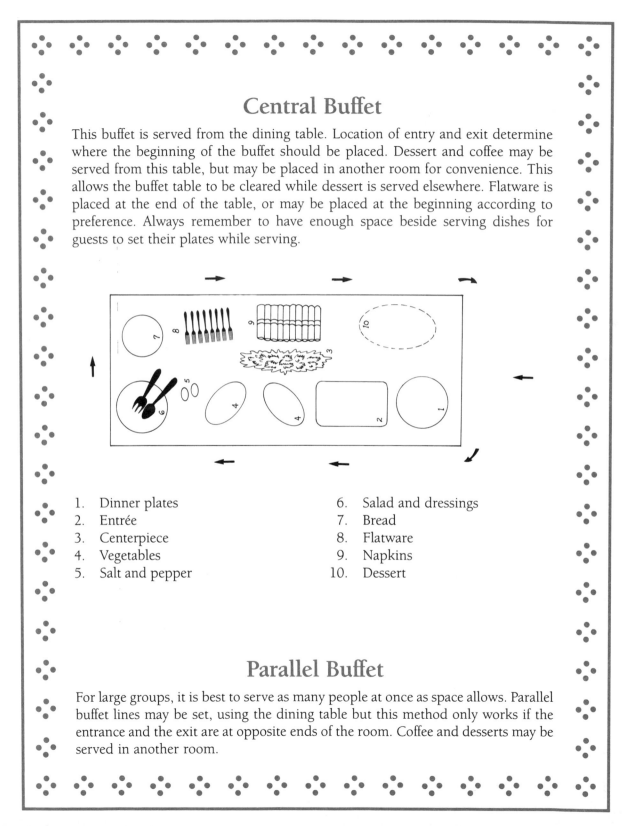

1. Dinner plates
2. Entrée
3. Centerpiece
4. Vegetables
5. Salt and pepper
6. Salad and dressings
7. Bread
8. Flatware
9. Napkins
10. Dessert

Parallel Buffet

For large groups, it is best to serve as many people at once as space allows. Parallel buffet lines may be set, using the dining table but this method only works if the entrance and the exit are at opposite ends of the room. Coffee and desserts may be served in another room.

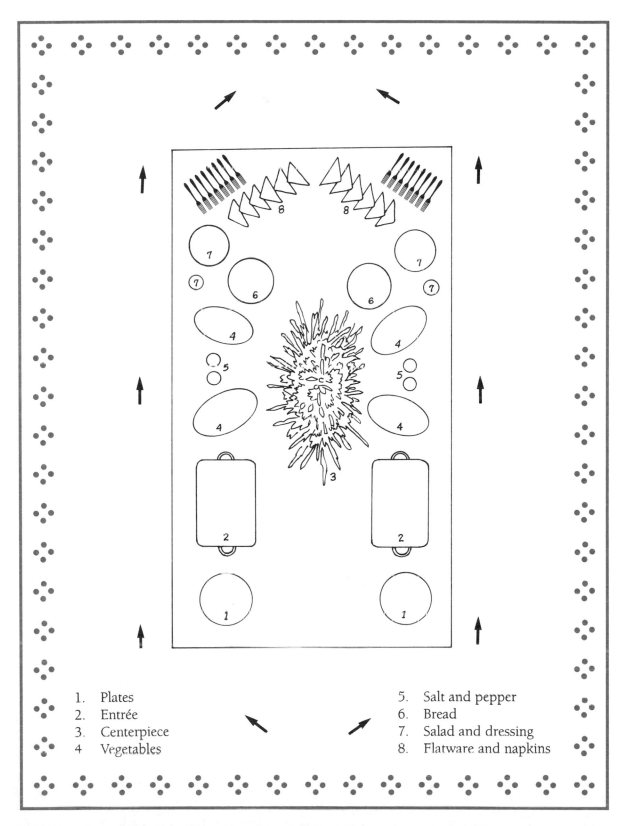

1. Plates
2. Entrée
3. Centerpiece
4. Vegetables
5. Salt and pepper
6. Bread
7. Salad and dressing
8. Flatware and napkins

Circular Buffet

A buffet placed on a round table works best for small groups. This is illustrated below with all items on the buffet table, except beverages and desserts. These are placed in a separate area to avoid congestion.

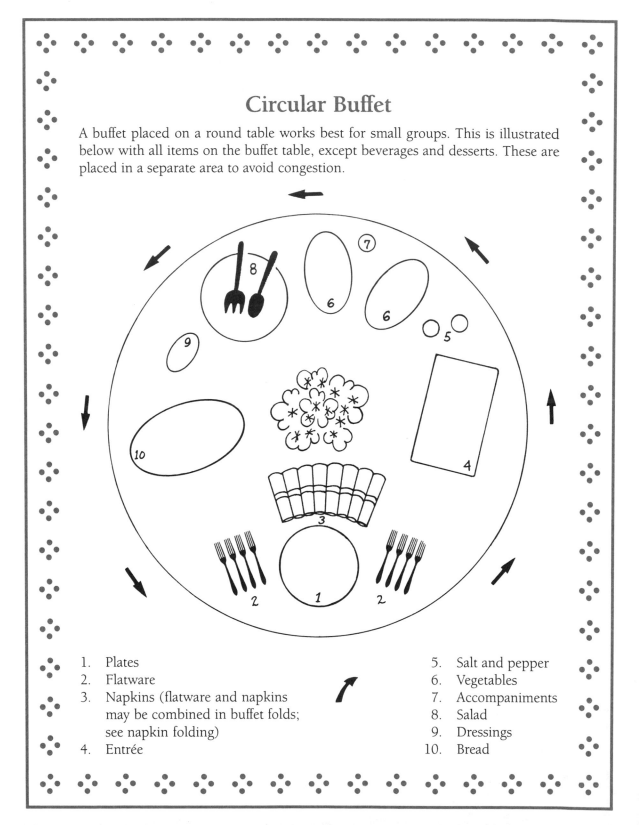

1. Plates
2. Flatware
3. Napkins (flatware and napkins may be combined in buffet folds; see napkin folding)
4. Entrée

5. Salt and pepper
6. Vegetables
7. Accompaniments
8. Salad
9. Dressings
10. Bread

Beverage Tables

We have emphasized that separate beverage tables are preferable for any kind of buffet. For a small seated buffet, the beverage table should be in the dining room adjacent to the sideboard. Guests may serve themselves or hosts may serve the guests from the table. For a larger buffet, the beverage tables should be located in a different area, away from the buffet table. This prevents congestion and allows guests to seat themselves and get drinks at their convenience.

Wine Tables

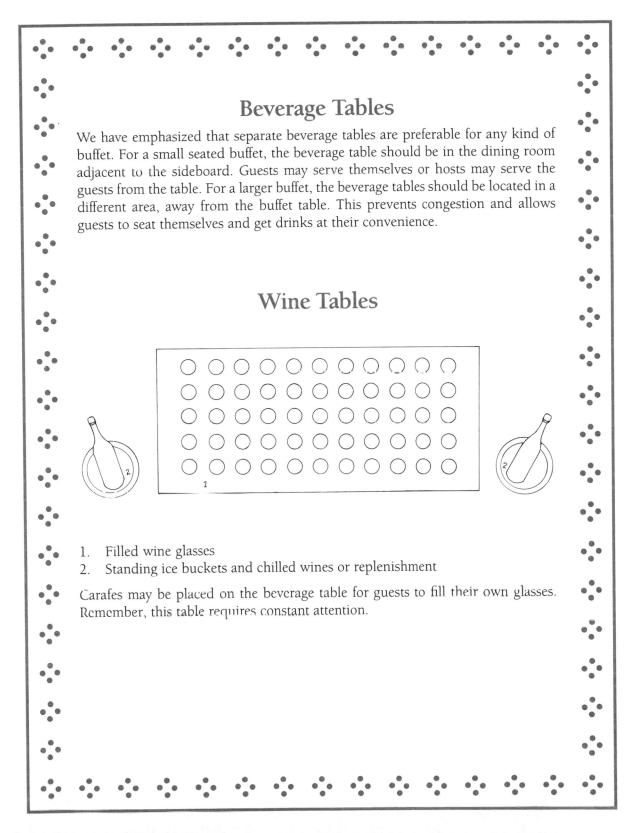

1. Filled wine glasses
2. Standing ice buckets and chilled wines or replenishment

Carafes may be placed on the beverage table for guests to fill their own glasses. Remember, this table requires constant attention.

Wine and Water

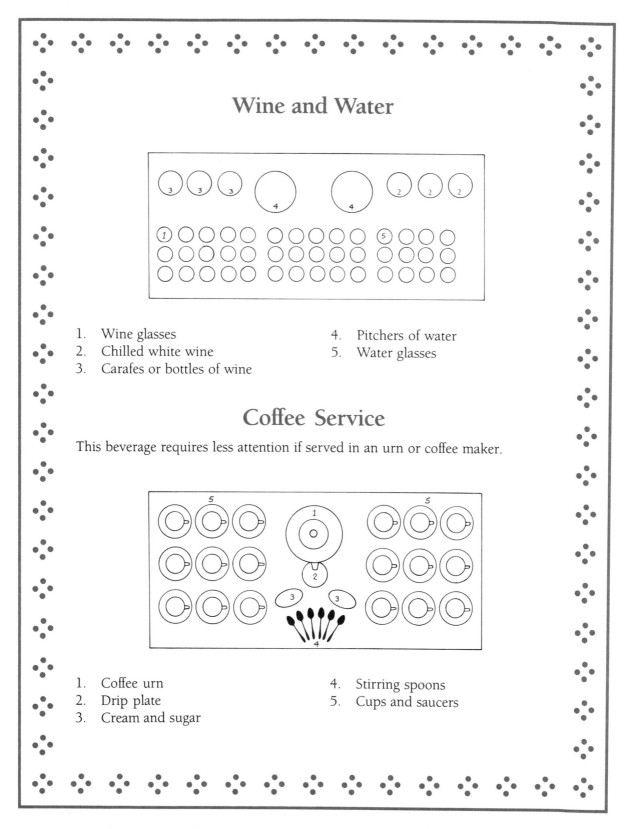

1. Wine glasses
2. Chilled white wine
3. Carafes or bottles of wine
4. Pitchers of water
5. Water glasses

Coffee Service

This beverage requires less attention if served in an urn or coffee maker.

1. Coffee urn
2. Drip plate
3. Cream and sugar
4. Stirring spoons
5. Cups and saucers

Fancy Tea Table

An afternoon tea is an elegant and pleasant way to entertain friends. This is an occasion to use your finest linen and best china and silver. A tea cannot be too elaborate. Coffee is served at one end of the table and tea at the other. Plates may be stacked with small folded napkins placed on each plate. Tea sandwiches, fancy cakes, cookies, nuts and mints are elaborately spread on both sides of the table, between the tea and coffee service. A friend or helper should assist with serving the coffee and tea.

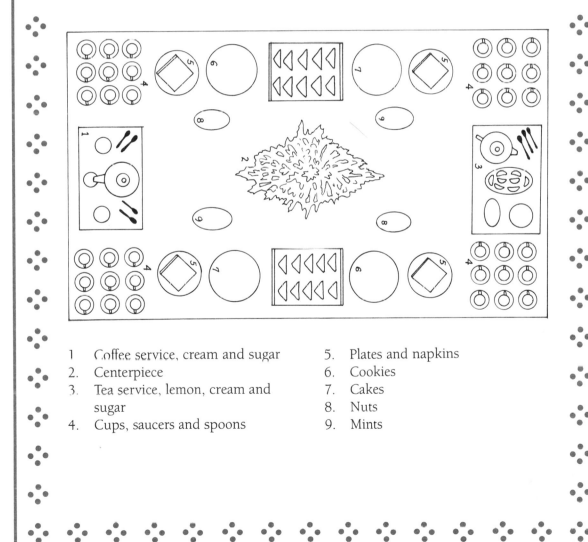

1. Coffee service, cream and sugar
2. Centerpiece
3. Tea service, lemon, cream and sugar
4. Cups, saucers and spoons
5. Plates and napkins
6. Cookies
7. Cakes
8. Nuts
9. Mints

GARNISHING

Presenting food and drink in an attractive and appealing manner should be a daily consideration of all cooks. Garnishes may be purely decorative or edible embellishments that add charm and style to any meal. They may be intricately sculpted figures that visually enhance a dish or a simple sprinkling of chopped basil. Some foods are not attractive and need garnishing. A plain loaf of pâté is not very tempting by itself. However, when it is molded in an attractive shape and covered with shaved almonds it becomes visually appealing.

Explore the vegetable and fruit sections in the market and think of new ways to use fresh produce as food decoration. Experiment with new ways of preparing and serving food that add flourish to old favorites. For a new approach, try piping cooked mashed potatoes onto a greased cookie sheet and lightly browning under the broiler. Many new and creative garnishing possibilities are limitless once you look at food with a creative approach.

We have illustrated several garnishes to help you begin. Once you familiarize yourself with the basic techniques, experiment and create your own new garnishes.

Quick and Simple Garnishes

Avocado slices
Basil leaves
Broccoli florets
Butter curls
Curly cabbage and lettuce leaves
Dill and parsley sprigs
Dried fruits
Frosted grapes
Green pepper rings
Hard-cooked eggs, sliced, quartered
    or crumbled

Lemon, lime and orange wedges,
    slices, twists and bows
Notched cucumber rounds
Nuts
Pickle fans
Pimiento bows
Piped fillings and borders
Serrated vegetable sticks
Spinach leaves

Quick Containers for Dips and Sauces

Artichokes
Avocados
Bread, hollowed

Egg plant
Onions
Pumpkins

Peppers
Squash
Tomatoes

Carved Decorative Baskets and Containers

Fancy baskets and containers may be carved and constructed from an endless variety of fruits and vegetables. A sharp knife is a pre-requisite for this garnish. Regardless of the kind of produce you are carving, the concept is the same; study the vegetable to determine where the first cuts should be made. A carved container sits better if a level slice is cut from the bottom. Cut and hollow, then scallop or serrate rims and edges to decorate.

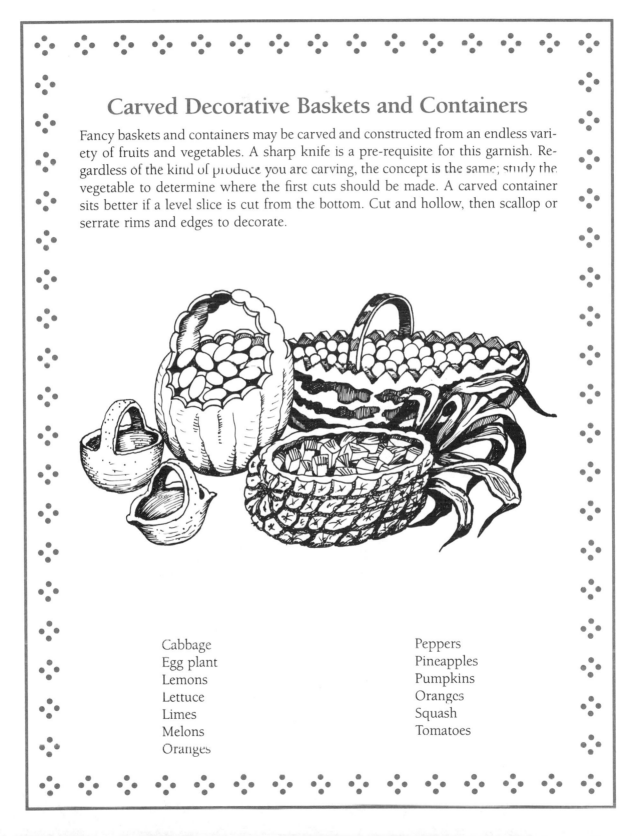

Cabbage
Egg plant
Lemons
Lettuce
Limes
Melons
Oranges

Peppers
Pineapples
Pumpkins
Oranges
Squash
Tomatoes

Decorative Carvings and Flowers

Harder, crisper vegetables or fruits may be used to make carved figures or flowers. Pieces may be placed around a tray or combined to build a flower arrangement in a carved container. This is a colorful way to serve crudités with dips.

* ⁂ Green onion stems cover skewers on which flowers are speared.

* ⁂ Use bundles of watercress, parsley or mint, sprigs of dill, sprays of chives or curly lettuce such as chicory or escarole to fill an arrangement.

* ⁂ Place carved flowers in cold water to curl and frill tips.

* ⁂ Flowers carved from white vegetables may be colored. Place flowers in water that has been colored with a few drops of food coloring.

* ⁂ Vegetables may be cut into varied shapes with small canapé cutters.

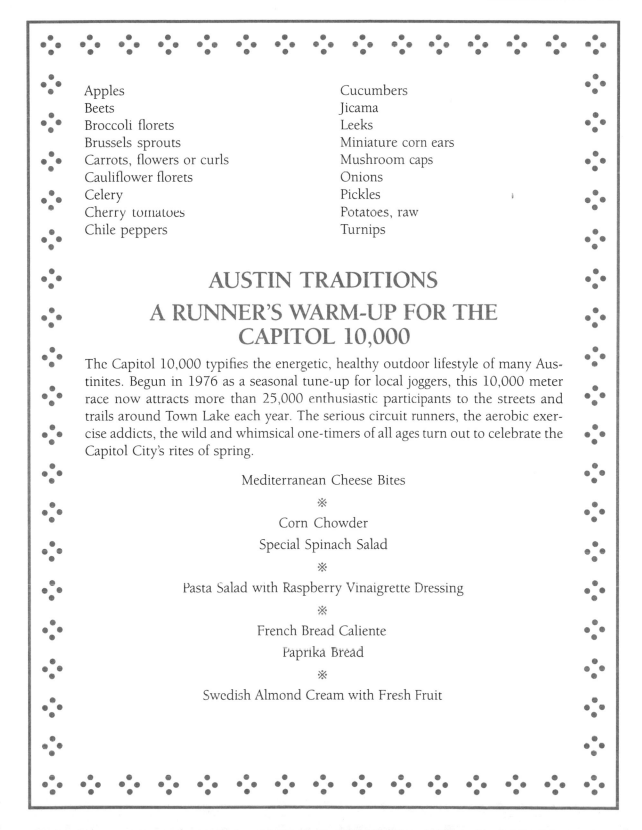

Apples
Beets
Broccoli florets
Brussels sprouts
Carrots, flowers or curls
Cauliflower florets
Celery
Cherry tomatoes
Chile peppers

Cucumbers
Jicama
Leeks
Miniature corn ears
Mushroom caps
Onions
Pickles
Potatoes, raw
Turnips

AUSTIN TRADITIONS
A RUNNER'S WARM-UP FOR THE CAPITOL 10,000

The Capitol 10,000 typifies the energetic, healthy outdoor lifestyle of many Austinites. Begun in 1976 as a seasonal tune-up for local joggers, this 10,000 meter race now attracts more than 25,000 enthusiastic participants to the streets and trails around Town Lake each year. The serious circuit runners, the aerobic exercise addicts, the wild and whimsical one-timers of all ages turn out to celebrate the Capitol City's rites of spring.

Mediterranean Cheese Bites

※

Corn Chowder
Special Spinach Salad

※

Pasta Salad with Raspberry Vinaigrette Dressing

※

French Bread Caliente
Paprika Bread

※

Swedish Almond Cream with Fresh Fruit

LEGENDS OF GOLF BRIGHT AND EARLY BRUNCH

Held at Onion Creek Golf Course in the lovely rolling hills outside Austin, the Legends of Golf is the nationally televised highlight of golf's senior tour. This exciting best ball competition has featured some of the finest golfers ever to play the game . . . Gene Sarazen, Jimmy Demaret, Sam Snead, Don January, Gene Littler, Billy Casper, Arnold Palmer and Gary Player. The four-day tournament attracts over 100,000 spectators to enjoy the popular opening pro-am, the outstanding professional play and the glorious Austin spring weather.

Fresh Fruit Compote

※

Sausage Toasties

※

Sourdough Biscuits and Raspberry Muffins
Homemade Jams and Butters

※

Brunch Egg Casserole and Chile Cheese Grits
Grapefruit Sorbet and Lemon Thins

※

Tea and Lemonade Cooler
Coffee

THE BLUEBONNET TRAIL
AND
TAILGATE PICNIC IN THE COUNTRY

A picnic at the Lyndon Baines Johnson State Park is the perfect complement to a tour of the Texas Hill Country west of Austin. Bluebonnets, Indian Paint Brushes and Mexican Hats blanket the gently rolling hills. This colorful display of native wildflowers reaches its peak in late March and early April. Complete your tour with a visit to the Johnson Ranch. You will easily understand why the late president so loved this rich, rugged land along the banks of the Pedernales River.

Asparagus and Celery Vinaigrette
Cold Curried Tomato Soup

※

Vegetable Rice Salad
Deviled Cornish Hens
Pickled Peaches

※

Redeemer Bread

※

Three Flavor Pound Cake

※

White Wine and Iced Tea

A CASUAL BUFFET BEFORE AN EVENING AT AUSTIN CITY LIMITS

Austin night spots have long provided a showcase for young talent and today the city ranks as a center for the pop and country music recording industry. Austin City Limits, a local institution since 1974 is taped before a live audience on the campus of The University of Texas and has a loyal national following of 14 million viewers. This popular public television program has featured such famous locals as Willie Nelson, George Strait, Jerry Jeff Walker, Marsha Ball, Stevie Ray Vaughan and The Fabulous Thunderbirds. A taping session is a great way to spend an evening in Austin.

Jalapeño Cheese Spread

※

Marinated Green Bean Salad

Topped Baked Tomatoes

Red Pepper Rice

Brisket

※

Sourdough French Bread

※

Mud Pie

※

Coffee

FOURTH OF JULY PICNIC ON THE SHORES OF TOWN LAKE

The Fourth of July in Austin is an old-fashioned, all-American good time with family, friends and outdoor fun. The nation's birthday celebration begins with neighborhood parades throughout the city featuring proud youngsters with bikes and pets decorated in red, white and blue. The hot afternoon is spent with the multitudes at Willie Nelson's famous 4th of July Picnic, with friends at one of the city's many parks, or with family in your own back yard. Toward sundown, Austinites gather on the shores of Town Lake for a rousing concert under the stars by the Austin Symphony Orchestra and the traditional fireworks extravaganza.

Beer Cheese with Crackers and Homemade Bread

Spicy Cracker Snacks

※

Curried Chicken Salad

Spinach Pasta Salad

Marinated Vegetable Salad

※

Best Brownies and Whoopie Pies

※

Lemon Almond Ice Tea

UT FOOTBALL FESTIVITIES

Hook 'Em Horns! In Texas, football is king, and in Austin, football means the Longhorns of The University of Texas. Home games reunite Texas Ex's from across the state for a weekend of great food, fellowship and good times. After a light lunch, more than 75,000 loyal fans pack Memorial Stadium in the shirt sleeve weather of a Texas fall to cheer for the Horns and enjoy the University's famous "Show Band of the Southwest". Win or lose, friends gather for post-game festivities at Scholz Beer Garten, then it is on to the nightlife of Austin's Sixth Street to complete the celebration.

Salsa Fresca　　　※　　　Chile Con Queso

Gringo Bean Dip

Green Chile Pinwheels

Fiesta Guacamole

※

Austin Fajitas

Mexican Rice

※

Pralines and Sherbet Macaroon Delight

※

Sangria　　　　Margaritas　　　　Beer

LATE NIGHT DINNER AFTER THE SYMPHONY

An evening at the Symphony has become a delightful tradition in Austin since the first public concert in 1911. Today, the 90-member Symphony under the direction of Sung Kwak flourishes as a major professional symphonic organization. Austin, too, has grown as a cultural center in an urbane university community. Broadway shows, lively community theatre, rock concerts, ballet and a new lyric opera are but a few of the city's rich offerings in the performing arts.

Chicken Liver Pâté with Cognac

※

Mushroom Soup with Parmesan

※

Caesar Salad

※

Swan's Path Scallops
Broccoli with Lemon Dressing

※

Rich Dinner Rolls

※

Satin Sin Mousse and Truffles with Champagne

※

Café Brulôt

REFRESHMENTS
FOR
THOSE COUNTLESS CHRISTMAS AFFAIR
COMMITTEE MEETINGS

A Christmas Affair is a delightful three-day shopping extravaganza featuring more than 100 specialty shops from as far away as New York and California and attracting visitors from throughout Texas. Sponsored by The Junior League of Austin, this outstanding fundraising event now in its eleventh season has raised more than $1,000,000 for the League's community projects. Always fresh and exciting with a new theme each year, the festivities surrounding this event traditionally mark the beginning of the holiday season in Austin.

Baked Brie with Fruit

※

Baked Cheese Puffs
Pear Bread and Cherry Muffins
Cinnamon Quickies

※

Special Fruit Tea
Coffee

FESTIVE HOLIDAY BUFFET

A rich cultural heritage and tremendous recent growth have brought a unique variety to Austin's secular and religious holiday celebrations. Spanish luminarios light the path to the traditional English Wassail Bowl and delicious German pastries. Festive home entertaining of family and friends is prevalent throughout the city. Children of all ages eagerly await the lighting of the towering, man-made Christmas tree, a colorful spiral of over 3,000 lights, and a drive through Santa's Village on Town Lake during Yule Fest. The warm fellowship of the holiday season is often reflected in the weather. It is not unusual to play a round of golf or a set of tennis on Christmas afternoon. Austinites who favor the more traditional "snow and hot toddies" leave town to ski the Rockies.

Eggnog and Cranberry Punch

❋

Snow Pea and Shrimp Appetizers

Hot Clam Rounds

Fresh Vegetable Tray with Sour Cream Horseradish Dip

Wild Rice Salad ❋ Cranberry Apple Salad

Spinach and Artichokes and Raspberry Carrots

Elegant Pork Tenderloin

❋

Butter Rolls

❋

Wine Cake Pecan Pie Brandy Snaps

❋

Flavored Coffees

INDEX

Recipes used in the menus of Austin Traditions are designated in the index with an M.

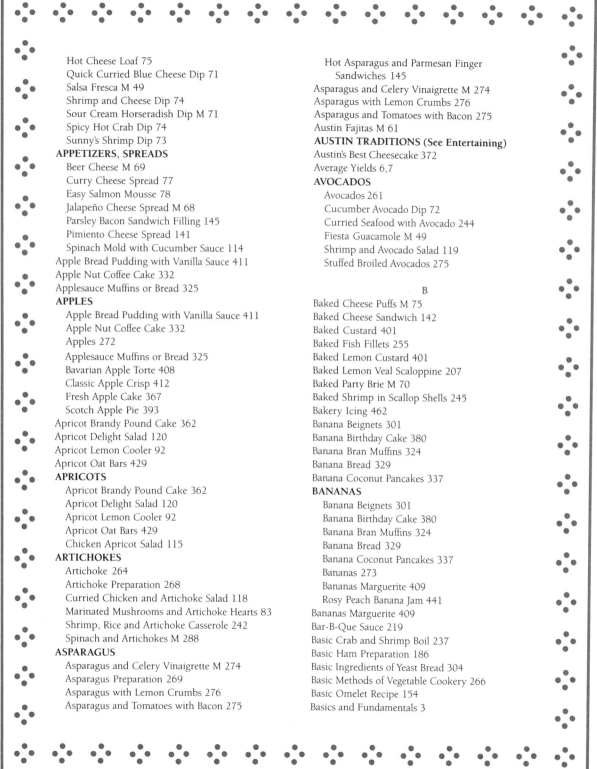

NOTES

NOTES

NOTES

The Junior League of Austin Cookbooks

5416 Parkcrest, Suite 100
Austin, Texas 78731
Telephone: 1-888-903-0888 or 1-512-467-9455
Fax: 1-512-454-7518
Email: cookbook@jlaustin.org
Website: www.jlaustin.org/store/products.asp

Name

Street Address

City   State   Zip

Telephone   Email

Your Order	Quantity	Total
Necessities and Temptations at $19.95 per book		$
The Collection at $19.95 per book		$
Austin Entertains at $28.95 per book		$
Texas Trio (all three cookbooks) at $60.00 per set		$
Shipping and handling at $4.00 per book		$
Total		$

Method of Payment: [ ] VISA   [ ] MasterCard
[ ] Check payable to The Junior League of Austin Cookbooks

Account Number   Expiration Date

Cardholder Name

Signature

All proceeds from the sale of our cookbooks will be used to support community
projects of the Junior League of Austin, Inc.

Photocopies accepted.

If you would like to see **Necessities and Temptations** carried in your area, please send us names and addresses of bookstores or gift stores. THANK YOU!

_____

_____

_____

_____

_____

_____

-------------------------------- cut here --------------------------------

If you would like to see **Necessities and Temptations** carried in your area, please send us names and addresses of bookstores or gift stores. THANK YOU!

_____

_____

_____

_____

_____